Contemporary Issues in Leadership

FIFTH EDITION

edited by
William E. Rosenbach
and Robert L. Taylor

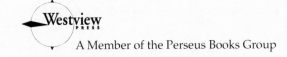

Westview
PRESS

A Member of the Perseus Books Group

Copyright © 2001 by Westview Press, A Member of the Perseus Books Group

Westview Press books are available at special discounts for bulk purchases in the United States by corporations, institutions, and other organizations. For more information, please contact the Special Markets Department at The Perseus Books Group, 11 Cambridge Center, Cambridge MA 02142, or call (617) 252-5298.

Published in 2001 in the United States of America by Westview Press, 5500 Central Avenue, Boulder, Colorado 80301-2877, and in the United Kingdom by Westview Press, 12 Hid's Copse Road, Cumnor Hill, Oxford OX2 9JJ

Find us on the World Wide Web at www.westviewpress.com.

Library of Congress Cataloging-in-Publication Data
Contemporary issues in leadership / edited by William E. Rosenbach
and Robert L. Taylor.—5th ed.
    p.   cm.
  Includes bibliographical references.
  ISBN 0-8133-6456-6
  1. Leadership.   I. Rosenbach, William E.   II. Taylor, Robert L. (Robert Lewis), 1939–

HM1261 .C69   2001
303.3'4—dc21

                                                                2001024876

The paper used in this publication meets the requirements of the American National Standard for Permanence of Paper for Printed Library Materials Z39.48–1984.

10   9   8   7   6

Contents

List of Illustrations   vii
Preface   ix

PART 1
THE HUMAN DIMENSION   1

1   What Makes a Leader? *Daniel Goleman*   5

2   A New Vision of Leadership,
Marshall Sashkin and William E. Rosenbach   19

3   To Give Their Gifts: The Innovative, Transforming
Leadership of Adaptive Work, *Richard A. Couto*   43

4   Do You Have the Will to Lead? *Polly LaBarre*   65

5   Inside Hewlett-Packard, Carly Fiorina Combines
Discipline, New-Age Talk, *David P. Hamilton*   73

PART 2
DEFINING VALUES   79

6   Moral Person and Moral Manager: How Executives
Develop a Reputation for Ethical Leadership,
Linda Klebe Trevino, Laura Pincus Hartman, and Michael Brown   85

7   Politics or Porcelain? *Robert Birnbaum*   101

8   Crisis, Culture, and Charisma: The New Leader's Work in
Public Organizations, *Matthew Valle*   111

9   Leading Learning Organizations, *Peter Senge*   125

10   A View About "Vision," *Neal Thornberry*   131

11   The Evolving Paradigm of Leadership Development,
      Robert M. Fulmer   143

12   Followers for the Times: Engaging Employees in a
      Winning Partnership, *Earl H. Potter III,*
      William E. Rosenbach, and Thane S. Pittman   163

PART 3
RETROSPECTIVES   183

13   Plato on Leadership, *T. Takala*   187

14   Napoleon's Tragic March Home from Moscow:
      Lessons in Hubris, *Mark J. Kroll, Leslie A. Toombs, and*
      Peter Wright   209

15   The Greatest Man Churchill and Truman Ever Met,
      Albert R. Hunt   229

16   The Antileadership Vaccine, *John W. Gardner*   233

PART 4
DILEMMAS AND PARADOXES   241

17   The End of Leadership: Exemplary Leadership Is
      Impossible Without Full Inclusion, Initiatives, and
      Cooperation of Followers, *Warren Bennis*   247

18   Do We Really Want More Leaders in Business?
      Andrea Giampetro-Meyer, Timothy Brown,
      S.J., M. Neil Browne, and Nancy Kubasek   261

19   We Won't See Great Leaders Until We See
      Great Women Leaders, *Harriet Rubin*   275

20   Narcissistic Leaders: The Incredible Pros,
      the Inevitable Cons, *Michael Maccoby*   281

21   Level 5 Leadership: The Triumph of Humility and
      Fierce Resolve, *Jim Collins*   297

About the Editors and Contributors   *311*

Illustrations

Exhibits

1.1   Can emotional intelligence be learned?   11

20.1 Fromm's fourth personality type   285
20.2 The rise and fall of a narcissist   291
20.3 Working for a narcissist   293

21.1 The level 5 hierarchy   299
21.2 Not by level 5 alone   301
21.3 The yin and yang of level 5   304

Tables

1.1   Five components of emotional intelligence at work   7

2.1   Transformational leadership measures   39

3.1   Lessons of innovative, transforming leadership for
      adaptive work   59
3.2   The common tasks and distinguishing elements of
      innovative, transforming leadership—values   60
3.3   The common tasks and distinguishing elements of
      innovative, transforming leadership—creativity   61
3.4   The common tasks and distinguishing elements of
      innovative, transforming leadership—inclusiveness   62
3.5   The common tasks and distinguishing elements of
      innovative, transforming leadership—initiative   63

8.1   Guidelines for creating and communicating
      organizational vision   118

11.1 The evolving paradigm of leadership development   145
11.2 Representative best practices in leadership development   151

11.3   Advantages/disadvantages of multiple perspectives   154

14.1   Examples of the sources of hubris   223
14.2   Examples of the implications of hubris   224

Figures

6.1   The two pillars of ethical leadership   88
6.2   Executive reputation and ethical leadership   95

8.1   Leadership processes in stable environments   114
8.2   Leadership processes in turbulent environments   115

12.1 Follower styles   171

14.1 Sources and implications of hubris   213

17.1 Organizational networks   253

Preface

In preparing for previous editions of this book, we found that the leadership literature had become broader and had crossed more disciplinary boundaries with each edition. This is particularly true for this fifth edition. In a significant change from previous books, we include only four of the pieces from the fourth edition, and you will find that the twenty-one chapters reflect a broad, multidisciplinary approach to leadership. The chapters come from a variety of academic, professional, and popular publications published in the United States and abroad. We believe that the enlarged perspective of leadership provides a deeper understanding of the topic. But it also results in confusion, dilemmas, and paradox. The differences in leadership research and writings, the absence of consensus on what effective leadership really is and how one does it and sustains it, is a reflection of the diversity of people, organizations, and cultures. The search for easy and simple answers to the leadership questions is a futile one, in our opinion, because something as ambiguous and complex as leadership defies an easy answer.

Though confusion about the relationship between management and leadership continues to exist, we find that confusion to be not as great as it once was. The assumptions that management and leadership are the same thing, or, if not, that one is better than the other, or that if you are good at one you will be good at the other, or that if you are the boss then you are the leader have been successfully challenged. Most of us agree that good management *and* good leadership are necessary for groups and organizations to succeed by effectively accomplishing their goals and objectives. There is now general agreement that management and leadership are both sources of influence, but one is based on positional power and the other on personal power. Therefore, in this edition you will not find the leadership-versus-management argument.

At the same time, we note that our literature review identified countless articles and books that described leadership as a set of tools and techniques. In many ways, this was discouraging because we believe that many writers use the term "leadership," but their propositions truly relate to management and management training. Through electronic and manual searches, we identified a list of nearly 1,100 possible articles written since the last edition in 1998. After screening those that actually described management issues, the number was reduced by nearly three-fifths. Of the remaining pieces, a large number were scholarly research articles in which the statistical methods all too often overshadowed the substance of the conclusions. Our ultimate review of approximately 100 articles yielded seventeen that we believe reflect the best of contemporary thought.

Much to our delight, the concept of followership continues to gain recognition as a legitimate area of leadership study as scholars explore the dynamic, reciprocal relationships between those who lead and those who are led. The literature describes varying follower styles just as it does leadership style. Models of follower behavior are emerging in the literature and are described in this edition. Through observation, empirical studies, and anecdotal evidence, the role of the follower is becoming more appreciated and recognized. Thus, our prior focus on followership is affirmed and plays a prominent role in this edition. However, since we believe that the follower is an integral part of leadership, we do not isolate the examination of followership in a separate part but integrate it throughout this edition.

This edition differs in organization as well as content. The current literature is characterized by a variety of well-researched and presented works based on a wide variety of methodologies. Recognizing that scholars continue to produce a large amount of high quality empirical research, we continue our preference for excellent qualitative, interdisciplinary research.

We have organized the book into four sections. Part 1 focuses on the individual as a leader, on what is required of a person to motivate others to follow her or him, and on what is necessary for success in the leadership endeavor. The values that define the leader, the followers, the organization, and the future are the emphases in Part 2. In Part 3, we take a retrospective view of leadership issues and examine enduring leadership lessons from the past and apply those lessons to the present. Finally, in Part 4, we present some of the more troubling dilemmas and paradoxes of the study and practice of leadership.

In this edition we recognize the critical need for effective leadership in government, not-for-profit organizations, business, military, education, and social movements. We drew upon a wide variety of journals and authors for ideas, opinions, and perspectives so that a diverse body of readers can study leadership without the constraints of a specific frame of reference.

We are indebted to the authors and publishers of the readings included in this edition as well as to our students and colleagues who continue to ask questions about leadership that have no easy answers. Our special thanks to Knight Miller, Cynthia McDonald, Laura Ahrens, and Stacy Hannings, who discovered a myriad of articles in expected and unlikely places and also assisted us with many of the mundane chores associated with a project such as this. We thank our colleagues from around the world who provided suggestions, meaningful feedback, and thoughtful criticism, which resulted in a much better book. We recognize the continuing support from Leo Wiegman of Westview Press. Without the caring and professional support of Rosalyn Sterner, Marda Numann, and especially Kara Rosenbach, the manuscript would not have been completed—they really are the best. Finally, we treasure the support of Colleen and Linda, particularly their understanding of our crazy way of working together.

William E. Rosenbach
Robert L. Taylor

PART ONE

THE HUMAN DIMENSION

Leadership is widely discussed and studied but continues to remain an elusive and hazy concept. Although the study of leadership has emerged as a legitimate discipline, one still finds little agreement about what leadership really is. There are almost as many definitions of leadership as there are people attempting to define it. Today, as in the past, the definitions are very often bounded by the academic discipline or the experience of those attempting definition. In 1984, Pulitzer Prize–winner James MacGregor Burns wrote that we know a lot about leaders but very little about leadership. However, Walter F. Ulmer, Jr., former president and CEO of the Center for Creative Leadership, believes that we know more than we used to about leaders, but much of our knowledge is superficial and fails to examine the deeper realms of character and motivation that drive leaders, particularly in difficult times. If one is to begin to understand what leadership is, it is worthwhile to examine what leadership is not. Leadership is not hierarchical, top-down, or based on positional power and authority. While effective managers must practice good leadership and effective leaders must possess managerial skills, leadership is not management or some principle of it. To understand leadership, one must understand its essential nature—that is, the process of the leader and followers engaging in reciprocal influence to achieve a shared purpose. Leadership is all about getting people to work together to make things happen that might not otherwise occur or prevent things from happening that would ordinarily take place.

In this book we distinguish between two basic types of leadership. *Transactional* leadership clarifies the role followers must play both to attain the organization's desired outcomes and to receive valued personal rewards for satisfactory performance, giving them the confidence necessary to achieve those outcomes and rewards. Transactional leadership is the equitable transaction or exchange between the leader and followers whereby the leader influences the followers by focusing on the self-interests of both. The self-interest of the leader is satisfactory performance and the self-interests of the followers are the valued rewards gained in return for good performance. Used well, and in appropriate situations, transactional leadership will result in good performance. Transactional leadership is simply good management and might be considered managerial leadership.

Transformational or *transforming* leadership involves strong personal identification of followers with the leader. The transformational leader motivates followers to perform beyond expectations by creating an awareness of the importance of mission and the vision in such a way that followers share beliefs and values and are able to transcend self-interests and tie the vision to the higher-order needs of self-esteem and self-actualization. Transformational leaders create a mental picture of the shared vision in the minds of the followers through the use of language that has deep meaning from shared experiences. In addition, they are role models—in their daily actions they set an example and give meaning to the shared assumptions, beliefs, and values. Transformational leaders empower, or better yet, enable the followers to perform beyond expectations by sharing power and authority and ensuring that followers understand how to use it. They are committed to developing the followers into partners. In the end, transformational leaders enable followers to transform purpose into action.

"Can leadership be taught?" is the wrong question. A more relevant question is "Can leadership be learned?" The answer is a resounding yes! The potential for good leadership is widely dispersed in our society, not limited to a privileged few. Learning about leadership means learning to recognize bad leadership as well as good. Learning about leadership involves understanding the dynamic relationship between leader and followers; recognizing the differing contexts and situation of the leadership landscape; and understanding the importance of the behavioral sciences, biography, the classics, economics, history, logic, and related disciplines, all of which provide the perspective so important to leadership effectiveness. Individuals committed to improving their leadership effectiveness will take advantage of opportunities to improve their skills as speakers, debaters, negotiators, problem clarifiers, and advocates. Would-be leaders will also follow Thomas Cronin's advice to "squint with their ears." Most important, the developing leader learns to appreciate her or his own strengths and weaknesses. We recall Colin Powell's response to a student's question regarding how one could best prepare to be an effective leader. General Powell responded by advising students to study past and present leaders but not to get too "hung up" on role models because they need to be authentically themselves and to learn from their own mistakes. We strongly believe that leadership can be learned from multiple perspectives. We agree with John Gardner that what you learn after you know it all is what really matters.

What leaders do is important, but how they do it is of equal concern. Although much research has focused on identifying the one best style, no single style or personality is best for all situations. The leader acting alone can often accomplish relatively simple tasks, but the more ambiguous and complex the situation, the greater the need for a participative style. Participatory decisions, however, are time consuming; the path to consensus is often long and tedious. Thus, timing as well as the situation is involved in leadership style. When decisions must be made quickly, the leader must act alone with available information and, very often, on intuition.

All successful leaders have a global orientation. They must thoroughly understand not only the microcosm of their organization but also where the organization fits in the larger perspective. To create a vision of the future, the leader must understand the environment in which the organization exists today and the one in which it will exist tomorrow. Leaders serve an increasingly diverse constituency and must seek and value that diversity if they are to transform their vision into action.

According to Thomas Cronin, students of leadership must develop their capacities for observation, reflection, imagination, invention, and judgment. They must also learn to communicate and listen effectively and develop their abilities to gather and interpret evidence, marshal facts, and employ the most rigorous methods in the pursuit of knowledge. They need to develop an unyielding commitment to the truth, balanced with a full appreciation of what remains to be learned. Students of leadership learn from mentors who lead by example and who make desirable things happen. We agree!

Leadership Perspectives

In "What Makes a Leader?" (Chapter 1), Daniel Goleman, the premier expert on emotional intelligence, describes why emotional intelligence is the crucial component of leadership and how it is displayed in leaders. Superb leaders have very different ways of leading, and different situations call for different styles of leadership. The author has found, however, that effective leaders are alike in one crucial way: They all have a high degree of what has come to be known as emotional intelligence. The author discusses each component of emotional intelligence and shows how to recognize it in potential leaders and how it can be learned.

In "A New Vision of Leadership" (Chapter 2), Marshall Sashkin and William E. Rosenbach propose that there has been a paradigm shift in leadership theory and practice. They review the evolution of the concept of transactional and transformational leadership and examine three empirically derived models. They describe Bernard Bass's Transactional/Transformational Leadership Theory and his and Avolio's Multifactor Leadership Questionnaire, Kouzes and Posner's model of transformational leadership and their Leadership Practices Inventory, Sashkin's Visionary Leadership Theory and The Leadership Profile developed by Sashkin and Rosenbach. They also discuss apparent paradoxes of leadership that are really not paradoxes at all if viewed from the perspective of transformational leadership. The chapter concludes with a discussion of some of the criticism of the concept of transformational leadership.

In Chapter 3, "To Give Their Gifts: The Innovative, Transforming Leadership of Adaptive Work," Richard A. Couto posits that social capital is critical to adaptive work because it reduces social and economic disparities and extends and strengthens communal bonds. It is moral resources and public goods that we invest in one another as members of a community. He proposes that the purpose—the "what"—of innovative, transforming leadership of adaptive work is to advocate and provide increased amounts and improved forms of social capital. He then describes the "how" and the "why" of innovative, transforming leadership for adaptive work.

In Chapter 4, "Do You Have the Will to Lead?" Polly LaBarre of *Fast Company* interviews philosopher Peter Koestenbaum for answers to these age-old questions: How do we act when risks seem overwhelming? What does it mean to be a successful human being? Koestenbaum explains how those questions apply to the new world of leadership and why, as a leader, everything is your responsibility, because you could always have chosen otherwise.

The *Wall Street Journal* reporter David P. Hamilton describes the leadership style of CEO Carly Fiorina in Chapter 5, "Inside Hewlett-Packard, Carly Fiorina Combines Discipline, New-Age Talk." Her style is a combination of transactional and transformational leadership, which is described through examples at H-P. The long-term business results are not yet determined. Absent misfortune or misstep, we predict that history will show her to be an effective leader in a turbulent environment.

1

What Makes a Leader?

DANIEL GOLEMAN

Every businessperson knows a story about a highly intelligent, highly skilled executive who was promoted into a leadership position only to fail at the job. And they also know a story about someone with solid—but not extraordinary—intellectual abilities and technical skills who was promoted into a similar position and then soared.

Such anecdotes support the widespread belief that identifying individuals with the "right stuff" to be leaders is more art than science. After all, the personal styles of superb leaders vary: some leaders are subdued and analytical; others shout their manifestos from the mountaintops. And just as important, different situations call for different types of leadership. Most mergers need a sensitive negotiator at the helm, whereas many turnarounds require a more forceful authority.

I have found, however, that the most effective leaders are alike in one crucial way: they all have a high degree of what has come to be known as *emotional intelligence*. It's not that IQ and technical skills are irrelevant. They do matter, but mainly as "threshold capabilities"; that is, they are the entry-level requirements for executive positions. But my research, along with other recent studies, clearly shows that emotional intelligence is the sine qua non of leadership. Without it, a person can have the best training in the world, an incisive, analytical mind, and an endless supply of smart ideas, but he still won't make a great leader.

In the course of the past year, my colleagues and I have focused on how emotional intelligence operates at work. We have examined the relationship between emotional intelligence and effective performance, especially in leaders. And we have observed how emotional intelligence shows itself on the job. How can you tell if someone has high emotional intelligence, for example, and how can you recognize it in yourself? In the following pages, we'll explore these questions, taking each of the components of emotional intelligence—self-awareness, self-regulation, motivation, empathy, and social skill—in turn.

Evaluating Emotional Intelligence

Most large companies today have employed trained psychologists to develop what are known as "competency models" to aid them in identifying, training, and promoting likely stars in the leadership firmament. The psychologists have also developed such models for lower-level positions. And in recent years, I have analyzed competency models from 88 companies, most of which were large and global and included the likes of Lucent Technologies, British Airways, and Credit Suisse.

In carrying out this work, my objective was to determine which personal capabilities drove outstanding performance within these organizations, and to what degree they did so. I grouped capabilities into three categories: purely technical skills like accounting and business planning; cognitive abilities like analytical reasoning; and competencies demonstrating emotional intelligence such as the ability to work with others and effectiveness in leading change.

To create some of the competency models, psychologists asked senior managers at the companies to identify the capabilities that typified the organization's most outstanding leaders. To create other models, the psychologists used objective criteria such as a division's profitability to differentiate the star performers at senior levels within their organizations from the average ones. Those individuals were then extensively interviewed and tested, and their capabilities were compared. This process resulted in the creation of lists of ingredients for highly effective leaders. The lists ranged in length from 7 to 15 items and included such ingredients as initiative and strategic vision.

When I analyzed all this data, I found dramatic results. To be sure, intellect was a driver of outstanding performance. Cognitive skills such as big-picture thinking and long-term vision were particularly important. But when I calculated the ratio of technical skills, IQ, and emotional intelligence as ingredients of excellent performance, emotional intelligence proved to be twice as important as the others for jobs at all levels.

Moreover, my analysis showed that emotional intelligence played an increasingly important role at the highest levels of the company, where differences in technical skills are of negligible importance. In other words, the higher the rank of a person considered to be a star performer, the more emotional intelligence capabilities showed up as the reason for his or her effectiveness. When I compared star performers with average

TABLE 1.1   Five Components of Emotional Intelligence at Work

	Definition	*Hallmarks*
Self-awareness	the ability to recognize and understand your moods, emotions, and drives, as well as their effect on others	self-confidence realistic self-assessment self-deprecating sense of humor
Self-regulation	the ability to control or redirect disruptive impulses and moods the propensity to suspend judgment—to think before acting	trustworthiness and integrity comfort with ambiguity openness to change
Motivation	a passion to work for reasons that go beyond money or status a propensity to pursue goals with energy and persistence	strong drive to achieve optimism, even in the face of failure organizational commitment
Empathy	the ability to understand the emotional makeup of other people skill in treating people according to their emotional reactions	expertise in building and retaining talent cross-cultural sensitivity service to clients and customers
Social skill	proficiency in managing relationships and building networks an ability to find common ground and build rapport	effectiveness in leading change persuasiveness expertise in building and leading teams

ones in senior leadership positions, nearly 90% of the difference in their profiles was attributable to emotional intelligence factors rather than cognitive abilities.

Other researchers have confirmed that emotional intelligence not only distinguishes outstanding leaders but can also be linked to strong performance. The findings of the late David McClelland, the renowned researcher in human and organizational behavior, are a good example. In a 1996 study of a global food and beverage company, McClelland found that when senior managers had a critical mass of emotional intelligence capabilities, their divisions outperformed yearly earnings goals by 20%. Meanwhile, division leaders without that critical mass underperformed by almost the same amount. McClelland's findings, interestingly, held as true in the company's U.S. divisions as in its divisions in Asia and Europe.

In short, the numbers are beginning to tell us a persuasive story about the link between a company's success and the emotional intelligence of its leaders. And just as important, research is also demonstrating that people can, if they take the right approach, develop their emotional intelligence. (See Exhibit 1.1)

Self-Awareness

Self-awareness is the first component of emotional intelligence—which makes sense when one considers that the Delphic oracle gave the advice to "know thyself" thousands of years ago. Self-awareness means having a deep understanding of one's emotions, strengths, weaknesses, needs, and drives. People with strong self-awareness are neither overly critical nor unrealistically hopeful. Rather, they are honest—with themselves and with others.

People who have a high degree of self-awareness recognize how their feelings affect them, other people, and their job performance. Thus a self-aware person who knows that tight deadlines bring out the worst in him plans his time carefully and gets his work done well in advance. Another person with high self-awareness will be able to work with a demanding client. She will understand the client's impact on her moods and the deeper reasons for her frustration. "Their trivial demands take us away from the real work that needs to be done," she might explain. And she will go one step further and turn her anger into something constructive.

Self-awareness extends to a person's understanding of his or her values and goals. Someone who is highly self-aware knows where he is headed and why; so, for example, he will be able to be firm in turning down a job offer that is tempting financially but does not fit with his principles or long-term goals. A person who lacks self-awareness is apt to make decisions that bring on inner turmoil by treading on buried values. "The money looked good so I signed on," someone might say two years into a job, "but the work means so little to me that I'm constantly bored." The decisions of self-aware people mesh with their values; consequently, they often find work to be energizing.

How can one recognize self-awareness? First and foremost, it shows itself as candor and an ability to assess oneself realistically. People with high self-awareness are able to speak accurately and openly—although not necessarily effusively or confessionally—about their emotions and the impact they have on their work. For instance, one manager I know of

---

EXHIBIT 1.1   *Can Emotional Intelligence Be Learned?*

For ages, people have debated if leaders are born or made. So too goes the debate about emotional intelligence. Are people born with certain levels of empathy, for example, or do they acquire empathy as a result of life's experiences? The answer is both. Scientific inquiry strongly suggests that there is a genetic component to emotional intelligence. Psychological and developmental research indicates that nurture plays a role as well. How much of each perhaps will never be known, but research and practice clearly demonstrate that emotional intelligence can be learned.

One thing is certain: emotional intelligence increases with age. There is an old-fashioned word for the phenomenon: maturity. Yet even with maturity, some people still need training to enhance their emotional intelligence. Unfortunately, far too many training programs that intend to build leadership skills—including emotional intelligence—are a waste of time and money. The problem is simple: they focus on the wrong part of the brain.

Emotional intelligence is born largely in the neurotransmitters of the brain's limbic system, which governs feelings, impulses, and drives. Research indicates that the limbic system learns best through motivation, extended practice, and feedback. Compare this with the kind of learning that goes on in the neocortex, which governs analytical and technical ability. The neocortex grasps concepts and logic. It is the part of the brain that figures out how to use a computer or make a sales call by reading a book. Not surprisingly—but mistakenly—it is also the part of the brain targeted by most training programs aimed at enhancing emotional intelligence. When such programs take, in effect, a neocortical approach, my research with the consortium for Research on Emotional Intelligence in Organizations has shown they can even have a *negative* impact on people's job performance.

To enhance emotional intelligence, organizations must refocus their training to include the limbic system. They must help people break old behavioral habits and establish new ones. That not only takes much more time than conventional training programs, it also requires an individualized approach.

Imagine an executive who is thought to be low on empathy by her colleagues. Part of that deficit shows itself as an inability to listen; she interrupts people and doesn't pay close attention to what they're saying. To fix the problem, the executive needs to be motivated to change, and then she needs practice and feedback from others in the company. A colleague or coach could be tapped to let the executive know when she has been observed failing to listen. She would then have to replay the incident and give a better response; that is, demonstrate her ability to absorb what others are saying. And the executive could be directed to observe certain executives who listen well and to mimic their behavior.

With persistence and practice, such a process can lead to lasting results. I know one Wall Street executive who sought to improve his empathy—specifically his ability to read people's reactions and see their perspectives. Before beginning his quest, the executive's subordinates were terrified of working

(Continues)

(Continued)

with him. People even went so far as to hide bad news from him. Naturally, he was shocked when finally confronted with these facts. He went home and told his family—but they only confirmed what he had heard at work. When their opinions on any given subject did not mesh with his, they, too, were frightened of him.

Enlisting the help of a coach, the executive went to work to heighten his empathy through practice and feedback. His first step was to take a vacation to a foreign country where he did not speak the language. While there, he monitored his reactions to the unfamiliar and his openness to people who were different from him. When he returned home, humbled by his week abroad, the executive asked his coach to shadow him for parts of the day, several times a week, in order to critique how he treated people with new or different perspectives. At the same time, he consciously used on-the-job interactions as opportunities to practice "hearing" ideas that differed from his. Finally, the executive had himself videotaped in meetings and asked those who worked for and with him to critique his ability to acknowledge and understand the feelings of others. It took several months, but the executive's emotional intelligence did ultimately rise, and the improvement was reflected in his overall performance on the job.

It's important to emphasize that building one's emotional intelligence cannot—will not—happen without sincere desire and concerted effort. A brief seminar won't help; nor can one buy a how-to manual. It is much harder to learn to empathize—to internalize empathy as a natural response to people—than it is to become adept at regression analysis. But it can be done. "Nothing great was ever achieved without enthusiasm," wrote Ralph Waldo Emerson. If your goal is to become a real leader, these words can serve as a guidepost in your efforts to develop high emotional intelligence.

---

was skeptical about a new personal-shopper service that her company, a major department-store chain, was about to introduce. Without prompting from her team or her boss, she offered them an explanation: "It's hard for me to get behind the rollout of this service," she admitted, "because I really wanted to run the project but I wasn't selected. Bear with me while I deal with that." The manager did indeed examine her feelings; a week later, she was supporting the project fully.

Such self-knowledge often shows itself in the hiring process. Ask a candidate to describe a time he got carried away by his feelings and did something he later regretted. Self-aware candidates will be frank in admitting to failure—and will often tell their tales with a smile. One of the hallmarks of self-awareness is a self-deprecating sense of humor.

Self-awareness can also be identified during performance reviews. Self-aware people know—and are comfortable talking about—their limitations and strengths, and they often demonstrate a thirst for constructive criticism. By contrast, people with low self-awareness interpret the message that they need to improve as a threat or a sign of failure.

Self-aware people can also be recognized by their self-confidence. They have a firm grasp of their capabilities and are less likely to set themselves up to fail by, for example, overstretching on assignments. They know, too, when to ask for help. And the risks they take on the job are calculated. They won't ask for a challenge that they know they can't handle alone. They'll play to their strengths.

Consider the actions of a mid-level employee who was invited to sit in on a strategy meeting with her company's top executives. Although she was the most junior person in the room, she did not sit there quietly, listening in awestruck or fearful silence. She knew she had a head for clear logic and the skill to present ideas persuasively, and she offered cogent suggestions about the company's strategy. At the same time, her self-awareness stopped her from wandering into territory where she knew she was weak.

Despite the value of having self-aware people in the workplace, my research indicates that senior executives don't often give self-awareness the credit it deserves when they look for potential leaders. Many executives mistake candor about feelings for "wimpiness" and fail to give due respect to employees who openly acknowledge their shortcomings. Such people are too readily dismissed as "not tough enough" to lead others.

In fact, the opposite is true. In the first place, people generally admire and respect candor. Further, leaders are constantly required to make judgment calls that require a candid assessment of capabilities—their own and those of others. Do we have the management expertise to acquire a competitor? Can we launch a new product within six months? People who assess themselves honestly—that is, self-aware people—are well suited to do the same for the organizations they run.

Self-Regulation

Biological impulses drive our emotions. We cannot do away with them—but we do much to manage them. Self-regulation, which is like an ongoing inner conversation, is the component of emotional intelligence that frees us from being prisoners of our feelings. People engaged in such a conversation feel bad moods and emotional impulses just as everyone else does, but they find ways to control them and even to channel them in useful ways.

Imagine an executive who has just watched a team of his employees present a botched analysis to the company's board of directors. In the gloom that follows, the executive might find himself tempted to pound on the table in anger or kick over a chair. He could leap up and scream at the group. Or he might maintain a grim silence, glaring at everyone before stalking off.

But if he had a gift for self-regulation, he would choose a different approach. He would pick his words carefully, acknowledging the team's poor performance without rushing to any hasty judgment. He would then step back to consider the reasons for the failure. Are they personal—a lack of effort? Are there any mitigating factors? What was his role in the debacle? After considering these questions, he would call the team together, lay out the incident's consequences, and offer his feelings about it. He would then present his analysis of the problem and a well-considered solution.

Why does self-regulation matter so much for leaders? First of all, people who are in control of their feelings and impulses—that is, people who are reasonable—are able to create an environment of trust and fairness. In such an environment, politics and infighting are sharply reduced and productivity is high. Talented people flock to the organization and aren't tempted to leave. And self-regulation has a trickle-down effect. No one wants to be known as a hothead when the boss is known for her calm approach. Fewer bad moods at the top mean fewer throughout the organization.

Second, self-regulation is important for competitive reasons. Everyone knows that business today is rife with ambiguity and change. Companies merge and break apart regularly. Technology transforms work at a dizzying pace. People who have mastered their emotions are able to roll with the changes. When a new change program is announced, they don't panic; instead, they are able to suspend judgment, seek out information, and listen to executives explain the new program. As the initiative moves forward, they are able to move with it.

Sometimes they even lead the way. Consider the case of a manager at a large manufacturing company. Like her colleagues, she had used a certain software program for five years. The program drove how she collected and reported data and how she thought about the company's strategy. One day, senior executives announced that a new program was to be installed that would radically change how information was gathered and assessed within the organization. While many people in the company complained bitterly about how disruptive the change would be, the manager mulled over the reasons for the new program and was convinced of its potential to improve performance. She eagerly attended training sessions—some of her colleagues refused to do so—and was eventually promoted to run several divisions, in part because she used the new technology so effectively.

I want to push the importance of self-regulation to leadership even further and make the case that it enhances integrity, which is not only a personal virtue but also an organizational strength. Many of the bad things that happen in companies are a function of impulsive behavior. People rarely plan to exaggerate profits, pad expense accounts, dip into the till, or abuse power for selfish ends. Instead, an opportunity presents itself, and people with low impulse control just say yes.

By contrast, consider the behavior of the senior executive at a large food company. The executive was scrupulously honest in his negotiations with local distributors. He would routinely lay out his cost structure in detail, thereby giving the distributors a realistic understanding of the company's pricing. This approach meant the executive couldn't always drive a hard bargain. Now, on occasion, he felt to the urge to increase profits by withholding information about the company's costs. But he challenged that impulse—he saw that it made more sense in the long run to counteract it. His emotional self-regulation paid off in strong, lasting relationships with distributors that benefited the company more than any short-term financial gains would have.

The signs of emotional self-regulation, therefore, are not hard to miss; a propensity for reflection and thoughtfulness; comfort with ambiguity and change; and integrity—an ability to say no to impulsive urges.

Like self-awareness, self-regulation often does not get its due. People who can master their emotions are sometimes seen as cold fish—their considered responses are taken as a lack of passion. People with fiery temperaments are frequently thought of as "classic" leaders—their outbursts are considered hallmarks of charisma and power. But when such people make it to the top, their impulsiveness often works against them. In my research, extreme displays of negative emotion have never emerged as a driver of good leadership.

Motivation

If there is one trait that virtually all effective leaders have, it is motivation. They are driven to achieve beyond expectations—their own and everyone else's. The key word here is *achieve*. Plenty of people are motivated by external factors such as a big salary or the status that comes from having an impressive title or being part of a prestigious company. By contrast, those with leadership potential are motivated by a deeply embedded desire to achieve for the sake of achievement.

If you are looking for leaders, how can you identify people who are motivated by the drive to achieve rather than by external rewards? The first sign is a passion for the work itself—such people seek out creative challenges, love to learn, and take great pride in a job well done. They also display an unflagging energy to do things better. People with such energy often seem restless with the status quo. They are persistent with their questions about why things are done one way rather than another; they are eager to explore new approaches to their work.

A cosmetics company manager, for example, was frustrated that he had to wait two weeks to get sales results from people in the field. He finally tracked down an automated phone system that would beep each of his salespeople at 5 P.M. every day. An automated message then prompted them to punch in their numbers—how many calls and sales they had made that day. The system shortened the feedback time on sales results from weeks to hours.

That story illustrates two other common traits of people who are driven to achieve. They are forever raising the performance bar, and they like to keep score. Take the performance bar first. During performance reviews, people with high levels of motivation might ask to be "stretched" by their supervisors. Of course, an employee who combines self-awareness with internal motivation will recognize her limits—but she won't settle for objectives that seem too easy to fulfill.

And it follows naturally that people who are driven to do better also want a way of tracking progress—their own, their team's, and their company's. Whereas people with low achievement motivation are often fuzzy about results, those with high achievement motivation often keep score by tracking such hard measures as profitability or market share. I know of a money manager who starts and ends his day on the Internet, gauging the performance of his stock fund against four industry-set benchmarks.

Interestingly, people with high motivation remain optimistic even when the score is against them. In such cases, self-regulation combines with achievement motivation to overcome the frustration and depression that come after a setback or failure. Take the case of another portfolio manager at a large investment company. After several successful years, her fund tumbled for three consecutive quarters, leading three large institutional clients to shift their business elsewhere.

Some executives would have blamed the nosedive on circumstances outside their control; others might have seen the setback as evidence of personal failure. This portfolio manager, however, saw an opportunity to prove she could lead a turnaround. Two years later, when she was promoted to a very senior level in the company, she described the experience as "the best thing that ever happened to me; I learned so much from it."

Executives trying to recognize high levels of achievement motivation in their people can look for one last piece of evidence: commitment to the organization. When people love their job for the work itself, they often feel committed to the organizations that make that work possible. Committed employees are likely to stay with an organization even when they are pursued by headhunters waving money.

It's not difficult to understand how and why a motivation to achieve translates into strong leadership. If you set the performance bar high for yourself, you will do the same for the organization when you are in a position to do so. Likewise, a drive to surpass goals and an interest in keeping score can be contagious. Leaders with these traits can often build a team of managers around them with the same traits. And of course, optimism and organizational commitment are fundamental to leadership—just try to imagine running a company without them.

Empathy

Of all the dimensions of emotional intelligence, empathy is the most easily recognized. We have all felt the empathy of a sensitive teacher or friend; we have all been struck by its absence in an unfeeling coach or boss. But when it comes to business, we rarely hear people praised, let alone rewarded, for their empathy. The very word seems unbusinesslike, out of place amid the tough realities of the marketplace.

But empathy doesn't mean a kind of "I'm okay, you're okay" mushiness. For a leader, that is, it doesn't mean adopting other people's emotions as one's own and trying to please everybody. That would be a nightmare—it would make action impossible. Rather, empathy means thoughtfully considering employees' feelings—along with other factors—in the process of making intelligent decisions.

For an example of empathy in action, consider what happened when two giant brokerage companies merged, creating redundant jobs in all their divisions. One division manager called his people together and gave a gloomy speech that emphasized the number of people who would soon be fired. The manager of another division gave his people a different kind of speech. He was upfront about his own worry and confusion, and he promised to keep people informed and to treat everyone fairly.

The difference between these two managers was empathy. The first manager was too worried about his own fate to consider the feelings of his anxiety-stricken colleagues. The second knew intuitively what his people were feeling, and he acknowledged their fears with his words. Is it any surprise that the first manager saw his division sink as many demoralized people, especially the most talented, departed? By contrast, the second manager continued to be a strong leader, his best people stayed, and his division remained as productive as ever.

Empathy is particularly important today as a component of leadership for at least three reasons: the increasing use of teams; the rapid pace of globalization; and the growing need to retain talent.

Consider the challenge of leading a team. As anyone who has ever been a part of one can attest, teams are cauldrons of bubbling emotions. They are often charged with reaching a consensus—hard enough with two people and much more difficult as the numbers increase. Even in groups with as few as four or five members, alliances form and clashing agendas get set. A team's leader must be able to sense and understand the viewpoints of everyone around the table.

That's exactly what a marketing manager at a large information technology company was able to do when she was appointed to lead a troubled team. The group was in turmoil, overloaded by work and missing deadlines. Tensions were high among the members. Tinkering with procedures was not enough to bring the group together and make it an effective part of the company.

So the manager took several steps. In a series of one-on-one sessions, she took the time to listen to everyone in the group—what was frustrating them, how they rated their colleagues, whether they felt they had been ignored. And then she directed the team in a way that brought it together: she encouraged people to speak more openly about their frustrations, and she helped people raise constructive complaints during meetings. In short, her empathy allowed her to understand her team's emotional makeup. The result was not just heightened collaboration among the members but also added business, as the team was called on for help by a wider range of internal clients.

Globalization is another reason for the rising importance of empathy for business leaders. Cross-cultural dialogue can easily lead to miscues and misunderstandings. Empathy is an antidote. People who have it are attuned to subtleties in body language; they can hear the message beneath the words being spoken. Beyond that, they have a deep understanding of the existence and importance of cultural and ethnic differences.

Consider the case of an American consultant whose team had just pitched a project to a potential Japanese client. In its dealings with Americans, the team was accustomed to being bombarded with questions after such a proposal, but this time it was greeted with a long silence. Other members of the team, taking the silence as disapproval, were ready to pack and leave. The lead consultant gestured them to stop. Although he was not particularly familiar with Japanese culture, he read the client's face and posture and sensed not rejection but interest—even deep consideration. He was right: when the client finally spoke, it was to give the consulting firm the job.

Finally, empathy plays a key role in the retention of talent, particularly in today's information economy. Leaders have always needed empathy to develop and keep good people, but today the stakes are higher. When good people leave, they take the company's knowledge with them.

That's where coaching and mentoring come in. It has repeatedly been shown that coaching and mentoring pay off not just in better performance but also in increased job satisfaction and decreased turnover. But what makes coaching and mentoring work best is the nature of the relationship. Outstanding coaches and mentors get inside the heads of the people they are helping. They sense how to give effective feedback. They know when to push for better performance and when to hold back. In the way they motivate their protégés, they demonstrate empathy in action.

In what is probably sounding like a refrain, let me repeat that empathy doesn't get much respect in business. People wonder how leaders can make hard decisions if they are "feeling" for all the people who will be affected. But leaders with empathy do more than sympathize with people around them: they use their knowledge to improve their companies in subtle but important ways.

Social Skill

The first three components of emotional intelligence are all self-management skills. The last two, empathy and social skill, concern a person's ability to manage relationships with others. As a component of emotional intelligence, social skill is not as simple as it sounds. It's not just a matter of friendliness, although people with high levels of social skill are rarely mean-spirited. Social skill, rather, is friendliness with a purpose: moving people in the direction you desire, whether that's agreement on a new marketing strategy or enthusiasm about a new product.

Socially skilled people tend to have a wide circle of acquaintances, and they have a knack for finding common ground with people of all kinds— a knack for building rapport. That doesn't mean they socialize continually; it means they work according to the assumption that nothing important gets done alone. Such people have a network in place when the time for action comes.

Social skill is the culmination of the other dimensions of emotional intelligence. People tend to be very effective at managing relationships when they can understand and control their own emotions and can empathize with the feelings of others. Even motivation contributes to social skill. Remember that people who are driven to achieve tend to be optimistic, even in the face of setbacks or failure. When people are upbeat, their "glow" is cast upon conversations and other social encounters. They are popular, and for good reason.

Because it is the outcome of the other dimensions of emotional intelligence, social skill is recognizable on the job in many ways that will by now sound familiar. Socially skilled people, for instance, are adept at managing teams—that's their empathy at work. Likewise, they are expert persuaders—a manifestation of self-awareness, self-regulation, and empathy combined. Given those skills, good persuaders know when to make an emotional plea, for instance, and when an appeal to reason will work better. And motivation, when publicly visible, makes such people excellent collaborators; their passion for the work spreads to others and they are driven to find solutions.

But sometimes social skill shows itself in ways the other emotional intelligence components do not. For instance, socially skilled people may at times appear not to be working while at work. They seem to be idly schmoozing—chatting in the hallways with colleagues or joking around with people who are not even connected to their "real" jobs. Socially skilled people, however, don't think it makes sense to arbitrarily limit the scope of their relationships. They build bonds widely because they know that in these fluid times, they may need help someday from people they are just getting to know today.

For example, consider the case of an executive in the strategy department of a global computer manufacturer. By 1993, he was convinced that the company's future lay with the Internet. Over the course of the next year, he found kindred spirits and used his social skill to stitch together a virtual community that cut across levels, divisions, and nations. He then used this de facto team to put up a corporate Web site, among the first by a major company. And, on his own initiative, with no budget or formal status, he signed up the company to participate in an annual Internet industry convention. Calling on his allies and persuading various divisions to donate funds, he recruited more than 50 people from a dozen different units to represent the company at the convention.

Management took notice: within a year of the conference, the executive's team formed the basis for the company's first Internet division, and he was formally put in charge of it. To get there, the executive had ignored conventional boundaries, forging and maintaining connections with people in every corner of the organization.

Is social skill considered a key leadership capability in most companies? The answer is yes, especially when compared with the other components of emotional intelligence. People seem to know intuitively that leaders need to manage relationships effectively; no leader is an island. After all, the leader's task is to get work done through other people, and social skill makes that possible. A leader who cannot express her empathy may as well not have it at all. And a leader's motivation will be useless if he cannot communicate his passion to the organization. Social skill allows leaders to put their emotional intelligence to work.

It would be foolish to assert that good-old-fashioned IQ and technical ability are not important ingredients in strong leadership. But the recipe would not be complete without emotional intelligence. It was once thought that the components of emotional intelligence were "nice to have" in business leaders. But now we know that, for the sake of performance, these are ingredients that leaders "need to have."

It is fortunate, then, that emotional intelligence can be learned. The process is not easy. It takes time and, most of all, commitment. But the benefits that come from having a well-developed emotional intelligence, both for the individual and for the organization, make it worth the effort.

2

A New Vision of Leadership

MARSHALL SASHKIN
WILLIAM E. ROSENBACH

Looking through the history of the study of leadership, we find that the earliest coherent thrust centered on an approach now referred to as the "Great Man" or "Great Person" theory. For a full generation, leadership scholars concentrated on identifying the traits associated with great leadership. At first it seemed obvious; are not great leaders exceptionally intelligent, unusually energetic, far above the norm in their ability to speak to followers, and so on? However, when these "obvious" propositions were subjected to test, they all proved false. Yes, leaders were found to be a bit more intelligent than the average, but not much more. And yes, they were more energetic and dynamic—but not significantly so. True, they were better-than-average public speakers, but again their overall advantage was not very great. And so it went: Each of these and other leadership myths evaporated under the glare of scientific scrutiny.

What followed was a focus on the behavior of leaders. If the key was not *who* they were, perhaps the crux of leadership could be found in *what* they did. In fact, researchers were able to identify two crucial types of leader behavior: behavior centered on task accomplishments and behavior directed toward interpersonal relations. Their peers typically reported individuals who consistently exhibited high levels of both of these types of behavior as leaders. Those who engaged in a high level of task-related activity but only an average level of relationship-centered behavior were sometimes still designated leaders. Those who engaged only in a high level of relationship behavior were rarely designated leaders by their peers. Finally, those who did little in the way of either task- or relationship-centered activity were never seen as leaders.

A previous version of this article with the title "A New Leadership Paradigm" appeared in the third edition of this book.

Perhaps, then, the essence of effective leadership is engaging in high levels of both task-oriented and relationship-centered activity. To test this possibility, researchers trained factory foremen in the two types of behavior and put them back on the job. For a while things did seem to improve, but the effects were short-lived. After only a few weeks the foremen went back to their old behaviors; performance and productivity also returned to their prior levels. Although further research showed that even sustained high levels of the new behaviors had limited long-term effects on employees' performance, productivity, or satisfaction, the leadership-training programs developed in the early 1960s are still popular. Serious students of leadership, however, soon recognized the need to look further for answers to the riddle of effective leadership.

Some took a new path, suggesting that leadership effectiveness might require different combinations of task and relationship behavior in different situations. Theoretically, the most effective combination would depend upon certain situational factors, such as the nature of the task or the ability level of employees reporting to a certain supervisor. Another somewhat different path was to combine the situational hypothesis with some variations of the personal characteristics approach. Like earlier attempts, however, these efforts to explain effective leadership met with limited results. The puzzle remained unsolved.

Earlier in this century, Chester Barnard commented that leadership "has been the subject of an extraordinary amount of dogmatically stated nonsense." More recently, Joseph Rost observed that leadership as good management is what the "twentieth-century school of leadership" is all about. Rost argues for the development of a whole new paradigm of leadership that includes the dynamic interplay between leaders and followers. Later on, we will have more to say about Rost's interesting and important ideas. But first we will examine the ground-breaking work of political scientist and historian James MacGregor Burns, who has had the most influence on leadership research and theory over the past fifteen years.

Burns's work served to reacquaint scholars with a critical distinction first raised by the famous German sociologist Max Weber—the difference between economic and noneconomic sources of authority. This important distinction was one basis for Weber's discussion of charisma and charismatic leadership. Burns amplified and focused this issue, using examples such as Gandhi and Roosevelt, illustrations that made the distinction between *leaders* and *managers* so striking that it could not be ignored. The work of Burns led to the development of several new approaches to the study of what many now refer to as "transformational" leadership. That term is now widely used to contrast this "new leadership" with the old "transactional" leadership (or *management*) approach.

The transactional approach is based on economic and quasi-economic transactions between leaders and followers and appeals to followers' self-interest. In contrast, the new transformational approaches appeal to followers beyond their self-interest and incorporate the idea that leadership involves what Weber called noneconomic sources of authority or influence. In his widely acclaimed 1978 book *Leadership*, Burns defined transformational leadership as occurring when one or more persons engage with others in such a way that leaders and followers raise one another to higher levels of motivation and morality. In other words, both leader and followers—as well as the social system in which they function—are transformed.

Explorations in the New Paradigm

Burns's early work was crucial for the establishment of the new transformational paradigm, but he did not carry forward his concept by developing a clear theory or any direct measures. It was left to others, inspired by his original work, to build on it by defining theory and creating measures. The first and one of the most important of these follow-up efforts was initiated by Bernard M. Bass. Bass had long been recognized as a serious leadership researcher and scholar and had taken responsibility for updating and preparing new editions of Ralph Stogdill's classic *Handbook of Leadership*. Perhaps Bass's immense breadth of background knowledge led him to try to turn Burns's new concept into a more rigorous and measurable theory.

Leadership and Performance Beyond Expectations

Bass's first contribution was to identify a serious error in Burns's work. Burns thought transactional (managerial) and transformational leadership were the end points of a continuum. This belief resembled an error made many years earlier by traditional leadership researchers, who thought that "relationship orientation" and "task orientation" were end points of one leadership dimension. They soon found, however, that they were really two independent dimensions, that a person could exhibit one, the other, both, or neither. Bass realized that transactional leadership is simply different from, not inconsistent with, transformational leadership. A person might exhibit just one, the other, both, or neither.

Bass demonstrated this point by creating a measuring tool, the Multifactor Leadership Questionnaire (MLQ). The MLQ is filled out by a leader as well as by others who report on that person. This variety of perspectives gives what is called a "360 degree" picture of the leader. The MLQ was developed by getting several hundred people to give descriptions of leaders and leadership, by identifying specific actions and characteristics contained in those descriptions, and by then translating those behaviors and characteristics into specific questions. These questions were put into a single, long questionnaire that was administered to hundreds more people. Their answers were then analyzed using factor analysis, a statistical technique that groups together all the questions that seem to fit with one another, producing a relatively small set of categories. This process helps clarify the underlying meaning of the specific questions.

Bass refined the MLQ repeatedly by revising the questions and administering them to new groups of people. Ultimately, he concluded that the questionnaire was able to measure the two forms of leadership and, within each, to identify several more specific categories.

With respect to the old transactional, or managerial, side of leadership, Bass found three subcategories very much like some of those identified by earlier researchers.

- *Laissez-faire*—This component refers to a tendency for the leader to abdicate responsibility toward his or her followers, who are left to their own devices. Laissez-faire leadership really indicates an absence of leadership.
- *Contingent reward*—Often called reward-and-punishment or simply carrot-and-stick leadership, this approach means that the leader rewards followers for attaining performance levels the leader had specified. Performance-contingent strategies are by no means completely ineffective; in general, they are associated with both the performance and satisfaction of followers.
- *Management by exception*—This type of transactional leadership involves managers taking action only when there is evidence of something not going according to plan. There are two types of MBE: *active* and *passive*. The former describes a leader who looks for deviations from established procedure and takes action when irregularities are identified. The passive form describes a tendency to intervene only when specific problems arise because established procedures are not being followed.

The MLQ also taps four specific aspects of transformational leadership. Each of these is different from the forms of transactional leadership just described, because there is no tit-for-tat, no reward (or punishment) from the leader in exchange for followers' efforts.

- *Charisma*—For Bass and, in a statistical sense, for the MLQ, this is the most important dimension assessed by the instrument. Followers see leaders as charismatic when the leader provides emotional arousal—that is, a sense of mission, vision, excitement, and pride. This feeling is typically associated with respect and trust of the leader.

- *Inspiration*—Transformational leaders who inspire their followers set high expectations, use symbols to focus efforts, express important purposes in simple ways, and are specifically concerned with communicating a vision to followers.
- *Individualized consideration*—This aspect of transformational leadership is similar to the old notion of relationship behavior. Individualized consideration means that the leader gives personal attention to followers. The leader builds a personal, considerate relationship with each individual, focusing on that person's needs. Leaders who show individualized consideration toward followers also help followers learn and develop by encouraging personal responsibility. In the process, the leader exhibits trust and respect, which followers then come to feel toward the leader.
- *Intellectual stimulation*—Transformational leaders often provide followers with a flow of new ideas, challenging followers to rethink old ways of doing things. In one sense, this aspect of transformational leadership is related to the older form of task-focused managerial (transactional) leadership, because the focus is on the actual content of the work. The difference is that instead of giving structure and directions, transformational leaders stimulate followers to develop their own task structure and figure out problems on their own.

Bass developed these dimensions of leadership to identify specific categories and types of transactional and transformational leadership behavior. The MLQ could then be used as a coaching and development tool, not just to aid in research or to assess individuals' potential in order to hire or promote the person most likely to succeed. Bass and his associates have made substantial contributions in this regard, developing training programs for navy officers and school superintendents, among other groups, based on this approach to transformational leadership and the MLQ.

However, we believe that the MLQ and Bass's theory have some important deficiencies. Although Bass argues that the MLQ is a measure of *behavior*, when one looks at the actual questions it becomes evident that the most important transformational leadership dimension, charisma, is measured by attitudinal questions, not by leader actions. This approach is actually quite sensible, because charisma is the *result* of transformational leadership rather than its *cause*. Max Weber was the first to use the term *charisma* to describe leaders. There was something special about them that he didn't understand, so he used the ancient Greek word meaning "gift of the gods." That seemed the only available explanation.

We now know that charisma is neither magical nor mysterious. It is simply the feeling that most people have about another person when that person behaves toward them in certain ways. (Later, we will look at some of the specific behaviors associated with charisma.) The chief flaw in Bass's approach is his continued acceptance of charisma as some mysterious quality of the leader. It is true that people often attribute certain special characteristics to leaders because of the way those leaders behave and the feelings they arouse. However, this doesn't really tell us anything about either the personal qualities or behaviors leaders display that produce charismatic effects. To understand transformational leadership we must explore, identify, and measure both the specific actions and the personal characteristics of leaders.

Although Bass's work has been very important in helping to clarify and make concrete Burns's ideas, it ignores some important aspects of transformational leadership that are rooted in the *personal characteristics* of individual leaders. Nor does Bass address the *culture* of the organization.

However, before looking at characteristics of leaders or organizational culture, we need to examine transformational behavior more closely. We will draw on the empirical and behavior-focused work of two other leadership researchers, James M. Kouzes and Barry Z. Posner.

Five Behavioral Dimensions of Leadership

Not long after Bass began theorizing about transformational leadership, researchers on the other side of the country took up the same general problem. Kouzes and Posner were also affected by Burns's work; however, rather than having people describe great leaders and then using those descriptions to construct a questionnaire, they asked managers to write detailed memoirs of their own greatest, most positive leadership experience. These "personal best" cases, some of which ran on for ten pages or more, were analyzed to identify common threads. Only then did the researchers begin to construct questions about leadership behavior.

Kouzes and Posner, like Bass, developed a very long list of questions. They asked hundreds of managers to answer these questions, describing exceptional leaders they had known personally (instead of concentrating on great leaders in history as did Bass). Like Bass, Kouzes and Posner examined the results using factor analysis. They identified five clear factors, all describable in terms of reasonably concrete behaviors. Ultimately (and again like Bass) Kouzes and Posner constructed a questionnaire to measure transformational leadership: the Leadership Practices Inventory (LPI).

The LPI has five scales, one for each of the five types of leadership behavior. We will briefly define each.

- *Challenging the process*—This means searching for opportunities and experimenting, even taking sensible risks, to improve the organization.
- *Inspiring a shared vision*—This sounds a lot like Bass's category, but it is focused less on inspiration per se and more on what leaders actually do to construct future visions and to build follower support for the vision.
- *Enabling others to act*—Leaders make it possible for followers to take action by fostering collaboration (as opposed to competition) and supporting followers in their personal development.
- *Modeling the way*—Leaders set examples by their own behaviors. They also help followers focus on step-by-step accomplishments of large-scale goals, making those goals seem more realistic and attainable.
- *Encouraging the heart*—Leaders recognize followers' contributions and find ways to celebrate their achievements.

The five practices of exemplary leadership identified by Kouzes and Posner are, in our view, much more specific and behaviorally focused than the transformational leadership dimensions developed by Bass. We don't mean that Bass's dimensions or his MLQ are not useful: His ideas were crucial for moving beyond Burns's groundbreaking concepts, and the MLQ can be a valuable tool for executive development. Still, Kouzes and Posner have taken a big step beyond Bass toward a much clearer behavioral explanation of transformational leadership. Yet even this work is not the final word. There's more to transformational leadership than behavioral practices.

The Visionary Leader

At about the same time Bass and Kouzes and Posner were working on their models of transformational leadership, Marshall Sashkin was constructing the first draft of his Leader Behavior Questionnaire (LBQ). Sashkin originally based the LBQ on the work of Warren Bennis, who studied ninety exceptional leaders. Bennis looked for some common factors, some things that would explain just what these leaders did that made them so successful. He identified several commonalties that he called, at various times, "competencies," "behaviors," and "strategies."

Sashkin took five of those behavior categories and developed a question-naire based on them. The categories were:

- *Clarity*—Sashkin's first category of transformational leadership behavior involves focusing the attention of others on key ideas, the most important aspects of the leader's vision. In practice, this means (for example) coming up with metaphors and analogies that make clear and vivid what might otherwise be abstract ideas.
- *Communication*—The second behavior is more general, dealing with skills such as active listening and giving and receiving feedback effectively. These actions ensure clarity of communication.
- *Consistency*—Leaders establish trust by taking actions that are consistent both over time and with what the leader says. Trust, of course, exists in the minds and hearts of followers and is not an obvious aspect of leader behavior. But consistency over time and between words and actions produces trust in followers.
- *Caring*—The fourth behavior is demonstrating respect and concern for people. Psychologist Carl Rogers called this behavior "unconditional positive regard." By this he meant caring about and respecting another person regardless of one's feelings or judgments about that person's actions. Caring is shown not just by "big" actions such as ensuring job security but also by many everyday actions, such as remembering people's birthdays or even something as basic as learning and using their names.
- *Creating opportunities*—Bennis originally associated this behavior with risk taking and risk avoidance, but the underlying issue is more complicated. Transformational leaders do empower followers by allowing them to accept challenges—taking on and "owning" a new project, for example. But transformational leaders also are careful to plan ahead and not to ask more of followers than they know the followers are capable of. Followers might honestly feel a sense of risk in accepting a challenge, but a transformational leader does all that is possible to ensure that any risk is relatively low, that with the right resources and (if necessary) help the follower can and will be successful.

The similarity between these categories and the five leadership practices identified by Kouzes and Posner is striking; in some cases even the words are the same. Sashkin used the categories identified by Bennis to create a questionnaire with a scale for each category and five questions on each scale. Then, like Kouzes and Posner, he collected data and used factor analysis to show that the five dimensions are replicated in people's real experience.

However, there is an interesting difference between the approach taken by Kouzes and Posner and that taken by Sashkin. Kouzes and Posner started by capturing significant experiences and, from those experiences, generated questions that identified their five practices. Sashkin, however, came from the opposite direction, developing measures of the five behaviors on the basis of Bennis's concepts and then validating his measure by analyzing reports of significant experiences. The fact that these two independent research efforts, coming from different directions, wound up in essentially the same place gives us confidence that these researchers are on to something, that the behaviors they've identified are real and important.

In the course of his study of leadership, Sashkin concluded that there had to be more to transformational leadership than just the five behaviors. He identified three specific personal characteristics that mark the differences among exceptional transformational leaders, average leaders, transactional leaders (managers), and nonleaders. None of these characteristics is a *trait* in the strictest sense, because all of them are learnable and changeable. Sashkin developed questionnaire scales to assess the extent to which leaders act on the basis of each of these three characteristics. The three scales were then added to the LBQ.

The first and perhaps most basic characteristic is self-confidence. Psychologists call this "self-efficacy" or "internal control." It is, in essence, the belief that one controls one's own fate. The second characteristic concerns the need for power and the way that need is manifested. Getting things done in organizations depends on one's power and influence and how that power is used. Finally, exceptional leaders have vision, but that vision is not an aspect of charisma or inspiration or some trait like creativity. Vision is based on the ability to think through what's happening, to determine causes, and to identify how complicated chains of cause and effect actually work. Only then can a person begin to figure out how to bring about the outcomes he or she wants. We will briefly describe the nature of each of these three personal characteristics.

- *Self-confidence.* The great American writer Mark Twain probably said it best: "If you think you can . . . or think you can't . . . you're probably right." Often we defeat ourselves before we start. Sometimes it's almost intentional. In the comic strip Calvin and Hobbes, Calvin, a precocious seven-year-old, asks his best friend, a stuffed tiger named Hobbes, whether he believes the stars control our fate. "Naw," says Hobbes. "Oh, I do," replies Calvin. "Life's a lot more fun when you're not responsible for your actions." However, by denying control, Calvin denies all of the vast possibilities of leadership. How can someone who has no faith in himself or herself become a leader of others?

Self-confidence or self-efficacy is a prerequisite to leadership. And it is not a trait. Self-efficacy is learned. Did you ever hear someone scold a child by saying, "Johnny, that's not how you do it! Can't you do anything right?!" Well, every time that happens, Johnny learns that he cannot control his fate. That's not a good lesson for success, let alone leadership. Parents and teachers must help children learn that they can control their own fate. But it's never too late; even adults can learn, and that's one of the most important jobs of leaders—teaching followers that they *can* do things for themselves. This is the first paradox of leadership: To become a leader, one must believe in one's own ability to achieve results for one's self, but the *real* job of a leader is not doing it but teaching others that *they* can do it.

- *Power.* Harvard psychologist David McClelland has studied human motivation for about half a century. Early on he came to believe that three motives, or needs, play particularly important roles: the need to achieve, the need for power and control, and the need for friendship and human interaction. McClelland thought of needs not as fixed or inborn traits but rather as habits that people develop in the course of their lives. His particular focus for many years was on the need to achieve, which he believed might relate to business success. He thought it might be possible to actually "teach" people to need achievement, which should make it more likely for them to actually attain their goals.

In an important real-world experiment, McClelland found that small business entrepreneurs could learn to "need" achievement and that this enhanced their business success. But when he looked at managers in organizations, he found that the need for *power*, not achievement, was most strongly associated with success. Organizations are set up because there is work to do that can't be done by just one person, that requires people to work together to achieve goals. The process is controlled by the exercise of power and influence. Managers who have an extremely high need to achieve tend to burn out; they get frustrated about things not getting done and try to do everything themselves. But that's not really possible; one gets things done, in large organizations, by using influence and relying on others.

McClelland went on to observe that some managers with a high need for power appeared to be quite effective, while others were very ineffective. Looking more closely at this second group, McClelland character-ized them as using power primarily to benefit themselves—to get status, to get "perks," and even just to get others to obey them and be sub-servient. In contrast, the effective managers used power to empower oth-ers, to delegate and to legitimate employees' taking charge and taking real responsibility for accomplishments.

People who use power to manipulate others to serve their own self-centered ends are often seen as charismatic. In fact, that's often how such leaders dupe others into doing as they, the leaders, wish. This helps ex-plain why one must be careful about measures of charisma, such as that contained in Bass's MLQ, and about reasonable-sounding theories that glorify charismatic leadership. In the United States people tend to associ-ate charisma with admirable leaders such as Franklin Roosevelt and John Kennedy. But in Europe charisma is often identified with tyrants such as Napoleon and Hitler. Roosevelt and Kennedy certainly used charisma, but they did not use it to control followers by promising that the follow-ers could become more like *them* (i.e., the leaders) by obeying the leader's every command. Instead, these and other great leaders who might be cited as positive models, people such as Gandhi or Churchill, appealed to what Abraham Lincoln called "the better angels of our nature." These are simply the basic values about what is right, what is good, what should be done, and what should be avoided that guide us toward positive long-run goals.

Nontransformational leaders who use charisma to get what they want appeal primarily to the self-serving side of human nature. They say (in effect), "If you do as I wish you'll be like me and have all the wonderful things I have." Psychologists call this an appeal to narcissism, or self-love. Of course, such leaders are really lying—their narcissistic appeals are designed only to get followers to do as the leader wants. Their charisma is artifice, a result of behaviors that they have carefully learned and rehearsed for the specific purpose of manipulating followers.

In contrast, transformational leaders seek power not for self-aggran-dizement but in order to share it. They empower others to take an active role in carrying out the value-based mission or vision defined by the leader. That vision is based on what the organization and followers need, not what the leader wants personally. Thus, transformational leaders ap-peal to followers' *values*, emphasizing that certain important values serve as the common basis for our ideals and goals.

This brings us to the second paradox of leadership: While it may seem that charismatic and transformational leaders are complete opposites, the power need is common to both. Thus the paradox: The same power need that gives us a Gandhi can also produce a Hitler. Those who have worked closely with even an exceptional transformational leader have probably seen in that person at least a touch of the self-serving tyrant. Again, the paradox: The source is the same—the power need—but how that need is channeled makes all the difference.

- *Vision.* The term vision is commonly applied to leadership. Many speak of leaders' vision and the importance of constructing a vision. Few observers, however, are able to explain exactly what vision means. Some seem to think it means that leaders come up with an image of an ideal future condition and then explain it to others and convince them to do what's necessary to attain the vision. But visionary leaders don't simply think up a vision and sell it to followers. If it is more than just a slick sales pitch, the long-term ideal that leaders come up with will always derive (at least in part) from followers' ideas.

Developing a vision doesn't mean dreaming. It means thinking, and thinking hard. That's what the groundbreaking work of social psychologist Elliott Jaques tells us. After years of study, Jaques concluded that when organizations are working well, they have leaders who possess the perspective necessary to deal with problems of the degree of complexity common to their particular hierarchical level.

Most organizations, Jaques found, need no more than six levels of hierarchy. But they also need people at each level who can think about chains of cause and effect and see how things work. At the higher levels these leaders must figure out how several causal chains affect one another over relatively long periods of time and must decide what to do to achieve desired outcomes. Jaques calls this ability "cognitive power," the ability to think in complex ways. Cognitive power isn't the same thing as intelligence, nor is it a fixed, unchangeable trait. Successful leaders *learn* to use cognitive power effectively. What's the time span over which you are comfortable in planning? A few months? A year? Two years? What's the longest-term project you are working on right now? That should tell you something about the time-span limits you're comfortable with.

Transformational leaders transform organizations by first using their cognitive power to understand complex causal chains and then acting to design outcomes that will benefit the organization and advance the leader's vision. But transformational leadership is much more than that. While a substantial degree of cognitive power is required in order for top-level leaders to be effective, such effectiveness results as much from the leader's success in developing followers' cognitive abilities as from the exercise of his or her own. A transformational leader with the degree of cognitive power required for a top-level position makes important long-term strategic decisions. But how much do these decisions affect what actually goes on in the organization on a daily, weekly, monthly, and yearly basis? It is the thought and action of managers and employees at lower levels that most affect current and short-term future operations. The finest long-term plan and the wisest long-range actions will surely fail if those who must act today and tomorrow are not capable of doing so. Thus, it is more important for top-level leaders with great cognitive power or vision to help followers expand and improve on their *own* vision than it is for leaders to simply exercise their cognitive power. This is the third paradox of leadership.

- *Personal Characteristics.* The personal characteristics of effective leaders are somewhat different from what traditional "trait" theories of leadership addressed. These characteristics are not obvious as the foundations of leadership, yet that's exactly what they are. More important, these foundations are not something people are born with; they are developed. At least to some extent, that development can be planned and carried out over one's life and career. Indeed, transformational leaders teach followers to develop these characteristics for themselves, rather than simply using their own capabilities to do things for followers.

Incorporating the three personal characteristics into his Visionary Leadership Theory (VLT), Sashkin modified his LBQ to include a total of eight scales—the five original scales developed to assess certain types of leader behavior, along with three new scales designed to examine how the three specific characteristics important for transformational leadership show up in leaders' actions. But there was still more to the transformational leadership equation. Behavior is a function of the person and the situation or context. What about that context? Sashkin addressed this question by looking at organizational culture in terms of the situational context of transformational leadership.

The Leader's Role in Shaping the Organization's Culture

Edgar H. Schein has said that the only important thing leaders do may well be constructing culture. They somehow help define and inculcate certain shared values and beliefs among organizational members. Values define what is right or wrong, good or bad; beliefs define what people expect to happen as a consequence of their actions. The values and beliefs shared by people in an organization are the essence of that organization's culture.

The elements of organizational culture are not just selected by chance or at random. They deal with the most important and fundamental issues faced by people in organizations. These issues include *adaptation*—how people deal with external forces and the need to change; *goal achievement*—the nature of organizational goals, how they are defined, and their importance; *coordination*—how people work together to get the job done; and *the strength of shared values and beliefs*—that is, the degree to which people in the organization generally agree that these values and beliefs are important and should guide their actions. We will briefly consider each issue and the values and beliefs relevant to that issue.

- *Adaptation.* Consider two specific beliefs about change and adaptation. The first goes like this: "We really just have to go along with outside forces; what we do can't really make much difference." Such a belief has some pretty clear implications for action—or inaction. After all, why bother? Contrast this outlook with the belief, "We can control our own destiny." The former belief may be more accurate in an objective sense. However, it also pretty much ensures that nothing will be done and that what is done will not, in fact, make a difference, because no one expects it to. Even if the second belief is not as accurate, it certainly helps make it more likely that action will be taken. And perhaps that action will have a positive effect, especially because people expect it to.

These beliefs dealing with change and adaptation are actually the organizational analog of self-efficacy, the belief that one's destiny is a matter of self-control. Therefore, it is crucial that leaders teach followers self-efficacy. Only then is it likely that the organization will develop the sort of culture that makes successful adaptation to change more likely.

- *Goal Achievement.* "Every person, every department, has its own goals; the organization is best served by competition among them." Does that sound like a typical organizational value? Unfortunately it is; it's unfortunate because organizations are not well served by such a value. Contrast it with this one: "We are all here to serve our customer by identifying and meeting the customer's needs, whatever they may be." That value says a lot about how goals are defined and what goal achievement is all about. And, unlike the first value, this one really does benefit the organization.

The issue of goals relates to the leader's need for power and how that need can be played out—to benefit the organization by empowering others, or to benefit only the individual through narcissistic self-aggrandizement. Leaders' empowerment of others is so important because it models the value of achievement in a larger, organizational sense, not just for their own benefit or the benefit of their department.

- *Coordination.* Many organizations seem to operate on the maxim, "Every person for him- or herself; we all compete to be best." But this is not a very functional value when the very essence of organization is to perform tasks that require the coordinated work of several individuals and groups. In contrast, the value "We all must work together" is a much better expression of the reality of organization. Only when people work together effectively can an organization prosper.

We spoke of vision or cognitive power as the means by which leaders think through complicated cause-and-effect chains and decide how to create desirable outcomes. This process entails looking at the organization as a system and thinking about how it fits together, which happens, of course, through the coordinated efforts of organization members. Leaders, then, must help followers develop their cognitive power, their own vision so that followers are able to coordinate their efforts effectively.

- *Shared Values and Beliefs.* In some organizations one hears people say, "Everyone has the right to his or her own philosophy." Although that might seem to be a sound democratic ideal, it makes poor organizational sense. Such a principle destroys the potentially positive effect of the three issue-focused beliefs and values just identified. If everyone can buy into or reject them at will, how can these values and beliefs be expected to have any consistent impact? "Everyone here is expected to adhere to a common core of values and beliefs" is itself a value that strengthens a positive, functional approach toward adapting, achieving goals, and coordinating efforts. Of course, such a value would make alternative beliefs and values even more dysfunctional. That's why "cultural strength," the degree to which values are shared among the members of an organization, is a poor predictor of organizational effectiveness.

But How?

All this may seem reasonable, especially because it is relatively easy to see how the personal characteristics required for effective leadership relate to the fundamental aspects of organizational culture. Still, we must ask how leaders construct cultures—that is, how they go about defining and inculcating values and beliefs. There are many ways that leaders do this, but three general approaches are of special importance and impact. First, leaders develop a clear, simple, value-based philosophy, a statement of organizational purpose or mission that everyone understands. This task is anything but simple. A philosophy does not spring fully formed from the brow of the leader. Leaders must use their cognitive power to assess the organization's context, its environment, and the key factors in that environment; they must solicit input from others; and they must convince top level executives that all this is possible.

Second, leaders empower others to define organizational *policies* and develop *programs* that are explicitly based on the values and beliefs contained in the philosophy that in fact put those values and beliefs into organizational action. For example, hiring and promotion policies should take into account values consistent with those in the organization's philosophy as well as applicants' knowledge and skill. Reward systems and bonus programs must be based on the values of cooperation and innovative action instead of on competition over a limited pool of resources.

Finally, leaders inculcate values and beliefs through their own individual behaviors, their personal *practices*. Leaders model organizational values and beliefs by living by them constantly and consistently. That is why the leadership behaviors we described earlier are extremely important. Many people think of these behaviors as tools with which leaders explain their vision to followers and convince them to carry out that vision. Although this is not totally untrue, the far more significant reason these behaviors are important is that leaders use them to demonstrate and illustrate the values and beliefs on which their visions are founded. That's why transformational leadership takes so much time and effort—and why transformational leaders must be good managers with strong management skills. These leaders use everyday managerial activities—a committee meeting, for example—as opportunities to inculcate values. In a meeting the leader may guide a decision-making process while making it clear that final authority and responsibility rests with the group. By so doing, the leader takes what might otherwise be a bureaucratic process and instills the value of empowerment into it. Whenever possible, leaders "overlay" value-inculcating actions on ordinary bureaucratic management activities. Without a sound base of management skills, this would not be possible.

The Leadership Profile

Thus, Sashkin's Visionary Leadership Theory brings us full circle, from the easiest-to-observe behaviors to a deeper understanding of the personal source of visionary leadership to the more subtle and fundamental expression of leadership through culture building. Ultimately, VLT leads to the recognition that transformational leaders' own personal behaviors play a large part in shaping organizational culture. This comprehensive theory goes beyond behavior to incorporate personal characteristics. Even more, it includes the organizational context of transformational leadership—that is, culture building. It is the only analysis of leadership that attends to all three factors—behavior, personal characteristics, and the organizational context—thus paying heed to the basic equation of behavior as a function of person and environment.

The latest work by Sashkin and Rosenbach incorporates an assessment of transactional as well as transformational leadership within a revised questionnaire instrument, The Leadership Profile (TLP). The first two LBQ scales both measured aspects of communication, so they were combined into a single scale, *communication leadership*. The last two scales were measures of the leader's culture building efforts and were also combined to form a single scale labeled *principled leadership* because it is by defining and inculcating values and beliefs—principles—that leaders must build culture. This allowed the construction of two new transactional leadership scales, *capable management* and *reward equity*.

With the development and validation of this new assessment, VLT incorporates a complete approach to leadership, including the baseline of sound management, identifying the specific behavioral dimensions of transformational leaders, and extending to the personal characteristics of transformational leaders. With the complete theory in mind, we are prepared to examine our most basic assumption: that there really is such a thing as transformational leadership.

Is There Really Such a Thing as Transformational Leadership?

We began by trying to define what most of those now involved in studying transformational leadership refer to as a "paradigm shift." A paradigm is a way of thinking, a frame of reference. Sometimes—generally not very often—we are forced to change the way we look at and think about things. When this happens it's most often because of some major change in scientific knowledge. When Copernicus, for example, concluded that the sun, not the earth, was the center of the solar system, he caused a radical scientific paradigm shift. Similarly, the proposal that what we had thought of as leadership is really something rather different—management/supervision—forced many researchers to take a step back and rethink their basic assumptions about leadership in organizations. Others concluded that this "discovery" was nothing more than a wrong-headed assertion, that a full understanding of leadership could still be had in the context of the existing paradigm.

The existing paradigm, of course, is based on the notion of transactions or exchanges: Leaders provide followers with rewards for doing as the leader wishes or administer punishments if the wishes are not heeded. In the 1950s various social scientists, George Homans (a sociologist) and Edwin Hollander (a social psychologist) in particular, developed detailed models of "social exchange." These models show how people exchange not just money for doing a job but also "sentiments." A person might, for example, exchange friendship for certain favors. This sounds a bit crass, and the fact is that whenever such exchanges become obvious they automatically lose their value. No one would consciously say, "I'll be your buddy if you'll drive me to work." But that's exactly what people do all the time without explicitly saying so.

The examples above are purposely simplistic and extreme for the sake of clarity. The social exchange model is really more subtle and complex than we have made it appear. Still, it may seem at first glance that transformational leadership is obviously more than an exchange of work for money and certainly goes beyond an exchange of sentiments, such as commitment and caring from the leader in exchange for followers' acceptance of the leader's agenda. Edwin Hollander has recently suggested that there is an exchange, an exchange that goes beyond money or sentiments. In exchange for their willingness to carry out the leader's vision, followers receive intangible but very real and useful rewards, such as a new, clear, and practical understanding of how to design and carry out projects that require interdepartmental coordination Thus, exchange can take at least three forms. At its simplest, leader-follower exchange involves concrete rewards for actions. In its simple social version, leader-follower exchange consists of sentiments for actions, friendship for favors. But in what may be its most sophisticated form, leader-follower exchange balances followers' committed actions against the intangible but practically useful insights and understandings they receive from leaders.

Is it possible, then, that what we have called transformational leadership could be reinterpreted within the traditional paradigm of transaction and exchange? We are not convinced. Our objection is based on the essence and nature of transformation. Leaders transform organizations, but they also transform followers, a process that involves much more than simply exchanging useful insights for followers' actions.

Transformational leadership, then, is more than a form of transactional leadership in which the transactions are subtle and intangible. But that doesn't mean that Hollander's extended social exchange model can be dismissed. It's easy to say that simple observation of a transformational leader in action yields no sign of social exchange, but it would be foolish to reject the social exchange model on that basis, because if social exchange is actually operating, that is exactly how it would have to appear. Remember, when a social exchange process is obvious, it tends to lose its utility; most people reject the thought of an exchange that involves "buying" feelings. Anyone actually involved in the transformational "exchange" would be expected to deny that such an exchange existed.

Our disagreement with the social exchange approach is not based on the notion that there is an "obvious" difference between transactional and transformational leadership. Rather, our view is based on evidence—the evidence provided by Bass's research. Remember, Bass was able to define and measure several aspects of transactional leadership and to show that these were clearly independent of the dimensions of transformational leadership. If there were really no difference—if these were all simply transactions, with some just more open than others—it's hard to imagine that Bass would have been able to show such a clear separation. Some of our own recent research adds support to Bass's work by showing that two very different approaches to measuring transformational dimensions yield consistent results.

We believe that the conceptual distinctions we have made provide clear theoretical support for our view. Transformational leadership is used to construct a value-based culture. But it requires the context of transactional leadership, the everyday bureaucratic and managerial activities that form the "text," with values and culture the "subtext." It is clear to us that these are very different activities and processes. Transactional leadership—management—is the "paper" on which transformational leaders define values and describe organizational cultures. Without management there could be no leadership. Thus, both are important—but they are different.

Current "Transformational" Leadership Approaches as Wolves in Sheep's Clothing

Some may argue that there is no such thing as transformational leadership or that it is simply a form of charisma; others insist that current transformational theory is still ill defined. One scholar, Joseph Rost, feels that a paradigm shift has not yet occurred; he views the present transformational leadership theories as merely providing an *opportunity* for a transition. What is especially lacking in current transformational theories, according to Rost, is a full and complex consideration of the role of followership. Leadership, he argues, involves more than leaders getting followers to carry out leaders' wishes. A distinction between leaders and followers is crucial, but the concept of follower must, according to Rost, take on a new meaning. Followers must be seen as active, not passive, and as themselves engaging in leadership, not just in followership. We agree with Rost that leadership involves more than leaders getting followers to carry out leaders' wishes; that is, motivating followers as does a transactional or charismatic leader.

Rost has emphasized that both leaders and followers make important contributions. Although we agree with Rost that there must be mutual contributions, we disagree on the *nature* of those contributions. Rost appears to us to say or suggest that leaders' and followers' contributions are similar in nature. We, however, believe that leaders' essential contributions are quite different from the contributions of followers. Leaders' contributions include synthesizing and extending the purposes of followers as well as constructing conditions under which followers can be transformed into leaders. Thus, in terms of a vision or common purpose, the relationship between leaders and followers need not and cannot be equal—but it *must be equitable*, that is, fair. To us this means that the contributions of leaders and of followers, which are inherently unequal in kind, must be equal in effort and in commitment to one another and to a shared vision.

We do not disagree with Rost's definition of leadership as "an influence relationship among leaders and followers who intend real changes that reflect their mutual purposes." We do, however, find this definition to be incomplete; what gets lost in Rost's argument, we think, is the leader as a source of vision or motive. Rost and some others seem to think that transformational leaders exist primarily to focus and help carry out the visions of followers. There is some truth to this and in this sense leaders are, as Robert Greenleaf has so beautifully said, servants. However, transformational leaders do not simply identify and build a clear vision from the visions of followers. They also identify what followers themselves might wish to envision but have not and perhaps cannot. And they provide followers with conditions that permit followers to achieve the goals and aims they share with leaders; leaders enable followers themselves to change, to realize more fully their potential. In sum, transformational leadership involves real, unique contributions from both followers and leaders, a point that Rost says he agrees with but which seems to us to be missing in meaningful detail from his approach.

Conclusion

We believe that a paradigm shift has indeed occurred over the past decades with respect to leadership research, theory, and practice. This shift has as its source Burns's pioneering ideas. That work led to a variety of new transformational approaches; we have reviewed the most important in this chapter. While different in many ways, these new approaches are nonetheless consistent. The new transformational leadership para-

TABLE 2.1   Transformational Leadership Measures

Multi-Factor Leadership Questionnaire (Bass and Avolio)	*Leadership Practices Inventory (Kouzes and Posner)*	*The Leadership Profile (Sashkin and Rosenbach)*
Laissez-faire	Challenging the process	Transactional leadership
Transactional leadership	Search for opportuni-	Capable management
Contingent-reward	ties	Reward equity
Management by	Experiment and take	Transformational leader-
exception	risks	ship behaviors
active	Inspiring a shared vision	Communication lead-
passive	Envision the future	ership
Transformational	Enlist others	Credible leadership
leadership	Enabling others to act	Caring leadership
Charisma	Foster collaboration	Creative leadership
Individual considera-	Strengthen others	Transformational leader-
tion	Modeling the way	ship characteristics
Intellectual stimula-	Set the example	Confident leadership
tion	Plan small wins	Follower-centered
Inspiration	Encouraging the heart	leadership
	Recognize contribu-	Visionary leadership
	tion	Principled leadership
	Celebrate accomplish-	
	ments	

digm confirms the unity of the concepts of leadership and followership. It accomplishes this in ways that, on the surface, appear to be paradoxical. However, the paradoxes we have described are paradoxes only if one tries to look at them from the perspective of the old transactional, or management, paradigm. When we apply the new transformational paradigm we see that what at first appeared to be paradoxical actually makes logical sense.

The most general paradox involves the apparent inconsistency between being a manager and being a leader. This apparent paradox is resolved by recognizing that effective transformational leaders use transactional, managerial roles not simply to define, assign, and accomplish tasks and achieve goals but also to educate, empower, and ultimately transform followers. By doing so, leaders wind up transforming their organizations. The transactional approach views the sort of skills and behaviors defined and described by Bass, Kouzes and Posner, and Sashkin as essential managerial activities, important for communicating clearly the terms of exchange between managers and their subordinates. But leaders don't just communicate directions, they communicate values.

What the transactional paradigm cannot explain is that leaders use these interaction skills not to convince followers to do as the leaders want but to become more self-confident, to use power and influence in a positive way, and to develop more complex thinking skills. These outcomes are more than rewards accepted in exchange for compliance; they are true transformations in followers, transformations that lead to transformation in the organization.

Our outlook does not, however, deny the need for management. From the vantage point of the new paradigm, management is more important than ever; only by using the context of management activities can leaders transform followers and organizations. Through this new transformational leadership paradigm, the study and practice of leadership itself has been transformed.

Notes

The authors gratefully acknowledge the helpful comments on earlier drafts of this chapter from Edwin P. Hollander, Barry Z. Posner, Joseph C. Rost, and Walter F. Ulmer, Jr. We accept full responsibility for our interpretation and presentation of their views.

Suggested Readings

Organizations and Management by Chester I. Barnard (Cambridge, MA: Harvard University Press, 1948). Chester Barnard was an executive at AT&T for many years. He was also a serious management thinker and his work is still considered important by both scholars and thoughtful managers.

Bass & Stogdill's Handbook of Leadership (3rd edition) by Bernard M. Bass (New York: Free Press, 1990). This is a comprehensive reference resource that organizes just about everything ever written on the topic of leadership.

Leadership and Performance Beyond Expectations by Bernard M. Bass (New York: Free Press, 1985). This was the first formal attempt to apply Burns's idea of transformational leadership to leadership in organizations instead of nations.

Leaders: The Strategies for Taking Charge by Warren Bennis and Burt Nanus (New York: Harper & Row, 1985). This very readable book reports the authors' study of ninety exceptional chief executives and a model of organizational leadership based on what they learned.

Leadership by James McGregor Burns (New York: Harper & Row, 1978). Burns's work is the most important original source for the concept of transformational leadership. His book is also very readable.

"Legitimacy, Power, and Influence: A Perspective on Relational Features of Leadership" by Edwin P. Hollander, in *Leadership Theory and Research: Perspectives and Directions*, edited by Martin M. Chemers and R. Ayma (New York: Academic Press, 1993). This is the most clear and current statement of the "pure" transactional approach. The author tries to interpret and explain transformational leadership in terms of the older transactional paradigm (though misunderstanding the nature of transformational leadership by confusing it with charisma).

Executive Leadership by Elliott Jaques and Stephen D. Clement (Arlington, VA: Cason Hall, 1991). This very readable explication of Jaques's important theory of organization and leadership is based on his concept of "cognitive power" and the notion that individuals' levels of cognitive power must be matched to their positional levels in the organizational hierarchy.

The Leadership Challenge by James M. Kouzes and Barry Z. Posner (San Francisco: Jossey-Bass, 1987). These authors used much the same approach as Bass did to create a tool for measuring leadership, but they did not start from a theoretical base, and their focus was more behavioral. The five aspects of leadership they identified and measured, however, are very similar to and consistent with the five "strategies" originally defined by Bennis and the five behavior categories defined and measured by Sashkin.

"Power Is the Great Motivator," by David C. McClelland and David H. Burnham (*Harvard Business Review*, March–April 1976, pp. 100–110). This is a very readable report of McClelland's ground-breaking work on how the need for power comes into play in organizations and how it can be used for good or for ill.

Structure and Process in Modern Societies by Talcott Parsons (New York: Free Press, 1960). This is a very unreadable (but important) reference source. Parsons was one of the most important modern social scientists. He developed a very simple, perhaps even elegant, way of understanding what goes on in organizations and why.

Leadership for the Twenty-first Century by Joseph Rost (New York: Praeger, 1991). Rost provides an exceptional overview of the history of leadership study, as well as a leading-edge analysis of the new paradigm of transformational leadership.

"Understanding and Assessing Organizational Leadership" by Marshall Sashkin and W. Warner Burke, in *Measures of Leadership*, edited by Kenneth E. Clark and Miriam B. Clark (West Orange, NJ: Leadership Library of America/Center for Creative Leadership, 1990). This is the most accessible synopsis of Sashkin's Visionary Leadership Theory, including extensive data and research results up to 1990.

"Assessing Transformational Leadership and Its Impact" by Marshall Sashkin, William E. Rosenbach, Terrence E. Deal, and Kent D. Peterson, in *Impact of Leadership*, edited by Kenneth E. Clark, Miriam B. Clark, and David P. Campbell (Greensboro, NC: Center for Creative Leadership, 1992). This update of Sashkin's earlier report focuses on additional research evidence for his approach and explains how transformational leaders achieve their effects.

Organizational Culture and Leadership (2nd edition) by Edgar H. Schein (San Francisco: Jossey-Bass, 1992). Schein applies Parson's concepts in an understandable manner, clarifying the underlying nature of organizational culture and identifying many of the values and categories of values that are the most important ingredients of organizational culture.

3

To Give Their Gifts

The Innovative, Transforming Leadership of Adaptive Work

RICHARD A. COUTO

"Leadership," Jacqueline Reed tells us, "sets up an opportunity for others to give their gift, for others to contribute to community." Reed directs the Westside Health Authority in Chicago, Illinois. This nonprofit, community-based organization is itself composed of several neighborhood programs and associations that train people to provide and to advocate for the resources and services they need to improve the quality of life in inner-city Chicago. Reed's succinct, profound view of leadership expresses the insights of people who are steeped in the difficult work of social change and reflection upon it.[1]

Like Reed, I have given some thought to the topic of leadership—recently, for instance, through my participation in the Kellogg Leadership Studies Project. Yet after several years of intense scholarly deliberations, many Project participants still returned to a fundamental question: What is the central problem with which leadership deals? Larraine R. Matusak, a former W.K. Kellogg Foundation program officer and Director of the Kellogg National Fellowship Program, lamented, "We keep coming back to the question, What? What is leadership for?" This paper provides one answer to that question. It develops a specific model of innovative, transforming leadership of adaptive work by drawing on the recent work of several prominent leadership scholars: Howard Gardner, James MacGregor Burns, and Ronald A. Heifetz.

Reprinted from Proceedings of the 1998 Annual Meeting of Leaders/Scholars Association, with permission of James MacGregor Burns Academy of Leadership, University of Maryland at College Park, pp. 43–52.

Social capital is critical to adaptive work because it reduces social and economic disparities and extends and strengthens communal bonds. It is the moral resources and public goods that we invest in one another as members of a community. This paper proposes that the purpose—the "what"—of innovative, transforming leadership of adaptive work is to advocate and provide increased amounts and improved forms of social capital. Too, this paper uses the four-year effort of the Kellogg Leadership Studies Project to construct a framework to analyze leadership in a manner that incorporates the concise, cogent, and compelling insight of "Jackie" Reed.

Innovative, Transforming Leadership for Adaptive Work

The work of Howard Gardner provides us the "innovative" part of our leadership formulation. Gardner explains leadership across domains or fields, such as physics or art, and not within them. He concerns himself less with outstanding leaders and creative people in a particular field and more with leaders attempting to lead people in the general public in common efforts—leaders who cross the borders of domains and offer new human possibilities. Gardner couples this concern with his finding that we have "unschooled minds" that are developed by the age of five. By this age, we have well-established theories about the world, social relationship, and values. He holds that adults continue to theorize about the world with the simple truths they developed as children.[2] Leaders working with a broad and diverse array of people from the general public and leaders working in efforts to change some fundamental aspect of human relations and conduct have to accept this mind or try to change it. Storytelling provides the primary method of access to the unschooled minds and fundamental, childlike beliefs of followers.

Gardner then distinguishes leaders by the stories they relate, which involves embodying stories more than merely telling them.[3] An ordinary leader, for Gardner, "relates the traditional story of his or her group as effectively as possible." This story provides us with valuable insight into the taken-for-granted assumptions of the unschooled mind and unbroken connection of the child-adult theoretical realm. Ordinary leaders reinforce the familiar. They do not provide an inkling of how a group will or must change. Innovative and visionary leaders, however, do. An innovative leader may bring new attention or a "fresh twist" to a familiar but ignored story and reassert traditional and familiar values. Margaret Thatcher and Ronald Reagan, for example, both did much to reinvigorate the values of market economies and limited government in the 1980s. A visionary leader creates a new story or stories that are familiar to only a few and succeeds in relating them effectively so that they reassemble parts of the unschooled mind and permit people to do new theory building about fundamental values and beliefs. Gardner cites as visionary leaders the great religious leaders of the past, Moses, Confucius, Jesus, Buddha, Mohammed, and more contemporary leaders such as Mahatma Gandhi and Jean Monnet, the champion of European unity.[4] Gardner's primary interest is in innovative and visionary leaders.

The borders of innovative stories meld with the boundaries of ordinary stories on one side and with those of visionary stories on the other. As innovative leaders, Reagan and Thatcher told ordinary stories extraordinarily well. They "put forth a simple nostalgic message in which they personally believed, one that they could articulate persuasively and one that, despite minor inconsistencies, they appeared to embody in their own lives."[5] Both "reactivated beliefs and values that had been dormant . . . for many years."[6] Both did so in a simplistic and divisive way that stressed differences among people and appealed to the childlike need to be better than "them." Both awakened new pride in old nationalism as well as fear of those with whom "we" differed. Both excelled in telling stories and embodied the values they espoused with the apparent unshakable confidence of the five-year-old mind. As Gardner says of Thatcher, with equal applicability to Reagan, she saw "the world in stark black and white terms and could not tolerate ambiguity or subtlety."[7]

Our interest is in those innovative leaders at the other end of the spectrum, where innovative and visionary leaders bump into each other. Gardner's visionary leaders relate stories of common bonds among people that imply new forms of association and larger degrees of social responsibility. "The formidable challenge confronting the visionary leader is to offer a story, and an embodiment, that builds on the most credible of past syntheses, revisits them in the light of present concerns, leaves open a place for future events, and allows individual contributions by the persons in the group."[8]

Visionary leadership that transforms society occurs rarely. It occurs more frequently within a domain,[9] such as community health, and in specific organizations, such as a community health program, because the range of truth and values is narrower, more developed, and more thoroughly shared. Leaders can access values and stories of people within a domain more easily than they can the values and stories of people from a wide array of domains/professions, countries, or socioeconomic backgrounds. Within their own programs and in terms of its values, some leaders indeed may be visionaries. We prefer, however, to leave the term "visionary leader" to such truly historic figures as Gardner cites. Instead, we wish to develop the concept of "innovative leaders" who embody old values, such as sharing, in new stories, such as poverty. The relevance of their stories and old values present "new trusts" applicable to diverse domains. In this manner, they resemble visionary leaders.

The stories of these innovative leaders, like the stories of visionary leaders, tell of "potential life experiences" of groups marginalized by the current distribution of social, economic, and political resources.[10] These innovative stories and truths differ radically from those of Thatcher and Reagan, which diminished social responsibility by focusing on individual responsibility as the root cause of disparities in social, economic, and political resources. Despite this fundamental difference, the common elements of innovative leadership are the stories and values of the five-year-old mind that may be taken from one context and applied to many others. *Innovative leadership, for us, will refer to new stories that reinforce old values of social responsibility and the worth of all individuals and groups.*

James MacGregor Burns's lengthy and thorough study, *Leadership*, provides a foundation for a discussion of leadership in general and the meaning of "transforming" in our formulation of leadership. Burns distinguishes transforming from transactional leadership, which exchanges psychological, political, and economic things of value. Each party to the transaction knows the other and has sufficient sense of his or her motives and resources to determine common purpose that can be advanced in a bargaining process. The bond of leader and follower is temporary and limited. Formal organizations, such as bureaucracies and groups, and established processes, such as voting, provide the context of transactional leadership.[11]

In contrast with transactional leadership, informal organizations and processes of change provide the context of transforming leadership. Transforming leadership "occurs when one or more persons *engage* with others in such a way that leaders and followers raise one another to higher levels of motivation and morality."[12] Transforming leadership fuses the common but initially separate purposes of leaders and followers into an enduring effort of mutual support. Burns offers as examples of transforming leadership the Founding Fathers and the drafting of the Constitution, political reform such as the New Deal, and the political revolutionary leadership of America, France, Russia, and China.

Although transforming leadership incorporates transactional leadership, Burns's readers have treated them as distinct and placed more emphasis on transforming than on transactional leadership. It is not enough, however, to have grand visions of transformation. Effective leadership gets things done, and that is largely the task of transactional leadership. Transforming and transactional leadership combine in "extended and complex structures of group relationships." In them, major transforming leaders, such as Lenin and Woodrow Wilson, led and are led by less well-known men and women. The relationship of these primary, secondary and tertiary figures makes up a "crucial component of transactional leadership."[13]

Here we find parallels between Gardner's visionary leader and Burns's transforming leader. Gardner's innovative leader achieves some measure of success by conveying new stories to others and learning new stories from others as well. Burns's transforming leader has a vision of a new state of human affairs and works with others to reach it. Innovative leadership, like transforming leadership, extends from old to new truths; from familiar to unfamiliar stories; and from exchanges of mutual benefit that further common interests to the successful call for sacrifice to further an uncommon state of affairs.

Transforming leadership exceeds transactional leadership primarily because "it raises the level of human conduct and ethical aspiration of both leader and led, and thus it has a transforming effort on both."[14] Burns, just like Gardner, offers as the best modern example of transforming leadership Mahatma Gandhi, "who aroused and elevated the hopes and demands of millions of the Indians and whose life and personality were enhanced in the process."[15]

Burns gives us the central idea that leadership entails a group: change *within* the group, and/or change by the group. "The leader's fundamental act is to induce people to be aware or conscious of what they feel to feel their true needs so strongly, to define their values so meaningfully, that they can move to purposeful action."[16] The transforming leader shapes, alters, and elevates the motives and values and goals of followers into "significant change."[17]

"Significant change" entails the abolition of some caste-like restriction that impairs the recognition of the human worth of a group of people and the public expression of their values and needs. Here we find a parallel between Burns's transforming leader and Gardner's visionary leader. Significant change begins with new stories that express new or neglected values of human worth. Burns is concerned with the social, political, and economic circumstances and nature of significant changes as well as their psychological character. He points out that transforming leadership more likely comes from outside formal organizations and institutions, entails involuntary changes of an organization, and depends on causal factors and conditions that transforming leaders do not create or control. Burns deals with leadership within social movements and politics; revolutionary leadership where politics and social movements overlap. *Transforming leadership helps a group move from one stage of development to a higher one and in doing so addresses and fulfills better a human need and possibility.*

Ronald Heifetz provides us the final element of our leadership formulation—adaptive work. Heifetz defines leadership as the activity of *adaptive work of a group that attempts to reduce the gap between its values and its practice.*[18] Implicitly, the gap between values and practice is a problem, and the task of leadership is to raise practice to the level of values. Heifetz distinguishes adaptive work from technical work in a way that distinguishes leadership from expertise.

Conveniently, given our central concern with community health, Heifetz uses the relation of physician and patient to explain the difference between adaptive and technical work. The symptoms and signs of illness that a patient presents may provide the physician a clear definition of the problem and the appropriate treatment. The physician may take care of the problem with little effort on the part of the patient beyond applying an ointment or taking the appropriate medicine. Other symptoms and signs of illness may provide the physician a clear definition of the problem, but the appropriate treatment will entail more effort from the patient. Diabetes and heart conditions require behavioral changes of life style—diet, exercise, smoking and drinking, for example—as well as medication. Part of the solution is mechanical and technical, but part of the solution is also the adaptive work of the patient to narrow the gap between the value of increased health and the practices that can improve or imperil health. In some cases, such as advanced breast cancer, the symptoms and signs of illness signal an unclear problem for which there is no mechanical and technical answer. The illness signals the problem of death, which is the real problem. Dealing with the illness may impede the patient's adaptive work "of facing and making adjustments to harsh realities that go beyond the health condition and that include several possible problems":[19] making the most out of life, providing for children, completing professional tasks, and preparing loved ones. Both patients and physicians have adaptive work in this case. The practice of medicine may impede the human value of preparing for death.

Clear problems and solutions call for technical answers of experts. Unclear problems and solutions call for leadership and a willingness to act in the face of doubt. For Heifetz, part of leadership requires the ability to tell when adaptive work and not technical answers are needed. This is an early and difficult task for leadership.

Even the toughest individual tends to avoid realities that require adaptive work, searching instead for an authority, a physician, to provide the way out. And doctors, wanting deeply to fulfill the yearning for remedy, too often respond willingly to the pressures we place on them to focus narrowly on technical answers.[20]

It is not difficult to equate Heifetz's patient-physician relationship with Gardner's child-adult relationship. Avoiding the requirement of adaptive work mirrors the five-year-old mind's seeking refuge in the assurance of an adult, the ordinary innovative leader, that the world is black and white, that all questions have answers, and all problems have satisfactory solutions that may be imposed by those in authority. In summary, Gardner, Burns, and Heifetz permit us to understand that *innovative, transforming leadership of adaptive work entails new stories about the nature of problems and solutions that permit people to conduct the tasks of significant change.*

Social Capital—The "What" of Innovative, Transforming Leadership of Adaptive Work

The work of Gardner, Burns, and Heifetz makes problems and problem solving central to leadership. But what is the problem? How can we tell if a solution is "significant change"? Gardner and Burns implicitly and explicitly make the problem of leadership a problem of morality. The highest forms of innovative and transforming leadership, which we are tracing here, attempt to bring individuals and groups to a higher and better level of human existence. Innovative, transforming leadership has the task to see and to say the potential life experiences and human dignity of groups of people who are denied them by others. It solves problems of the social, economic and political practices of organizations and institutions that restrict or distort that potential life experience and human dignity of some people and groups to a degree that compromises and contradicts democratic values of equality and responsibility. Heifetz's idea of adaptive work incorporates these values and others. For Heifetz however, adaptive work clarifies and tests values. It does not presuppose one set of values over another.

Even if we accept, as we do, that democratic values are the values of leadership, we still have a problem. Which democratic values are we discussing? Margaret Thatcher and Ronald Reagan did adaptive work just as surely as Martin Luther King, Jr. and Lyndon Baines Johnson. According to Gardner, however, Thatcher and Reagan fall on the innovative/ordinary end of the spectrum and King and Johnson on the innovative/visionary side. Within a democracy, we find tensions and paradoxes, if not contradictions, of competing values: majority rule and minority rights; individual rights and common responsibilities; liberty and equality; and freedom from and freedom through collective action, including government. We also find competing patterns of representation and participation. Even the five-year-old unschooled mind has a theory of democracy beset with contradictions. "What's mine is mine and what's yours is yours" bumps into "All for one and one for all." Likewise, the special individual worth a child feels has to be moderated with concern for the welfare and feelings of other children. The adaptive work of innovative, transforming leadership, for us, sees, speaks to, and solves problems of equity, human needs, human dignity, and social responsibility. It falls on minority rights, common responsibilities, equality, and freedom through the collective-action side of the democratic constellation of values. It falls on the "all-for-one-and-one-for-all" concern for side of the proto-theory of democracy in the five-year-old mind.

Put in simplest terms, the adaptive work of innovative, transforming leadership, as we are dealing with it, relates directly to increasing the amounts and improving the forms of social capital. Social capital produces and reproduces people in community through the public provision of goods, such as health, housing, and education, and moral resources, such as charity, trust, and cooperation. Social capital promotes social and economic equity and communal bonds. Democracy requires that some people provide, directly and indirectly, as well as advocate for the public provision of new forms and increased amounts of social capital. Without innovative, transforming leadership for the adaptive work of increased amounts and new forms of social capital, democratic practice risks contracting to an illusion covering the undemocratic realities of oligarchy and rigid and increasing economic divisions and their social correlates.

An innovative leader who established services for victims of domestic violence has explained the idea of social capital in practical terms. The speaker recounted how economic decline and increased unemployment in a local steel plant had strained the resources of families and contributed to increased acts of violence towards women and children. She reported turning an unused inner-city church rectory into a shelter for women and children who were no longer safe in their own homes and had no other place to go. After securing this space, she and her colleagues found beds, furniture, and volunteers to repair and paint the shelter. They also found other volunteers to staff the shelter and provide counseling and referrals to the women and children who found refuge there.

Somewhere in the middle of this account, the speaker observed, "We didn't go about this in a very businesslike way." In fact, she and her colleagues had been very businesslike. They had found a market in which a new demand for services had an inadequate supply of providers. They accumulated resources to meet that demand and instituted services. Only lack of a profit motive distinguishes their efforts from those of a "business." Their domestic violence shelter had little chance to make a profit and to offer a financial reward to those who instituted it. Risking the time and effort to uncover resources to invest in people without money to pay for the shelter's services distinguished the shelter from "business." The distinction was particularly sharp at the time: it was the 1980s, the greed-is-good era.

The leadership behind this domestic violence shelter was unbusinesslike only in that it was not tied to profit making. Ordinarily, social capital is spent to produce and reproduce people as a labor force of human capital. James Coleman, a prominent sociologist who provides a social science narrative of social capital, distinguishes social capital from three other forms of capital: financial, physical, and human. Monetary wealth comprises financial capital. Physical capital entails tools, machinery, and other productive equipment. Human capital is made up of people in the production process. Social capital is the relationship among persons involved in the production process. Social capital functions as the aspects of social structure valuable to entrepreneurs who can use them as resources to realize their interests.[21] These four forms of capital are related to each other, most obviously in a business organization created by owners of financial capital to earn a profit. Financial capital entrepreneurs turn financial capital into physical capital in the forms of tools and buildings. They produce human capital by recruiting or training people with the knowledge and skills required in production. They produce social capital by investing in the design of obligations and expectations, responsibility and authority, and norms and sanctions among the people within the organization in order to achieve effectiveness and efficiency.[22] Human capital resides in people; social capital resides in the relations among them.[23]

The ties between social and human capital mean a strong emphasis on the private provision of social capital. We look to the laborer's wage as the first and primary source of the goods and resources that people need to produce and continue community. We look to the employer as the secondary source of social capital. Public provision of social capital, such as education, is linked to the needs of local employers in the local economy. We spend most social capital to produce and reproduce people as a labor force and smaller amounts on people as citizens, parents, community members, or other public roles. Our public policies also depend upon work-related social capital—primarily the wage—to provide the financial means to get housing, transportation, and cultural and recreational opportunities. Health care insurance is another work-related form of social capital dependent upon a person's place in the economy.

When a group of people have a subordinate role in the economy, the social capital invested in them is modest. When people have no role in the economy, social capital may not be invested in them at all. Low-wage, low-skill workers or large populations of surplus labor in inner cities and rural areas have less social capital because of their low value as human capital. Areas of high unemployment and low income generally have low amounts and poor forms of social capital: health care, leisure, housing, educational services, the goods and moral resources that we depend upon to support communities.

Appalachia illustrates clearly the history, rise and fall, and ordinary ties of social capital to financial, physical, and human capital. The coal, steel, and textile towns that dot the map of Appalachia graphically depict the relation of social capital and the work place. For the first half of this century, private capital produced and reproduced a work force for the industries it created through social capital investment.[24] When the need for this labor force diminished, social capital dried up and coal towns began a decline that is apparent in the region. Steel towns[25] and some textile towns have followed that decline. Where the demand for a skilled labor force declines, so does incentive to invest social capital.

The forms and amounts of social capital vary from place to place at the same time and from time to time in the same place.[26] American forms of social capital invest public goods and moral resources to produce and sustain people as laborers, primarily. This limits the community that is produced to the labor force. The innovative/ordinary leadership of Ronald Reagan and Margaret Thatcher emphasized this value. Since 1980, American policy makers have argued over whether the sources of the few forms and limited amounts of social capital, such as job training or welfare and health care for children in poverty, should be public or private. Less often, we argue about the adequacy of the size and forms of social capital. The welfare reform measures of 1996 indicated that American workers and low-income family members need to face new and larger social and economic problems with fewer forms and smaller amounts of public social capital. In this context, community becomes an indirect consequence of public policies and financial capital to shape a work force and to minimize the costs of human and social capital. Coleman's social capital disappears without work.

Inadequate services for victims of domestic violence, problems of homelessness, inadequate health care, poor schools, environmental degradation, and areas of chronic poverty, such as Appalachia, may be understood as the consequence of inadequate amounts of social capital. This single issue has two sides: first, increased amounts of social capital—more housing, health care, educational services—and new forms of social capital—investments of goods and services in people separate from their market value as human capital. This is the "what" of the adaptive work of innovative, transforming leadership: provision and advocacy of increased amounts and new forms of social capital that decrease social and economic disparities and increase and improve communal bonds. The first problem for innovative, transforming leadership is to increase the amounts and improve the forms of social capital to see, say and solve the general problem of reducing human and social problems to economics and the inevitable, absolute values driven by extra-human forces of the market. Social capital, the goods and moral resources that produce people in community, permits us a measure for Burns's "purposeful action" and "significant change." Social capital, in its broadest forms, also helps us to understand Gardner's innovative leadership. The increase and improvement of social capital embody the narratives of innovative/visionary leadership. Finally, we use the increase and improvement of social capital as the central element of adaptive work.

The "How" of Innovative,
Transforming Leadership of Adaptive Work

Identifying the adaptive work of innovative, transforming leadership as increased amounts and improved forms of social capital leaves us with other questions of how leaders go about this work. This leads us to the question of how leaders go about any work. After almost five years of discussions and written work on this last questions, the members of the Kellogg Leadership Studies Project identified some promising avenues for answers. In his work with this group, Burns revisited his original work on leadership. He conceived leadership anew as interactive networks that empower their members, in the sense of transferring tangible resources and increasing moral resources, to achieve, by the most democratic means feasible, an improved expression of human values and conditions. Burns emerged from the Kellogg Project with a new perspective on leadership—an initiative for change through empowerment.[27]

Burns turned his attention to values and initiative. Leadership entails conflict over the human and social consequences of putting one set of values into practice rather than another. Burns's transforming leaders conflict over what adaptive work to do, what old or new truths to innovate. He is concerned also with a leader who gets things done: "the special kind of initiator, the *innovator* who not only proposes a change to meet a need but a means of realizing it."[28] Values help explain the initiative of innovative, transforming leaders and their adaptive work. Values also distinguish their inclusiveness and creativity. Successful innovative, transforming leaders do adaptive work that includes those neglected or injured by current practices.

They recognize differences among people, search the differences out, and include people with differences in their organizations and processes. This marks the fundamental difference between ordinary and visionary leaders. Ordinary leaders narrate stories that extol old truths of human differences as the basis of practices of exclusion. Visionary leaders narrate stories that offer new truths of human bonds as a basis of practices of inclusion. This work requires the creativity to express the fundamental, five-year-old's values of caring, equity, and justice. The values of a leader or of a context of leadership—political, business, or community—spill over into where they take initiative; whom they include in the purpose and process of their work; and the distinguishing criteria of their creativity. Thus we assume all leadership has values that affect directly its initiative, inclusiveness, and creativity.

The three other common elements of leadership that the Kellogg Leadership Studies Project identified are change, conflict, and collaboration.

- *Change*—Leaders take initiative as "the first step toward change." Burns presumes that change means moving from one state in the web of relations to another. But this change may be to formalize and activate an informal web or it may be to energize a formal web that has ossified.[29]
- *Conflict*—If change is the lure of leadership, conflict is the companion of change. Conflict is also the avenue to see clearly the values of an individual as well as a web of relations. It makes the unspecified and perhaps even unintended consequences of a set of actions clearer.
- *Collaboration*—Power is central to leadership and shared power is central to collaboration. Collaboration imparts a sense of agency, of being an agent of history, a person and group capable of improving events, circumstances, and conditions.

Change entails conflict and collaboration. Change also implies values. Subsuming change under values, however, obscures the central point that there are conflicting values contested in change efforts and that collaboration requires working together because of similar values or despite conflicting values. By separating the value-related distinguishing characteristics of leadership from the change-related tasks common to leadership, we construct an analytical framework of all leadership, including one that is helpful to analyze innovative, transforming leadership of adaptive work.

The "Why" of Innovative, Transforming Leadership of Adaptive Work

These two dimensions—values and change and their related factors—permit us to describe further the innovative, transforming leadership of adaptive work in terms of new forms and increased amounts of social capital.

The forms and amount of social capital support the initiative of some people to undertake innovative, transforming leadership. A sense of responsibility for the depletion of the moral resources and public goods that sustain people in community causes them to act. They draw attention to externalities, such as the consequences of market transactions that are subsidized at the expense of community. Toxic wastes, for example, subtract from the minimal environmental quality required to sustain community. Dumping them in a manner that threatens a community subsidizes fundamental capital at a cost to social capital. The public learns of these subsidies and externalities through the conflictive and collaborative efforts of innovative, transforming leaders and other organizations and institutions. Innovative, transforming leaders are also moved to action by important omissions in the provision of social capital. Security from physical harm, for example, seems a primary prerequisite to community. Yet, many women and their children did not have this security until others took initiative to provide safe spaces for them. An expanded realm of human rights, inclusiveness and values is the girder for this call to action to expand and increase social capital. A sense of responsibility to redress inadequate social capital springs from a sense that human services like health care and the other factors that support community, i.e., environmental quality, are human rights. This sense of responsibility is conveyed in embodied narratives (see Table 3.3) about how the market failed by either producing the poor health or poor environment or by not improving the condition. Therefore, the conditions of our communities fall within the realm of individual and social responsibility and ability and not within the suprahuman external forces of the market.

Obviously, acting to improve and increase forms of social capital means change. Innovative, transforming leaders do their adaptive work by providing new forms of social capital as well as new amounts. They bring children's services where there were none and incorporate in them development strategies for the children and their parents. The human needs they address take place in a context, and innovative, transforming leaders follow those needs to their causes and consequences and deal with them there, if possible. If a child's success in school depends upon parental involvement with homework and schoolwork, then parents must be qualified for their role. Improving children's chances of success in school may require formal preparation for their parents and classes to provide high school equivalency diplomas. The adaptive work of innovative, transforming leaders takes the context of a human need and problem into account. Their change efforts take a system of organizations and institutions into account. They often describe their efforts as holistic.

As change agents of adaptive work, innovative, transforming leaders become alternative sources of social capital, but only after they develop sources of alternative social capital. They not only provide social capital, such as shelter services, but they acquire financial and physical capital that supports their services. This means that they cajole and convince organizations and institutions, such as banks, to do things they would not ordinarily do, such as provide loans for low-cost housing. In conducting this work, they secure "risk" social capital to invest in new ideas premised on new or existing social values.

The adaptive work of innovative, transforming leaders deals with inter- and intrapersonal change as well as with the practices of organizations and institutions. Often we find the deliberate attempt to break down interpersonal barriers, real and perceived, of race, ethnicity, gender, class, physical ability, and other human differences that transmute into social divisions. The adaptive work of organizations and programs of innovative, transforming leaders includes different people in the provision and eligibility for services. Differences among people with disabilities are set aside to realize and assert what they have in common. Such personal changes bring on forms of empowerment. The transformation of social capital goes beyond the empowerment that instills new attitudes or behaviors. The empowerment of innovative, transforming leaders transfers resources to an individual or a group that enable them to change their condition as well as to deal with it. The holistic and systemic approach implies changing the practices of organizations and institutions, not learning to cope with them.

Coping, however, is part of the adaptive work of innovative, transforming leaders. Successful change comes about because they can combine a sense of what is necessary with a sense of what is possible. Curiously, successful change comes when leaders take to heart the lessons about the limits and problems of local organizing from their own efforts or those of others. The patience to cope, the courage to change, and the wisdom to tell which is appropriate at the time works in change efforts on the individual and organizational level.

Change will bring on conflict, as will the implicit or explicit criticism of existing practices of organizations and institutions that stimulates innovative, transforming leaders. The gap between values and practices may not be obvious to everyone. Likewise, those with different values, who prize individual liberty over social equality, may find no gap in such practices as income redistribution to the wealthy through tax reform. Market failures resulting from benefits to one group, such as saved costs, prompts them to continue negative externalities or the underproduction of social capital. Redressing a market failure entails conflicting with someone's profitable practice—and that is likely to create conflict. Is there a gap between practice and values? What values are at stake? How can practices be changed to benefit some and to cut the losses of others? The closer we approach visionary leadership, the clearer conflicting values emerge and the more likely power and violence will protect existing practices.

The conflict is not entirely external. Groups differ over how much change is needed and what is the best way to achieve it. Differences over strategies and tactics will divide people who share a common goal. The ordinary work of innovative, transforming leaders entails holding a group together despite differences and resolving differences and conflicts over group values and practices. Acting on new values and in contrast with existing practices means internal personal conflict as well as internal group conflict. To some degree, innovative, transforming leaders share the values they oppose and have been socialized to accept the practices they seek to change. This may raise grave self-doubt within individuals about whether they are right and whether they have the right to change the practices with which they disagree. These doubts will arise within the organization of innovative, transforming leaders. The effort to increase social bonds and to include different groups in the organization inevitably runs into resistance, and group cohesion becomes threatened by inclusion and participating in broad networks of new people and unfamiliar and unpopular groups. Innovative, transforming leaders have adaptive work within their own groups to bring the values of inclusiveness into line with practices of exclusion premised on prejudice towards those perceived as different.

Collaboration solves some of the conflicts within change efforts of innovative, transforming leadership of adaptive work. Groups find threats to their cohesion when they are unable to set priorities and to agree on strategies and tactics. Collaboration increases cohesion by forging agreement for group action including conflict. Collaboration does not eliminate conflict. It resolves and manages conflict within groups that permits them more cohesion for united action in conflict or cooperation with others.

Collaboration entails networks. In some cases, innovative, transforming leadership conducts its adaptive work by establishing new networks through chapters of its organization. In the case of smaller organizations, it uses networks of committees and small groups. In both instances, innovative, transforming leadership does the adaptive work of developing the leadership potential of other members within the group. This action promotes effectiveness but not efficiency. Emerging leaders present the possibility of conflict over priorities, strategies, and tactics. Apart from working within its group, innovative, transforming leadership for adaptive work also forms coalitions with groups that have common programs or problems. Again, especially at first, this form of collaboration may promote effectiveness and inefficiency as well. As these coalitions and associations become more formal and effective, the tension between group cohesion and network participation diminishes. Again, conflict and collaboration relate to each other.

Networks inevitably mean new forms of collaboration. Innovative, transforming leadership requires assistance for its adaptive work. Those who are successful in dealing with conflict; in fostering inclusiveness and dealing with prejudice and discrimination within their program; in finding and providing alternative social capital; and in the host of other adaptive tasks of innovative, transforming leadership, may be called upon to help others deal with those tasks. Networks of innovative, transforming leadership for adaptive work create markets for collaborative assistance.

Not all forms of innovative, transforming leadership for adaptive work are equally successful. It succeeds most often when social capital combines private and public resources and has market and government sources. Housing, for example, has ties to public regulation of lending, government programs such as Farmers Home Administration and Section 8 Public Housing, and the private market. Innovative, transforming leadership of adaptive work succeeds best when different streams of resources are available from which to find sources of social capital.

TABLE 3.1   Lessons of Innovative, Transforming Leadership for Adaptive Work

Change	Conflict	Collaboration
• Transformative democratic achievements took place, in part, because of the lessons on the limits and problems of local organizing • Testing new ideas and providing "risk" social capital • Psychosymbolic and psychopolitical empowerment • Viewing human needs and services as a right and not a commodity • Deliberate means to intentional breakdown of interpersonal barriers, real and perceived, or race, gender, and class • External threats to social capital that create human needs and the urgency of responding to them • Providing new forms of social capital, not merely new amount • Alternative sources of social capital and sources of alternative social capital	• Group cohesion may be threatened by a group's inability to select one or a few clear threats to social capital on which to focus • The democratic task of increasing social bonds, promoting equality, and extending communal ties to new groups may also threaten group cohesion • Mitigating the social consequences of market failures • An early warning system of the depletion of social capital • Warning of important omissions in the provision of social capital • Deliberate means to intentional breakdown of interpersonal barriers, real and perceived, of race, gender, and class • Quarrels about leverage points in networks robbed the group of its cohesion	• Leadership successfully creates increased cohesion by establishing new networks through chapters or among groups with common programs or problems • Most success in those areas of social capital that are mixed between market and public goods: housing, health care, and culture • Meeting the unique market demands of other community-based organizations • Coalitions and associations reduce the tensions between group cohesion and network participation

SOURCE: Richard Couto, *Making Democracy Work Better: Mediating Structures, Social Capital, and the Democratic Prospect* (Chapel Hill: University of North Carolina Press, 1999).

TABLE 3.2   The Common Tasks and Distinguishing Elements of Innovative Transforming Leadership—Values

Distinguishing Elements	*Common Tasks*		
Values	*Change*	*Conflict*	*Collaboration*
All people have intrinsic value worthy of investment. Cultural diversity is a strength. People have the right to self-determination in their own communities. Mutuality and interdependency are valued over individualism. Participation in the governmental process is a responsibility of a healthy community. Community education and employment are major preventative health measures.	Change is not a value by and in itself, but a value as a means to other values. The pursuit of these fundamental values requires change and leadership. Change may be both incremental and quantum. Both are judged by their relation to advancement of values of social and economic justice.	Worthwhile conflict occurs over values. It pushes up the dysfunctional practices and issues of a system. Conflict comes from the initial statement that there is adaptive work to be done—practices that must be changed to serve better values or to better serve the same values. Conflict occurs internally, among competing values, within a person.	Collaboration has value as the expression of relationships that constitute social reality and the prospects for social change. Collaboration supports change in programs and practices that build a better future. Collaboration provides a legacy of value for others in the fruits of its actions but collaboration, as process, provides a valuable legacy for others. Collaboration entails the continuation of past values that others acted on previously.

TABLE 3.3   The Common Tasks and Distinguishing Elements of Innovative, Transforming Leadership—Creativity

Distinguishing Elements	*Common Tasks*		
Creativity	*Change*	*Conflict*	*Collaboration*
• Vision • Imagination • Reflective practice • Critical thinking	Greatest success in areas of public and private mix in the provision of social capital—health care, housing, and artistic expression. Transforming change may occur within limited opportunities and because of the limits to change learned in previous change efforts. Reflection upon mistakes in past practices permits improvement in later practices.	Conflict may occur over what targets to select for social capital investment. Creativity reduces dissipating conflicts within a group and chooses wisely the conflict between and among groups. Creativity resolves conflicts. Creative use of networks may reduce the conflict inherent in leaders' participation in networks and away from groups.	Chances for collaboration increase with a shared vision of expanded social capital. Seeing new roles for institutions in the provision of new amounts and improved forms of social capital. Seeing past the obstacles to change and to follow new opportunities. To recognize the relevance of other successful efforts to one's own adaptive work. Coalitions and associations may group cohesion, if done creatively. To share with others the lessons acquired in successful and unsuccessful adaptive work.

TABLE 3.4   The Common Tasks of Leadership and the Distinguishing Elements of Innovative, Transforming Leadership—Inclusiveness

Distinguishing Elements	Common Tasks		
Inclusiveness	Change	Conflict	Collaboration
All people have intrinsic value worthy of social capital investment. Cultural diversity contributes to social capital by increasing the forms of community and exemplifying the variety of means that people use to sustain themselves in community. People have the right to be included in decisions about resources in their own communities. Mutuality and interdependency are valued over individualism.	Economic, social, and technologic changes affect the factors to produce and sustain people in community. Change should be in the direction of increased amounts and new forms of social capital. New forms and increased amounts of social capital decrease social and economic disparities and increase and improve communal bonds. Change in social capital begins with establishing personal relationships with other members of disinvested communities.	Worthwhile conflict entails fighting for increased amounts and improved forms of social capital and against changes that deplete stocks of social capital. Financial capital and public policy will minimize the forms of social capital and limit them to people as members of a new labor force rather than as members of a broader community. Conflict is often required to gain inclusion for groups with too little social capital into the decision-making process. Inclusiveness may entail internal, personal conflict between self-esteem and the depreciating judgments of others that are internalized. Conflict, when successful, may be a prelude to collaboration.	Collaboration has value as horizontal and vertical networks. Collaboration increases moral resources of trust, cooperation, honesty, integrity. Collaboration provides a foundation of moral resources for later inclusive change efforts. The moral resources of collaboration are a starting point for the acquisition of new and improved forms of social captial. Moral resources are not the sum total of social captial, but a means to its provision as well.

TABLE 3.5   The Common Tasks and Distinguishing Elements of Innovative, Transforming Leadership—Initiative

Distinguishing Elements	Common Tasks		
Initiative	Change	Conflict	Collaboration
Initiative comes from meeting one's own needs and learning of the public nature of one's apparently individual, private problem. Initiative stems from a sense of calling, often reluctantly accepted or related to an involuntarily imposed condition, e.g., a disabling injury inflicted by violence.	Some threat to existing forms and amounts of social capital appears. Some change is required to increase the amount and to improve the forms of social capital to a point to meet some basic needs of groups of people. A vision of the achievement of some services ordinarily available to the general public but withheld from "extraordinary" group spurs determined resistance to practices of exclusion. Impatience and frustration with the thought of a future without changes in insufficient amounts and inappropriate forms of social capital. Hopes for change are tempered by one's own and other's experience.	Conflict to stimulate the social imagination about forms and amounts of social capital and its public provision. Conflict over economic, social, and political practices that diminish social capital or ignore its provision. Defense of one neglected set of democratic values.	A heavy emphasis on process and the development of people in the process of making change. Emphasis on shared and familiar values. Building on legacies that are common or that provide an analogy for current efforts. Self-consciously building a legacy for continued initiatives for change.

Notes

1. This paper is part of a work in progress titled *To Give Their Gifts: Health, Community, and Leadership,* Vanderbilt University Press, 2002.

2. Howard Gardner, *Leading Minds: An Anatomy of Leadership* (New York: Basic Books, 1995), pp. ix–x.

3. Ibid., p. 9.

4. Ibid., pp. 9–11.

5. Ibid., p. 235.

6. Ibid., p. 241.

7. Ibid., p. 237.

8. Ibid., p. 56.

9. Ibid., p. 11.

10. Ibid., p. 223.

11. James MacGregor Burns, *Leadership* (New York: Harper & Row, 1978), p. 19ff.

12. Ibid., p. 20.

13. Ibid., p. 289.

14. Ibid., p. 20.

15. Ibid., p. 20.

16. Ibid., p. 44.

17. Ibid., p. 425.

18. Ronald A. Heifetz, *Leadership Without Easy Answers* (Cambridge, MA: Belknap/Harvard University Press, 1994), pp. 19–27.

19. Ibid., p. 76.

20. Ibid., p. 76.

21. James William Coleman and Donald R. Cressey, *Social Problems* (New York: Harper & Row, 1990), p. 305.

22. Ibid., p. 313.

23. Ibid., p. 304.

24. See, for example, Crandall A. Shifflet, *Coal Towns: Life, Work, and Culture in Company Towns of Southern Appalachia, 1880–1960* (Knoxville, TN: University of Tennessee Press, 1991); and William Serrin, *Homestead: The Glory and Tragedy of an American Steel Town* (New York: Vintage Press, 1993).

25. Serrin, *Homestead* (1993).

26. Hirofumi Uzawa, *Preference, Production, and Capital: Selected Papers of Hirofumi Uzawa* (New York: Cambridge University Press, 1988) p. 341.

27. James MacGregor Burns, "Empowerment for Change," *Rethinking Leadership* (College Park, MD: The Academy of Leadership Press, 1998).

28. Ibid., p. 28.

29. Ibid.

4

Do You Have the
Will to Lead?

POLLY LABARRE

Philosopher Peter Koestenbaum poses the truly big questions: How do we act when risks seem overwhelming? What does it mean to be a successful human being?

Who hasn't stared out an airplane window on yet another red-eye and thought, What exactly is the point of this exercise? Or sat through a particularly senseless meeting and wondered, How in the world did I get here? Or wrestled with a set of strategic choices—all of which seem hard and unpleasant—and said, What happened to the fun part of being in business? According to Peter Koestenbaum, those uncomfortable questions—those existential quandaries—are at the root of issues that great leaders deal with all the time, and they influence every decision that must be made.

A classically trained philosopher with degrees in philosophy, physics, and theology from Stanford, Harvard, and Boston University, Koestenbaum has spent half a century pondering the questions that give most of us headaches: Why is there being instead of nothing? What is the ultimate explanation of the universe? What does it mean to be a successful human being? After fleeing pre–World War II Germany with his parents, Koestenbaum was raised in Venezuela; later, he emigrated to the United States to pursue his studies. He taught at San Jose State University for 34 years, and during that period he focused on creating a "practical philosophy"—a philosophy that is linked to education, psychology, and psychiatry. His many books include "The Vitality of Death" (Greenwood, 1971), "The New Image of the Person" (Greenwood, 1978), and "Managing

Anxiety" (Prentice Hall, 1974). One of his books, "Leadership: The Inner Side of Greatness" (Jossey-Bass, 1991), has been translated into several languages, and Koestenbaum is now at work on a new book, tentatively titled "Diamond Reverse Engineering."

More than 25 years ago, Koestenbaum traded the cloistered halls of academia for the front lines of the global economy. It's not unheard-of for this philosopher, now a tireless 71-year-old with thick glasses and a flowing beard, to visit clients across three continents in a single week. His agenda: to apply the power of philosophy to the big question of the day— how to reconcile the often-brutal realities of business with basic human values—and to create a new language of effective leadership. "Unless the distant goals of meaning, greatness, and destiny are addressed," Koestenbaum insists, "we can't make an intelligent decision about what to do tomorrow morning—much less set strategy for a company or for a human life. Nothing is more practical than for people to deepen themselves. The more you understand the human condition, the more effective you are as a businessperson. Human depth makes business sense."

Koestenbaum's wisdom makes sense to leaders at such giant organizations as Ford, EDS, Citibank, Xerox, Ericsson, and even one of Korea's chaebols. All of these companies have welcomed him into their offices to roam free as a resident sage, company therapist, and secular priest. His involvement with them ranges from one-on-one coaching sessions to decade-long engagements featuring intensive leadership seminars. At Ford, Koestenbaum contributed to the company's 2,000-person Senior Executive Program throughout the 1980s. In more than a decade at EDS, he led seminars and coached hundreds of top executives, including then-chairman Les Alberthal. He also coached Alexander Krauer, a prominent Swedish industrialist, when Krauer was chairman of Ciba-Geigy. Picking up on that momentum, another leading Swedish industrialist, Rolf Falkenberg, founded the Koestenbaum Institute to disseminate the philosopher's teachings across Scandinavia.

"Everything I do," says Koestenbaum, "is about using themes from the history of thought to rescue people who are stuck." His logic: Change— true, lasting, deep-seated change—is the business world's biggest and most persistent challenge. But too many people and too many companies approach change by treating it as a technical challenge rather than by developing authentic answers to basic questions about business life. "We've reached such explosive levels of freedom that, for the first time in history, we have to manage our own mutation," declares Koestenbaum. "It's up to us to decide what it means to be a successful human being. That's the philosophical task of the age. Nothing happens unless you make it happen. As a leader, everything is your responsibility, because you always could have chosen otherwise."

In an interview with *Fast Company*, Koestenbaum explains how age-old questions apply to the new world of work.

Why does being a leader feel so hard today?

Because reckoning with freedom is always hard—and the powerful paradoxes of the new economy make it even harder. We're living in a peculiar time: It's marked by a soaring stock market, the creation of tremendous wealth, an explosion in innovation, and the acute alienation that occurs when the global economy hits the average individual. What I call the "new-economy pathology" is driven by impossible demands—better quality, lower prices, faster innovation—that generate an unprecedented form of stress. People feel pressure to meet ever-higher objectives in all realms of work, wealth, and lifestyle—and to thrive on that pressure in the process.

This condition is exacerbated by the pornographic treatment of business in media and culture. The message is, You're living in the best country in the world at the best time in history; you have an amazing degree of freedom to do what you want, along with an unprecedented opportunity to build immense wealth and success—and to do it more quickly than ever before. Of course, the average individual has as much of a chance of launching a skyrocketing IPO as he or she has of becoming a movie star.

What's even more disturbing is that the ascendancy of shareholder value as the dominant driving force in business has resulted in a terrible insensitivity to basic human values. That's the real "stuck point" for leaders: How do we cope with a brutal business reality and still preserve human values? How do we handle competition without becoming either the kind of fool who allows it to crush us or the kind of fool who forgets people?

Resolving that paradox requires something like an evolutionary transformation of who we are, how we behave, how we think, and what we value. We've reached such an incredible level of freedom that, for the first time in history, we have to manage our own mutation. It's up to us to decide what it means to be a successful human being. That's the philosophical task of the age.

In some sense, of course, that has been the task of every age. There's nothing in today's economic disruptions that equals the horror of World War II. According to some estimates, nearly 100,000 people were killed during every week of that war. In 1935, when I was a seven-year-old boy, I once stood in the Alexanderplatz, a square in Berlin, and watched Hitler parade by in his Mercedes, just a few feet away. I'll never forget the mothers with babies in their arms, the children holding up swastikas. That leaves a mark on you that can't be erased—and it leaves you with questions that you have to confront: Who am I to have witnessed such acts? How am I to live meaningfully in a world such as this?

The new economy just happens to be the form that our existential challenge takes today. As always, the real obstacle is existence itself.

That's a heavy burden to place on leaders. They must not only guide organizations but also wrestle with basic philosophical questions.

There's a terrible defect at the core of how we think about people and organizations today. There is little or no tolerance for the kinds of character-building conversations that pave the way for meaningful change. The average person is stuck, lost, riveted by the objective domain. That's where our metrics are; that's where we look for solutions. It's the come-on of the consulting industry and the domain of all the books, magazines, and training programs out there. And that's why books and magazines that have numbers in their titles sell so well. We'll do anything to avoid facing the basic, underlying questions: How do we make truly difficult choices? How do we act when the risks seem overwhelming? How can we muster the guts to burn our bridges and to create a condition of no return?

There's nothing wrong with all of those technical solutions. They're excellent; they're creative; they're even necessary. But they shield us from the real issues: What kind of life do I want to lead? What is my destiny? How much evil am I willing to tolerate?

Reflection doesn't take anything away from decisiveness, from being a person of action. In fact, it generates the inner toughness that you need to be an effective person of action—to be a leader. Think of leadership as the sum of two vectors: competence (your specialty, your skills, your know-how) and authenticity (your identity, your character, your attitude). When companies and people get stuck, they tend to apply more steam—more competence—to what got them into trouble in the first place: "If I try harder, I'll be successful," or "If we exert more control, we'll get the results we need."

The problem is, when you're stuck, you're not likely to make progress by using competence as your tool. Instead, progress requires commitment to two things. First, you need to dedicate yourself to understanding yourself better—in the philosophical sense of understanding what it means to exist as a human being in the world. Second, you need to change your habits of thought: how you think, what you value, how you work, how you connect with people, how you learn, what you expect from life, and how you manage frustration. Changing those habits means changing your way of being intelligent. It means moving from a nonleadership mind to a leadership mind.

What are the attributes of a "leadership mind"?

Authentic leaders have absorbed the fundamental fact of existence—that you can't get around life's inherent contradictions. The leadership mind is spacious. It has ample room for the ambiguities of the world, for conflicting feelings, and for contradictory ideas.

I believe that the central leadership attribute is the ability to manage polarity. In every aspect of life, polarities are inevitable: We want to live, yet we must die. How can I devote myself fully to both family and career? Am I a boss or a friend? A lover or a judge? How do I reconcile my own needs with those of my team? Those paradoxes are simply part of life. Every business interaction is a form of confrontation—a clash of priorities, a struggle of dignities, a battle of beliefs. That's not an invitation to wage an epic battle of good versus evil or right versus wrong. (Chances are, your boss is less of an SOB than he is an agent of the cosmos.) My point is, you have to be careful not to bang your head against the wrong door. Polarities are in the nature of things. How we act, how we respond to those polarities—that is where we separate greatness from mediocrity.

That doesn't mean that we don't have to make decisions. Tough choices are a daily requirement of leadership. Leaders have to hire and fire, to sign off on new strategies, and to risk investments—all of which can lead to stress and guilt. The presence of guilt is not a result of making the wrong choice but of choosing itself. And that is the human condition: You are a being that chooses.

A young, ambitious guy whom I worked with at Amoco got a double promotion that required a transfer to Cairo. He went home to his new wife and young baby and said, "Great news, we're moving to Cairo." Appalled, his wife said, "You're moving alone. I'm going home to my mother." That was the first test of leadership in that family. There was no viable compromise: If he relinquished his promotion, he would resent his wife for ruining his career; if she just went along with the move, she would hate him for squashing her ideals for her baby and herself. What to do?

After some discussion, they might have been tempted to believe that maturity required them to deny their feelings and to sacrifice on behalf of each other. But that actually leads to illness, depression, and the end of affection. Instead, they went back to the fundamentals: Is it my career, or is it our career? Is it your baby, or is it our baby? Are we individuals, or do we operate as a team? What are our values? That marriage had to grow up by the equivalent of five years in about two weeks. They ended up going to Cairo, but their relationship had been transformed: She understood that his career was important to her; he recommitted to his values as a participant in the family. What matters is not what they ended up choosing, but how. They took the courageous step to redefine, from the inside out, who they truly were. The how is what gives you character. The what, which at first appears paramount, is ultimately of no emotional significance.

Managing polarity teaches us that there are no solutions—there are only changes of attitude. When you grapple with polarities in your life, you lose your arrogant, self-indulgent illusions, and you realize that the joke is on you. To get that message makes you a more credible human being—instantly.

It's one thing for a leader to embrace the contradictions of the new economy. But how does he or she persuade colleagues to go along with this kind of thinking?

The best leaders operate in four dimensions: vision, reality, ethics, and courage. These are the four intelligences, the four forms of perceiving, the languages for com-

municating that are required to achieve meaningful, sustained results. The vision-ary leader thinks big, thinks new, thinks ahead—and, most important, is in touch with the deep structure of human consciousness and creative potential. Reality is the polar opposite of vision. The leader as realist follows this motto: Face reality as it is, not as you wish it to be. The realist grapples with hard, factual, daily, and nu-meric parameters. A master in the art of the possible, the realist has no illusions, sees limits, and has no patience for speculation.

Ethics refers to the basic human values of integrity, love, and meaning. This di-mension represents a higher level of development, one ruled not by fear or pleasure but by principle. Courage is the realm of the will; it involves the capacity to make things happen. The philosophic roots of this dimension lie in fully understanding the centrality of free will in human affairs. Courage involves both advocacy—the ability to take a stand—and the internalization of personal responsibility and ac-countability.

The real challenge of leadership is to develop all four of these often-contradictory modes of thinking and behaving at once. Leaders tend to operate on two dimensions at most—which has more to do with a lack of insight into human nature than with corrupt intent. Reality dominates, and the second-most-common attribute is ethics: Consider the statement "People are our most important asset." Unfortunately, those are often empty words—not just because too few people make the connection be-tween profits and human values, but also because there is no adequate understand-ing of what it means to be a human being in a brutally competitive environment. "Vision" might be one of the most overused words in business, but in fact vision— in the sense of honing great thinking and fostering the capacity for ongoing inven-tiveness—is rarely practiced. And courage is demonstrated even more rarely.

When we talk about courage, we usually mean having guts or taking risks. But you talk about courage as if it were an almost mythic quality—one that lies at the heart of leadership success.

It goes back to the beginning of our discussion. Aristotle believed, correctly, that courage is the first of the human virtues, because it makes the others possible. Courage begins with the decision to face the ultimate truth about existence: the dirty little secret that we are free. It requires an understanding of free will at the arche-typal level—an understanding that we are free to define who we are at every mo-ment. We are not what society and randomness have made us; we are what we have chosen to be from the depth of our being. We are a product of our will. We are self-made in the deepest sense.

One of the gravest problems in life is self-limitation: We create defense mecha-nisms to protect us from the anxiety that comes with freedom. We refuse to fulfill our potential. We live only marginally. That was Freud's definition of psychoneuro-sis: We limit how we live so that we can limit the amount of anxiety that we experi-ence. We end up tranquilizing many of life's functions. We shut down the centers of entrepreneurial and creative thinking; in effect, we halt progress and growth. But no significant decision—personal or organizational—has ever been undertaken without being attended by an existential crisis, or without a commitment to wade through anxiety, uncertainty, and guilt.

That's what we mean by transformation. You can't just change how you think or the way that you act—you must change the way that you will. You must gain control over the patterns that govern your mind: your worldview, your beliefs about what you deserve and about what's possible. That's the zone of fundamental change, strength, and energy—and the true meaning of courage.

Does developing the will to transform mean that you can actually will others to change?

Taking personal responsibility for getting others to implement strategy is the leader's key polarity. It's the existential paradox of holding yourself 100% responsible for the fate of your organization, on the one hand, and assuming absolutely no responsibility for the choices made by other people, on the other hand. That applies to your children too. You are 100% responsible for how your children turn out. And you accomplish that by teaching them that they are 100% responsible for how they turn out.

So how do you motivate people? Not with techniques, but by risking yourself with a personal, lifelong commitment to greatness—by demonstrating courage. You don't teach it so much as challenge it into existence. You cannot choose for others. All you can do is inform them that you cannot choose for them. In most cases, that in itself will be a strong motivator for the people whom you want to cultivate. The leader's role is less to heal or to help than to enlarge the capacity for responsible freedom.

Some people are more talented than others. Some are more educationally privileged than others. But we all have the capacity to be great. Greatness comes with recognizing that your potential is limited only by how you choose, how you use your freedom, how resolute you are, how persistent you are—in short, by your attitude. And we are all free to choose our attitude.

5

Inside Hewlett-Packard, Carly Fiorina Combines Discipline, New-Age Talk

DAVID P. HAMILTON

At a company event in June, Carly Fiorina told employees that she envisions a remade Hewlett-Packard Co. as "a winning e-company with a shining soul."

Pacing back and forth in a smart business suit, pausing only for an occasional sip of bottled water, Ms. Fiorina exhorted employees to "aspirational performance" and asked them to commit "your hearts, your minds and your souls" to her mission. H-P, she said, "must be known as much for its strength of character as it is for the strength of its results."

The staid company long known as the Gray Lady of Silicon Valley has a new chief executive who often sounds like a New Age inspirational speaker. But the first outsider to take the reins in H-P's 60-year history also has used what she calls "well-placed shocks" to goad the technically accomplished—but slow-moving— manufacturer into the Internet age.

Soon after arriving about a year ago, she unveiled plans for a major corporate reorganization. Her top executives told her it would take a year to pull off; she ordered it done in three months. It was.

Without layoffs or a merger, Ms. Fiorina, 45 years old, aims to overhaul a company of 85,000 employees making everything from scientific instruments and laser printers to "big iron" server computers and PCs.

So far, H-P seems to be responding. The company's revenue growth, which had slowed to just 3% in the late 1990s, has accelerated again—to 15%. Its share price has jumped 25% since she took over, to a split-adjusted $111.25, though that is down from its 52-week high of $155.50.

Not long ago, the company seemed in danger of missing the Internet era altogether, as it was overshadowed by such competitors as Sun Microsystems Inc. and International Business Machines Corp. H-P still has plenty of heavy lifting to do. For example, Sun continues to best H-P in sales of large server computers to companies integrating the Internet into their operations.

Running Ragged

Some remaining executives and employees, including those who applaud Ms. Fiorina's changes, admit that keeping up with her can be wearing. A number of veterans worry about preserving the "H-P Way," a revered corporate tradition of employee support and innovation.

Unless subordinates consciously carve out time for their own initiatives, Ms. Fiorina's requests and directives can consume the entire day, says Robert Wayman, H-P's chief financial officer. He has cut back on outside commitments and canceled a family vacation to keep up.

"I don't think anyone is sleeping very much," Antonio Perez, another top executive, said in November. Since then, he has retired from H-P but praises the Fiorina shakeup. He says he left the company only because he wanted a shot at being a chief executive himself, which he has done at Gemplus SA, a French maker of "smart" cards.

Similar turnaround attempts at other troubled, conservative companies have foundered when leaders demanded what turned out to be too much change too quickly. In June, Procter & Gamble Co. ousted reformer CEO Durk Jager after just 17 months. Xerox Corp. dumped its outsider chief executive, Richard Thomen, in May; managers there say they don't know when the company will return to profitability.

H-P could run into similar problems adjusting to sudden change. Founded in a Silicon Valley garage in 1939 by William Hewlett and David Packard, the paternalistic company was long governed by a few simple maxims: Treat employees with respect, plan for the long term, and hold bureaucracy to a minimum by dividing business units when they get too big.

Those ideas served H-P well for decades, but by the mid-1990s, it was stagnating. When Ms. Fiorina arrived, H-P had splintered into 83 autonomous businesses that had no overarching strategy. Most of the units exercised nearly total authority over their budgets, often to the detriment of broader goals.

Just over a year ago, H-P lost a Chinese banking-system deal worth roughly $50 million to rival IBM. The main stumbling block: A midlevel H-P manager in the U.S. declined to spare $50,000 to build a prototype of the system for the would-be customer. "Things like that happened all the time," Cheng-Yaw Sun, H-P's general manager in China, says with a sigh.

Ms. Fiorina, a former executive at Lucent Technologies Inc., quickly saw parallels between H-P and her former company. Like Lucent during its 1996 spin-off from AT&T Corp., H-P needed to take several bold steps simultaneously to dislodge an entrenched culture, Ms. Fiorina says.

She actually had experienced that culture many years earlier, when she worked briefly as a secretary at Hewlett-Packard. That was before she tried law school, dropped out and eventually received an MBA. She later joined AT&T and, following the Lucent spin-off, rose to head the telecommunications-equipment provider's global-services business.

In her first three months as H-P's chief executive, she unleashed a new advertising campaign, starring herself and emphasizing the H-P brand over the former hodgepodge of product names. She tore up the company's profit-sharing program in favor of a strict performance-based bonus system.

Most dramatically, she launched a plan to consolidate H-P's 83 businesses into only 12. She also aligned the reduced number of divisions into two "front-end" groups that would focus on customer activities, such as marketing and sales, and two "back-end" organizations devoted strictly to designing and making computer and printer products.

Old-time H-P executives were shocked. "I was a deer caught in the headlights when she described the front and back end," says Carolyn Ticknor, who now presides over the merged printer unit. Several of these executives protested that employees weren't ready for a major reorganization.

Some executives fretted that managers wouldn't wield "real" authority if they couldn't control both product development and marketing. "It took some of the glory, if you wish, out of the job," says Mr. Perez, the departed executive.

Consternation rippled through the ranks. Managers who had long aspired to run their own autonomous units, known as P&Ls, short for profit & loss, suddenly saw most of those jobs disappear.

Dented Pride

Few parts of H-P resented the changes as much as the proud laser- and inkjet-printer divisions, which together contributed roughly two-thirds of the company's profits. Neal Martini, who ran much of the laser-printer operation, learned he would lose his authority over sales, marketing and manufacturing. He says he watched valued but fed-up colleagues leave for other jobs and often found himself grousing at the office coffeepot.

"The feeling was, here was Carly, who wasn't a long time in the H-P culture, who doesn't understand our business and the H-P Way, and doesn't understand our strengths, particularly in businesses that were viewed as so successful for so long," he says. "It initially felt like a big disempowerment."

The changes were so anguishing that "in the middle of this thing, I didn't sleep for nights," says Vyomesh Joshi, a vice president in the inkjet division. But as Mr. Martini, Mr. Joshi and their colleagues dutifully remodeled their operations, they started to see some advantages of the new organization.

H-P's laser and inkjet printers, for instance, had always used incompatible software and network connections, making it difficult for customers to swap a laser printer for an inkjet. With its design teams merged, H-P plans to introduce a fully compatible line of inkjet and laser printers this fall. Messrs. Martini and Joshi have remained with the company in senior positions in the merged printer division.

Ann Amazon

In a few areas, the results have already been striking. Frustrated customers had long complained that large purchases required them to deal separately with several H-P divisions. So Ms. Fiorina tapped Ann Livermore, who previously ran the server-computer division, to consolidate dealings with the company's top 100 customers.

One of Ms. Livermore's early successes in her new role came with Amazon.com. Ms. Fiorina personally helped persuade the online retailer to install 20 of H-P's top-of-the-line servers to run its site over the busy Christmas season last year. At a party at Amazon in February, Ms. Livermore cornered two executives and offered to supply the company's entire computer infrastructure. The Amazon executives just laughed and asked if H-P was willing to buy a nearby building and fill it with staff to win the deal, she says.

It didn't quite come to that, although Ms. Livermore's sales team did camp out in Amazon's conference rooms for days, eventually proposing to supply Amazon not only with servers, but also printers and personal computers. The deal, worth hundreds of millions of dollars over 18 months, would have been unthinkable at the old H-P, whose disparate divisions couldn't have worked together so easily.

The day after announcing the deal in May, Ms. Fiorina dubbed Ms. Livermore "Ann Amazon, warrior woman" at a morale-boosting session attended by hundreds of employees.

That was a sweet vindication for Ms. Livermore, who was passed over for the top job last year and found herself flooded with offers from the likes of Compaq Computer Corp. and Dell Computer Corp. Ms. Fiorina, however, implored Ms. Livermore to stay and boosted her stock-options package, a bonus that could be worth millions, says a person familiar with the situation.

While she can be generous to keep a top performer, Ms. Fiorina doesn't mind ruffling feathers. During a business-review meeting last August, Bill Russell, then Ms. Livermore's deputy, confessed that sales of the company's Unix servers were lagging so badly that H-P risked missing its financial targets for the quarter.

"I got fairly well lambasted on the point of what we were going to do about it," says Mr. Russell. Ms. Fiorina's pointed questions taught him, he says, that "whatever we thought was good enough, wasn't good enough now." Within days, top executives had cobbled together plans to tighten expenses and close a few big deals earlier enough to meet the targets.

Labs Rebound

The new pressure on H-P's businesses has produced some unexpected consequences. One of the biggest came at the company's previously de-moralized basic-research division, H-P Laboratories.

Ms. Fiorina took an early interest in the labs, seeing them as a key source of innovation. She has made a habit of passing through the research area every month, once bringing along H-P's entire board. On one visit, she dropped by a lab working on "Cool Town," an effort to use basic Web technology, which is available to anyone, to build a "pervasive" computing environment in which gadgets from PCs to wristwatches can communicate.

"They show me this incredible stuff," Ms. Fiorina recalls, "and then they tell me, 'our funding is about to get cut off'" by the labs administration.

That quickly changed. With its finances secure, Cool Town is thriving. Sales and marketing managers frequently bring customers to tour the project.

The high-level patronage has reinvigorated morale throughout the labs. Until Ms. Fiorina arrived, Stan Williams, a researcher in nanotechnology, the science of manipulating atomic structures, had planned to move his lab to Agilent Technologies Inc., a test-and-measurement company spun off from H-P earlier this year. Now, H-P is building a new multimillion-dollar nonfabrication facility. It may not generate commercially useful work for years, but the investment could help H-P retain researchers in a field that one day could allow more powerful silicon chips to be "grown" by means of subatomic chemistry and physics, rather than manufactured in complex factories.

Ms. Fiorina wants H-P eventually to be known for three main specialties: Internet infrastructure such as servers; information appliances, from

PCs and hand-held devices to "intelligent" printers; and e-services that will anticipate users' needs. It's a tall order, not least because aggressive competitors such as Sun, Dell and IBM have so far been more successful in many of those markets.

Ms. Fiorina, however, predicts that her troops will leap ahead of these rivals. "This is a company of people who can do things no one else can do," she says.

PART TWO

DEFINING VALUES

Values are the underpinnings of effective leadership. Values are the ideals and beliefs that influence our choices and actions. Values are also the standards by which we judge or measure our actions, character, decisions, policies, and organizational objectives. One of the primary roles of a leader is to manage the values of the organization, since values serve as a transforming focus for achieving the shared vision.

The degree to which values are embraced and shared at all levels determines the strength of the organizational culture that serves as the guideline for how leaders and followers behave. The way leaders create trust among followers is by clearly and consistently communicating their values and expectations and then reinforcing and modeling them. Credibility is built, over time, by how consistent the leaders' actions are with their words.

According to James MacGregor Burns, ethics are the moral dynamics of the heart of leadership—we agree. Right-versus-wrong decisions are not particularly difficult for courageous leaders. However, ethical judgments or dilemmas are particularly tough because they involve right-versus-right choices where one must choose between two or more values to which one is committed. Dealing with these types of ethical dilemmas becomes what Joseph L. Badracco, Jr. calls "defining moments" and often determines the future standards of an organization.

Leaders cannot assume that everyone in an organization shares the same cultural and personal values. There are many kinds of diversity in today's organizations, and dealing with diversity effectively—seeking it and valuing it—can give an organization a strategic advantage because diversity, if managed well, leads to innovation. However, leaders must also understand and deal with one of many leadership paradoxes: Ethical values are the most diverse from culture to culture.

Identifying and building consensus for values is not the sole domain of the leader. In fact, our premise is that the leader and followers must work together, and we place significant emphasis in the role of followers as a requisite to effective leadership. With increasing rates and magnitude of change, the consequences of each decision seem greater. Thus, there is an emphasis on participatory decision-making and on addressing both the short and the long term.

Whether we ask successful leaders to describe the relationship they have with their followers or ask successful followers to describe the relationship they have with their leaders, we get essentially the same description. Again, our experience is that when followers are asked what attribute the want in a leader, the response is, most often, "honesty and integrity." Each understands the perspective of the other and both recognize that they can be successful in the long term only if they share success. However, leadership theory and practical applications derived from theory focus, too often, only on the role of the leader in creating success, thereby undervaluing the role of the follower. In far too many organizations, the leadership role is seen as the only avenue to personal success, and therefore it is developed, encouraged, appreciated, and rewarded, whereas followership is not.

Contemporary organizations can no longer depend upon the leader alone. We must study and appreciate the role of the follower in the dynamics of group and organizational success. Most of us are followers more often than we are leaders. Followership dominates our lives and our organizations, and leaders come from the ranks of the followers. In fact, few leaders can be successful without first having learned the skills of following. Aristotle's *Politics*, Plato's *Republic*, Homer's *Odyssey*, and Hegel's *Phenomenology of Mind* affirm the mastery of followership as the sine qua non of leadership: Qualities that we associate with effective followers are the same qualities that we find in effective leaders. The experience of following also gives leaders perspective and enables them to share vision, communicate with empathy, treat people as individuals, and empower followers to achieve shared goals and objectives. Effective leaders realize that they are also followers and purposefully set the example when performing that role. Thus, a major tenet of developing effective leadership is understanding, experiencing, and modeling effective followership.

In organizations where good followership is appreciated, effective followers and leaders are very comfortable moving from one role to the other. Fortunately, more and more organizations are recognizing that good followership leads to a strategic advantage and have begun to develop and reward effective followers.

In an attempt to get around the stereotypes associated with followership, many organizations refer to their followers with terms such as "constituents," "associates," "members," or "colleagues." The term "subordinate" has begun to fade from the vocabularies. However, what we call people in our organizations matters much less than how we treat them. No matter what they are called, followers who are treated with disdain by those in charge are clearly regarded as subordinates.

Followers want to feel a sense of partnership with the leader in accomplishing goals and defining a path to the future. Social, economic, and technological conditions have encouraged a better educated and more sophisticated constituency; superior education, skills, and access to information are no longer the sole purview of leaders. As a result of the blurred differences between followers' abilities and their own, leaders must more actively involve followers in organizational processes.

If leaders are to develop good followers, they must encourage participation in the creation of the vision, mission, and goals, while allowing their ideas to be modified and "owned" by everyone. Separating the individual from leadership creates "we," building a true sense of involvement and empowerment among followers.

Failure to recognize interdependencies between leader and follower can have serious consequences for both. These interdependencies are critical to a leader's success and ensure an ongoing pattern of leadership development. In many ways, leaders serve followers—certainly a reversal of traditional perceptions. But effective leaders create opportunities, help provide necessary resources, delegate authority, and vigorously support the decisions made and actions taken. Often, leaders must watch while others do things differently than they would have. Helping people learn by allowing them to make mistakes takes true courage and results in organizational learning. This is how leaders develop effective followers, who, in turn, are learning the elements of effective leadership.

Many leaders thrive on having followers revere them. Unfortunately, the organization becomes completely dependent upon that leader— everything happens because of that leader. Truly effective leaders have people around them who are bright, critical, courageous, and independent. Decisions are made at the organizational level having the most information. Followers are given the means and responsibility to do the job; creativity and innovation are prized. Thus, leaders are best evaluated on the basis of organizational success and according to how well they develop their followers.

Leadership Perspective

In an outstanding piece, "Moral Person and Moral Manager: How Executives Develop a Reputation for Ethical Leadership" (Chapter 6), Linda Trevino, Laura Hartman, and Michael Brown outline the perceptual differences between you as a moral person and you as a moral leader. You are defined as a person by how others perceive who you are, what you do, and what you decide. They note that you must clearly communicate these elements to those you lead. The second aspect is that of moral manager. Here the authors cite the importance of being a role model, communicating regularly about ethics and values while using rewards to ensure that everyone in the organization accepts and adheres to those standards. The result is a shared pride, commitment, and loyalty that are they key elements in attracting and retaining the best people.

In "Politics or Porcelain?" (Chapter 7) Robert Birnbaum examines transactional and transformational leadership in the context of academe. He argues that the effectiveness of an academic leader may depend less on getting the community to follow the leader's vision and more on influencing the community to face its problems. The world, he says, reveres transformational leaders, but the world, particularly the academic world, works because of transactional leaders.

Matthew Valle, in "Crisis, Culture and Charisma: The New Leader's Work in Public Organizations" (Chapter 8) suggests that the changing nature of public service requires a "new" leadership. This is an important addition to this text because Valle specifically addresses the public sector organization, where accountability for performance is based on perceptions of service rather than profit. There are external and internal environmental forces impacting public organizations, especially as responsibilities for social needs are shifted from one venue to another. Valle describes the interactions of the environment, the followers, and the leader, characterizing this interplay as a combination of crisis, culture, and charisma. Leadership is now the development of an adaptive organizational culture in response to environmental changes.

In Chapter 9, "Leading Learning Organizations," Peter Senge notes that future challenges will require more than isolated, heroic leaders. He describes a unique mix of three types of leaders in learning organizations: local line leaders, executive leaders, and internal networkers. All must lead in ways that differ from traditional leadership models.

Vision is presented as an essential element of leadership in Neal Thornberry's "A View About 'Vision'" (Chapter 10). There are many interpretations of vision, and the concept is not well understood by those who are setting the stage for future action in organizations. Thornberry describes the key components of vision and argues that much of the ability to be visionary can be taught. Vision is not a passing fad; it is an increasingly important part of an organization's struggle to be fast, flexible, and competitive. He draws several conclusions that will help leaders manage the visionary process.

Robert Fulmer provides a powerful review of the changes in leadership development with his article "The Evolving Paradigm of Leadership Development" (Chapter 11). With increased emphasis on developing high potential people and the cost of creating worthwhile learning experiences, Fulmer identifies the major shifts in leadership development, providing examples of best practices. He sees participants moving from passive listeners to active learners; programs moving from independent events to ongoing processes; purpose moving from knowledge to action; focus moving from the past to the future; presenters moving from limited roles to general partners; presentations moving from form to substance; and location moving from academe to the business setting. The uncertainty of knowing the precise nature of organizational life in the future necessitates these shifts. Incorporating all of them is necessary for effective leadership development.

Finally, in Chapter 12, "Followers for the Times: Engaging Employees in a Winning Partnership," Earl Potter, William Rosenbach, and Thane Pittman provide a comprehensive perspective on followership. They argue that in order to understand follower style, followers' actions in two fundamental and distinctly different dimensions have to be recognized. The dimension of *performance initiative* concerns the actions followers take to ensure they will be effective performers in their assigned tasks and responsibilities, both now and in the future. Equally important are the actions followers take to make their relationships with their leaders more effective. These *relationship initiatives* round out the picture of what is required for followers to act as full partners with their leaders. Variations in the extent to which followers take performance and relationship initiatives constitute differences in follower style. The authors argue that understanding these styles, follower personalities, leader behaviors, and the organizational contexts that promote various styles allow both leaders and followers to think about ways to be more effective in their groups and organizations.

6

Moral Person and Moral Manager

How Executives Develop a Reputation for Ethical Leadership

LINDA KLEBE TREVINO
LAURA PINCUS HARTMAN
MICHAEL BROWN

Plato asked, which extreme would you rather be: "an unethical person with a good reputation or an ethical person with a reputation for injustice?" Plato might have added, "or would you rather be perceived as ethically neutral—someone who has no ethical reputation at all?" Plato knew that reputation was important. We now understand that reputation and others' perceptions of you are key to executive ethical leadership. Those others include employees at all levels as well as key external stakeholders.

A reputation for ethical leadership rests upon two essential pillars: perceptions of you as both a moral person *and* a moral manager. The executive as a moral person is characterized in terms of individual traits such as honesty and integrity. As moral manager, the CEO is thought of as the Chief *Ethics* Officer of the organization, creating a strong ethics message that gets employees' attention and influences their thoughts and behaviors. Both are necessary. To be perceived as an ethical leader, it is not enough to just be an ethical person. An executive ethical leader must also find ways to focus the organization's attention on ethics and values and to infuse the organization with principles that will guide the actions of all employees. An executive's reputation for ethical leadership may be more important now than ever in this new organizational era where more em-

Reprinted with permission, from the *California Management Review* 42, 4 (Summer 2000), pp. 128–142.

ployees are working independently, off site, and without direct supervision. In these organizations, values are the glue that can hold things together, and values must be conveyed from the top of the organization. Also, a single employee who operates outside of the organizational value system can cost the organization dearly in legal fees and can have a tremendous, sometimes irreversible impact on the organization's image and culture.

Moral Person + Moral Manager = A Reputation for Ethical Leadership

These ideas about a dual pillar approach to ethical leadership are not brand new. As the opening quotation suggests, the emphasis on reputation goes back to Plato. Chester Barnard addressed the ethical dimension of executive leadership sixty years ago. Barnard spoke about executive responsibility in terms of conforming to a "complex code of morals"[1] (moral person) as well as creating moral codes for others (moral manager).

If Plato and Barnard had this right, why bother revisiting the subject of ethical leadership now? We revisit the subject because, in our 40 structured interviews (20 with senior executives and 20 with corporate ethics officers), we found that many senior executives failed to recognize the importance of others' perceptions and of developing a reputation for ethical leadership. To them, being an ethical person and making good ethical decisions was enough. They spoke proudly about having principles, following the golden rule, taking into account the needs of society, and being fair and caring in their decisions. They assumed that if they were solid ethical beings, followers would automatically know that. They rejected the idea that successful ethical executives are often perceived as ethically neutral. Furthermore, they assumed that good leaders are by definition ethical leaders. One senior executive noted, "I don't think you can distinguish between ethical leadership and leadership. It's just a facet of leadership. The great leaders are ethical, and the lousy ones are not."

However, a *reputation* for ethical leadership cannot be taken for granted because most employees in large organizations do not interact with senior executives. They know them only from a distance. Any information they receive about executives gets filtered through multiple layers in the organization, with employees learning only about bare-bones decisions and outcomes, not the personal characteristics of the people behind them. In today's highly competitive business environment, messages about how financial goals are achieved frequently get lost in the intense focus on the bottom line. We found that just because executives know themselves as good people—honest, caring, and fair—they should not assume that others see them in the same way. It is so easy to forget that employees do not know you the way you know yourself. If employees do not think of an executive as a clearly ethical or unethical leader, they are likely to think of the leader as being somewhere in between— amoral or ethically neutral.

Interestingly, perceptions of *ethically neutral leadership* do not necessarily arise because the leader *is* ethically neutral. In fact, many of the senior executives we spoke with convinced us that it was impossible for them to be ethically neutral in their jobs, given the many value-laden decisions they make every day. Rather, the perception of ethically neutral leadership may exist because the leader has not faced major *public* ethical challenges that would provide the opportunity to convey his or her values to others. As one executive noted, "They haven't had to make any decisions on the margin ... once you're faced with [a major public ethical dilemma], you bare your soul and you're one or the other [ethical or unethical]." On the other hand, a reputation for ethically neutral leadership may exist because the leader has not proactively made ethics and values an explicit and evident part of the leadership agenda. Executives must recognize that if they do not develop a reputation for ethical leadership, they will likely be tagged as "ethically neutral." As a result, employees will believe that the bottom line is the only value that should guide their decisions and that the CEO cares more about himself and the short-term financials than about the long-term interests of the organization and its multiple stakeholders.

Figure 6.1 provides a summary of our study's findings.

Pillar One: Moral Person

Being an ethical person is the substantive basis of ethical leadership. However, in order to develop a reputation for ethical leadership, the leader's challenge is conveying that substance to others. Being viewed as an ethical person means that people think of you as having certain traits, engaging in certain kinds of behaviors, and making decisions based upon ethical principles. Furthermore, this substantive ethical core must be authentic. As one executive put it, "If the person truly doesn't believe the ethical story and preaches it but doesn't feel it ... that's going to show through. ... But, [a true ethical leader] walks in [and] it doesn't take very long if you haven't met him before [you think] there's a [person] with integrity and candor and honesty."

Traits

Traits are stable personal characteristics, meaning that individuals behave in fairly predictable ways across time and situations and observers come to describe the individual in those terms. The traits that executives most often associate with ethical leadership are honesty, trustworthiness,

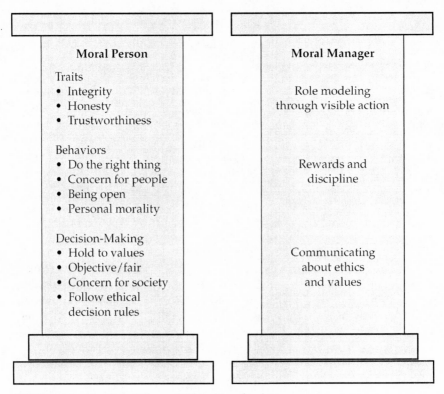

FIGURE 6.1   The Two Pillars of Ethical Leadership

and integrity. A very broad personal characteristic, *integrity* was the trait cited most frequently by the executives. Integrity is a holistic attribute that encompasses the other traits of honesty and trustworthiness. One executive said that the average employee would say that the ethical leader is "squeaky clean." They would think "I know that if I bring an issue to him or her that I can count on their honesty and integrity on this because I've seen their standards and that one, integrity, is one that's very important to them."

Trustworthiness is also important to executives. Trust has to do with consistency, credibility, and predictability in relationships. "You can't build a long-term relationship with a customer if they don't trust you." Finally, *honesty*, *sincerity*, and *forthrightness* are also important. "An ethical leader . . . tends to be rather candid, certain, [and is] very careful to be factual and accurate. . . . An ethical leader does not sugarcoat things . . . he tells it like it is."

Behaviors

"Your actions speak so loudly, I can't hear what you're saying." That is the sentiment expressed by one executive. Although traits are clearly important to ethical leadership, behaviors are perhaps more so, and these include: "The way you act even when people aren't looking." "People are going to judge you not by what you say but by what you do." "People look at you and understand over time who you are personally as a result of their observations." Important behaviors include "doing the right thing," showing concern for people and treating people right, being open and communicative and demonstrating morality in one's personal life.

First and foremost, executives said that ethical leaders *do the right thing*. One retired CEO talked about the founder of his firm, a man who "was known for his strong belief that there is only one way to do business and that's the right way."

Second, executive ethical leaders *show concern for people* through their actions. They treat people well—with dignity and respect.

> I think [the ethical leader] treats everybody with dignity—meaning everybody—whether they're at the lowest level or higher levels . . . everyone gets treated with dignity and respect. I've also found that if you treat people with dignity and respect and trust, they almost invariably will respond in that fashion. It's like raising children. If you really don't trust them, they don't have much to lose by trying to get away with something. If they feel you trust them, they are going to think long and hard before they do something that will violate that trust.

Several of the executives used the military example. "In the military, the troops eat before the officers. . . . Leaders take care of their troops. . . . A leader is selfless, a leader shares credit, a leader sees that contributors are rewarded."

Being open means that the executive is approachable and a good listener. Employees feel comfortable sharing bad news with the ethical leader. One executive said, "An ethical leader would need to be approachable so that . . . people would feel comfortable raising the tough issues . . . and know that they would be listened to." Another put it this way: "In general, the better leaders that I've met and know are more than willing to share their experiences of rights and wrongs, successes and failures." These leaders do not kill the messenger who brings bad news. They encourage openness and treat bad news as a problem to be addressed rather than punished.

Finally, *personal morality* is associated with ethical leadership. We asked explicitly about personal morality because our interviews with execu-

tives took place during the Monica Lewinsky scandal in the Clinton Presidency and the topic was prominent in everyone's mind. When we asked
whether personal morality was linked to ethical leadership, most executives answered yes. "You can not be an ethical leader if your personal
morality is in question. . . . To be a leader . . . what you do privately reflects on that organization. Secondly, to be a leader you have a greater
standard, a greater responsibility than the average person would have to
live up to."

Decision Making

In their decision-making role, executive ethical leaders are thought to
hold to a solid set of ethical values and principles. They aim to be *objective and
fair*. They also have a perspective that goes beyond the bottom line to include *concerns about the broader society and community*. In addition, executives said that ethical leaders rely upon a number of ethical decision rules
such as the golden rule and the *"New York Times Test."* The *"New York
Times Test"* says that, when making a decision, ethical leaders should ask
themselves whether they would like to see the action they are contemplating on tomorrow morning's front page. This question reflects the ethical leader's sensitivity to community standards.

To summarize, the "moral person" pillar of ethical leadership represents the substance of ethical leadership and it is an important prerequisite to developing a reputation for ethical leadership because leaders become associated with their traits, behaviors, and decisions as long as
others know about them. With the moral person pillar in place, you
should have a reputation for being an ethical person. You can think of
this as the ethical part of the term "ethical leadership." Having a reputation for being a moral person tells employees what *you* are likely to do—
a good start, but it does not necessarily tell them what *they* should do.
That requires moral managing—taking the ethics message to the rest of
the organization.

Many of the executives we interviewed thought that being an ethical
person who does the right thing, treats people well, and makes good decisions was necessary *and* sufficient for being an ethical leader. This is not
surprising because executives know other executives personally. They
have served under them, worked with them, and observed their behavior at close hand. Therefore, in their minds, an executive's ethical traits,
behaviors, and decisions are automatically associated with a reputation
for ethical leadership. However, some of the executives and even more of
the ethics officers noted that being an ethical person was not enough. To
develop a reputation for ethical leadership with employees, leaders must
make ethics and values a salient aspect of their leadership agenda so that
the message reaches more distant employees. To do this, they must be

moral managers as well as moral persons. As one executive expressed it: "Simply put, ethical leadership means doing the right thing, and it means communicating so that everyone understands that [the right thing] is going to happen at all times . . . I think that most of the people I've been in business with adhere to the first but do less well with the second. And, in my experience, it is something that has to be reinforced constantly . . . the second part is the hardest."

Pillar Two: Moral Manager

In order to develop a reputation for ethical *leadership*, a heavy focus on the leadership part of that term is required. The executive's challenge is to make ethics and values stand out from a business landscape that is laden with messages about beating the competition and achieving quarterly goals and profits. Moral managers recognize the importance of proactively putting ethics at the forefront of their leadership agenda. Like parents who should explicitly share their values with their children, executives need to make the ethical dimension of their leadership explicit and salient to their employees. Executives who fail to do this risk being perceived as ethically neutral because other more pervasive messages about financial success take over. One CEO put it this way:

> We do some good things [turn down unethical business opportunities, develop people, champion diversity], but compare the number of times that we recognize those [ethical] achievements versus how much we recognize financial achievements—it's not close. I mean, I cringe . . . saying that . . . I'm not saying we don't work at these other things, but . . . the recognition is still very much on financial performance and . . . it's true in almost all organizations . . . And that's what's wrong. That's what's out of kilter.

Our study identified a number of ways moral managers can increase the salience of an ethics and values agenda and develop a reputation for ethical leadership. They serve as a role model for ethical conduct in a way that is visible to employees. They communicate regularly and persuasively with employees about ethical standards, principles, and values. Finally, they use the reward system consistently to hold all employees accountable to ethical standards.

Role Modeling Through Visible Action

Role modeling may seem similar to the "doing the right thing" category above. However, role modeling emphasizes *visible action* and the perceptual and reputational aspects of ethical leadership. Some ethical behaviors will go completely unnoticed while others will be noticed and will contribute to a reputation for ethical leadership. Effective moral managers recognize that they live in a fishbowl of sorts and employees are watching them for cues about what's important. "You are demonstrating by your example on and off the job, in other words, 24 hours a day, seven days a week, you're a model for what you believe in and the values." In addition, "if you're unethical . . . people pick up on that and assume because you're the leader that it's the correct thing to do . . . that not only are you condoning it, but you're actually setting the example for it."

The effective moral manager understands which words and actions are noticed and how they will be interpreted by others. In some cases, visible executive action (without any words at all) is enough to send a powerful message. One executive offered the following as an example of the power of executive action.

> Some years ago, I was running one of our plants. I had just taken over and they were having some financial troubles. . . . Most of our management was flying first class. . . . I did not want . . . my first act to be to tell everybody that they are not gonna fly first class anymore, so I just quit flying first class. And it wasn't long before people noticed it and pretty soon everybody was flying coach. . . . I never put out a directive, never said a word to anybody . . . and people noticed it. They got the message . . . People look to the leader. If the leader cuts corners, they say its okay to cut corners around here. If the leader doesn't cut corners, we must be expected not to do any of that around here.

Negative signals can also be sent by visible executive action and moral managers must be particularly sensitive to these. For example, what kind of signal does it send when your organization's ethics policy prohibits employees from accepting any kind of gift from a prospective client and then employees see a group of senior executives sitting in a client's box enjoying a professional football or basketball game? Unless the CEO is wearing a large sign that says "we paid for these tickets," the message is clear. Ethics policies do not apply equally to everyone. It becomes much easier for an employee to rationalize receiving gifts. According to one interviewee, many executives "wouldn't think twice about it because you don't intend to do anything wrong." However, employees are generally not aware of your *intent*. They see the actions and make inferences based upon them.

Communicating About Ethics and Values

Many executives are uncomfortable talking about ethics and wonder about those who do. In our interviews, some executives expressed concern about the leader who talks about ethics too much. "I distrust people who talk about it all the time. I think the way you do it [ethical leadership] is to demonstrate it in action . . . the more a person sermonizes about it, the more worried I am . . . sometimes you have to talk about it, but mostly you don't talk about it, you just do things." However, moral managers need to talk about ethics and values, not in a sermonizing way, but in a way that explains the values that guide important decisions and actions. If people do not hear about ethics and values from the top, it is not clear to employees that ethics and values are important. You may not feel comfortable talking about ethics if it means discussing the intricacies of Aristotle or Kant. However, talking about ethics with your employees does not mean that at all. It means talking about the values that are important to you and the organization. It is a bit like teaching children about sex. Parents can choose to avoid the uncomfortable subject, hoping that their children will learn what they need to know in school; or, they can bring an expert home who knows more than they do about the physiology of the human reproductive system. However, what parents really want their children to know about and adopt is a set of values the family believes in such as love, respect, and responsibility. To be most effective, that message must come from parents, in words and in actions. Similarly, the message about the values guiding decisions and actions in business should come from senior leaders.

The Reward System

Using rewards and discipline effectively may be the most powerful way to send signals about desirable and undesirable conduct. That means rewarding those who accomplish their goals by behaving in ways that are consistent with stated values. "The most senior executive should reward the junior executive, the manager, the line people who make these [ethical] decisions . . . reinforcement is very important."

It also means clearly disciplining employees at all levels when they break the rules. A financial industry executive provided the following two examples.

> If there's a situation within the corporation of sexual harassment where [the facts are] proven and management is very quick to deal with the wrongdoer . . . that's leadership. To let the rumor mill take over, to allow someone to quietly go away, to resign, is not ethical leadership. It is more difficult, but you send the message out to the organization by very visible, fair, balanced behavior. That's what you have to do.

> If someone has taken money, and they happen to be a 25-year employee who has taken two hundred dollars over the weekend and put it back on Monday, you have to . . . fire that person. [You have to make] sure everybody understands that Joe took two hundred dollars on Friday and got

[fired] . . . [they must also] be assured that I did have a fact base, and that I did act responsibly and I do care about 25-year people.

Another financial industry executive talked about how he was socialized early in his career. "When I was signed . . . to train under a tough, but fair partner of the firm . . . he [said] there are things expected from you . . . but if you ever make a transaction in a client's account that you can't justify to me was in the best interest of the customer, you're out. Well that kind of gets your attention."

An airline executive said, "we talk about honesty and integrity as a core value; we communicate that. But then we back it up . . . someone can make a mistake. They can run into the side of an airplane with a baggage cart and put a big dent in it . . . and we put our arm around them and re-train them. . . . If that same person were to lie to us, they don't get a second chance . . . When it comes to honesty, there is no second chance."

The moral manager consistently rewards ethical conduct and disciplines unethical conduct at all levels in the organization, and these actions serve to uphold the standards and rules. The above reward system examples represent clear signals that will be noticed and that demonstrate clearly how employees are held accountable and how the leader backs up words with actions.

In summary, to develop a reputation for ethical leadership, one must be strong on both dimensions: moral person and moral manager. The ethical leader has a reputation for being both a substantively ethical person and a leader who makes ethics and values a prominent part of the leadership agenda.

What Does Ethical Leadership Accomplish?

The executives we talked with said that ethical leadership was good for business, particularly in the long term, and avoids legal problems. "It probably determines the amount of money you're spending in lawsuits and with corporate attorneys . . . you save a lot of money in regulatory fees and lawyer fees and settlement fees." They also said that ethical leadership contributes to employee commitment, satisfaction, comfort, and even fun. "People enjoy working for an ethical organization" and it helps the organization attract and retain the best employees. "If the leadership of the company reflects [ethical] values . . . people will want to work for that company and will want to do well." Finally, employees in an organization led by an executive ethical leader will imitate the behavior of their leader and therefore the employees will be more ethical themselves.

Next, we combine the two pillars of ethical leadership into a two by two matrix that can help us think about the kinds of reputation an execu-

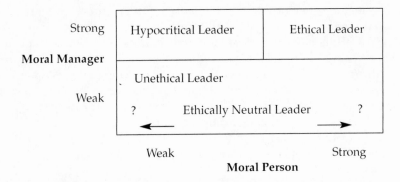

FIGURE 6.2   Executive Reputation and Ethical Leadership

tive can develop (see Figure 6.2). As noted, the combination of strong moral person and strong moral manager produces a reputation for ethical leadership. However, what happens if the leader falters in one of these areas? The matrix suggests the following possibilities: one may develop a reputation as an unethical leader, a hypocritical leader, or an ethically neutral leader.

The Unethical Leader

A leader who is perceived to be weak on both dimensions will develop a reputation for unethical leadership. A number of executives we spoke with named Al Dunlap as a prime example of someone with a reputation for unethical executive leadership. *Business Week* recently published excerpts from John Byrne's book about Dunlap entitled *Mean Business*.[2] The article describes Dunlap as the "no-nonsense executive famous for turning around struggling companies—and sending their shares soaring in the process." However, Dunlap was also known for tirades against employees "which could reach the point of emotional abuse." "He was condescending, belligerent and disrespectful." "At his worst, he became viciously profane, even violent. Executives said he would throw papers or furniture, bang his hands on his desk, and shout so ferociously that a manager's hair would be blown back by the stream of air that rushed from Dunlap's mouth." He used the promise of huge rewards to get "employees to do things they might not otherwise do." In order to make the numbers that Dunlap demanded, creative accounting techniques were employed and "dubious techniques were used to boost sales." He also lied to Wall Street analysts. "Despite the chaos inside the company, Sunbeam's chief kept up a steady drumbeat of optimistic sales and earnings forecasts, promises of tantalizing new products, and assurances that the

Dunlap magic was working." In the end, the lies could no longer cover up what was really going on. Wall Street abandoned the company and the board of directors fired Dunlap. Sunbeam was left crippled and the company continues to struggle today.

On the moral person dimension, Dunlap was found to be dishonest, he treated people horribly and made decisions based upon the financial bottom line only, disregarding the interests of multiple stakeholders in the process. On the moral manager dimension, his own behavior, communications, and the reward system were used to send a single consistent message. The bottom line was the only thing that mattered.

The Hypocritical Leader

A leader who is not perceived to be a strong ethical person but who attempts to put ethics and values at the forefront of the leadership agenda is likely to be perceived as a hypocritical leader who "talks the ethics talk" but does not "walk the ethics walk." In such cases, people tend to see the talk only as window dressing. They watch for actions to match the words and if there is a mismatch, the words are dismissed. As suggested above, some executives expressed concern about the leader who talks about ethics too much. In terms of the leader's reputation for ethical leadership, communicating about ethics and values, without the actions to match, is probably worse than doing nothing at all because talk without action places a spotlight on the issue that would not otherwise be there. As a result, employees become cynical and distrust everything the leader says. They also figure that they too can ignore ethical standards if they perceive that the leader does so.

The Ethically Neutral Leader

This category generated a lot of comment. Half of the executives rejected it out of hand. The other half recognized its existence and almost all of the twenty corporate ethics officers we talked with readily acknowledged it. On the moral person dimension, it is most appropriate to say that this person is perceived to be *not clearly unethical*, but also not strongly ethical. Consider what people say about ethically neutral leaders. In terms of traits, the ethically neutral leader is seen as more self-centered than other-centered. In terms of behaviors, ethically neutral leaders are less open to input from others and they care less about people. They are less compassionate. In terms of decision-making, ethically neutral executive leaders are thought to have a narrower view than do ethical leaders. They focus on financial ends more than the means that are of interest to ethical leaders. They also are more likely to base decisions upon the

short-term bottom line and they are less concerned with leaving the organization or the world a better place for the future. Interestingly, much of
the emphasis seems to be on what the ethically neutral leader is *not* (not
open to input, not caring, not focused on means, not concerned with
leaving a legacy). This is important because it means that to perceive ethical leadership, followers need evidence of positive ethical traits, behaviors, and decision processes. Lack of awareness of these positive characteristics leads to the perception that the leader is ethically neutral.
Clearly, employees must be aware of these positive attributes in order for
them to infer the existence of ethical leadership.

When asked to talk about ethically neutral leaders, people said virtually nothing about moral managing (role modeling, communicating, the
reward system). Given that employees make sense of the messages they
do get, the ethically neutral leader's focus on the short-term bottom line
gets employees' attention—by default. If that is what the leader is focusing on, it must be the only thing that is important. One executive said,
"Ethics hasn't been on the scorecard for what's important here . . . it's
kind of like quality. Quality is something that we slipped away from and
someone had to say, 'It's important.' Maybe the same is true of ethics . . .
we need a Deming . . . to remind us of how important it is."

Perhaps the most important outcome of ethically neutral leadership
is that employees then think that ethics is not particularly important to
the leader, "So they're left deciding on their own what's important in a
particular situation." This means that they are acting without clear
guidance about the ethics and values of the organization. The leader
has not demonstrated it, has not thought through it, has not given an
example of it, has not talked about it, and has not discussed it in an
open forum.

Cultivating a Reputation for Ethical Leadership

Given the importance of ethical leadership, we offer the following practical
steps executives can take to cultivate a reputation for ethical leadership.

Share Your Values: Who You Are as an Ethical Person

"Ethical leadership is not easy . . . the temptations and the rewards for
unethical behavior are great. So, ethical leadership requires a discipline, a
mental and personal discipline that is not easy to come by." Some senior
executives arrive in their leadership positions with all of the necessary
cognitive and emotional tools to be an active ethical leader. Part of the
reason many of them ascend to senior leadership positions is because
they have a reputation for integrity, for treating people well and for do-

ing the right thing. They have likely had a lifetime of personal and work-related mentors and experiences that have molded and reinforced their values. By the time they reach the executive level, these values are so solid, that when challenged, the leader holds to them without question.

On the other hand, senior executive positions have a way of challenging your values in ways you may not have been challenged before. If you think that this aspect of your leadership needs work, devote energy to developing this side of yourself. Read books. Attend workshops and seminars with other senior executives who share your concerns. Work with a personal coach. Talk with your spiritual advisor about how your values can be applied in your work.

It then becomes particularly important to share this side of yourself. Find out what employees know about you and how they think of you in ethical leadership terms. You may be a strong ethical person, but your employees may have no way of knowing that. Most people do not have an accurate view of how others see them, especially when it comes to ethics. Surveys consistently find that most people think of themselves as above average and more ethical than their peers. However, the only way to honestly assess where you stand in terms of others' perceptions is to ask for candid input. A leader should "always have someone who can tell the emperor that he has no clothes." So, ask those closest to you. You can also survey your employees to find out how much they know about you as an ethical leader. Be open to what you learn and do not be surprised if employees say they simply do not know. For example, if you have not been outspoken on ethics and values issues, or you have not managed a highly public crisis that provided an opportunity for employees to learn about your values, you may be surprised to learn that employees do *not* know much about this aspect of your leadership. They may even see you as "neutral" on the ethics dimension. Talk to your communications people and your ethics officer, if you have one, about how you might successfully convey your values to employees on a regular basis. Figure out a way to open the lines of two-way communication on ethics and values issues. Ask employees to share the ethical dilemmas they face and to let you know what kind of guidance they would like from you.

Assume the Role of Moral Manager: Chief Ethics Officer of Your Organization

Ethical leadership means that the person, the leader, who is exercising that leadership is well-grounded in a set of values and beliefs that we would view as being ethical. However, in a leadership sense . . . it means that the leader sets an example because ethical leadership doesn't just mean that leader, it means the entire organization. If there isn't an observed ethical leadership at the top, you won't find it in the organization.

As noted, moral management requires overt action on the part of the executive to serve as a role model for ethical behavior in highly visible ways, to communicate about ethics and values, and to use the reward system to hold people accountable. James Burke, former CEO of Johnson & Johnson, provides an excellent example of highly visible action that gets everyone's attention. Soon after Burke assumed the presidency of Johnson & Johnson, he brought together 28 senior managers to challenge the age-old corporate credo. He asked them to talk about whether they could really live by the document that had been hanging on corporate walls for years. "If we can't live by this document then it's an act of pretension and we ought to tear it off the walls, get rid of it. If we can live with it but want to change it that's okay too, if we can agree on what the changes should be. And, we could also leave it the way it is." According to Burke, people "stayed up all night screaming at each other." When they were done, they had updated the credo. They then took it to J&J sites around the world, released a revised credo in 1979, and committed the organization to it. Less than three years later, the Tylenol poisoning occurred and lots of folks were waiting to see whether management would live up to the credo values. As every student of business ethics and corporate crisis management knows, they did, and the case is now held up as a premier example of good business ethics. Burke does not take credit for J&J's success in handling the corporate crisis. He attributes the success to the value system that had been articulated. However, clearly he was responsible for guiding the organization through the values articulation process and for making the credo prominent in the corporate culture and consciousness. As another executive put it, "all the written statements in the world won't achieve ethics in an organization unless the leader is perceived as being very serious and committed."

Following the Tylenol crisis, in 1985 Burke launched the credo survey process. All employees were surveyed regarding the company's performance with respect to the credo. Based upon the results, managers held feedback and problem-solving sessions with their employees and developed action plans to address problems. The survey process continues today on a biannual schedule under Burke's successor, Ralph Larsen, and remains a valuable way to keep attention focused on the credo and the values it represents.

To better integrate the credo into the reward system, Larsen instigated a "standards of leadership" program which holds leaders at all levels accountable to the credo values.

At the important succession planning meetings, when upward mobility in the company is discussed, "Credo Values" is first on the agenda. "Business Results" is next in line. The following behaviors associated with Credo values are noted: "Behaving with honesty and integrity. Treating others with dignity and respect. Applying Credo values. Using Credo survey results to improve business. Balancing the interests of all constituents. Managing for the long term."[3]

Finally, violations of credo policy are handled swiftly and clearly. In one incident that involved infiltration of a competitor's sales meeting, President Larsen wrote the following to his management, "Our behavior should deeply embarrass everyone associated with Johnson & Johnson. Our investigation revealed that certain employees had engaged in improper activities that violated our policies. These actions were wrong and we took steps, immediately, to discipline those involved and guard against a recurrence of this kind of activity."[4]

Conclusion

Being an ethical leader requires developing a reputation for ethical leadership. Developing a reputation for ethical leadership depends upon how others perceive the leader on two dimensions: as a moral person and as a moral manager. Being a moral person encompasses who you are, what you do, and what you decide as well as making sure that others know about this dimension of you as a person. Being a moral manager involves being a role model for ethical conduct, communicating regularly about ethics and values, and using the reward system to hold everyone accountable to the values and standards. Ethical leadership pays dividends in employee pride, commitment, and loyalty—all particularly important in a full employment economy in which good companies strive to find and keep the best people.

Notes

1. C. Barnard, *Functions of the Executive* (Cambridge, MA: Harvard University Press, 1938 and 1968), p. 279.

2. J. A. Byrne, "Chainsaw," *Business Week*, October 18, 1999, pp. 128–149.

3. L. Foster, *Robert Wood Johnson* (State College, PA: Lillian Press, 1999), pp. 645–646.

4. Ibid., p. 646.

7

Politics or Porcelain?

ROBERT BIRNBAUM

As we approach the millennium, we face a crises of academic leadership, requiring new paradigms of virtual entrepreneurial agility so that colleges and universities can become the right-sized, results-oriented, consumer-focused learning organizations needed in our postmodern age. I have no idea what the previous sentence means, but I read it in an article somewhere, so it must be true. Perhaps you read the same article.

To strengthen academic leadership, we are told, we must reform structures, adopt more rationalized management systems, and increase the power of executive leadership to make faster, more efficient, and more effective decisions. There are few data to support the claimed value of such recommendations, a curious inconvenience for the rationalists who espouse them, but the logic is self-evident if one believes that change and progress are synonymous.

The arguments appear to be based on four ideas whose validity is authenticated more by repetition than by evidence. First, society is facing unprecedented crises. Second, weaknesses in higher education have contributed to these crises and improvement of higher education will help solve them. Third, academicians are part of the problem, and technology is part of the solution. Finally, implementing improvements will require stronger academic leadership. The consequences of ignoring the situation are dire. If higher education doesn't respond, then others will. Peter Drucker, an internationally recognized management guru, is among those who suggest that universities as we know them will disappear in thirty years.

We have heard variations on these themes in the past, and I don't believe they are any more accurate today than they were a hundred years

Reprinted from *Academe* 85, 3 (May–June 1999), pp. 15–19, with permission of American Association of University Professors.

ago. Clark Kerr's wonderful observation about universities being among the few institutions of western society that have survived from medieval times essentially unchanged speaks not only to their resilience but also, and of even greater importance, to their centrality to our notions of culture and civilization. You can bet on Drucker's prediction if you like; my money is on Kerr.

Today, universities exhibiting that stability are criticized as conservative, self-absorbed, and unconnected to the real world—increasingly irrelevant curiosities in a kind of institutional Jurassic Park. It is claimed by some that universities are dinosaurs, about to lose an evolutionary race with the emergence of more agile institutions that are swifter, less expensive, more flexible, more consumer oriented, and more responsive to the needs of industry and government. Virtual institutions will out-compete us if we do not change our ways, and if *they* don't, Disney U. or Microsoft U. or Motorola U. or Murdoch U. surely will. It is assumed that losing this competition will be harmful and must be avoided at all cost. The possibility that instead it might be advantageous for universities to focus on what we have traditionally done best by ceding some educational activities to the new forms and sectors is seldom considered.

Why this fall from grace? Daniel Seymour, a consultant and champion of the quality movement in higher education, says in *Once Upon a Campus* that it may be that society "expects the same thing in a college education that [it expects] in a toaster oven or a new home—utility. Skip the rhetoric. Forget about the cute accessories or the quaint features. People want to be assured that what they purchase today will be useful tomorrow."

What academic leaders can do about it is unclear. University presidents are held in high regard, and wield vast de facto if not de jure power. Nevertheless, groups such as the Association of Governing Boards of Universities and Colleges insist that presidents have to become even tougher and more decisive and be willing to make changes and to take risks. Universities are exceptionally complex organizations. As a student of leadership and a past university chancellor, I am bemused by the assumption that a president who had all the power in a university would know what to do with it.

Importance of Academic Leadership

Americans in general think that leadership is important. When we criticize social conditions, national policies, or organizational performance, we are quick to identify failures of leadership as the cause and to prescribe stronger leadership as the solution. We write countless books and articles about leadership. Yet despite the enormous attention we give to leadership, we still disagree about its meaning, how it should be exercised, how individuals should be prepared for it, or what its consequences are.

There is a lot of advice out there on leadership. Some of it is sound, some of it is foolish, and sometimes it is difficult to tell the difference. In general, successful leaders don't need the advice, and unsuccessful leaders don't understand it. I belong to the school of leadership that asserts that while leaders are important as a class, as individuals most university leaders have less influence most of the time than most of us are willing to believe. Some have labeled this position as cynical, but I prefer instead to think of it as realistic, particularly when applied to leadership in pluralistic democratic systems in general and in academic institutions in particular.

It may appear unreasonable to say that it is difficult for university presidents to provide leadership. After all, the legal structure of must U.S. universities appears to provide the basis for considerable presidential authority. Presidents are appointed by, and are the agents of, boards of trustees, which have total authority for institutional policies and decisions. Yet many presidents confirm that the appearance of authority is often an illusion. The authority of presidents is constrained by external forces such as declining resources, increased governmental controls, and greater institutional complexity. Perhaps even more important are the internal constraints, particularly the countervailing power of the faculties who assert their professional authority over all issues related to education.

How much of a difference do leaders make? Why is it that universities on average don't change even as their leaders are replaced? Why is it that change at the top is seldom followed by change at the middle and bottom? The reality is that university leaders are only one element in the process of reform. Not all leaders will want to support reform (after all, they achieved their success in the current system and are therefore likely to support it). But even selecting the most reform-minded leader will not by itself lead to change unless the reforms are supported in other ways. Faculty leadership, governmental leadership, corporate leadership, and public support and understanding all play a role. Presidents can lead only where their institutions and society permit them to go, and excessive attention to executive leadership may obscure the importance of history, culture, and leadership dispersed throughout the institution.

Transformational and Transactional Leadership

One way of thinking about the influence of executive leaders in the university is to consider their roles in terms of transformational and transactional leadership. Transformational leaders are those who create a new vision of an institution's future, and then, because of their personal charisma, self-confidence, and ability to change the ways in which others perceive reality, induce followers to higher levels of performance and motivate them to support changes desired by the leader. The transformational perspective argues that presidents must assertively articulate a clear vision for change, remain distant from their followers, and take risks if they are to be effective. It considers collegial leadership an oxymoron, bridles at the concept of consensus, identifies campus governance as the greatest barrier to change, and calls for the Lilliputians to unshackle the president.

In contrast to the transformational view, others propose that university leadership usually is, and ought to be, primarily transactional in nature. Transactional leadership is based on the principle of a fair social exchange in which leaders provide their followers with a sense of direction and recognize their needs and efforts. In exchange, through mutual regard and two-way influence, followers provide the leader with responsiveness to the leader's efforts. Good transactional leaders initially secure the support of followers by demonstrating their support of institutional values and their ability to contribute to the institution's goals. After establishing this relationship, they are then in a position to make changes that followers will accept because they believe in the leader's competence and commitment.

Transformational leadership emphasizes the potential power of leaders; transactional leadership notes the potential influence of followers. Transformational leadership looks for major changes of policy and direction; transactional leadership is likely to move in smaller, incremental steps. Transformational leadership captures our imagination; transactional leadership is more ordinary and less dramatic. Transformational leadership assumes that presidents, through their unusual personal attributes, can overcome all obstacles and inspire others to unusual achievements; transactional leadership recognizes that leadership must operate within limitations imposed by institutional history, culture, and structure. Transformational leaders can sometimes achieve spectacular successes or be equally spectacular failures; transactional leaders may be less likely to reflect either of these extremes, and more likely to encourage modest steady improvement. The world reveres transformational leaders, but the world works because of transactional leaders.

Transformational and transactional leadership are not different types as much as they are two idealized extremes on a leadership continuum. It is tempting to suggest that universities can be improved by selecting transformational leaders, but research suggests that the charisma required of truly transformational leaders is rare. Good transactional leadership, on the other hand, may be exercised by most of the accomplished people who become university leaders and therefore may be a more realistic way of understanding how leaders can make a difference to their institutions. And it may be the influence gained through good transactional

leadership that opens the way for some leaders to have an almost transformational effect on their institutions when the time is ripe.

I have described the ordinary, and occasionally extraordinary, accomplishments of transactional presidents in *How Academic Leadership Works*,
an analysis of college and university leadership based on a five-year research study. A fourth of the presidents in the study were identified as
failures; half were mostly successful, providing good stewardship and
leaving their institutions little better than they found them (no mean feat
today!). The remaining fourth were what I called exemplary presidents,
based on evidence that they enjoyed the support of campus constituen-
cies while at the same time institutional morale and performance improved. The exemplary presidents displayed characteristics of transactional leadership: they were selected in ways considered by their
followers to be legitimate, they listened respectfully to others and were
open to their influence, they honored the institution's history and took
time to learn about its moods, they worked collaboratively with faculty
leaders and encouraged leadership by others, they downplayed the bureaucratic aspects of their roles, and they constantly sought feedback on
their own performance. Exemplary presidents were seen by others as
committed to transcendent values for which their institutions could serve
as vehicles, such as furthering the growth and development of students,
or creating new knowledge. These presidents were able to use the influence they had gained as transactional leaders to get people in the institution to focus their energies on diminishing the discrepancies between
the espoused values and beliefs of the campus community and its actual
behavior.

This analysis of exemplary presidents suggests that the effectiveness of
an academic leader may depend less on getting the community to follow
the leader's vision and more on influencing the community to face its
problems. If this is so, what are the problems? For some, the problem is
getting the university to reform its programs and procedures and to become more responsive to "the needs of society." Some even presume to
know what those needs are! For others, the problem is getting the university to become more efficient and to produce more "output" at lower
cost. And everyone has Good Ideas that he or she believes will save
higher education from disaster.

Leadership for What?

Ideas are important, and they have consequences. I frequently remind
my students of the old aphorism, "There is nothing more powerful than a
good idea whose time has come." I recently tried to track down the
source, and was surprised to discover that I had it wrong. In the last di-
ary entry before his death, Victor Hugo wrote, "There is one thing

stronger than all the armies in the world; and that is an idea whose time has come." What I had remembered as a "good idea" was in reality "an idea"—any idea, good, bad, or indifferent—as long as its time had come. In a nation obsessed with angels, alien abductions, creationism, and New World Order conspiracies, I was naïve to believe that the quality of an idea would be related to its degree of acceptance. Worthy ideas might not find strong advocates. And bad ideas might prevail.

A number of new ideas about the university are currently being proposed. Increased acceptance of these ideas is offered as proof of their quality, and resistance is cited as further evidence of institutional intransigence and ivory-tower escapism. The important thing is reform, and never mind that we have no real basis for suggesting that the overall effects of these reforms might be beneficial. The goal is change, and the faster the better. We may have lost the way, but at least we are making good time. Everyone can put together a personal list of Ten Bad Ideas Whose Time Has Come. Here is mine; you may feel free to substitute your own: (1) The purpose of the university is to serve the economy. (2) Faculty tenure should be abolished. (3) The number of part-time faculty should be increased. (4) Virtual institutions can substitute for real ones. (5) Curriculums should be based on employers' needs, rather than student interests. (6) Every student should be required to purchase a computer. (7) Every course should make use of computers. (8) Trustees (or other public officials) should be more assertive in academic matters. (9) Outsourcing of services and instruction should be increased. (10) Research universities should give greater attention and more resources to undergraduate teaching.

Sound arguments can be made for or against each of these ideas individually, and each makes great sense for certain kinds of educational enterprises. But not for the university. The ideas ignore the university as an institution, overemphasize it as an instrument of economic policy, underemphasize it as a creator and conservator of civilization, fail to reflect the wide diversity of institutional types of missions, and tend to de-skill the faculty. But a university is not just a storehouse for facts or a producer of credentials for work. It is a place with a physical and social presence, an institution whose existence symbolizes the values of the culture that supports it and that represents the best of that culture. It is a community of faculty members and students connected to each other by more than modems, not a convenience store where isolated and disembodied individuals measure out virtual units of teaching or learning.

While some see the purpose of leadership as encouraging institutions to adopt new educational programs, others see it as moving institutions to adopt the new management techniques believed to be successful in business and government. Those of us with graying hair will remember program budgeting, inflicted on higher education in the 1960s. Today, we are coping with Continuous Quality Improvement, Benchmarking, and Business Process Re-engineering. Even newer reforms, with even more forbidding names, are on the horizon. The principles and procedures of many of these innovations are in conflict with academic norms and culture. In my research on the use of these new techniques over the past forty years, I have uncovered little evidence that they improved the institutions that adopted them. Still, the demands continue that universities model themselves more closely after business firms. One of the major challenges facing higher education leaders is protecting nonrational academic values from the pressures of rationalized management systems.

Narrative of Education

Whether we are talking about leaders influencing the adoption of new programmatic ideas or new management ideas, the major issue for leaders should really be *why* we want to do something, rather than *how* we do it. In his recent book, *The End of Education*, New York University professor and social critic Neil Postman refers to the importance of purposes when he says, "For school to make sense, the young, their parents, and their teachers must have a god to serve or, even better, several gods. If they have none, school is pointless." What Postman means by a "god" is a compelling narrative of ideals, purpose, and continuity that provides participants with meaning. Every culture has its own narratives. The educational narratives of the past have been stories of personal virtues, civic participation, democracy, and social equality. The narrative gods of the present appear to be economic utility, consumerism, and technology—weak foundations on which to excite the imagination or build a just social order.

Although Postman writes about school systems, the lack of a compelling narrative is higher education's major leadership problem as well. Our past narratives spoke to a liberating education, to critical thinking, to full involvement in citizenship, to personal growth, and to social justice. What are the narratives that drive us now? Are they as worthy? Can we help create new ones? Many of the new programs and management innovations that higher education leaders are being urged to adopt are very sophisticated, but the narrative supporting them is simple. It goes like this: business and industry are highly efficient and customer oriented. Higher education is not. Higher education could become more efficient if it adopted the management techniques of business, such as outsourcing, benchmarking, or re-engineering. But the faculty won't permit it because they are protecting their own selfish interests, and presidents are too timid to stand up against them. Therefore, other public advocates must act if the situation is to be corrected.

This is a simplistic narrative, and its simplicity is its power. Leaders tell stories to at least two audiences. In the battle for narrative supremacy, the sophisticated story developed for an expert audience is likely to lose out to the less sophisticated story that appeals to what Harvard psychologist and educator Howard Gardner has called the five-year-old mind. If you doubt this, consider the ascendance of the narrative of educational technology that will improve all of higher education. It has led to huge expenditures of money and effort, while experts continue to question whether any data indicate that the goals of lower cost and higher quality have been—or can be—met. The five-year-old mind wins again!

What We Know Now About Academic Leadership

I recently attended a meeting of college and university presidents whose institutions were each engaged in a program of planned change. As they discussed their various programs, I was surprised by two things. First, each appeared to accept the premise that something was wrong with higher education and that one role of leadership was to fix it. Some of the wounds they described seemed self-inflicted. Second, while there was a great deal of discussion about efficiency and competition, there was a conspicuous absence of discussion identifying higher education as a public good that refines social interaction and serves communal as well as individual interests. It's not that the participants didn't believe in these educational purposes—it's just that they weren't included in the stories they were telling.

We are losing the battle of the narratives, and without a compelling narrative we are increasingly vulnerable to those who have one. We are unable to defend the university in ways that make sense to others. We are at the mercy of new demands and management techniques, because if we are seen as being no different from business, then we can be—and increasingly will be—judged by business standards. Institutional leaders today are under enormous pressure to change. We find it hard to defend what we do, while those who clamor for change are loud and insistent. Our sensitivity to the complexity of the problems appears to drain us of all conviction, while the passionate intensity of those who see simplicity in both the problems and their solutions sounds a clarion call. As part of an open system, higher education clearly must be responsive to changes in the environment. At the same time, we should not lose sight of the fact that interactions in an open system are a two-way street, and that, within limits, we can also influence the environment that then influences us. Leaders should not only facilitate change, but should also seek to protect that which should endure.

Do we know anything about academic leadership that may be helpful to us today? I am sure that leadership is culturally defined, socially constructed, and situationally dependent. Other than that, little is certain. I can offer the following statements about leadership that I believe apply to most organizations, including universities. These statements sound simple, but they are subtle. They are supported by a considerable body of research. If they are correct, they have significant implications for how academic leaders should be chosen and for defining the limits of what they might be able to achieve.

- The basic function of leadership is to help others clarify, and become committed to, the essential purposes of the organization.
- Leadership presumes followership; effective leadership cannot be imposed, but must be granted.
- Followers grant leadership to those seen as legitimately selected, who have institutionally relevant expertise, and who endorse and represent the institution's values.
- Leaders' initial conformity to what followers expect increases the likelihood that they will subsequently be able to innovate successfully.
- Effective leadership is informed more by judgment and experience than by science.

In a letter to his wife, the American patriot John Adams proposed that education for a democracy might pass through three developmental stages. He wrote, "I must study politics and war that my sons may have liberty to study mathematics and philosophy. My sons ought to study mathematics and philosophy, geography, natural history, naval architecture, navigation, commerce, and agriculture, in order to give their children a right to study painting, poetry, music, architecture, statuary, tapestry, and porcelain." We have been exceptionally successful in exploiting this second developmental stage, but we appear increasingly reluctant to make the evolutionary advance from studying politics to studying porcelain. Academic leaders cannot by themselves make this choice, but collectively perhaps we may influence and inform the public debate about the purposes of higher education, either by reviving old narratives or by creating new ones.

8

Crisis, Culture, and Charisma

The New Leader's Work in Public Organizations

MATTHEW VALLE

This paper argues that the changing nature of public service requires new leadership and that the primary goal of leaders in public organizations today should be the development of, as the organization's primary core competence, an adaptive organizational culture. The changing nature of public service will be discussed in terms of the external and internal environmental forces impacting public organizations, the expanded and diverse missions that make up the work of the members of these organizations, and the style of leadership appropriate in order to take steps to create the organizational energy necessary for action. The model presented emphasizes the interaction of the environment, the followers, and the leader and describes this interaction as a combination of crisis, culture, and charisma.

In an era of increasing public pressure and dwindling budgets, the challenge of leadership in public organizations grows more acute each day. Given the pervasive stereotypes about public leaders,[1] the increasingly uncertain regulatory environments in which they operate,[2] and the constraints, controls, and processes of public management,[3] leaders in public organizations are faced with substantial, if not insurmountable, obstacles to effective management. It may go without saying that tomorrow's regulatory and administrative problems will differ markedly from today's. Consider, for example, the changing landscape of public administration: the number of stakeholder groups has swelled and all groups

Reprinted with permission, from *Public Personnel Management* 28, 2 (Summer 1999), pp. 245–257.

are becoming increasingly vocal; demographic changes are causing shifts in federal, state, and local responsibilities; there is increasing downward pressure on the ability of public organizations to levy taxes, often in combination with an increase in the level of unfunded mandates; and the continuing pervasive and interactive nature of the global economy and global markets inject a higher degree of chaos than was previously experienced.[4] In such an environment, it is not so difficult to explain the exodus of high quality leaders[5] and the drain of managerial talent may continue unabated unless some mechanism exists for new leaders in public organizations to enact environments that facilitate mission accomplishment, personal growth and productivity, and a rebirth of organizational energy.

Public organizations today need leaders capable of coping with continual environmental change, but the real work of new leaders in public organizations is to prepare the members of their organizations to cope with, and adapt to, changes of mission, environment, and/or direction. Such leadership will require individuals who have the ability to correctly assess current environmental threats and opportunities, both within and outside the organization, and take steps to create the organizational energy necessary for action.[6] In this paper, I will argue that leaders in public organizations must focus their efforts on developing, as the organization's primary core competence, an adaptive organizational culture. It is through such a culture that public organizations, and their leaders, will learn how to succeed in the face of constantly changing responsibilities.

The Central Role of Crisis in Public Organizations

Intuitively, we know that leadership in public organizations today is different. This is primarily because of the increasingly turbulent nature of the environments in which public organizations operate.[7] Changes in environment require corresponding changes in the methods by which the organization plans, organizes, and directs its energies toward mission accomplishment. Such is the province of leadership. The primary function of leadership is to guide the organization and its members toward their objectives, but those objectives have become more elusive and dynamic in public organizations. Leadership under these circumstances requires continual environmental scanning in order to assess threats and opportunities. The environment in which public service organizations operate today more closely mirror the private sector with constantly evolving technological focus and the interplay of local and global market forces. Actually, the turbulent nature of the environment surrounding most public organizations can be more accurately described as one of crisis.

One normally associates crisis with severe societal, economic, or political upheaval, but there are crises continually impacting organizations which are relatively pervasive but less severe.[8] Crisis may be perceived if the current situations the organization faces are of such a varied nature that simple resolution based upon reference to past actions or procedures becomes problematic. Affective reactions based upon such perceptions may include increased levels of perceived stress and decreased levels of personal satisfaction for organizational members. Behavioral reactions to crisis situations may include detrimental physical effects and increases in absenteeism and turnover. The response of the organization to these new realities is determined, in great part, by the ability of organization leaders to guide members toward the successful resolution of the crisis. The methods leaders use to guide members are the result of a series of choices that reflect how leaders and followers interact.

Leadership and Culture in Public Organizations

In the past, leaders in public organizations have placed great emphasis on developing stable and predictable organizational structures and work processes.[9] The purpose of leadership in such organizations was (and still may be) to train employees to anticipate problems by focusing on specific rules, procedures, and policies for handling matters requiring organizational action. This type of leadership is often referred to as transactional. A transactional leader guides and motivates followers by clarifying role and task requirements so that goals may be achieved.[10] Rewards accrue to those who follow the rules. Transactional leaders take corrective action only when there is a deviation from the rules or procedures. What is perhaps unintentionally made clear to employees in this type of system is that thinking and acting "outside the box" have no place in this organization. Effectiveness is measured by adherence to standards, rules, and procedures. Such an approach may prove efficient and effective if the tasks required of the organization are stable and predictable and can be completed with reference to specified rules. In manufacturing organizations, rules and procedures (i.e., work processes) enhance standardization, which subsequently impacts efficiency and the quality of the effort and output. Discipline is required in such organizations to produce outputs that conform to specifications. However, if the problems faced by public organizations are not routine, work processes may degenerate to fitting square pegs in round holes, no matter how square they may be.

The culture that develops under this "rule-driven" organizational system may be referred to as anticipatory.[11] An anticipatory system is one that takes present action based upon an expected future state. The term

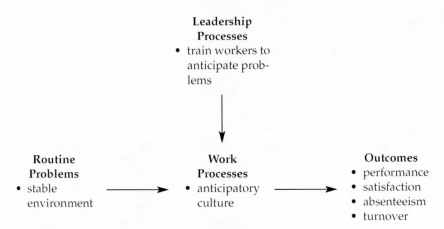

FIGURE 8.1   Leadership Processes in Stable Environments

refers to any system in which decisions are made by reference to an established algorithm or problem-solving guide. By nature, anticipatory cultures are passive and reactive. Work processes emphasize learning the rules and procedures to guide decisions. Employees develop a reactive stance toward problems; workers engage in a deterministic search for the correct application of standards to problematic issues. The identification and exploitation of opportunities (unforeseen problems) may not even occur in such organizations. Remember, action is taken only on expected future states. Figure 8.1 shows the relationship between routine problems, leadership, and the anticipatory culture of these organizations.

If the majority of the problems public organizations face could be classified as routine, then such a system of anticipation would be the most efficient form in which to conduct the work of the organization. In some systems leaders try to isolate the technical core (i.e., the workers) from their external environment by sorting, classifying, and filtering until what arrives for disposition is a neatly packaged, clearly solvable "problem." Much of the work done by transactional leaders is along those lines. Increasingly, however, leaders in public organizations are not able to isolate their technical core from the chaos of their environments. Therefore, if public organizations are operating in increasingly turbulent environments, is it possible to structure work processes to achieve stability when the parameters for stable operation are constantly shifting? What is the appropriate fit of organizational structure and environment in these new circumstances? And, perhaps a more practical question, do leaders in public organizations have the ability to restructure their organizations to achieve a good fit? The good news is that such a reorganization is implicit in the cultural change leaders must initiate in public orga-

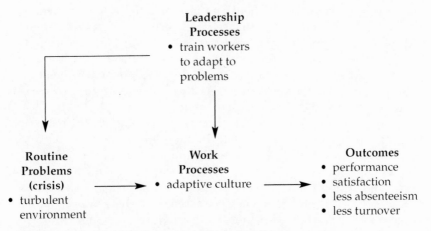

FIGURE 8.2   Leadership Processes in Turbulent Environments

nizations in order to cope with, and adapt to, the increasing complexity of their environments. And it is posited that such a change can occur without the physical shift of personnel and resources that is normally associated with organizational change.

The New Leader's Work

Public organizations which are subject to continual crises, whether acute or chronic, severe or less severe, need to develop mechanisms to cope with the demands of their ever-changing situations. Figure 8.2 suggests a new model for leadership in public organizations that focuses on the relationships between the culture of the subordinates in the organization; the situational context, or environment, in which the organization operates (i.e., crisis); and the leadership essential to facilitate effectiveness. This model emphasizes the interaction of leader, follower, and situation to understanding how leaders in public organizations may accomplish their expanded missions in the face of pressure from increasing numbers of stakeholders.

The primary means by which leaders facilitate the successful resolution of organizational tasks in turbulent environments is to build a culture with a core competence which values and excels at adaptation. In manufacturing terms, such a distinctive competency would be referred to as "flexibility," and that description holds for service operations in general, and public organizations specifically.[12] There is no flexibility in a system which requires rote adherence to written procedures. If crises by nature are varied and of random impact and importance, basic transactional leadership does not go far enough toward providing the necessary guidance concerning comprehensive plans of action for every possible contingency. Some famous public servants recognized this limitation of leadership in rapidly changing environments. George Patton was fond of saying, "Never tell people how to do things, tell them what to do and they will surprise you with their ingenuity."[13] Adaptive cultures foster innovation and creative solutions, and Patton's armies were known to be highly adaptive, and dramatically successful.

An organizational culture which values adaptation, by necessity, makes use of a wider range of skills by more members. In order to accomplish the substantial tasks of information gathering and evaluation in complex environments, adaptive organizational cultures must seek information and support from diverse elements within their structure. Also, by necessity, organizational members are forced to share information, resources, and ideas. Job scope and subsequent responsibilities for outcomes are expanded. Organizational units, which previously acted as separate units (i.e., co-acting groups), must now interact in order to accomplish the mission. And while the structure of the organization may appear on charts as functional and stable, the operation of the organizational elements may be perceived as more "team-like" and dynamic. A structure that was developed to operate mechanistically can become organic for problem identification and resolution and revert to mechanistic processes in executions.[14] Such an ambidextrous approach allows for the "virtual" shift of people and resources. It is not necessary to physically restructure the organization with teams in mind if the de facto practice is for the members within the organization to operate as members of rapidly forming and adjourning teams.

This process is by no means as simple as it sounds. Real culture change is a slow and tedious process. Most organizational cultures are the result of critical incidents at founding and during the entrepreneurial stage of development. Leaders in public organizations do not often have the luxury of starting anew. The requirements of the new work of public organizations dictate that we have new workers, but, in most cases, it is not necessary to search outside the organization for those people. Most experts agree that culture change can be managed in one of two ways:[15] 1) by using a symbolic approach, leaders attempt to influence cultural norms and values by shaping surface elements (e.g., symbols, stories, ceremonies) and continually managing meaning; and 2) by using organizational development interventions (e.g., process consultation, team development), leaders can help guide members through the stages of identifying and accepting new norms and values. Shaping team players requires careful selection, training, and rewards. For those organizational members who cannot adapt to the realities of the new organization, transfer, relocation, or perhaps termination (as a last resort) may be necessary. Most likely, organizational members can be taught to be team players. Training in problem-solving skills, communication, negotiation, conflict management, etc. can help turn individuals into team players. Team-building training is a slow process, but it is a necessary and ultimately worthwhile intervention if workers are to engage in the kind of interaction required of units to "do more with less." And finally, regardless of how egalitarian the concept of work-place teams may appear to be, unless the reward systems are structured to reinforce appropriate group and team behaviors (e.g., interaction and cooperation), the mission will never be adequately accomplished. Appropriate reward structures ensure the proper match between actions and outcomes.

Leaders who communicate new meanings to be shared (i.e., crisis becomes "challenge") forge a common vision that guides the interacting teams.[16] Such challenges will most likely arise in the external environment, but it is also possible for crises to be internally generated.[17] The link between leadership and crisis in the model shown as Figure 8.2 is meant to indicate that leaders can also generate or highlight crises. Research suggests that some executives may create states of non-equilibrium as a means to achieve organizational self-renewal and creativity.[18] By being proactive in the selection of relevant or advantageous crises to address, the leader can shape the situation to his/her advantage. In doing so, the leader moves his/her organization from a reactive stance to a proactive stance. Leaders may even go so far as to change the contingencies of the environmental context, or enact their own environments.[19]

The new work of leaders in public organizations does not stop with creating the appropriate adaptive culture or enacting situational crises. There are new personal requirements imposed on the leader as a result of the shift in focus. Given the nature of the new environmental realities, the leader must rely less on concrete task and performance direction, and more on framing and guiding the work tasks so that they align with the organization's mission and focus. Such work entails exhibiting those characteristics and emulating the behaviors associated with charismatic or transformational leaders.[20] These leaders should be able to provide their followers with a compelling vision or sense of purpose, and should be able to communicate that vision clearly.[21] Vision formation and communication serve as guides to action (e.g., the "what" but not necessarily the "how," as Patton suggested).[22] Charismatic or transformational leaders can positively transform and empower their followers[23] and achieve many positive organizational changes.[24] By verbalizing a focused vision leaders contribute to the integration of activities. Osborne and Gaebler suggested in their book *Reinventing Government* that leaders in public organizations should stick to steering (purpose and problem definition) as opposed to rowing (developing solutions).[25] Instead of rules and proce-

TABLE 8.1   Guidelines for Creating and Communicating Organizational Vision

Understand the design and use of forums. Forums allow organizational members the chance to discuss ideas and plans in an attempt to develop shared meanings. Many leaders underestimate the value of these informal discussion sessions.

Seize opportunities to provide interpretation and give direction in difficult and uncertain situations. This is your chance to change the interpretation of crises, threats, and problems into challenging tasks for the organization. It is at these times that visionary leadership is most in demand.

Reveal and name real needs and real conditions. Make sense out of difficult problems by framing issues in terms that organizational members can understand.

Help followers frame and reframe issues and strategies. Name and explain the "what" of the problems, but let the followers suggest the "how" part of solving the problems.

Offer compelling visions of the future. Give organizational members a scenario of how the problem will unfold and how it will eventually be solved.

Champion new and improved ideas. Gather ideas from many sources. Foster an environment which values innovation and experimentation.

Detail actions and expected consequences. Explain what the consequences of the difficulties are and give the members a plan of action for solving those problems.

SOURCE: Adapted from J.M. Bryson, *Strategic Planning for Public and Nonprofit Organizations: A Guide to Strengthening and Sustaining Organizational Achievement* (San Francisco: Jossey-Bass, 1995) p. 221–224.

dures guiding action, the vision and goals espoused by the leadership of the organization serve as the coordination and control mechanisms. Table 8.1 provides a listing of useful guidelines for creating and communicating organizational vision.[26]

Charisma is not something endowed by divine forces, as was once believed.[27] Charisma is an attribute. It is a manifestation of the belief among followers that the leader possesses or exhibits charismatic qualities. And even though it seems that charisma, as an all-or-nothing quality, is overused in daily conversations about leaders and leadership, it is possible for formerly non-charismatic individuals to be trained to act more charismatically.[28] Charismatic leaders are not necessarily boastful or flamboyant. Sam Walton exercised a style of quiet leadership which was perceived to be very charismatic (and successful). For followers to attribute charisma to an individual, they must hold a particularly strong emotional reaction to, identification with, and belief in that person.[29]

Followers of charismatic leaders have been found to accept the leader without question, trust in the leader's beliefs, show willing obedience to the leader, identify with the leader, and try to emulate him/her.[30] The bond which develops between the leader and followers, if nurtured, can produce some pretty substantial changes. Individuals working under a charismatic leader have been found to have higher task performance, task adjustment, and adjustment to the leader and the group.[31] The attribution of charisma depends on the simultaneous interaction of the situational context (i.e., crisis), the characteristics of the followers (i.e., norms, values, culture), and the qualities exhibited by the leader. The charismatic bond may ultimately represent a manifestation of the need of followers during times of crisis for centralized authority.[32] In return for obedience and service, the followers expect that charismatic leaders will provide direction and focus. Such "framing" or guidance may serve as a stress reduction mechanism and could, perhaps, lead to less absenteeism and turnover. There may be great danger in such bonds in that some leaders may abuse the relationship by pursuing leader-driven instead of follower-driven goals,[33] and that is always a possibility. However, power which is controlling or coercive will eventually destroy the bonds between leader and follower. When charismatic leadership is directed toward the accomplishment of organizational goals and to the benefit of the organization, increases in productivity, performance, and satisfaction will be the result.[34] Remember, it is not the person alone which engenders the attribution of charisma, but the vision the person communicates (i.e., the path out of crisis) that is responsible for the charismatic bond between leader and followers.

Implications for Public Organizations

Public organizations have been characterized as diverse and fragmented.[35] Perhaps it is time to rethink our conception of the basic work of public organizations. Upheaval and change are becoming the standard operating procedure for many public organizations, yet these organizations continue to focus on the mechanics of rule interpretation and application instead of developing the distinctive competence of adaptation in their human resources. The problem is not change itself, but the lack of leadership for change.

New leaders in public organizations must first recognize the realities of their changing environments. Public administration is no longer a stable industry; nor is it a place for those who cannot innovate and inspire. Leadership in public organizations must be fundamentally customer-oriented and purposefully entrepreneurial. When leaders view their subordinates as their immediate customers, they enact an environment of reciprocity. The subordinates, in turn, can then figure out how best to serve their external customers. Entrepreneurism can be stimulated by the creation of crisis. Identifying new missions and programs can help generate new ideas and insights concerning public service.

What is certain is that no one element alone can bring about the needed changes. The new leadership is a combination of some pretty old, but effective ideas. It is about what all leadership is about—the interaction of environment, followers, and the leader; and crisis, culture, and charisma. Vision is the glue which binds the three elements. A clear vision can be translated into action, policy, and job-related behavioral guidelines.[36] Without clear vision, the stimulation or identification of crisis will only lead to further fragmentation and dilution of effort. Without effective communication, the vision remains nothing more than an unfulfilled idea. Motivation is nothing without direction, and even the best organizations can suffer failure unless the path to the communicated goals is made clear. And, without crisis and a corresponding vision, there is little chance that charismatic qualities will be attributed to the leader. Without such an attribution, leaders can never hope to lead their organizations to perform beyond expectations, no matter how much they might wish for it.

In the absence of increased budgets for equipment and resources, public organizations have but one resource left with which to accomplish their expanded and diverse new missions—people. If we are to continue to experience the same kind of productivity gains in service operations (like public government) that we have experienced in recent years in the manufacturing sector, we must increasingly rely on improvements in human productivity. Selection, training, and appropriate reward systems can help leaders build adaptive organizational cultures, which will not only succeed in crisis environments, but excel. In biological terms, such organizations will survive because they represent successful adaptations to their environment. Leadership is the key to the survival of the fittest public organizations. Unless leaders in public organizations engage in the new work of adaptive culture formation and training, the only practical outcome is extinction.

This discussion of the new work of leaders in public organizations has only scratched the surface and outlined the "what" to do and not the "how" to do it. As with any complex and formidable task, the first and primary step is for someone to decide that the work must be done. Harnessing the interactive elements of crisis, culture, and charisma presents new leaders in public organizations with a powerful strategic weapon for survival, but beyond that, these tools help in the broader, yet unchanging, mission of providing high quality public service at the lowest cost possible. It appears to be time for some new leaders to take the first and requisite step.

Notes

1. Lipset, S. M. and Schneider, W. 1987. *The Confidence Gap: Business, Labor, and Government in the Public Mind*. Baltimore, MD: Johns Hopkins University Press.

2. Bryson, J. M. 1995. *Strategic Planning for Public and Nonprofit Organizations: A Guide to Strengthening and Sustaining Organizational Achievement*. San Francisco, CA: Jossey-Bass; Rainey, H. G. 1991. *Understanding and Managing Public Organizations*. San Francisco, CA: Jossey-Bass.

3. Chase, G. and Reveal, E. C. 1983. *How to Manage in the Public Sector*. Reading, MA: Addison-Wesley.

4. Bryson, J. M. 1995. *Strategic Planning for Public and Nonprofit Organizations: A Guide to Strengthening and Sustaining Organizational Achievement*. San Francisco, CA: Jossey-Bass.

5. Volcker Commission. 1989. *Leadership for America: Rebuilding the Public Service*. Lexington, MA: Heath.

6. Prahalad, C. K. and Bettis, R. 1988. "The dominant logic: A new link between diversity and performance," *Strategic Management Journal*, 7: 485–501.

7. Chase, G. and Reveal, E. C. 1983. *How to Manage in the Public Sector*. Reading, MA: Addison-Wesley; Rainey, H. C. 1991. *Understanding and Managing Public Organizations*. San Francisco, CA: Jossey-Bass.

8. Madsen, D. and Snow, P.G. 1991. *The Charismatic Bond: Political Behavior in Time of Crisis*. Cambridge, MA: Harvard University Press.

9. Bryson, J. M. 1995. *Strategic Planning for Public and Nonprofit Organizations: A Guide to Strengthening and Sustaining Organizational Achievement*. San Francisco, CA: Jossey-Bass.

10. Burns, J. M. 1978. *Leadership*. New York, NY: Harper and Row; Bass, B. M. 1985. *Leadership and Performance Beyond Expectations*. New York, NY: Free Press; Bass, B. M. 1990. "From transactional to transformational leadership: Learning to share the vision," *Organizational Dynamics*, Winter: 19–31.

11. Rosen, R. 1985. *Anticipatory Systems*. New York, NY: Pergamon.

12. Porter, M. E. 1990. "The competitive advantage of nations," *Harvard Business Review*, 90(2): 73–93.

13. Puryear, E. F. 1987. *19 Stars: A Study in Military Character and Leadership*. Novato, CA: Presidio Press.

14. Duncan, R. B. 1976. "The ambidextrous organization: Designing dual structures for innovation," in Ralph H. Killman, Louis R. Pondy, and Dennis Slevin (Eds.), *The Management of Organization*, 1: 167–188. New York, NY: North Holland.

15. Wagner, J. A. and Hollenbeck, J. R. III. 1998. *Organizational Behavior: Securing Competitive Advantage*. Upper Saddle River, NJ: Prentice-Hall.

16. Lipton, M. 1996. "Demystifying the development of an organizational vision," *Sloan Management Review*, Summer: 83–92.

17. Avolio, B. J. and Bass, B. M. 1988. "Transformational leadership, charisma and beyond," In J. G. Hunt, B. R. Baliga, H. P. Dachler, and C. A. Schreisheim (Eds.), *Emerging Leadership Vistas*. Lexington, MA: Lexington; Boal, K. B. and Bryson, J. M. 1988. "Charismatic leadership: A phenomenological and structural approach," In J. G. Hunt, B. R. Baliga, H. P. Dachler, and C. A. Schreisheim (Eds.),

Emerging Leadership Vistas. Lexington, MA: Lexington; Kets de Vries, M. F. R. 1989. *Prisoners of Leadership.* New York, NY: Wiley.

18. Hughes, G. D. 1990. "Managing high-tech product cycles," *Academy of Management Executive*, 4(2): 44–55.

19. Weick, K. E. 1979. *The Social Psychology of Organizing.* Reading, NM: Addison-Wesley.

20. Avolio, B. J. and Bass, B. M. 1988. "Transformational leadership, charisma and beyond," In J. G. Hunt, B. R. Baliga, H. P. Dachler, and C. A. Schreisheim (Eds.), *Emerging Leadership Vistas.* Lexington, MA: Lexington; Boal, K. B. and Bryson, J. M. 1988. "Charismatic leadership: A phenomenological and structural approach," In J. G. Hunt, B. R. Baliga, H. P. Daclier, and C. A. Schreisheim (Eds.), *Emerging Leadership Vistas.* Lexington, MA: Lexington.

21. Bennis, W. 1984. "The four competencies of leadership," *Training and Development Journal*, 15–19.

22. Lipton, M. 1996. "Demystifying the development of an organizational vision," *Sloan Management Review*, Summer: 83–92.

23. House, R. J., Spangler, W. D., and Wyocke, J. 1991. "Personality and charisma in the U.S. Presidency: A psychological theory of leadership effectiveness," *Administrative Science Quarterly*, 36: 364–396; Block, R. 1993. *Stewardship: Choosing Service over Self-Interest.* San Francisco, CA: Berrett-Koehler.

24. House, R. J., Spangler, W. D., and Wyocke, J. 1991. "Personality and charisma in the U.S. Presidency: A psychological theory of leadership effectiveness," *Administrative Science Quarterly*, 36: 364–396.

25. Osborne, D. and Gaebler, T. 1992. *Reinventing Government.* Reading, MA: Addison-Wesley.

26. Bryson, J. M. 1995. *Strategic Planning for Public and Nonprofit Organizations: A Guide to Strengthening and Sustaining Organizational Achievement*, pp. 222, 223. San Francisco, CA: Jossey-Bass.

27. Weber, M. 1947. *The Theory of Social and Economic Organizations.* (A. M. Henderson and T. Parsons, trans.). New York, NY: Free Press.

28. Howell, J. M. and Frost, P. J. 1989. "A laboratory study of charismatic leadership," *Organizational Behavior and Human Decision Processes*, 43(2): 243–269.

29. Bass, B. M. 1985. *Leadership and Performance Beyond Expectations.* New York, NY: Free Press; Conger, J. A. and Kanungo, R. N. 1987. "Towards a behavioral theory of charismatic leadership in organizational settings," *Academy of Management Review*, 12(4): 637–647.

30. House, R. J. and Baetz, M. L. 1979. "Leadership: Some empirical generalizations and new research directions." In B. M. Staw (Ed.), *Research in Organizational Behavior.* Greenwich, CT: JAI.

31. Howell, J. M. and Frost, P. J. 1989. "A laboratory study of charismatic leadership," *Organizational Behavior and Human Decision Processes*, 43(2): 243–269.

32. Madsen, D. and Snow, P. G. 1991. *The Charismatic Bond: Political Behavior in Time of Crisis.* Cambridge, MA: Harvard University Press.

33. Howell, J. M. 1988. "The two faces of charisma: Socialized and personalized leadership in organizations," in J. A. Conger and R. N. Kanungo (Eds.), *Charismatic Leadership: The Elusive Factor in Organizational Effectiveness.* San Francisco, CA: Jossey-Bass.

34. Howell, J. M. and Frost, P. J. 1989. "A laboratory study of charismatic leadership, *Organizational Behavior and Human Decision Processes*, 43(2): 243–269; House, R. J. and Baetz, M. L. 1979. "Leadership: Some empirical generalizations and new research directions," in B. M. Staw (Ed.), *Research in Organizational Behavior*. Greenwich, CT: JAI.

35. Rainey, H. G. 1991. *Understanding and Managing Public Organizations*. San Francisco, CA: Jossey-Bass.

36. Lipton, M. 1996. "Demystifying the development of an organizational vision," *Sloan Management Review*, Summer: 83–92.

9

Leading Learning Organizations

PETER SENGE

I think of three types of leaders in learning organizations, roughly corresponding to three positions:

1. Local line leaders, who can undertake meaningful organizational experiments to test whether new learning capabilities lead to improved business results.
2. Executive leaders, who support line leaders, develop learning infrastructures, and lead by example in the gradual process of evolving the norms and behaviors of a learning culture.
3. Internal networks, or community builders, the "seed carriers" of the new culture, who can move freely about the organization to find those who are predisposed to bringing about change, assist in experiments, and aid in the diffusion of new learnings.

Here I'll sketch what we are learning about these three types of leaders.

Local Line Leaders

Nothing can start without committed local line leaders, individuals with significant business responsibility and "bottom-line" focus. They have units that are large enough to be meaningful microcosms of the organization, and yet they have enough autonomy to undertake meaningful change.

Reprinted with permission, from author and *Executive Excellence*, April 1996.

In effect, they create subcultures that may differ significantly from the mainstream culture. To be useful in creating experimental laboratories, they must also confront issue and business challenges that are seen as both important and recurring. For example, a unique cross-functional task force may be important but less useful for a learning experiment than a team that manages a process that is ongoing, generic, and vital for future competitiveness, such as a product development team, a sales team, or a business division.

The key role played by local line leaders is to sanction significant practical experiments. Without serious practical experiments aimed at connecting new learning capabilities to business results, there is no way to assess whether enhancing learning capabilities is just an appealing idea or really makes a difference.

We have seen no examples where significant progress has been made without leadership from local line managers, and many examples where sincerely committed CEOs have failed to generate any significant momentum.

· Executive Leaders

Our fervor with practical experiments led by local line managers has frequently made us blind to the necessary complementary roles played by executive leaders. Local line leaders benefit significantly from "executive champions" who can be protectors, mentors, and thinking partners.

Working in concert with internal networkers, executives can help in connecting innovative local line leaders with other like-minded people. They also play a mentoring role—helping the local line leaders to mature, to understand complex political concurrents, and to communicate their ideas to those who have not been involved.

Part of the problem in appreciating effective executive leadership in learning is that we are so used to the "captain of the ship" image of traditional hierarchical leaders. We think of top managers as the key decision-makers, the most visible and powerful people. Although undoubtedly some key decisions will always have to be made at the top, cultures are not changed through singular decisions, and decision-making power does not produce new learning capabilities.

When executives lead as teachers, stewards, and designers, they fill roles that are subtler, more contextual, and more long term than the traditional model of the power-wielding hierarchical leader suggests.

Effective executive leaders build an environment for learning in three ways: the first is through guiding ideas. Guiding ideas are different from slogans or the latest buzzwords. They are arrived at gradually, over many years, through reflection on an organization's history and traditions and on its long-term growth and opportunities.

The power of guiding ideas derives from the energy released when imagination and aspiration come together. Understanding this power has always been a hallmark of great leaders. The promise of learning organizations is the promise that this power will become deeply and widely embedded in a way that rarely, if ever, happens in traditional authoritarian organizations.

A second way to build operating environments for learning is through attention to learning infrastructure. Executives will increasingly come to realize that, in a world of rapid change and increasing interdependence, learning is too important to be left to change. "We have plenty of infrastructure for decision-making within AT&T," says Chairman Bob Allen. "What we lack is infrastructure for learning."

I have met many CEOs in recent years who have lamented that "we can't learn from ourselves," that significant innovations simply don't spread, or that "we are better at learning from competitors than from our own people." Yet those very same executives rarely recognize that they may be describing their own future job description. When we stop to think, certain questions arise: Why should successful new practices spread in organizations? Who studies these innovations to document why they worked? Where are the learning processes whereby others might follow in the footsteps of successful innovators? Who is responsible for these learning processes?

A third way to build operating environments for business is the executives' own "domain for taking action"—namely, the executive team itself. What is important, first, is that executives see that they, too, must change, and that many of the skills that have made them successful in the past can actively inhibit learning. They are forceful, articulate advocates, but they usually are not very good at inquiring into their own thinking or exposing the areas where their thinking is weak.

How radical are ideas like these about executive leadership? I think they will eventually lead to a very different mindset and, ultimately, skill set among executives. "Gradually, I have come to see a whole new model for my role as CEO," says Shell Oil's Phil Carroll. "My real job is to be the ecologist for the organization—to see the company as a living system and to see it as a system within the context of the larger systems of which it is a part. Only then will our vision reliably include return for our shareholders, a productive environment for our employees, and a social vision for the company as a whole."

Achieving such shifts in thinking, values, and behavior among executives is not easy. "The name of the game is giving up power," says Carroll. "Even among 'enlightened' executives, giving up power is difficult. Being the commander in chief is kind of fun."

Internal Networkers

The most unappreciated leadership role is that of the internal networkers, or community builders. Internal networkers are effective for the very reasons that top-management efforts to initiate change can backfire. One paradox may be that "no power is power."

Precisely because they have no positional authority, internal networkers are free to move about a large organization relatively unnoticed. When the CEO visits someone, everyone knows. When the CEO says, "We need to become a learning organization," everyone nods. But when someone with little or no positional authority begins identifying people who are genuinely interested in changing the way they and their teams work, the only ones likely to respond are those who are genuinely interested. And if the internal networker finds one person who is interested and asks, "Who else really cares about these things?" he or she is likely to receive an honest response.

The only authority possessed by internal networkers comes from the strength of their convictions and the clarity of their ideas. This, we find time and again, is the only legitimate authority when deep changes are required, regardless of one's position. The internal networkers have the paradoxical advantage that this is their only source of authority.

It is very difficult to identify the internal networkers because they can be people from many different positions. They might be internal consultants, trainers, or staff in organization development or human resources. They might be front-line workers, engineers, sales representatives, or shop stewards. They might be in senior staff positions.

What is important is that they move freely, with high accessibility. They understand the informal networks, whereby information and stories flow and innovative practices naturally diffuse.

The first vital function played by internal networkers is to identify local line managers who have the power to take action and who are predisposed to developing new learning capabilities. Much time and energy can be wasted working with the wrong people, especially in the early stages of a change process.

As practical knowledge is built, internal networkers continue to serve as "seed carriers," connecting people of like minds in diverse settings to each other's learning efforts. Gradually they may help in developing the formal coordination and steering mechanisms needed to leverage from local experiments to organization-wide learning.

The limitations of internal networkers likewise are not difficult to identify. Because they do not have a great deal of formal authority, they can
do little to directly counter hierarchical authority. If a local line leader becomes a threat to peers or superiors, they may be powerless to help her
or him. Internal networkers have no authority to institute changes in
structures or processes.

The leadership challenges in building learning organizations represent
a microcosm of the leadership issue of our time: how communities, be
they multinational corporations or societies, productively confront complex, systemic issues where hierarchical authority is inadequate for
change. None of today's most pressing issues will be resolved through
hierarchical authority.

In all these issues, there are no simple causes, no simple "fixes." There
is no one villain to blame. There will be no magic pill. Significant change
will require imagination, perseverance, dialogue, deep caring, and a willingness to change on the part of millions of people.

The challenges of systemic change where hierarchy is inadequate will,
I believe, push us to new views of leadership based on new principles.
These challenges cannot be met by isolated heroic leaders. They will require a unique mix of different people, in different positions, who lead in
different ways. Changes will be required in our traditional leadership
models.

10

A View About "Vision"

NEAL THORNBERRY

Any modern manager who has not heard the word "vision" used in relationship to his own or another organization must surely be undereducated regarding today's latest "buzz words." The term "vision" may actually lead in frequency of usage in the mahogany halls of senior management; ahead of "total quality," "reengineering," "strategic intent," and "competitive advantage."

The concept of vision is not the problem, but the fact that most business leaders who use the term don't really understand it and worse still, don't have the faintest idea how to create and deploy it. It's not entirely their fault since most of the literature and research on vision has accurately identified its importance and pointed out individuals who seem to be visionary, but has done little to help leaders at all levels in the organization actually do it (Krug and Oakley, 1993; Capowski, 1994).

Some of the fault lies in the nature of the concept. A simple definition of vision is, a picture or view of the future. Something not yet real but imagined. What the organization could and should look like. Part analytical and part emotional.

This definition is actually no more concrete to managers than the concept of vision itself. Herein lies both the challenge and difficulty of vision. It is very hard to define. In fact in some Spanish-speaking countries the translated words for vision are more closely defined as "Nightmare" or "Apparition." A definition some English-speaking managers may find closer to reality after trying to develop and implement a vision within their own companies.

Unfortunately the concept is itself very "woolly" or "fuzzy" which creates various individual interpretations with little consensus to be found.

Reprinted with permission, from *European Management Journal* 15, 1 (February 1997), pp. 28–34. Copyright 1997. Published by Elsevier Science, Ltd. All rights reserved.

The author was recently asked to review and evaluate the vision state-ment of an international finance company. Senior management had spent over a year trying to evolve this vision. Many meetings had been held and after much debate they arrived at an acceptable "vision" statement of which they were quite proud. They had it engraved on a gold plaque which was conspicuously displayed in the corporate boardroom. The plaque had the following elements:

- We aspire to be number one in our market place.
- We respect and value our customers and our employees.
- We will work diligently to build value for our shareholders and investors.

I will not bore you with further elements of this "vision statement," but as you can see, it really tells us nothing. The author was not popular with this company when he suggested that they had actually purchased this "vision" from some "vision" warehouse which sells the same generic statements to hundreds of other companies in all kinds of industries. They were not amused. One would be hard pressed to find a company that did not publicly agree with all of the above platitudes. Can you imagine a company that wants to be mediocre, is mean to their employ-ees, and tries to screw its customers?

What they had done was mix generic concepts and ideas. In their vi-sion statement they had mixed values with mission, but had not really created a picture of the future nor had they come to grips with their fun-damental purpose or reason for being.

Confusing Terminology

With one notable exception, the literature on vision has not been very helpful in sorting out and differentiating these concepts. Most vision statements, which the author has reviewed, seem to be a mix of strategy, goals and objectives, values and beliefs, slogans, purposes, etc. Vision statements should be designed to be vivid, memorable, inspiring, mean-ingful and brief. Some of these statements, especially those found in an-nual reports are boring at best and indecipherable to the general public and clearly they are not memorable. In addition, words alone rarely carry long-term meanings for people unless the message behind them can be vi-sualized. We recently asked over 200 managers from a large European IT company to tell us their company's vision. Some people had no idea what it was. For those who thought they knew, there was no consensus. A num-ber of these managers volunteered to go to their rooms to help us clear up the confusion. This in itself was indicative of a less than effective visioning process. The company's vision was neither clear nor memorable.

Key Components of Vision

Perhaps the most coherent differentiation of some of these concepts comes from the work of Collins and Porras (1991; 1994). They studied over 75 organizations and isolated 20 of those who seemed to have got this "vision" thing down. Among those were Procter and Gamble, 3M, Ford, Sony, and Compaq. They analyzed these organizations to determine what constituted the anatomy of vision. They found that the most obvious and memorable part of the vision was what they called the "Vivid Description." Bennis and others have called this the picture or painting of the future entity; that which the company aspires to become (Bennis and Goldsmith, 1994).

From the author's work at Babson College in the US and at Ashridge Management College in the UK, this is the part of vision which people actually remember. It is the part that gives direction, helps focus effort, and stays etched in one's mind. This is also the component of vision which is the most difficult for business leaders to comprehend and develop. It involves both an artistic and an emotional component that many managers feel ill equipped to cope with.

Purpose or Reason for Being

Collins and Porras further argue that visions also have other components which are necessary to support this vivid description. The first is purpose. It is the fundamental reason that the organization exists. Many of today's managers will say the purpose of their organization is to make a profit and to increase shareholder value. My friends in financial circles will not like my view, but ROE is not the organization's purpose. It may be a goal or mission, but purpose refers to the fundamental need in the marketplace that a company's goods or services fulfill.

The new President of an International Division of a financial services company with whom the author works, had an opportunity to communicate the purpose of his company to three hundred of his managers at a conference held in Canada. His speech was spent mostly in talking about his company existing for the purpose of building value for the company's shareholders. Rubbish—the real purpose of the company was to help people who can't get conventional banks to loan them money to buy the things that so many of us take for granted. This company exists to help low wage earners satisfy some of their physical and psychological needs through loans and revolving credit. It also gives their low wage earning customers respect and attention; something that typical banks do not. The shareholders are the least important for this purpose. If a company can't satisfy some basic human need or want in the marketplace, then there won't be any equity for shareholders to share. Furthermore, very few of the managers in the room were shareholders, so from an inspirational perspective this purpose fell on deaf ears.

The best way to understand purpose is to ask the question that Collins and Porras ask: "What would the world lose if your company went out of business tomorrow?" Purpose tends to be long term and often helps to define the industry that a business is really in. Automobile manufacturers are not really in the car business; their purpose is to provide transportation. Purpose should be inspiring. Company employees should be able to see how what they do affects other people, especially the customer whose wants and needs the employee is trying to satisfy.

Cultural Beliefs and Values

The second element of the overall vision deals with values and beliefs. A Swedish-German combine in the paper industry is spending a great deal of time and energy on just this one component of vision. They realize that in order to fulfill their vision, they will have to have values which support it. For example, they envision their future organization to be much flatter, leaner, and more decentralized. Yet many of their current values support hierarchy, power and authority, and the chain of command. Furthermore, the Germans have different values than the Swedes in terms of empowerment and delegation. This focus on values is seen as critical to the CEO because he knows that the company must create a new value system in order to meld both cultures together. Clearly managers' values have to change if power and decision making is to be pushed down to lower levels (*Business Week*, 1994; *Canadian Manager*, 1993).

Values are extremely important if an organization is to realize its vision. Jack Welch of GE has always believed in promoting risk taking. Yet, GE had traditionally "shot" risk takers who failed. Not exactly an action conducive to developing risk taking and entrepreneurship within the company. So Welch decided to reinforce this value by promoting someone even though they had taken a risk which failed and lost the company money. Welch felt that the risk was a good one and that it was well thought out. Risk taking wouldn't be risk taking if there weren't a significant chance for failure. Welch's action sent a real and symbolic message around GE that the company was serious about supporting a risk taking culture. Welch's vision of a new GE which was fast, flexible, and opportunity focused could only be realized if people live values which support this vision.

Mission, Goals, and Objectives

Mission, the third element of the visioning process, is not purpose although it is often used as a synonym. Mission is bounded by time and it usually involves some sort of target which can be either qualitative or quantitative. Welch wants GE businesses to be one or two in all of their marketplaces or GE will sell them. This mission can be measured in terms of market share, or volume or any number of indices. Operating plans can often be cascaded from a well developed and thought out mission statement.

The financial services company mentioned earlier has a mission of 15 percent growth annually. Missions usually allow for the derivation of specific goals, objectives, and measures so that the accomplishments of the mission can be determined. Collins and Porras describe mission as a "bold, hairy, audacious goal." What they are really saying is that mission should stretch the organization but be possible to achieve given the company's aggressive pursuit of that goal—to be number one, to be world class, etc. Although these are both very broad statements, companies who are serious in reaching these lofty goals can actually develop measures which will allow them to determine their degree of success. Since missions are time bounded, they force the company to try and achieve their missions by a certain period in time. Some missions are never accomplished but always sought. Toyota has a mission of producing zero defect automobiles. Unlikely to ever happen, but it has driven them to be the best in accomplishing much of this mission. Missions are milestones towards the realization of the vision.

A Painting of the Future

The last part of the Collins and Porras model is what they describe as the "vivid description." This is the crux of the vision concept. It embodies purpose, values, and mission in a picture of how the future organization will look and operate. This vivid description is a state to be aspired to. It is not yet real but what the organization would aspire to be in the future, given some realities of its current market position, financial health, competitors, etc. It is not strategy. Strategy refers to plans and actions to be taken to meet strategic targets and objectives; to achieve the organization's mission. Strategy is hard, the picture of the future is soft. It is a dream. Individuals dream all the time about the future. Why shouldn't an organization dream as well? Dreams which are built around a combination of reality and fantasy.

Isadore Sharp, founder and CEO of Four Seasons Resorts and Hotels, started his career as an architect and with his father built one small motel; but he *dreamed* of creating a luxury hotel where employees would want to bend over backwards to serve their guests. So he built his first luxury hotel in a seedy area on the outskirts of Toronto but with an inward looking courtyard and garden so that guests would see beauty regardless of where the hotel was actually situated. The reality for Sharp was that he had the skills to design and build motels, but dreamed of something greater and the rest is history. In fact, Sharp's dream or vision is so in-stilled in its culture that a hotel employee flew to a nearby city at his own expense to return a bag which he had forgotten to load for a hotel guest. Thus Sharp's dream is not only a reality in stone and brick, it is a reality in the hearts and minds of his employees (*Canadian Manager,* 1993).

If the reader is currently feeling a little unsettled about my use of lan-guage, you are in good company. Very few self-respecting CEOs, MDs, or division heads would admit to dreaming. Their world is the world of numbers, market share, ROI, etc. It is the world of management, not lead-ership or art. To lead, means to take people somewhere. In today's ex-tremely competitive and changing environment, that "somewhere" can be quite frightening. The "somewhere" part can be determined in part by careful analysis, planning, and strategy development. Taking people there requires the ability to paint that "somewhere" in an understandable and motivational picture and the courage to commit to this picture with one's heart and soul.

Visioning is not for the faint of heart. Many people in the organization will purposefully take issue with the picture. The colors aren't right, the frame is the wrong size, the picture is fuzzy, the cost is too high, the pic-ture is frightening, you're not a good artist, etc. This is probably the clearest line of demarcation between management work and the work of leadership.

Teaching Managers to Be Visionaries

One can argue whether the ability to be visionary can be taught at all. My experience at two business schools and in numerous training sessions suggests that much of it can be taught. There are, however, two elements that probably can't be taught. The first is conceptual ability and the sec-ond is courage. Conceptual ability is critical because it allows the indi-vidual to conceive of the future. To think in conceptual terms and to see the interrelationships between concepts, such as purpose, mission, val-ues, etc. Most higher-level managers in today's businesses have a fair de-gree of conceptual abilities or they wouldn't be where they are. There are exceptions. In some old line businesses like utilities, mining, and some el-ements of manufacturing, conceptual skills are not necessarily prized. With the recent upheavals in these industries, however, conceptual skills, like strategic planning, etc. have become much more important and we have seen a new brand of leader emerging.

Courage is about deciding where you want to go and then committing to it. We suspect that many managers are afraid to do this for fear that the direction might be wrong and therefore it is better to take no stand at all. If a leader is unwilling to put his or her stake into the ground then they are not really leaders. This kind of courage is also not easily taught. If one does not have the courage of one's convictions, then it will be very hard indeed to get others to have courage about these convictions. Interestingly, vision workshops have demonstrated that some people have very strong convictions and the courage to stand behind them, once they discover that they have convictions. This is no small thing. A number of the managers who attend these vision workshops start out with very little understanding of what they really care about. During the day and a half workshop they actually find out that they care very deeply, but were unaware of the depth of their caring or have not been able to communicate it.

In the Vision Workshop, we ask managers to practice communicating their vision to a small group of other people in the course who then critique this communication process. This vision presentation is video taped and reviewed. Participants often start out mouthing the platitudes about vision and mission that they have literally taken out of the company brochures or annual report. This is usually very boring and very predictable. An excellent antidote for insomnia. The real test comes when the platitudes are exhausted and there is nothing "out there" to rely on. This is the point where some participants are forced to look inwardly and get in touch with their own views and feelings about what is important. The workshop design also encourages listeners to challenge the presenter's vision. This often helps the presenter to further refine and hone his views and it helps him deal with the inevitable challenges that he will actually face when trying to implement his visions back in the organization.

An Asian manager from one of our sessions was surprised to find out how angry he was about the lack of individual ownership and responsibility shown by the employees and managers in his company. Everyone waited for orders and were quick to blame the person in charge. This anger helped him form a vision of his company as one which encouraged lateral communications, profit center orientation, and individual accountability. His company manufactured farm equipment, mostly tractors and tractor components. To express his vision of the future, he used a tractor metaphor, showing a drawing of a tractor which represented the current state of his company and another tractor which represented the desired future state. The first tractor was slow and outdated. It had weak internal parts which constantly broke down affecting the performance of every other part. The tractor was only effective on flat terrain not rolling hills or unpredictable landscapes. It did not have much pulling power and was unattractive to customers. It did not do very well in pulling or pushing.

The new tractor on the other hand was just the opposite; fast, powerful, attractive, capable of carrying a heavy load and good on all types of terrain. It is easy to see the connections between the tractor and the company, both in terms of how he sees the company today and what he wants it to be tomorrow. The picture of the new tractor is simple, it's easily remembered, it uses a metaphor which all employees, including those on the shop floor can understand, and it travels well.

This manager then made the connections for us. The terrain for his company is the competitive landscape. It used to be flat and predictable, now it is competitive and constantly changing. The tractor's weak parts are his internal departments which don't take responsibility to develop themselves, and the parts are not well integrated. This refers to lack of communication and cooperation among the various internal company departments. Making the new tractor or the new company requires some major changes in the way the tractor is made, the way the company operates. It is easy to see the power of this image.

On his first attempt at developing a vision, this manager used typical managerial tools. He stood over an overhead filled with goals and objectives, market share, etc. All-important data to be sure, but not visionary. He started with mission not vivid description and used a lot of supporting financial data. Neither motivating, nor inspirational. He made the mistake of thinking that mission is vision. Goals and objectives are data driven, while the tractor is clearly image or vivid description driven.

Art or Science?

The video tape reviews are quite remarkable because we are able to define the distinct line of demarcation, from the mouthing of someone else's words to the "real" person emerging. There is a distinct change in body language, tone, enthusiasm, conviction, and emotion that is clearly evident. Program participants are often unaware of this transition until they see it on tape. Once we have identified what the participant really cares about, then the development process becomes much easier. The biggest challenge for us as educators is knowing when the participant makes this transition. Some of these individuals are very adept speakers; highly literate, loquacious, and extremely good presenters. But all of us, teachers and participants alike, are usually able to see when the words and the emotions don't connect, in spite of excellent presentation and communication skills.

We are currently examining how we might employ techniques used by actors to help some of our workshop participants. This is where we see a connection between business and art which might be worth exploring. Actors are taught how to interpret text and convey it directly to an audience so that the text becomes real. He breathes life into words. We are asking corporate leaders to do the same. The difference is that corporate leaders must write their own script or it becomes obvious that they are "acting" and therefore suspect. But the actor's skill allows the translation to carry some emotion which does tend to support and reinforce the conceptual message.

The director of a large hospital in the UK, part of the NHS (National Health Service) had a very difficult time with the vivid description part of our workshop. She was all business, numbers oriented, and a very logical, detail-oriented thinker. The idea of painting a picture or showing emotion was too much for her. One of our theater consultants took her aside and worked with her on expressiveness. She asked her to imagine her mother as a patient in her hospital. How would your mother be treated and how would you like her to be treated? How would you personally feel and act if she were mistreated?

From this exercise came one of the best visions we have seen. The hospital director gave us two scenarios; the first involved a sickly old woman coming to a hospital. She described in painful imagery what this woman experienced. Insensitive treatment, being left on a trolley, unattended to for two hours, cursory examinations, and uncaring healthcare people. The second scenario involved the same woman attending another hospital and having a completely different experience. She then described the first hospital as illness, a virus with all the typical attributes of a virus: Spreading malaise, difficult to control, impersonal, etc. The second hospital was described as healthy, self-diagnosing and self-treating. She then made the links to her organization. Her hospital was the sick one where the old woman was treated poorly. The other was the one she wanted her hospital to become and she then laid out a plan for getting there. The picture was clear to all of us listening to her presentation and it was indelibly etched on our memories.

Again, she had planned to give a statistical and data-laden presentation as her first attempt at communicating her vision. She was pleased that with time and the right coaching she was able to develop and internalize a clear vision for herself; one that could be communicated easily to others. And this was from an individual who did not believe that she had the ability to be a visionary leader.

Is This Just a Fad?

But why should today's leaders worry about this vision thing at all? Is it just the latest fad which will go the way of Quality Circles or Job Enrichment? We don't think so. The difference is that many of today's organizations have taken out or significantly "downsized" the middle management or "glue" that has traditionally held organizations together. Flatter, leaner, meaner, downsized, right-sized all mean removal of layers of management which are supposed to provide order, integration, and direction. Many of today's companies have cross-functional team structures, self-directing groups and large spans of control.

The "glue" has weakened. So how does the organization keep itself integrated and organized? There is still some structure to be sure, but flattening requires everyone in the organization to be less managed and more self-directed. If you no longer have a boss who tells you what to do, you either need to have a vision of where to go or you have to guess. Today's managers don't have time to hold their employees by the hand so they need to get the right people. Give them the right information (desktops have allowed us to give just about any information to anyone), and let them make the right decisions. At the core of this information is what we want the organization to be. Thus the ability to paint, communicate, and anchor a vision (Bennis and Goldsmith, 1994) will become more, not less, important as organizations struggle to be fast, flexible, and competitive.

Conclusions

First, vision is neither rhetoric nor platitude. It provides organizational direction, aligns people so that they move in roughly the same line, and it forces senior management to come to grips with their strategic obligation. Others, lower down in the organization, should not have to guess as to where it is going. Developing a vision requires strategic planning, industry analysis, risk taking and decision-making, imagination and commitment. This doesn't mean that senior management should not get help from both inside and outside the organization to help them craft this vision, but in the end, it is *their* job to make sure that it gets done and it is *their* view not someone else's.

Second, a vision must give guidance. Thus wordy documents without a painting of what the company will be like when we arrive at our destination isn't very helpful. This painting must be understood and communicated throughout the organization. With rare exceptions, wordy documents do not travel well. Thus vision must be simple, easily communicated, and memorable. Paintings do this well, words do not. This means that senior management must communicate both the content and intent of this painting in symbolic, artistic ways as opposed to mere numbers and text. Slogans can help. For instance we all know that at Ford, "Quality is job one," and that GE "makes good things for life." Slogans can be extremely powerful reflections of both vision and values, and they are easily memorable. Also, we know that visions tend to get blocked or retranslated by middle and upper middle management. Effective leaders make sure that they deliver their messages to the lowest level as well. Sam Walton used to visit his distribution warehouses at midnight bringing coffee and doughnuts. He took this opportunity to communicate Wal-Mart's vision in a direct, informal manner.

Third, the visioning process requires that senior management get in touch with their leadership responsibilities. Namely, the ability to help plot the future course of the organization so that it develops and sustains a competitive advantage in the market place. This means that senior management must get in touch with what they really care about and where they think the organization should be going. It is very typical for senior managers to be so obsessed with the short-term quarterly numbers game, that this becomes their only field of "reference." One can look only at the quarterly numbers and go out of business in the process. The Japanese have taught us that there is real strength in planning for the long run, not just jumping for the "jelly bean" in the short run. This is a lesson that only some Western businesses have taken to heart. Japanese leaders are willing to accept short-term losses in pursuit of long-term success. Managers are not. So the visioning process is a real test of an organization's leadership.

Fourth, visions are crafted. They need thought to develop, nurturing, and practice to deliver effectively. These are not skills taught in business school. Thus, senior management may have to call upon creative help in developing their organization's vision. More than likely, this help will come from outside the organization unless it has some very talented and savvy communications people. This is that intersection between art and science. Don't be ashamed to get help from the non-business-oriented community. We have used some theater and broadcast consultants in our UK seminars to help participants with the visioning process. The theater people have been received with mixed reviews but they are excellent at challenging the closed and self-limiting attitudes of many of the senior managers with whom we have worked. The media people are excellent at asking participants to communicate their vision in "sound bites" which force participants to distill their visions into easily communicated and remembered messages. The broadcast people are also skilled at getting our participants to say things which they don't really mean. Working with them helps participants identify the traps that others may want to spring on them in the organization and they give them communication skills for dealing effectively with these traps.

Fifth, don't wait for perfection. Paintings are by nature imperfect. The colors may not be true to life, the brush strokes are not uniform, and the closer to the painting one gets, the more flaws one sees. The same is true of visions. They can be nit-picked to death. The real test is whether they convey a direction forward. There may be detours in the path and the road will be bumpy, but we know where we are heading. Get the vision out. Get feedback, refine it, develop it and re-communicate it. It is a process, not a destination. Things happen so that the painting of the future may change. The picture may be smaller, the colors brighter or less bright, or the painting needs re-framing. Still, we have an idea of where we are headed.

Sixth, have fortitude. Courage can be brought out in people who have it and may not know it. It takes courage to paint a picture of the future that may be inaccurate. It takes even more courage to set sail to unknown lands when sharks and storms await the ship on its journey. But if the captain does not have the courage to head for his destination, then the passengers are unlikely to have faith in the captain. Visioning is taking a risk. It is what we think leaders are paid for.

Finally, the ability to develop a vision is not the sacred territory for senior management alone. Unit managers can create visions for their units. Divisional heads can do the same. It helps if there is a corporate vision to connect to, but in its absence, people in the middle have to make their best guess. A middle manager at Toomey-Delong, a food brokerage company in Boston, attended one of our visioning seminars. He came back to his company, developed a vision for his account management group and then went to senior management and asked him to relate their vision to his. Interestingly, this pressure and that of his colleagues caused senior management to go through the same process, so it doesn't always have to start at the top.

References

Bennis, W. and Goldsmith, J. (1994) *Learning to Lead*. Addison-Wesley.
Business Week (1994) "It's warm not fuzzy." July 18, (Editor's Page).
Business Week (1994) "Managing by values." August 1.
Canadian Manager (1993) "Isadore Sharp, outstanding CEO of the Year." Spring.
Capowski, G. (1994) "Anatomy of a leader." *Management Review,* March.
Collins, J. and Porras, J. (1991) "Organizational vision and visionary organizations." *California Management Review,* 34. Fall.
Collins, J. and Porras, J. (1994) *Built to Last*. Harper Publishing.
Krug, D. and Oakley, E. (1993) *Enlightened Leadership*. Simon & Schuster.
Nice, R. C. (1994) "Empower the Leaders." *Credit Union Management,* April.
Quigley, J. (1993) *Vision: How Leaders Develop It, Share It. Sustain It*. McGraw-Hill.
Smith, R. (1994) "Inspirational leadership." *Executive Speeches,* Feb.–Mar.

11

The Evolving Paradigm of Leadership Development

ROBERT M. FULMER

Management training and education has become a big business, with annual corporate expenditures standing at $45 billion annually, up from $10 billion a decade ago. Approximately $12 billion is devoted to executive education, with almost one-fourth of this total spent at various university-based business schools. Respondents from one study, of major corporations, report that average costs for executive education at their companies have grown to approximately $2 million annually, with more than 1,000 executives at each firm targeted for training.

Along with this growth, executive education is undergoing a series of revolutions from which a new vocabulary is emerging. The term *executive education* now implies a much more sophisticated approach than *management training*. Moreover, the new lexicon has put the idea of "training *managers*" out of favor, in that it tends to define *managers* as bureaucrats who administer complexity and try to make the status quo more efficient. Even the status of the word *executive* in *executive education* is declining. Almost every organization is trying to create *leaders* who are capable of helping the corporation shape a more positive future.

The growing emphasis in leadership development is clearly on customized programs to help achieve specific corporate initiatives. The costs of these programs often run from $100,000 to $250,000 to develop and from $50,000 to $150,000 per session to deliver. Both universities and consulting firms tend to use their own internal staff for the majority of the program delivery. In university programs, about 10 percent of program content is delivered by professors from other universities and about 10 percent by non-university faculty. Approximately two-thirds of the rev-

Reprinted with permission, from *Organizational Dynamics* (Spring 1997), pp. 59–72.

enues received by consulting firms go directly into program delivery, whereas marketing and overhead leave only 55 percent of university revenues for delivery.

Mapping the New World

In a recent *Organizational Dynamics* article, Jay Conger wrote about "The New World of Leadership Development." The metaphor is apt. No matter how thoroughly Columbus compared his map to the terrain of the Caribbean on his initial trip to the New World, he would not have been able to find the Ganges River. These early maps were, of course, quite primitive. The map-maker could see what was in the immediate vicinity, but had no idea what might be over the next horizon. And Columbus, like some corporate explorers, was using a map designed for a totally different environment.

In a similar manner, our old maps are no longer adequate to describe contemporary competitive reality, and new forms of leadership development continue to evolve in an effort to help executives chart a course for whatever lies beyond the horizon. Seven major shifts seem to be taking place in the field of leadership development and are the focus of this analysis. Table 11.1 presents an overview of where we have been, where we are at present, and where "best practices" are headed.

Participants: From Passive Listeners to Active Learners

Attending a corporate learning event today is very different from the experience a generation ago. Many readers will recall what happened in the old days. Participants arrived at corporate or university programs with little understanding of the curriculum that lay before them. At check-in, someone handed them a series of books and an agenda that outlined how each hour was to be spent for the duration of the program. The notebook provided extensive amounts of blank paper, signaling that the participant's major role was to be a listener. He (only occasionally was it a she) was expected to take voluminous notes from the assembled presenters, who would share their insights and knowledge in discrete 90-minute segments.

That model has been passé for some time. In a later stage of program development, participants were expected to engage in case discussions, debate recommendations or alternatives, and sometimes make presentations based on their conclusions about class assignments. These assignments often involved a business case that had little direct relevance to the participants' situations back at the office; however, it was hoped that they

TABLE 11.1   The Evolving Paradigm of Leadership Development

	Past	Transition	Future
Participants	Listener	Student	Learner
Program design	Event	Curriculum	Ongoing process
Purpose	Knowledge	Wisdom	Action
Period	Past	Present	Future
Players	Specialists	Generalists	Partners
Presentations	Style	Content	Process/outcome
Place	University campus	Corp. facility	Anywhere

would be able to make applications when and if similar situations presented themselves.

In the new world, participants listen occasionally, interact frequently in simulated situations to test their skills or understanding, and frequently spend a significant portion of time demonstrating their ability to apply concepts to real challenges. It is impossible to predict what the end result of the learning experience will be. Participants generally take learning to the level most appropriate for their immediate concerns or level of motivation. Managers who are struggling with a recognized need to develop a dramatically new strategy will respond to a "Merlin Exercise" or "Invent the Future" project more enthusiastically than someone who wants to make the status quo just a little better.

In this kind of applied learning, some participants still make minimal effort and learn relatively little. Others will rise to demanding challenges, gain important knowledge, and make significant contributions to organizational goals. The majority of executive-level programs do not reinforce participants' learning with built-in formal assessments. However, informal assessment by peers, program administrators, and visiting senior executives almost always take place. Like so many other areas of life, leadership development usually rewards participants in direct relationship to their effort and contribution.

With almost universal pressure to do more with less, organizations are asking that educational providers reduce the major costs of development programs—namely, managers' time away from their jobs. This is especially essential when large numbers of people must be involved, as is the case when the program is expected to have company-wide impact. There appears to be widespread recognition that drawing participants from many vertical slices of the organization, rather than from one thin horizontal slice, yields more significant impact.

Program Design: From Unique Event to Never-Ending Process

Historically, most organizations saw executive development as a one- or two-time event. A person viewed as having the potential to become a CEO might be sent to the one-year Sloan program at MIT or the 13-week Harvard Advanced Management Program. If the organization saw an individual as having "significant potential," but not beyond upper middle management, he or she might be sent to a four-week program at a less well-known business school. In either case, it was an important "rite of passage." But each passage was a one-time trip, with little relationship to other developmental activities taking place in a progressive career.

During the 1980s, leading companies began to recognize the importance of reinforcing key career transitions with appropriate educational activities. One of the leading corporate models was described as a "slalom course." At each stage in an individual's career, he or she was expected to attend a program appropriate for that stage of development. A person promoted to a management job was expected to attend a "new manager program" within 30 days of the promotion. This would take place at a corporate facility where a carefully defined curriculum was presented to a group of recent "managers-elect."

Once individuals achieved the mid-management level, they were expected to make the pilgrimage to corporate headquarters, where they would again receive training appropriate for their new positions. After having satisfied the corporate requirement, other educational events were scheduled on a regional or divisional basis until the manager became an executive. At this point, the new executive was invited to attend the top level corporate program designed for heads of business units or major functions and would probably interact with the CEO or key members of the executive committee. This approach was often cited as a "best practice" because it had moved the educational process to an organized set of events that were planned over a person's entire career.

Universities for Learning Organizations

Realizing that learning could be translated into competitive advantage, some corporations erected college-sized institutions that would help them become "learning organizations." In 1993, Jeanne C. Meister identified 30 companies with corporate universities, most of which shared the common goal of seeing "training as a process of lifelong learning rather than a place to get trained." By 1996, she reported that almost 1,000 firms had begun or were actively investigating the feasibility of a corporate university. Some of these initiatives place emphasis on supporting employee career development, while others are tilted toward addressing key business issues or providing skills for key suppliers.

Arthur Andersen, for example, has a carefully designed career ladder with courses required at each stage in an employee's career. The company is developing a career tracking system that includes every employee throughout the world. In a somewhat similar vein, the GE Crotonville facility is organized around the concept that there are particular "moments of opportunity" in any career. The curriculum addresses these moments of opportunity, starting with new-employee and new-manager orientations and ending with programs designed for senior executives.

Most corporate universities share a major focus on building competencies and skills that are strategically aligned to meet the requirements of employees and the company. GE's Crotonville facility and Motorola University are leaders in placing emphasis on actions that drive the business, rather than knowledge acquisition.

While the corporate university movement must be viewed as a positive development because of its commitment to lifelong learning for employees, a danger looms on the horizon. Universities are not typically viewed as the most flexible, progressive, and change-oriented institutions. Practices that date back several centuries are still embraced at conventional universities, held in place by tradition rather than contemporary value. Any strength, if carried to excess, will become a weakness. Similarly, the commitment that led to the creation of a corporate university must be clearly monitored, kept flexible, and focused on change.

The Importance of Scale

As previously suggested, program design is no longer targeted to isolated individuals who have been "anointed" by senior management. Instead of the thin horizontal slice, the program design is likely to involve work groups or several vertical slices of the organization. In 1992, the average number of people targeted for a typical corporate program was over 1,000. Even in a medium-size organization, a participant pool of less than 200 was not considered large enough to build the leverage needed for significant impact. The Executive Conference at Johnson & Johnson, for example, was aimed at the top 700 managers in the firm. The Hoechst Celanese Middle Management Leadership Program (MMLP) included 1,100 managers in North America. At General Electric, the Work-Out program has involved a total of 220,000 people. On any given week, 20,000 GE employees will be participating in some stage of a Work-Out effort.

The pace of change and competition have caused the stakes for learning to increase significantly. Just as professionals in other disciplines must commit to a lifelong process of learning and updating their knowledge, so must the executive who plans to compete personally and organizationally. Much learning is self-directed. Individuals look for ways of sharpening their knowledge, but more importantly must develop the ability to access information and to learn more quickly. Organizations are looking for approaches that make a real difference. General Electric's Work-Out program is one of the most significant endeavors in this widened approach to corporate learning.

GE does not describe Work-Out as a training program. Rather: It is a process of concentrated decision-making and empowerment to resolve issues. A team of experienced, knowledgeable people with a stake in the issue is charged to develop solutions and action plans. They are sanctioned by the key stakeholder to proceed with implementation (or given clear reasons why not to proceed, or specify direction for further study). There is a follow-up to ensure completion of the action plans.

Work-Out is part of General Electric's drive to create a culture of speed, simplicity, and self-confidence in a manner consistent with continuous improvement. Expected results include:

- Boundaryless, cross-functional teamwork
- Empowered employees
- Building of trust
- Focus on customers
- Greater use of process thinking
- Improvement of business process

Purpose: From Knowledge to Action

In a simpler era, it was believed that each discrete stage of a person's career required specific types of new knowledge. Consequently, the purpose of management or leadership development was to provide that knowledge in advance of the times when it was required. As a functional specialist began to be considered for additional promotion, or sometimes immediately before becoming a general manager, he/she would be sent to a "general management program," often described as a mini-MBA. At this stage, the participant would be expected to learn how marketing programs or capital improvements had to be viewed in the context of corporate financial limitations, production capacity, or other environmental constraints.

Practice Fields for Learning

Knowledge of the tools and techniques used in other functional disciplines came to be viewed as broadening the arsenal of tools and techniques in an executive's repertoire. Most sophisticated programs provided opportunities for executives-in-training to choose appropriate tools for complex challenges and craft appropriate responses. Computerized simulations proved especially useful in the process of helping participants gain the wisdom to apply the knowledge acquired in other settings. Peter Senge and Fred Kofman have written eloquently in *Organizational Dynamics* about the importance of "practice fields," where managers have an opportunity to practice some of the concepts they are expected to apply.

In today's world, relatively few organizations provide for the use of practice fields. Unlike professional athletes or members of symphony orchestras, business managers seldom have an opportunity to practice their skills and receive feedback other than in the real world. Contemporary pressures are, however, pushing the application of knowledge toward the solution of actual problems in which managers can see, almost in real time, the results of their decisions.

Applications of Action Learning

In the late 1980s, Motorola University created what it called an Application Consulting Team (ACT) to facilitate the use, in the workplace, of knowledge gained from Motorola courses. ACT is staffed by managers with 20-plus years of experience who prefer to mentor, coach, and assist in the transfer of learning rather than continue with traditional management responsibilities. Another approach to action learning at Motorola University involves a number of corporate partnerships that focus on developing knowledge in mutually important arenas. The Six Sigma Institute illustrates this kind of partnership. In 1990, Motorola joined with ABB, Digital Equipment, Eastman Kodak, and IBM to accelerate the development of six sigma quality and transfer this knowledge in the most effective manner.

In still another example of action learning at Motorola, former Chairman Robert Galvin requested a workshop for over 100 Motorola Senior Executives to help them understand the market potential of selected Asian countries. Rather than bringing in experts to talk about the subject, participants were asked to analyze the existing competition and to determine how Motorola could compete in these markets.

After doing their homework, these executives traveled around the world to see local market developments firsthand. They were then asked to teach the concepts of globalization to the next 3,000 Motorola managers. In other words, they first studied the issue, then verified these impressions with first-hand observations and, finally, solidified this learning by teaching it to others.

This action-oriented approach to learning is illustrative of world-class learners in the evolving paradigm.

Period Focus:
From Past Tense to Future Perfect

Because of its real-world orientation, the case method has had tremendous impact on business education. Long associated with Harvard Business School, it is still used in a majority of executive development programs, both within companies and in business schools other than Harvard. Despite the many positive aspects of the case method, the system is inherently flawed in that the case is almost always a historical document. It reflects what could have been done, given a set of circumstances that existed in the past.

Seeking the Best of the Present

Companies now seek to know who is doing the best job in a particular area, even if that firm is not a direct competitor. Firms in a variety of industries, for example, may look at Wal-Mart as a benchmark for excellence in logistics management, or to ABB to understand the paradox of a global company that operates with 1,300 autonomous business units in 140 countries.

The growing awareness of "best practices" applies to leadership development as well, and this has improved the contemporary focus of many programs. Table 11.2 summarizes some of the best practices in leadership development reviewed in this article.

A few organizations currently use "future-oriented cases" or scenarios as a means of shifting the view from past to future. The proprietary "Johnson & Johnson 2002" case, for example, brings projections and future issues to life by encouraging problem solvers to consider the issues they *will* be addressing. Participants can challenge the conventional wisdom about how their industry or firm will evolve. Discussion, background research, and expert advice can dramatize the trends that are beginning to shape industry practices and demonstrate some of the important ways business will be different in the future.

For one future-oriented scenario, the Johnson & Johnson case writer conducted over 100 interviews in six countries to assess the key issues facing various client businesses. He then crafted a scenario that was used over a three-year period to stimulate top executives' thinking about the future of the company. Interestingly, during the first year, participants thought the case was "too far out." During the last year of its use, participants generally felt that the scenario was too conservative.

With future-oriented scenarios, participants begin to focus on how specific actions in their own organization can help create or mold the future. Their case discussions help them explore the assumptions that undergird

TABLE 11.2   Representative Best Practices in Leadership Development

Firm	Initiative	Significance
Arthur Andersen	Andersen Centre	645-acre campus with 130 class-rooms, 1,000 computer stations, and accommodations for 1,700 students
	Career Tracking System	Monitors progress and developmental needs of every employee around the world
General Electric	Crotonville Corporate University Facility	Comprehensive approach to life-long learning, built around "moments of opportunity"
	"Work-Out" Program	Action learning initiative that has involved over 220,000 people world-wide
Johnson & Johnson	Creating the Future	Anticipatory learning initiative for top 700 executives designed to challenge complacency and extend thinking horizons
	J&J 2002 Case	Future-oriented case based on interviews with 100 executives
	Flexible Educational Facility	Reduced need for "bricks and mortar" by creating flexible learning center in existing corporate facility
Motorola	Motorola University	Leader in Corporate University concept and lifelong learning, produced returns of 30:1 on targeted educational expenditures
	Asia Initiative	100 senior executives with responsibility to "learn then teach" challenger in Asia
	Application Consulting Training (ACT)	Utilizes mature managers to monitor, coach, and assist in transfer of learning
	Six Sigma Institute	Application and transfer of best practices (with AAB, Digital, Kodak, and IBM)
Phillips	Centurion Project	Large-scale strategic initiative designed to change corporate culture and improve productivity
	Professional Partnerships	Selected consultants to commit 90 days to facilitate corporate training

their views about the future. Arriving at a shared understanding or "mental model" becomes the starting point for effective utilization of scenario planning.

Creating a Future

Even this level of sophistication appears to be giving way to a conscientious attempt on the part of firms to anticipate where the action *could* be, rather than where it appears to be headed at the current moment. Gary Hamel and C.K. Prahalad have alerted large numbers of managers to the importance of "Competing for the Future." In concert with this kind of thinking, Johnson & Johnson recently completed a three-year initiative aimed at 700 senior managers around the world. The subject: dealing with the challenge of managing the next millennium.

As author/consultant Stan Davis has suggested, *future perfect* can mean "a future that is perfect"; it's also a verb tense that involves "speaking of the future as though it had already occurred." Jack Welch came close to this when he articulated GE's statement of strategic intent by saying, "We *will* be number one or two in every market where we compete."

Leading corporate initiatives for management or executive development are increasingly future-focused for anticipatory learning.

Players: From Limited Role to General Partners

In a more comfortable and predictable world, the major players in the field of executive development were specialists who became proficient in their roles—and in fulfilling management's expectations. Professors developed segments that could be inserted in a variety of program contexts. Business school administrators were expected to know the various areas of expertise that were available within their faculty and how these topics could be used in addressing the needs of an executive or organization.

Corporate human resource specialists became adept in knowing which university programs seemed to offer the best fit for the needs of their managers. Going to professional meetings of groups such as UNICON (The International University Consortium for Executive Education) was a pleasant, predictable event because people stayed in their appropriate roles.

Multiple Perspectives

During the 1980s, however, things began to shift. A person who had been a university director of executive education might suddenly move to become director of corporate management development for a Fortune 100 firm. Two or three years later, that same individual might be heading a successful consulting practice and providing executive programs in competition with his previous academic institution.

For example, Dr. John Bachmann was associate dean for executive education at the University of Tennessee (Knoxville) in the early 1980s. He then became director of corporate management development at Combustion Engineering. When a highly publicized leveraged buyout broke up Combustion, Bachmann left to become a principal in the IBIS Group, where he continues to work at the present time.

Dr. Ken Graham, who currently serves as associate dean for executive education at the University of Texas, began his career in executive education at Penn State University. Leaving the relative security of academia in the mid 1980s, Graham assumed responsibilities for management development at Beatrice Foods. When the stability of this firm began to disintegrate, Graham became a partner in the Burgundy Group, which provides customized computer simulations for organizations. He then moved back to industry, serving as vice president for human resource planning at Allstate Insurance before returning to academia in 1995.

There are perhaps a dozen individuals in the world today who have had this kind of high-level experience and can view leadership development from the perspectives of a university, consulting firm, and major corporation. The advantages and disadvantages of these vantage points are shown in Table 11.3.

Partnerships with Key Players

This increased level of "boundarylessness" in the field and the diversified experiences of its leading practitioners has led to new expectations. The ability to truly understand and "partner" with the individuals and organizations with whom they work is becoming essential for major players. University experience should provide an individual with exposure to cutting-edge thinking in a variety of disciplines. It should develop a commitment for honest inquiry and an attempt to seek new answers to old questions. Corporate experience adds the dimension of relevance. In a business setting, ideas have little currency unless they can be meaningfully applied in a specific situation.

Since most corporate executive educators operate without line authority, their ability to provide value-added service to their constituency is of critical importance, along with building relationships based on mutual understanding and trust. Consultants usually develop a set of business skills that allows them to operate with less-developed support systems than most corporations or business schools. Consequently, consultants often learn to listen more acutely than representatives of larger organiza-

TABLE 11.3   Advantages/Disadvantages of Multiple Perspectives

Vantage Point	Advantages	Disadvantages
University	Commitment to honest inquiry Exposure to cutting-edge thinking in diverse areas Potential for objectivity	Lack of perceived relevance Lack of flexibility, unwillingness to listen
Corporation	Relevance/action-oriented Value-added service orientation Understanding of needs Resources to fund innovative approaches	Parochial experience/perspective Lack of opportunity to explore, create and reflect on new concepts Past history may limit options
Consulting	Listening skills and responsiveness Networking and alliance-building Varied experience and exposure	Pressures for short-term profitability Focus on tools in existing repertoire

tions. Because their own staff resources are often quite limited, they become experts in networking and alliance building.

In the new paradigm, individuals with a blend of skills will build partnerships that enhance both organizational learning and personal/professional development. A number of businesses are developing partnerships with key academics or consultants who become a semipermanent part of the organization. This may be seen as part of a "shadow pyramid" composed of organizations and professionals to whom key challenges are farmed out. These may be specialized subcontractors who can do certain jobs better and cheaper. In leadership development, they may be highly trained, highly compensated professionals who are opposed to the constraints of working for a single organization. Yet, by spending 20 to 100 days or more per year with one organization, they leverage their skills, have tremendous impact, and invest both time and intellectual capital in becoming productive partners.

When, for example, Philips asked a number of academics and consultants to invest 90 days per year in the Centurion Project, the company made a major commitment to these individuals in terms of learning and income. On the other hand, the individuals who were given this opportunity brought with them high-level expertise and experience from a variety of other organizations. The same is true of any major corporate initiative, such as the GE Work-Out program or the Johnson & Johnson Creating Our Future initiative.

Presentations: From Style to Substance

In traditional executive programs, the assessments tended to value style more than content. Certain presenters were known to be good "closers." They left an audience with a feeling of excitement and enthusiasm, which often carried through to the evaluations that were conducted for other program modules.

Upon hearing about an academic study being conducted to determine what caused certain presenters to be "superstars" in executive education, one seasoned human resource vice president complained, "Why does anybody need a study to determine that? The answer is simple, 'it's entertainment.'" Neither the executive nor his comment was as naïve as might first appear. Content has to be presented in a way that is well-received and understood. For individuals unaccustomed to sitting in classrooms for days on end, a speaker's ability to present information in a timely and engaging way was a welcome attribute.

The Search for Relevance

Today, however, fewer sessions can be described as "fluff." Entertainment may still be important, but the value of relevant content has increased significantly. Not only must the message be presented well, it must also be seen as important. The challenge has shifted to an ability to process rather than present information. The most valuable executive educators are those who are able to elicit participant input in such a way as to help with the resolution of actual issues.

The ultimate test of relevance is the ability to see (and measure) significant change. Motorola has led the way with its research indicating that targeted educational efforts can generate a 30:1 return within three years. Moreover, the General Electric Work-Out program and the Philips Centurion Project illustrate how concepts introduced in the corporate classroom can be applied to real-life situations with observable results.

Corporate, university, and consultant leaders agree that almost every learning initiative now relies less on professor-led classroom time and more on small group work, facilitated to ensure application. This is not just a question of how time is divided among lecture, discussion, and case analysis. Case discussions are increasingly seen as ways of illustrating a concept or developing tools that will then be applied to a current challenge or issue. Several consulting firms, such as the Swedish MiL Institute, view action learning as their specialty. U.S. corporations such as General Electric, Motorola and Philip Morris have emerged as leaders in this arena.

Business Schools with a Bent for Action

British business schools have been much more innovative than their American counterparts in designing programs that take the learner out of the classroom and into the real world—usually that of the corporation sponsoring the program participants. In fact, MBA programs in several British institutions have strong action-learning components. Oxford, Cambridge, Ashridge, and Henley degree programs all intersperse classroom sessions with application projects. Management-level students in these programs may spend more time learning on the job than on the university campus.

There is a Chinese proverb that suggests "A good leader is one whom the people respect, the poor leader is the one whom people hate; but the great leader is one who, when the people have finished, they say 'we have done it ourselves.'" This concept can also be applied to contemporary leadership development. In some ways, it calls for a difficult adjustment by traditional educators. No longer revered simply for what they know, many of the "great lecturers" of the past have not been able to compete in the emerging paradigm, where respect is earned by what the teacher is able to stimulate others to know. A significant number (perhaps 1,500 in total) are making the adjustment to become great teachers—so that when their work is completed, participants say, "We have done it ourselves."

Place: From Ivory Tower to Factory Floor

As we have suggested, in the traditional era, education for executives was limited to a select handful of future senior leaders and delivered primarily by leading business schools. As recently as 1988, a report prepared for the American Assembly of Collegiate Schools of Business (AACSB) reported that two business schools, Harvard and Stanford, provided one-third of the total general management market. Corporate HRD directors, university program managers, and participants agreed with the importance of "getting away from traditional surroundings" in order to contemplate, listen and learn.

Location even played a part in some peoples' decision making. Occasionally, an executive would report, "I prefer to go to Sea Island, Georgia, in February rather than Chicago." One British interviewee commented,

"Management development's greatest contribution in the U.K. has been to the restoration of country houses." Hopefully, he was joking about how status conscious CEOs are about the size of their training centers. Commitment to learning can be measured in ways more important than investment in facilities.

University campuses are still important settings for leadership development. Participants report that it is easier to change their own paradigms and see things from a different perspective when they are in the midst of a bustling, academic environment. Nevertheless, more and more leaders are participating in learning programs that are conducted in their own educational facilities or even in a plant conference room.

Corporate Campuses

While "bricks and mortar" (dedicated facilities) are less important in the emerging environment, many corporate facilities boast campuses that compete with those at colleges. Arthur Andersen purchased a former college campus outside Chicago and operates satellite educational facilities in Europe and Asia. Andersen's annual worldwide investment in education exceeds $300 million dollars—about 7 percent of the company's total revenues. The Andersen Centre at St. Charles, Illinois, operates with a staff of 200 educational specialists. Over 60,000 trainees come to the St. Charles campus each year to study accounting practices, industry knowledge, or fundamental business skills (such as business ethics, negotiation, and presentation effectiveness). Slightly more than half of them work for Andersen. The remaining trainees are clients or outside customers.

Andersen has invested almost $150 million in the 645-acre St. Charles campus, which it purchased from Saint Dominic College in 1971. The facility can accommodate 1,700 overnight students. It boasts 130 classrooms, six auditoriums, two amphitheaters, five large conference centers, 1,000 computer work-stations, a staff complex, several restaurants, a barber shop, a shoe repair shop, a book store, a discotheque, and a nine-hole golf course. In addition to the professional staff of 200, the Centre employs 200 support personnel and a comparable number of operations people.

A few organizations, such as Andersen, General Electric, and Motorola, can justify the commitment to facilities because of their tremendous "through-put" of participants each year. Most, however, are finding it more efficient to make their commitment to "learning spaces" instead of conference centers or even hotel operations. Rather than invest in permanent facilities, Johnson & Johnson conducts its Executive Conference in a facility that takes approximately one-half of a floor in a New

Brunswick office building. Participants stay (with negotiated rates) at a Hyatt Hotel across the street. Rather than building a dedicated "case room," the Executive Conference series uses portable risers to create a tiered working area. The arrangement provides space to run wiring for individual computers that tie into the company's LAN system.

Breakout rooms for small group discussions are available on the same floor. Meals are served, buffet style, in a room adjacent to the company cafeteria. Since an Executive Conference may run ten times per year, the flexibility provided by this arrangement provides a cost effective alternative to going off-site to a specialized conference center or making the commitment to the fixed costs associated with a full-time corporate conference facility.

CSX Corporation, a $10 billion international transportation company offering a variety of container-shipping, intermodel logistics, and related services, announced in 1995 its commitment to create a "State of the Art CSX Learning Center" that would:

Provide a learning environment for present and future CSX leaders that fosters efficient individual growth and promotes effective inter-unit collaborative learning by:

- Creating a plan for effective physical space
- Providing the vision for the best use of technology

While this is to be a "world-class" facility, it will also use space in one of the corporate division's headquarters. The center has two large classrooms, an auditorium, break-out rooms, networking areas, and support services. CSX concluded that this type of facility would be the most effective solution to its needs rather than the creation of a separate campus for learning. Regardless of which alternative an organization chooses, it is clear that the caliber of ideas discussed is more important than the quality of facilities that are dedicated to learning.

In the future, learning will not be associated with a particular place. Individuals will log on to an interacting learning experience via networked computers. They will participate in video-conferencing with colleagues from around the world, eliminating the requirement for extensive travel time. When they do travel, it will be to a variety of places where people are being brought together for organizational and individual learning. This may be a hotel conference room in Singapore, a public conference center in Brussels, or a corporate meeting facility in New Jersey.

Federal Express provides a dramatic illustration of education that is not restricted by place. The company spent almost $70 million to create an automated educational system. Annually, it spends almost 5 percent of payroll to enhance learning among its 40,000 couriers and customer service agents through the use of interactive videodisks (IVD). Federal Express owns 1,225 IVD units in 700 locations. At each location, the curriculum is housed on 20 to 25 videodisks (the equivalent of 37,500 floppy disks) and updated monthly. Each employee receives four hours of company-paid study and preparation in addition to two hours of self-administered tests every six months.

While this is illustrative of the trend toward involvement of larger numbers of people in corporate initiatives, the FedEx program is not focused at the executive or leadership level. A better illustration of the movement might be the MIT effort to deliver "distance learning" by satellite to China. Given the population of China, even at the managerial level, and the distances involved for U.S.-based universities, new telecommunication technology is an essential form of distribution if MIT wishes to make a contribution to this emerging area.

Sterling Winthrop (formerly the pharmaceutical division of Kodak) provides a more basic example. The company offered a series of senior and middle management programs in 14 countries and on six continents during a three-year period. Basically, it was easier to transport three to five instructors/facilitators to distant locations than it was to bring people from every corner of the world to a central location.

Anytime, Anyplace, Gray Matter

This article has attempted to provide pilgrims in the new world of leadership development with a map showing the topography leadership development has traveled in the past several decades, as well as the pathways currently under construction by pioneers in the practice of organizational learning.

But maps merely chart the surface. They do not provide a fundamental understanding of reality. Despite Albert Einstein's writings on the relativity of time and space, we continue to see time, place, and matter in Newtonian terms. The new paradigm of physics continues to examine and redefine these notions of reality.

Similarly, the "reality" of business is being redefined. Stan Davis suggests that during the evolving "age of information," the rules of competition will become "anytime, anyplace, no matter." Davis is making the point that competition will favor the organization that is able to provide its goods or service whenever and wherever the consumer wants.

The third concept is perhaps more important. The world of "matter" that has traditionally been defined by "products" is becoming less important than the information that is used or collected about the consumer or organization for whom "value" is being provided.

This is also true in the field of leadership development. There is little in the way of notebooks, handouts, or facilities (matter) that can compete with the caliber of the ideas that are being discussed or the ability to learn new ways of responding to emerging challenges.

The kind of learning that results in competitive advantage will not be limited by time, space, or matter. The new paradigm will be focused on learning as an action-oriented, lifelong process where global partners work together to produce a positive, profitable future for all.

Selected Bibliography

Statistics cited in the introduction to the article are based on Nitin Nohria and James D. Berkley, "Whatever Happened to the Take-Charge Manager?", *Harvard Business Review*, Jan.–Feb. 1994, p. 130; Lori Bongiorno, "Corporate America's New Lesson Plan," *Business Week*, Oct. 25, 1993, p. 102; Gilbert Fushsberg, "Taking Control," The *Wall Street Journal*, Sept. 10, 1993, p. R4; and Albert A. Vicere, Maria Taylor, and Virginia Feddman, *Executive Education at Major Corporations: An International Study of Executive Development Trends* (Penn State University, 1993), p. 7.

The field research described in this manuscript is based on a study sponsored by the University Consortium for Executive Education (UNICON) and The Institute for the Study of Organizational Effectiveness (ISOE) and published by ISOE in 1995 as *Executive Education and Leadership Development: The State of the Practice*. The work of Robert M. Fulmer and Albert A. Vicere is expanded in their book, *Strategic Leadership Development: Crafting Competitiveness* (Oxford: Capstone Publishers, 1996). Other useful references are: Robert M. Fulmer and Albert A. Vicere, "Executive Development: An Analysis of Competitive Forces," *Planning Review*, Jan., 1996; Robert M. Fulmer and Ken Graham, "A New Era of Management Education," *Journal of Management Development*, Vol. 12, No. 3; and Robert M. Fulmer "Executive Learning as a Strategic Weapon," *Executive Development*, Vol. 3, No. 3.

The concept of microworlds was introduced in Peter Senge's *The Fifth Discipline: The Art and Practice of the Learning Organization* (New York: Doubleday, 1990). *Organizational Dynamics* published a collection of distinguished articles on this and other subjects relating to the learning organization, with articles by Kofman and Senge, Chris Argyris, William Isaacs, Edgar Schein, Dale Ulrich, Todd Jick, Mary Ann Von Glinow, Michael McGill, John Slocum, and David Lei in *The Learning Organization in Action: A Special Report from Organizational Dynamics* (New York: American Management Association, 1994). A review of simulations and practice fields is contained in J. Bernard Keys, Robert M. Fulmer, and Steven A. Stempf, "Microworlds and Simuworlds: Practice Fields for the Learning Organization," *Organization Dynamics*, Spring 1996, pp. 36–49. See also Peter Senge, et al., *The Fifth Discipline Fieldbook* (New York: Doubleday, 1994, pp. 30–37), along with Peter M. Senge and Robert M. Fulmer, "Simulations, Systems Thinking and Anticipatory Learning," *Journal of Management Development*, Vol. 12, No. 6 (1993).

Information about corporate universities reported in this article comes from several sources: the author's survey of these institutions, along with Jeanne C. Meister's UNI-CON presentation, March 17, 1996; Jeanne C. Meister, *Corporate Quality Universities* (New York: Richard D. Irwin, Inc., 1994); and Robert H. Miles, *Corporate Universities: Some Design Choices and Leading Practices* (Atlanta: Emory Business School, 1993).

The material on the GE Work-Out program is drawn from Noel M. Tichy and S. Sherman, *Control Your Destiny or Someone Else Will* (New York: Doubleday, 1993); Thomas A. Stewart, "GE Keeps Those Ideas Coming," *Fortune*, August 12, 1991, p. 42; and "Work Out: Continuous Improvement," unpublished GE document, March 15, 1995. See also Richard M. Hodgetts' conversation with Steve Kerr, *Organizational Dynamics*, Spring 1996, pp. 68–79.

Individuals interested in more information about future-oriented cases and scenarios should see John A. Gutman, "Developing Case Scenarios for Anticipatory Learning," *Journal of Management Development*, November 6, 1993, pp. 52–59. See also John A. Gutman, "Creating Scenarios and Cases for Global Anticipatory Learning," *American Journal of Management Development*, Vol. 1, No. 3 (1995).

The AACSB work on the future of management development was prepared by Lyman Porter and Larry McKibbon, *Management Development: Drift or Thrust into the 21st Century* (New York: McGraw-Hill, 1988). Other important sources for future-oriented thinking and learning are Gary Hamel and C.K. Prahalad, *Competing for the Future* (Boston: Harvard Business School Press, 1994); Stan Davis and Jim Botkin, *The Monster Under the Bed* (New York; Simon & Schuster, 1994, p. 96); Stan Davis, *Future Perfect* (Reading, MA: Addison Wesley, 1987); and J.A. Conger, "The New World of Leadership Development," *Organizational Dynamics*, Winter 1993, Vol. 21, No. 3, p. 46.

12

Followers for the Times

Engaging Employees in a Winning Partnership

EARL H. POTTER III
WILLIAM E. ROSENBACH
THANE S. PITTMAN

The truth is that when things are going smoothly, many people question whether organizations really need leaders. Familiar strategies and established procedures produce predictable results. The boss can leave town and things will go on as planned. In uncertain times, however, we look to leaders to define the path, create the plan and encourage the heart. These are complex and uncertain times. Global markets, instantaneous communications, the fast pace of change and new technologies make effective leadership essential. In these times the best earn star status and money. Those who want to be among the best have created a thriving market for books and articles on leadership. It is not possible to wander through an airport bookstore without tripping over several books or audiocassettes on the subject.

With established market dominance organizations don't really need followers whose whole being is engaged in the success of the enterprise. Solid performers who come to work on time will do. In uncertain times, however, when organizations have refocused on the customer to drive quality and the pace of change demands that employees learn new skills daily, the effective follower is an essential asset. So, where are the books on "followership"? There are only three of which we know and one is out of print!

More thought needs to be given to the follower—what good followers might be—what good followers must be—and how to develop good followers. A company that can succeed with followers who simply do what they are told poses leadership challenges that are different from the challenges of leading a team of creative, engaged followers. Conditions that call for proactive followers call for a particular approach to human resources development and leadership.

For example, every one of us has been in a classroom with a teacher who answers her or his own questions and every one of us in those situations has learned to out-wait the teacher. Some of us have also listened to teachers talk about these experiences in the classroom—and few of these are aware that their own behavior created passive students. Asking the question in different ways, waiting as long as it takes, and being clear about expectations for participation can turn passive students into active participants. Leaders face analogous challenges in understanding the impact of their own behavior on the willingness of employees to participate actively and fully in the life of the organization. But even with the right intentions and a clear understanding, leaders are often unable to harness their employees' latent capacity.

In a recent consulting opportunity with the chair of a science department in a major research university we worked with a leader who wanted to create a "self-managed" work team among his administrative staff. He was tired of establishing work schedules, resolving conflicts and approving routine requests. He had a research agenda on the "front burner." Moreover, there was an existing self-managed team among his lab technicians and he liked the way it worked. In this case, however, he was unable to move his employees. They wanted no part of increased responsibility—preferring security to freedom. Their average age was 26!

This leader knew what he wanted and by all evidence was able to work effectively with employees as partners. Still, he was unable to teach, enable and encourage his employees to accept a more complete partnership. He didn't have a model that he could use to frame the expectations he had of his employees and he didn't have a strategy that would get him to where he wanted to go. The model we will describe offers both.

The Follower as Partner

In many effective organizations, the relationship between a leader and her or his followers is best described as a partnership in which the initiatives of followers are just as important as those of their leaders. Partnership is not essential in all circumstances; but, where market demands are greatest and results are created or improved through the intellectual efforts of employees, followers must be partners. Two elements of organizational culture are important in developing partnership. The first is the drive for performance and the second is a commitment to effective relationships.

A secure position in the market can allow organizations to pay less attention to performance. American higher education has been a good case in point. Government and customer calls for increased accountability have often fallen on deaf ears. However, when the market gets its teeth into poor quality, new competitors begin to take advantage of unguarded opportunities and even stodgy old-line universities begin to increase their attention to performance.

The role of relationships in the effectiveness of organizations is becoming more and more prominent. When cultures require consensus or the need for shared purpose is essential, the quality of relationships is key. Those in which partners each assume that the other listens and seeks to understand are more effective. Where work units are interdependent and resources are limited, people in relationships that support the belief that the one who goes first "won't use up all the hot water" get more done. Moreover, the greater the need for coordination and collaboration the more important strong relationships are to efficient communication. Finally, between leader and follower the stronger the relationship, the more likely that substantive, honest communication will flow both ways.

The challenge for leaders is that in relationships where there are power differences, we tend to assume that the one with more power determines the character of the relationship. As long as this is true, followers must depend on leaders to create relationships that foster open, creative communication. When followers accept shared responsibility for the quality of the relationship with their boss, true partnership is possible. In pursuit of partnership, therefore, bosses may have special power but followers can have substantial influence in creating effective partnerships. The greatest gains occur in those organizations where leaders take an active role in creating partnerships AND build cultures that foster the independent initiative of followers who, with the same goals in mind, also work to create partnership. In these organizations when, inevitably, the leader missteps, the leader is not the only one who can take action to reestablish balance. Furthermore, in these organizations leaders need not shoulder the entire responsibility for creating culture—even in uncertain times. Thus, leaders who create partnerships with their followers make dependence on leaders less necessary even in the toughest of times.

The leader who works in partnership with followers is one who can accept the initiative of followers and act in ways that encourage followers to continue to take initiative. Either leader or follower can begin change in the organization but consistent culture throughout the organization remains the province of leadership. The most effective cultures are created intentionally—often built on models or visions of the ideal. Our model has emerged as we have worked in six different countries with organizations including a financial services company, a major private university, a federal emergency management training center, NASA's Kennedy Space Center and a variety of other settings. It offers an understanding that will support leaders and followers in choosing an approach to followership that fits the needs of organization. Such an understanding begins with understanding the way followers behave.

The Behavior of Followers

The behavior of followers differs in two important ways or along two dimensions—the amounts of Performance Initiative and Relationship Initiative. Performance initiative refers to the follower's active efforts to do a good job. A person who demonstrates a great deal of performance initiative finds ways to improve his or her own performance in the organization. These ways might include improving skills, sharing resources with team members and trying new strategies. Relationship initiative refers to the follower's active attempts to improve his or her working relationship with the leader. A person who demonstrates a high degree of relationship initiative behaves as if "you can't succeed if your boss fails." For this follower shared purpose and shared vision are essential and thus he or she assumes an active role in achieving and maintaining both.

Performance Initiative

One important aspect of followership relates to the follower's concern about her or his performance. Does the person find ways to take the initiative to improve his or her own performance in the organization? To assess this dimension of follower initiative, we need to consider: (1) the extent to which the follower thinks of ways to get her or his assigned job done, (2) the extent to which the follower treats himself or herself as a valuable resource, (3) how well the follower works with co-workers, and (4) what view the follower takes toward organizational and environmental change.

Followers differ in the extent to which they take positive initiatives in each of these domains. Effective followers are committed to high performance. They understand that their future depends on the future of the organization and are not content simply to do what they were asked to do yesterday. At the low end of this scale one still finds satisfactory performers. At the high end one finds experts who lead in their fields and whose contributions strengthen the bottom-line performance of the organization.

Doing the Job

Followers vary in the extent to which they strive to be as good as they can be at what they do. At one end of the continuum are followers who go through the motions, performing the tasks that are assigned to them just well enough to keep their jobs. If an aspect of an assigned task is not mentioned or emphasized by the manager, it is ignored. The definition of acceptable performance lies outside of the follower in the directives and regulations of the organization. Managers are continually challenged to think of a set of standards and rules that will squeeze adequate performance out of these reluctant performers. Performance at work is not important to the self-concept of these followers.

At the other end of this continuum are followers who care deeply about the quality of their performance. They take pride in what they do. They have their own standards, ones that are higher than the minimum prescribed by the organization. Work is an important and integral part of their lives. Creative managers try to find ways to free these followers to allow their enthusiasm and drive to work best for the organization.

Working with Others

Another important dimension of follower performance is working with others. At one extreme is the follower who does not work well with others. Some of these are continually involved in arguments and disputes, irritating everyone in the process. These followers actually interfere with the performance of others in the organization. Other followers at the low end of the scale do not have difficulties with others, but do not really work with others either. These see their performance as solely dependent on what they themselves do. They miss opportunities for synergy and by withholding their cooperation may limit the effectiveness of others.

At the high end of the scale are followers who take advantage of working with others. They may act as coaches, assume the role of leader when it serves the team, act as mentors for less experienced team members, and share expertise with co-workers. When followers work effectively with others, they are able to balance their personal interests with the interests of others, discovering common purpose and working to achieve common goals. These followers emphasize cooperation over competition and find their own success in the success of the whole group.

Self as a Resource

Some followers pay little attention to their own well-being, neglecting physical, mental, and emotional health. This behavior may yield short-term benefits for the organization, if the follower is effective in important ways. In the long run, however, such neglect is likely to lead to burnout or stagnation. For an organization with a throwaway approach to its employees, this may be acceptable. For the individual follower, however, such an approach obviously is not wise. Followers who will be effective over the long haul recognize that they are their own most valuable resource, and take care to maintain their own physical, mental and emotional health by balancing work and other interests (e.g., family and friends, community activities and relations, physical and nutritional fitness).

Embracing Change

The other dimension of follower initiative that we think is important to consider concerns the follower's orientation to change. Change can be threatening and confusing. The widespread popularity of the book, "Who Moved My Cheese?" underlines the importance of change as a threat to the time-honored and familiar. Even motivated, generally competent employees will resist change when the results of change are uncertain. Those most rooted in the way things are generally have vested interests in maintaining the status quo. These may actually sabotage efforts to change.

At the positive end of this dimension are the followers who look for new and better ways to do things because they are committed to continuous improvement. These followers see change as an opportunity for improvement for themselves and their organizations. Such followers anticipate or look for change. They can be extremely effective as agents for change, by explaining to their co-workers the advantages of doing things differently, showing by example how different doesn't have to mean worse. Followers oriented toward embracing change will anticipate new methods, contribute ideas for ways to make positive changes in the way the organization functions, and will be willing to try out different ways of being effective.

Relationship Initiative

The other absolutely vital, but typically neglected, dimension of follower initiative is the follower's relationship to the leader. Good leaders find it extremely difficult to lead followers who are in an adversarial or indifferent relationship with them. Conversely, even mediocre leaders can look good and do well if their followers are willing to do whatever they can to help. A follower's position on this scale is determined by evaluating the degree to which the follower: (1) understands and identifies with the leader's vision for the organization, (2) actively works to earn the leader's trust, (3) is willing to communicate in a courageous fashion with the leader and (4) works to negotiate differences with the leader.

Identifying with the Leader

Followers vary considerably in the extent to which they understand and sympathize with their leader's perspective. Many followers simply do not. Viewing the leader as someone apart and alien, they do not try to think about how things look from the leader's perspective or what the leader's goals or problems might be. More problematic is the case in which the follower has developed active hostility toward the leader. In these cases, the follower's thoughts about the leader's perspective are strongly affected by animosity and opposition. Followers who are thought to have "problems with authority figures," or who indeed are saddled with inept or unfriendly supervisors, are likely to identify only in a negative way with their leaders. In contrast, some followers have thought more dispassionately about their leaders, understand their aspirations and styles, and have developed sufficient respect for the leader to adopt those aspirations as their own. These followers understand the leader's perspective, do what they can to help the leader succeed, and take pride and satisfaction in the leader's accomplishments. Managers who try to make their own views, goals, aspirations, and concerns understood by their followers can make it much easier for their followers to adopt and identify with their perspective.

Building Trust

Followers can also take the initiative to act in ways that will build their leader's confidence and trust in them. This means that the follower will look for and take advantage of opportunities to demonstrate to the leader that she or he is reliable, discreet, and loyal. Followers who demonstrate these qualities to their leaders are more likely to be asked for their opinions and reactions to new ideas. Their leaders will be more likely to share their plans and doubts, to entrust them with important tasks, and when necessary to give them honest feedback that can be used for performance improvement. Followers who do not seek out such opportunities for building trust, who do not understand or see as important this aspect of their relationship with their leaders, are less likely to be in a position to help their leaders as much as they might.

Courageous Communication

Part of building trust includes being honest, even when that is not the easiest thing to do. This aspect of relationship initiative is important enough to consider in its own right. Some followers fear (often with good reason) being the bearer of bad news, and are likely to refrain from speaking unpleasant truths. This can range from the classic notion of the "yes man" to simply refraining from speaking one's mind when that might be uncomfortable for the speaker and listeners. But followers who take the initiative in their relationships with their leaders are willing to speak the truth even when others may not enjoy hearing the truth in order to serve the goals of the organization. A follower who exhibits courageous communication takes risks in order to be honest. Because leaders can suffer from being surrounded by people who are supportive to a fault, a follower who is willing to be honest when others shy away from voicing their real opinions and evaluations can be invaluable.

Negotiating Differences

Another aspect of relationship initiative concerns the follower's approach to differences that arise between leaders and followers. A follower who is oriented toward improving her or his relationship with the leader is in a position to negotiate or mediate these differences. In the case of a difference of opinion between a leader and follower, the follower may engage in open or hidden opposition to the leader's decisions, hiding his or her differences of opinion and quickly agreeing with the leader regardless of true personal opinion. Alternatively, the follower who is concerned about the leader-follower relationship will air these differences in order to have a real discussion that may persuade either party or lead to a compromise that is satisfactory to everyone. In the case of disagreements between a follower's leader and other co-workers, the follower can stir the pot for fun or step out of the way. Alternatively a follower can take advantage of an understanding of the points of view of both parties to try to help resolve the disagreements in a way that leads to creative solutions acceptable to the leader as well as the other followers.

Follower Styles

The performance initiative and relationship initiative dimensions are each complex. Moreover, each follower has an individual behavior pattern—a follower style—that is the result of a unique combination of the elements of these dimensions. Understanding individual patterns can help a manager think about how to develop optimal follower styles. Furthermore, managers can assess their own leadership and followership characteristics when considering how they function in their organizations with an eye toward self-improvement.

By thinking of the two dimensions of performance and relationship initiative together, we can define four different follower styles by looking at the four combinations of high and low performance initiative and high and low relationship initiative (see Figure 12.1). We have used the terms Contributor, Politician, Subordinate, and Partner to describe the follower styles represented by these four combinations. These terms are useful for thinking about different follower styles, but we want to emphasize two things. First, although these terms may have acquired positive or negative connotations, we use them in a less evaluative way. There is no "one

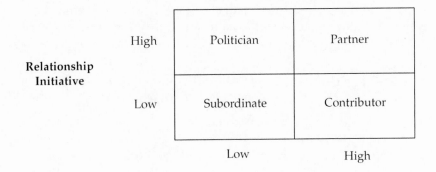

FIGURE 12.1   Follower Styles

best style" that will work for every person in every organizational setting. Each style can work well in certain organizational settings or with
certain personal characteristics of followers, and each can create problems when that style conflicts with the follower's personal characteristics
or with the nature of the organization in which he or she works. In addition, because organizations are often complex and multi-faceted, the de-
sirability of particular follower styles may vary from one part of the organization to another. However, we do believe that in general the most
effective organizations, particularly in times of rapid change and challenge, will be those that are characterized by a partnership between leaders and followers.

Before discussing the different follower styles, however, it is worth
thinking about how these styles arise. The easiest way to think about
personal styles is to assume that they reflect the personality of the individual. This is often the case, but there are other powerful influences on
follower style. Chief among them is the nature or style of the leader.
Some leaders demand or encourage a particular follower style, discouraging or preventing other approaches. In these cases, followers may exhibit that style whether or not it suits them personally. Similarly, organizations have structures and develop cultures and subcultures that
promote some styles and inhibit others. From a manager's point of
view, the personal, leadership, and organizational influences on follower style need to be evaluated. From the follower's point of view,
careful consideration should be given to what the leader and the organization desires or will allow. In some cases, it will be difficult, risky, or
impossible for a follower to adopt a different style even if he or she
wants to change. Conversely, if a follower's style is a reflection of long-

standing and stable personal characteristics, the leader and the organization will have a difficult (but not necessarily impossible) task if a change in follower style is desired.

The Contributor: High Performance Initiative, Low Relationship Initiative

A follower who exhibits this style shows many, if not all, of the positive characteristics associated with performance initiative: a focus on doing the job very well, working effectively with co-workers in the organization, embracing change, and taking care of personal resources for long-term health. The Contributor's follower style is admirable, and the person is probably known and respected for dedication to work of high quality. Clearly this is a follower style that would be valued highly by many organizations.

However, the Contributor style does not include positive initiatives toward improving the relationship with the boss. Followers with this style rarely seek to understand the perspective of the leader or to promote the leader's vision. Their interactions with the leader are not characterized by courageous communication, initiatives designed to build interpersonal trust (beyond being trusted to do the work well), or a mature approach to negotiating differences that arise with the leader. Although such followers are thorough and creative in obtaining the resources, information, and skills that are needed to do the job, they are not interested in the interpersonal dynamics of the "higher ups" in the workplace. There are ways in which followers with this style could do more to help their leaders, and in turn their organizations, to be more effective. Indeed, the respect they earn through performance initiative could make them very effective if they took relationship initiatives, but they do not.

The Contributor style may suit some individuals very well. An energetic focus on doing the work very well, and the satisfactions gained from succeeding at that, can be enough for many people, and realistically there may be little time or energy left for relationship initiatives. In addition, some people simply lack the skills or the interest that is required for successful relationship initiatives. The Contributor style may also arise as a complementary counterpart to a leader who has everything under control, and has no need for assistance through relationship initiative, or who has other people to serve that function. At the organizational level, the Contributor style may also be what is needed and rewarded by the organization in general or by the organizational unit in which the person works. The most pressing organizational need may be for people who put all of their energy into their own tasks, or there may be a division of labor such that enough other people are paying attention to relationship initiative to free Contributors to do nothing but produce.

However, the Contributor style may arise from less fortunate circumstances. At the individual level, the person may truly lack some important interpersonal skills that prevent relationship initiatives (and in that case, the "working with others" aspect of performance initiative may also be problematic). The person may have failed previously in (clumsy) attempts to establish a relationship with a leader, and may have been soured on that whole dimension. At worst, persons with a Contributor style may actively oppose the leader. A person who works very well with co-workers and very badly with anyone in authority can be a real problem. In such a case, getting the person to take positive relationship initiatives would be a real coup, but simply getting them to give up active opposition would also be a victory.

The Contributor follower style may also arise because the leader discourages or rejects any positive relationship initiatives. For example, a follower may be capable of and willing to take relationship initiatives, but a leader who has a traditional view of leader-follower relations and responsibilities (i.e., I lead, you follow, end of story) may find such initiatives to be inappropriate. Or the leader may have marginal competence or self-confidence, and may see persons attempting to take relationship initiatives as threats or rivals. In such cases, the problem lies with a leader who prevents followers from doing all that they could do to help the organization. Similarly, the structures of organizational units, or entire organizations, can act to prevent relationship initiative. If followers have little or no contact with their superiors, if the organizational structure is rigidly hierarchical with orders flowing only from the top down, or if the organizational culture does not recognize relationship initiatives as appropriate follower behavior, then the organization may be throwing away its own interpersonal assets.

Universities are often home to a wide range of contributors, professionals with external audiences who are rewarded for their personal achievement. In many cases university faculty fit this model. Many faculty members have little interest in the affairs of the administration and see little reason why they should work to understand the perspective of their "leaders." It is even likely that some faculty members do not acknowledge the members of the administrative team as their leaders in the first place. The Contributor style also typifies "backroom" software designers of the "mainframe era." As the backroom has become transparent and the customer has access to technical specialists, the role of the professional who can remain apart from the business of the organization has changed. More and more traditional contributors are being asked to relate their work and goals to the values and performance goals of the organization as a whole. This transformation poses a significant challenge for leaders in universities, research labs, and the computer and software industry as a whole.

The Politician: Low Performance Initiative, High Relationship Initiative

We refer to a person who shows a follower style that is low in performance initiative but high in relationship initiative as having a Politician style. We hasten to say that although we think this is a good descriptive term, it does suffer from the current highly negative reaction to politicians in government. In public organizations where a mix of career employees and those appointed by the elected leaders clash, the appointed followers often exhibit the Politician style. But the Politician style has its strong as well as its weak points. Followers such as these are unusually sensitive to interpersonal dynamics and are valuable for their ability to contribute when interpersonal difficulties have arisen or might arise. They understand better than most the perspective of the leader, her vision and goals, his problems and concerns, and act to support the leader, taking satisfaction in her or his success. They are willing to give honest feedback, even when many others lack the courage to do so, providing the leader with invaluable if unpleasant real information. They act in a manner that engenders trust, allowing the leader to discuss plans and concerns openly. They can provide valuable assistance to the leader because they are willing and able to give insights into group relationships, and they can be invaluable in the role of mediator and negotiator when differences with the leader arise.

Followers with a Politician style may be naturally inclined toward interpersonal relationships, and particularly oriented toward and good at understanding and connecting with people in authority. In personality terms, people who are high in dependency, for example, might be likely to adopt a Politician follower style. The prospects, difficulties, and intrigues of leadership may be particularly engaging, while the potential rewards to be gained from a performance initiative focus are not. However, a Politician style can also arise from necessity rather than from personal inclinations. For example, if the leader is sorely in need of people who can understand and translate his approach to others, a follower may need to devote a considerable amount of time and energy to relationship initiatives in order to help the leader succeed. Similarly, the organization or the follower's organizational unit may need followers to oil the relationship machine, and may arrange reward systems and structures to encourage followers to be oriented toward relationship initiatives. In all of these cases, a follower's desire, or at least willingness, to devote a considerable amount of energy and time to relationship initiatives, even at the expense of performance initiatives, may be adaptive and useful for the person and the organization.

But as with the Contributor style, Politician styles can have a less benevolent source and a less salutary effect for the organization. This is a follower style that can be chosen as a way to cover fundamental deficiencies in performance. A person interested in personal gain and power, or in being attached to power, might see this approach as an easy or quick way to advancement and success. Such a person would rather play the system than do his or her job, adopting an attachment to people in positions of authority as a route to success. Alternatively, certain kinds of leaders may demand this sort of focus from their followers. When the leader's success is clearly the main item on the agenda, and when the care and feeding of the leader's ego is a full-time job, a follower may show the Politician style through necessity. Organizations may unwittingly create this style by promoting people up to their level of incompetence, leaving them in jobs they cannot perform in any way other than to play politics within the system to survive. Any of these more negative causes behind the Politician style can be quite damaging to the organization and to the people who depend on the followers in question to perform their duties.

The Subordinate: Low Performance Initiative, Low Relationship Initiative

We fear that this is what most people think of when they hear the term "follower." But we hope that by now it is apparent that this is a limited view of followership. The subordinate is the stereotypical follower who does what he or she is told. A follower with a Subordinate style may be quite competent at his or her assigned tasks, and may rise in a seniority driven organization, but demonstrates neither a sensitivity to relationships with leaders nor a commitment to high performance.

As with the other follower styles, a Subordinate style may arise from personality characteristics; some people prefer to be given direction, and feel most comfortable when others take the responsibility for decisions about direction and procedure. In many cases, this may be a habit that has been acquired over the course of a lifetime. But it is also easy to see how leaders and organizations often demand such a style. Leaders who expect to give orders and have them followed or who are threatened by anything other than acquiescence to their decisions will have followers who behave as Subordinates. Similarly, if the organization requires and rewards nothing more than straightforward performance of a well defined job, the Subordinate style will likely predominate. In these cases, many of the people who show a Subordinate style are probably capable of more, and are probably unhappy in or unfulfilled by their work. In fact, studies of intergenerational differences in the workforce suggest that workers in Generation X and later may not stay with organizations that require nothing more than subordinate behavior.

On the other hand, the Subordinate style can be appropriate in some cases. It may suit the follower, the leader, or the organization. The subordinate is the only kind of valued follower in hierarchical organizations that operates only with orders from the top and obedience from the bottom or in production-line organizations where tasks are clearly defined and where deviation from prescribed methods or processes can create chaos. Similarly, when the job is one that may be waiting for the day when automation becomes possible and cost-effective, humans are serving where machines may soon arrive, and the job is designed so that initiative is not part of the picture. This style may also be inappropriate because improvements to the processes will come most often from the followers who are encouraged to show initiative and creativity for improvement, but unfortunately, for most cases, it is the most likely style. It is also the likely style of a somewhat or completely disaffected follower who is not interested in giving anything extra, or whose job is not one of his or her primary concerns. Or it can be the style of a follower who has discovered that the leader or the organization is not really interested in his or her ideas and initiatives.

The Partner: High Performance Initiative, High Relationship Initiative

Analyses of high-performance teams have revealed that the distinction between leader and follower is often more apparent than real, with team members slipping into and out of the role of leader so as to maximize team effectiveness. In these cases, the follower style is one of a Partner. The follower with a Partner style is committed to high performance and an effective relationship with the leader. Organizations that anticipate and keep pace with change in the global environment are characterized by leaders who encourage partnership and followers who seek to be partners. In these organizations Partners develop the kind of understanding that enables them to make contributions that anticipate market opportunities and customer needs.

Followers with a Partner style are often leaders-in-waiting. But they can also be people who do not particularly desire to have the lead or head position, but instead are concerned with doing whatever they can do to make their organization effective and successful. Clearly, organizations that are characterized by the Partner follower style are getting the most from their employees.

Developing Partners

It is true that each of the follower styles can be appropriate at some point in an organization's life. Furthermore, within each larger organization there will undoubtedly be subcultures where different follower styles are favored appropriately. Nevertheless, over the long run and particularly in times of change in strongly competitive markets, organizations need followers who are partners. Creating the right conditions for effective followership requires a clear understanding of practical steps that invite followers to partnership. The first of these is knowing what to look for in followers. The model we have described offers this picture. The next steps can be taken independently but leaders will be most effective when they take each of the steps below.

1. Model Partnership

The good news and the bad for every leader is that she/he is also a follower. Thus, every leader can understand what good leadership looks like to a follower. When you focus on followership, however, you gain insight into your own behavior as a follower—and you are able to assess whether or not you would like your organization full of folks who behave the way you do as a follower. Anyone who has ever sat at the boardroom table with a boss who has criticized his boss's position on a pending decision and watched her boss smile and agree in spite of real disagreement, knows what behavior is really valued in the organization. On the other hand, those leaders who engage their followers in planning how to present their case "in loyal opposition" teach partnership by example.

2. Hire Potential Partners

Lyle Spencer, former Vice President for Research of Hay-McBer Company, the leading source for research on competence in the workplace is fond of saying that, "You can teach a turkey to climb a tree but it's easier to hire a squirrel." We agree that there are folks whose personal preferences and innate competence favors partnership. This is not to say that leaders do not play a part in determining the expression of that competence. Turn arounds at Sears and American Airlines depended, in part, on creating new roles for current employees enabling them to use competencies that they already possessed. On the other hand, many organizations have created positions for people who are content to let others take responsibility for performance and relationships in the workplace.

With a clear picture of follower competence, i.e., the skills for and inclinations towards partnership, leaders can select employees who will move faster towards partnership than current employees may be able to move. This strategy does have a bit of the "be careful what you wish for" problem inherent in its results, however. To hire people who want to be partners you must decide that you are going to make room for partnership and develop the leadership strategies that support partnership. It is more possible to promise partnership to current employees who are sure that they want to be partners than it is to survive the failure to deliver on your promises. Fifty percent failure rates of reengineering projects across the country and the long list of TQM dropouts underscore this truth.

3. Assess Leaders for Their Ability to Foster Partnership

GE, Sears, Merck and Levi-Strauss have all made leadership development and assessment a cornerstone of their human asset management strategies. In each company CEOs have led the identification of leadership values and competencies that will enable employees to give their best to the organization. One of these goes so far as to say that there are two things a leader must do—get bottom line results and support the leadership values of the corporation. Success goes to those who do both. Those who can do neither "are history." The more interesting responses, however, are the responses to leaders who are strong in one area but not the other. If a leader doesn't get bottom-line results but supports corporate values, coaches will work with him or her. If a leader meets bottom-line goals but does not support corporate values, however, they will be looking for other employment.

4. Teach Partnership

Partnering requires the development of skills like active listening that need to be nurtured. The first step to developing partners is to be able to describe what you expect of employees. Some employees, however, who may be active problem solvers as parents or community leaders may not be able to imagine themselves in the roles you suggest as you describe partnership. If you have hired people with the potential to be partners and offer them leaders who know how to work with partners, simple skill development workshops should be enough. In employee development workshops at Cornell University we have worked with Contributors and Subordinates who want to be partners with leaders who don't understand partnership—and we have been able to help these followers create partnerships with their bosses. Teaching partnership skills is essential in organizations that want to develop partners—and potentially very powerful in every organization.

The success of the MASCO Corporation, a conglomerate that owns dozens of familiar brands in the home products industry, is based on its ability to recognize strength in the leadership teams of the companies it acquires. But MASCO leaders also recognize that leaders who have succeeded in command and control environments need to learn new skills in order to be successful in the future. The on-site MBA program MASCO has created in partnership with Eastern Michigan University brings leaders at various stages in their careers together for learning. The learning environment requires that senior managers become "learning partners" with their juniors. In more than one case, the lessons learned in this environment have been transformational. Strong leaders unaccustomed to listening to their juniors have developed team leadership skills that have enabled them to turn subordinates into Partners.

Leaders at Gold Paints, a winner of the New York State award for "Small Business of the Year," wanted to turn materials ordering over to shopfloor employees in order to create a "just-in-time" production process. Most of these employees did not have business management experience or basic accounting knowledge. In order to prepare employees for success Gold Paints created a year long course in basic business management skills before making the transition to new production processes. The results included improvements in efficiency, reductions in cost and a cadre of shopfloor employees whose taste of responsibility and success turned them into Partners who sought further opportunities to improve business results.

5. Reward Partnership and Take the Pain Out of Taking Initiative

There is a saying that "no good deed goes unpunished." Simply put, if we punish employees for telling us the truth—they won't.

6. Build Systems That Engage Partners

Learning systems that give employees access to the tools to do their work are one example. Dell Computers has created an employee driven, expert knowledge "warehouse" that employees can access to get information they need to do their jobs. The system "learns" in response to employee questions and feedback. Dell's research shows that user-driven learning by inquiry does a better job of building employees' understanding of the "big picture" than leader-driven briefings and workshops. Ramsoft, a computer services company, makes learning tools available to employees on a "24/7" basis. In Ramsoft's highly competitive labor market, this strategy helps keep highly motivated Partners in the company.

Collaborative business process redesign, GE's Workout model, TQM problem solving teams and community development workshops all offer systemic means for engaging employees as partners. Employees will only be successful in these processes, however, if steps 1–5 above are taken as well. Those organizations that invest in expensive organizational development strategies without developing partners find little value in group problem solving. When an organization is full of folks who behave as Subordinates, Contributors or Politicians, employees do not have the understanding, skill or sense of shared responsibility to be partners. The power of involvement strategies can only be realized in organizations that have taken the time to develop followers as partners.

Epilogue

It is counter intuitive but true that larger, complex organizations often offer employees the greatest freedom—especially if they are what Karl Weick has called "loosely coupled" organizations. In these situations, individual followers can create partnerships that significantly increase the probability of their own success—even when the organization as a whole "hasn't got a clue." The best will recognize this opportunity and grab it. So, one of the best strategies for change might be to leak some copies of this article to an employee association. Remember—true partners act in the best interest of the organization—and their boss. You can't lose!

References

Boccialetti, G. (1995). *It takes two: Managing yourself when working with bosses and other authority figures.* San Francisco: Jossey-Bass.

Branch, Shelly. "So Much Work, So Little Time." *Fortune,* June 3, 1997, pp. 115—117.

Case, John. "The Open-Book Revolution. Inc." June 1995, pp. 26—43.

Chaleff, I. (1995). *The courageous follower: Standing up to and for our leaders.* San Francisco: Berrett-Koehler Publishers.

Herman, Stanley M. *A Force of Ones: Reclaiming individual power in a time of teams, work groups, and other crowds.* San Francisco: Jossey-Bass, 1994.

Kelley, R. E. (1988). "In praise of followers." *Harvard Business Review,* Nov.–Dec., 142–148.

Kelley, R. E. (1992). *The power of followership.* New York: Doubleday/Currency.

Kouzes, James M., and Posner, Barry Z. *Credibility: How leaders gain and lose it, why people demand it.* San Francisco: Jossey-Bass, 1993.

LaBarre, Polly. "Grassroots Leadership—*The USS Benfold.*" *Fast Company,* April 1999, pp. 115–126.

Noer, David M. *Healing the Wounds: Overcoming the trauma of layoffs and revitalizing downsized organizations.* San Francisco: Jossey-Bass, 1993.

Organ, Dennis W. *Organizational Citizenship Behavior: The good soldier syndrome.* Lexington, MA: D. C. Heath, 1988.

Potter, E. H., Rosenbach, W. E., & Pittman, T. S. (2000). "Leading the new professional." In R. Taylor & W. Rosenbach (Eds.), *Military Leadership,* 4th edition. Boulder, CO: Westview Press.

Rosenbach, W. E., Pittman, T. S., & Potter, E. H. (1997). *The Performance and Relationship Questionnaire.* Gettysburg, PA.

Ryan, Kathleen D., and Oestreich, Daniel K. *Driving Fear Out of the Workplace: How to overcome the invisible barriers to quality, productivity, and innovation*. San Francisco: Jossey-Bass, 1991.

Sashkin, Marshall, Rosenbach, William E., and Sashkin, Molly G. "Development of the Power Need and Its Expression in Management and Leadership with a Focus on Leader-Follower Relations." Paper presented at the 12th scientific meeting of the A. K. Rice Institute, Washington, DC, May 12, 1995.

PART THREE

RETROSPECTIVES

The study of leadership spans the recorded history of humankind. Many of the classic writings chronicle the feats of the great leaders. Empires were built and conquests recorded with attribution given to the political and military leaders of the time. These stories are pervasive, and until the twentieth century, the study of leadership was primarily focused upon a few individual Great Man–leaders whose accomplishments were recorded by scribes or found in books.

There continues to be a quest for understanding leadership. Historians search for clues that will help us to understand how leaders are defined and to predict what they will do. Politics, the military, and religion provide rich resources from which we can gain perspective.

A more introspective approach to leadership began in the 1930s with the launch of the Ohio State and Michigan Leadership Studies. With the Industrial Revolution and the economic shift from agriculture to manufacturing, the focus of leadership studies turned to business. Agriculture was essentially a lone endeavor; manufacturing, transportation, and the emergence of markets made groups and teams of people integral to the economic engines. As we expanded and consolidated markets, companies and corporations began to play more important roles in our lives. Like the political societies, religious organizations, and military, our economic structures were composed of many people working together for a common goal. Thus, it was natural for the leadership focus to shift.

Increased attention to business leadership resulted in the first attempts to apply scientific methods to understand the causes and effects of leadership style, behaviors, and effectiveness. Interestingly, as scholars began to create research agendas that explored leadership and leader effectiveness, the methods changed and more sophisticated techniques were developed. In the late 1900s, academic researchers in many disciplines addressed the study of leadership with gusto. Groups, organizations, and most institutions of scholarly endeavor developed leadership themes as part of human development and scholarly work.

Why did leadership emerge as a popular topic of study? One reason may be that in the United States, our prosperity and access to education gave individuals many choices in their lives. At the same time, the rate of information exchange increased at exponential rates. People and organizations were overwhelmed with information, and the ability to discriminate and analyze appeared to be daunting. There seemed to be a reaching out—an external orientation as we looked to others to explain the chaos in their lives. This impacted our work life, spiritual life, and role in society. The focus was on leaders and their successes and failures. Responsibility was shifted from the individual to the group or organization, with the result that we placed the spotlight on our leaders. Demonstrated leadership became a criterion for recognition and a requisite for students competing for honors, workers competing for promotions, and candidates for key positions in the public and private sectors.

In our quest for leaders, businesses, government, and not-for-profit organizations established training programs and sponsored educational experiences in attempts to create a pipeline of candidates. Many could be described as management training, emphasizing tools such as effective communication, strategic planning, team building, and graduate education. The interest spread globally as people searched for the best ways in which to identify, encourage, develop, and reward those who were designated as the leaders in their lives.

The absence of a similar interest in followership, described in Part 2, once again seemed to highlight only the leader. In a sense, we are continuing the historical trend of looking only at leaders for the answers to our questions. Yet leadership is the interaction of followers and leaders and we reemphasize that the study of both roles is critical to understanding leadership.

The potential for effective leadership is widely dispersed in our society, and not limited to a privileged few. Learning about leadership means learning to recognize bad leadership as well as good. Learning about leadership involves understanding the dynamic relationship between the leader and follower; recognizing the differing contexts and situations of the leadership landscape; and understanding the importance of the behavioral sciences, philosophy, economics, logic, and related disciplines that provide the perspective so important to leadership effectiveness.

There are significant differences in business, political, religious, military, and social organizations. Each calculates the "bottom line" in different ways. Nonetheless, there are commonalities in organizational leadership, and we must explore all of the areas to identify those elements important to our effectiveness. Technology has made the boundaries in our lives less clear. We applied a broad search of the literature to highlight the diversity of sources for common ideas. With the exception of the arenas in which the leaders operated, the similarities are greater than the differences when examining leader effectiveness.

All too often, we ignore the lessons of history. The environment has changed, say some people. The circumstances have changed, say others. That we cannot relate to earlier times is a rationale too often advanced. Yet we appear to repeat events, and so the key is to identify important writings to ask: "Is anything really new?" As writers and scholars continue to purport new discoveries about effective leadership, history is the lens through which we can best understand the phenomenon of leadership. The enduring lessons of success and failure reflect the individual leader coping with the task at hand. While the economic, social, and technological environments continually change, the capacity of the human does not. We still have intellect and personality as our tools. It is how we use them that determines our capacity as leaders.

Leadership Perspectives

In "Plato on Leadership" (Chapter 13), T. Takala provides a perspective from the Greek philosopher Plato, describing him as the most influential leadership thinker of all times. This paper presents the various dimensions of leadership from Plato's discussions on ideal political governance and relates them to contemporary issues. Ethics, rhetoric, management of meaning, and charismatic leadership are also discussed. Plato's theory of an organization as a harmony-seeking entity was a precursor of the follower-as-partner construct in effective organizations. His concept of leadership as management of meaning helps us to understand leadership as a social process, which describes how leaders create, sustain, and induce change in organizations. Finally, the author describes Plato's notion of charisma, the gift of grace, as a necessary condition of effective leadership. All of these concepts are important in our study of contemporary leadership.

Mark Kroll, Leslie Toombs, and Peter Wright examine hubris as a common reason for leadership failure in "Napoleon's Tragic March Home from Moscow: Lessons in Hubris" (Chapter 14). Hubris is defined as the insolence or arrogance resulting from excessive pride or passion. A classic example was Napoleon's Russian campaign in 1812, in which he lost his army and, eventually, his empire. The authors compare the hubris of Napoleon with that reflected in the actions of contemporary business executives. The rush to make acquisitions at any price, grow organizations without limits, and stretch legal and ethical limits of accepted business conduct are the examples given. They suggest that introspection, listening to those who oppose, alter egos, and modeling behavior to best practices are issues relevant to leaders today. Although hubris is not characteristic of all organizations, its study provides yet another classic lesson.

Leadership in the broad context is described by Albert Hunt in "The Greatest Man Churchill and Truman Ever Met" (Chapter 15). Insights about General George C. Marshall highlight the importance of self-knowledge and self-confidence. Vision and integrity characterized General Marshall. At the same time, Hunt reflects on the miscalculations of this great person to suggest that the most effective leaders have, at one time or another, failed, but they have learned from their failures. Marshall was a politician, but he did not promote himself. Winner of the Nobel Peace Prize, Marshall served in key military and civilian roles, one of few people who were successful leaders in very different environments. While the author wonders if Marshall would be successful today, we are reminded that timing is an element of effective leadership. Perhaps there are others who, when subjected to historical review, might follow in Marshall's footsteps.

We conclude this part with John Gardner's essay from 1965, "The Antileadership Vaccine" (Chapter 16), in which he discusses the dispersion of power and our failure to cope with the "big question." This is a meaningful contemporary review despite the fact that nearly four decades have passed since he wrote it. In his opinion, the antileadership vaccine is administered by our educational systems and by the structure of our society, causing people to lose the confidence they need to assume leadership roles. Gardner notes that in training people for leadership, we have neglected the broader moral view of shared values, thus inhibiting vision, creativity, and risk taking. We appear to be approaching a point, he argues, at which everyone will value the technical expert who advises the leader or the intellectual who stands off and criticizes the leader, but no one will be concerned with the development of leadership itself. Alas, we can safely ask: "What is truly new?"

13

Plato on Leadership

T. TAKALA

Leadership has been one of the main topics among management writers during the last thirty years. This is understandable, of course, because the area of leadership has traditionally had a central position on management's agendas and it has been studied intensively. However, an evident defect can be found. One area of study has almost totally been neglected by the researchers. This category of leadership study can be called *"classical studies"* in which some classical (managerial) thinker is analyzed and studied thoroughly. But, by which criteria can one choose this kind of influential thinker to study? Plato, the Greek philosopher, can without any doubt be defined as one of the most influential leadership-thinkers of all times in addition to his other merits.

The purpose of the paper is to identify various dimensions of leadership emerging in Plato's discussions on ideal political governance and then generalize them to fit in with current discussions.

The term leadership has many meanings: it means different things to different people. It is a word taken from the common vocabulary and incorporated into the technical vocabulary of a scientific discipline without being precisely defined. As a consequence, it still carries extraneous connotations which create ambiguity of meaning. Stogdill states (1974) in his comprehensive review of leadership studies that "there are almost as many definitions of leadership as there are persons who have attempted to define the concept".[1]

The term *leadership-thinking* is also problematic, when the time context is as far away in the past as in the Era of Antiquity. However, it seems to me that it may be fruitful and fresh to look at such a phrase-like concept from quite an unordinary point of view. One might suspect the relevance

Reprinted with permission, from *Journal of Business Ethics* 17 (1998), pp. 785–798. Copyright 1998 by Kluwer Academic Publishers.

of searching out and considering the ideas of some ancient philosopher. In spite of that, I think that it is possible to get obvious intellectual benefit from this kind of consideration. Especially when developing the area of leadership thinking. Plato (427–347 B.C.), the great philosopher, can be seen as a very important source of ideas.

When one evaluates leadership studies made by earlier researchers, one can notice that the status of classicist studies is minor. However, it can be polemically argued that the whole Western administrative thinking bases on the principles presented in classical antiquity. The task of studying such remote objects, like ancient management thinkers or philosophers, becomes more important if this statement is accepted. But why study Plato? The influence of Plato on Western thought has been enormous. Recent philosophers and philosophy teachers often say that philosophy after Plato has been only remarks on Plato's work. So, the roots of Western administrative thinking go back to Plato's and Aristotle's work. Although part of their work has lost its relevance in the course of years, these two philosophers will always be very important as thinkers and sources of ideas.

Leadership—a Concept with Many Meanings

Next, it may be useful to take a glance at the concepts of leadership and management. Everyone who studies administrative sciences knows that these two matters are usually differentiated. To be a leader, to get things done, is the theme in common to both of them. Then, what differentiates these two concepts from each other? *Manager* is said to be some kind of an "instructor" who puts pieces together and manages the "things". Managers are concerned with making the organization function as an organization, that is, they evolve routines (source of efficiency), and make these routines relevant to the purposes of the organization (effectiveness). To put it another way, their major job is to facilitate the recombination of elements separated by the division of labor. At the same time, they need to keep on changing these routines, either because persisting internal problems make them unworkable, or because new external threats or opportunities require accommodation.[2]

Management is seen as an activity which is especially typical of large corporations, but it is said that there is *leadership* in every organization, not only in business organizations. On the other hand, a leader must be a person who takes care of people and emphasizes in his professional activity the social psychology of an organization. This categorization of management vs. leadership may be artificial, but it is commonly used in management literature. One must, however, note that a person who runs a business or leads a big organization acts situationally in both roles; sometimes as a manager and sometimes as a leader.

The term *leadership* is a relatively recent addition to the English language. It has been in use only about two hundred years, although the term leader, from which it has been derived, appeared as early as A.D. 1300 (Stogdill, 1974).[3] Most conceptions of leadership imply that at various times one or more group members can be identified as a leader according to some perceived differences between the person(s) and other members, who are referred to as "followers" or "subordinates". The definitions of leadership usually have a common denominator, the assumption that leadership is a group phenomenon involving interaction between two or more persons (Janda, 1960).[4] In addition, most definitions reflect the assumption that leadership involves an influence process whereby intentional influence is exerted by the leader on the followers. The definitions of leadership differ in many respects, including e.g. important differences in who exerts influence, the purpose of the attempts to influence, and the manner in which the influence is exerted.[5]

As stated above, *the concept "leader" is not necessarily related only to business life only, but it is an inevitable functional element in all social organizations*. In a way, each of us could be a leader, e.g. the leader of some political, religious or societal organization, or simply the head of the family. In his role the leader makes the norms of action, but he is also more than just a disciplinarian. He aids people to develop and grow up as individuals, he is a human constructor.

As we can see, these principles describe well the idea of classical paideia: to help people complete themselves as good human beings in a good society (polis) and with the guidance of a good leader.

The evolution of leadership theories began at the beginning of this century when the focus was on the leader's personality. The leader was defined as a Great Man who had some exceptional features of behavior. He was seen to have some identifiable traits of character which made him a great leader (see e.g. Banner and Blasingame, 1988). The early leadership theories attributed success in leadership to the possession of extraordinary abilities such as boundless energy, deep intuition, uncanny foresight, and irresistible persuasive powers. This massive research effort failed to find any traits which would guarantee success in leadership. Interest turned towards the behavioral theories, including the studies on leadership styles. The significance of the context, leadership situation, was noticed next. For example, Fiedler (1964) put forth his "contingency model of leadership". But now, it seems to me that a new *"syncretism"* has emerged. This means that all old elements are included, but in a very "scattered" way. There does not exist any strong mainstream in management or leadership studies which would have the power to overcome other rival trends of research.

The following division can be made if one wants to classify leadership studies from another perspective. The first category of leadership studies is about the manager's personal characteristics or about his professional role in the work community; "Leadership is a personal ability to direct the activities of a group towards a shared goal" (see e.g. Hemphill and Koons, 1957). The second category of studies considers the styles of leadership; e.g. the question which leadership style is effective or which is not (see studies made by Kurt Lewin, Rensis Likert and those applied to by e.g. Hersey and Blanchard). The third group of studies deals with the charisma or hero myths in managerial action, especially in the context of organizational culture. Leadership is often seen to represent some heroical activity. This class also includes studies on organizational symbolism (see e.g. Deal and Kennedy, 1982, Schein, 1985, Hofstede, 1980, Alvesson, 1987, Gahmberg, 1990).

One can, of course formulate several kinds of research categories but the above categorizing can help us to orient ourselves in the jungle of leadership studies. However I want to stress once again that kind of classicist approach used in this paper is unusual, but yet relevant. And now back into the world of Plato. Although Plato himself nearly always speaks about Polis, in which leadership really exists, we can try to change the term republic to the term (work) community, firm, or corporation. By this means we can get a heuristical tool for redefining the tasks of modern leadership.

Plato sketched out the idea of ideal community. *The point is that by following Plato one can try to sketch out those qualities of leadership which belong to modern ideal community. This means that we can try to apply Platonic thinking to modern organizations.*

Plato, His Philosophy and Leadership

Background of the Consideration

Ancient Greece (400 B.C.) has been regarded as the home of systematic administrative thinking; it has been seen as the place where the Western administrative thinking was born. The city-state (polis) was the administrative unit where pre-democratical experience was started and where it matured. It also ruled the whole societal life of the Greeks. Athens, Sparta, and Thebes were this kind of city-states. But what is important is the intimate relationship between the State and the individual citizen. The relationship was so close that it was not possible to think of a citizen living outside his state. This close relationship leaves its marks on the Grecian leadership thinking, too.

Plato, a Grecian philosopher, was the first thinker who presented a systematic political and administrative model to arrange the life in an ideal state (polis). The purpose (telos) of this kind of state is to educate people to become "good". Thus, the State has mainly a moral function in people's life. According to Plato, the State is like a human body where parts complement each other and act in harmony. Stating this, Plato represents himself as an early pre-modern functionalist, interpreted in the terms of organizational theory. Plato omits the organizational conflict; no conflict should exist between the parts in an ideal situation. This omitting of conflict appears also in the ideal state, where refined division of work, communism, equality etc. will prevail.

In *Polis* (Plato's dialogue: in English, the Republic) Plato states that politicians must act as the rulers of the new ideal state, because they have real knowledge (episteme) of what is "the Form of Good", and which are the aims of the state. They also have the skill to rule according to these aims. But, in the later written *Politikos* (Plato's dialogue), he does not any more speak about the forms according to which the ideal state can be ruled. Instead, he believes that the *art of ruling* (comp. leadership) can be found and based on scientific principles. This art is like the art of sailing which can be learnt. Political science, which is more than any individual art, takes care of law-making by "weaving these arts as one unity". But a just politician who knows the political science thoroughly and has moral strength, too, is rare. Because of that, it is better that the law stands above the ruler and the ruler must act according to the law.

Plato's Life and Work—an Overview

Plato and his "disciple" Aristotle (384–322 B.C.) were the great figures in Grecian thinking, and their influence on Western thinking and philosophy has been) enormous. Both Platonism and Aristotelian, as philosophies, have been the main trends of thinking in the Western world. The significance of these philosophies lies in the fact that they include in a very well formulated form a presentation of those issues which have occupied philosophers' minds through decades.[6]

Plato was born in Athens about in 427 B.C. He was the son of an aristocratic family which actively took part in the political life of Athens. It is evident that Plato planned to take part in politics, too, but due to violent and cruel social conditions (The Peloponnesian War was going on) he chose a more contemplative way of life. This decision was dramatic, because after that Plato never again managed to take part in day-to-day politics.

Democracy was the main form of government in Greece in those days. Athens, the forerunner of democracy, was the polis which had the leading position among other city-states. But, Plato's view of democracy was disapproving. He saw that aristocracy would offer a better alternative to rule, because the hegemony of *demos* would be a disaster to all parties of society. To Plato's mind Socrates' death might be the final step, and one that could release the bad and dysfunctional character of democracy. After this unfortunate event, Plato's literary career began. In his books, written in dialogical form, he set forth his political, ethical and epistemological ideas.[7] From the viewpoint of the leadership theme, Plato presented remarkable considerations in the following: Polis (The Republic), Politikos (The Statesman), and Nomoi (Laws) which remained the last work of Plato.

Plato's *epistemological* considerations and his own life were intimately connected with each other. We know that Plato tried to influence the formulation process of the constitution of the state Syracusa. In practice, his attempts met with a lot of misfortune and Syracusa kept the non-platonist model of constitution.[8] Plato himself had no luck and he had to escape from Syracusa. During the voyage he got into trouble when in Aigina buccaneers took him prisoner to sell him as a slave. Annikeris, a friend of Plato, bought him free. Plato continued his voyage to Athens where he devoted himself to literary work and founded his school called Academia.[9]

Forms in Platonic Ontology

Plato's view of the ultimate construction of reality can be characterized as idealistic. The ultimate nature of reality is ideal. Plato makes a drastic difference between the material (sense) world and the eternal world of Forms. Material particulars, single "things" (nominalia) are in the endless process of arising, changing and dying. In contrast with them, the Forms, i.e. the models of these changing things, are eternal, constituting the immaterial or ideal reality. For two reasons, the Forms are more real compared with the particular things which exist in the sense world. First, a Form exists in the same form eternally because it is unalterable by its nature. Instead, if a thing exists now, a time may come when it will vanish and thus it is not as real as the Form of it. Second, the Forms as the original models of all alterable material things are more real than their copies.

But there exists a hierarchy of Forms, as Plato states it. The most elementary is the *Form of Good*. He seems to think that each of the Forms is in a way part of the Form of Good. It is the most basic element in the cosmos; it is a principle that bears both existence and knowledge, as Plato puts it. He takes an analogy of seeing as an example. The Good (Demiurg) creates the ability to see and the ability to be invisible. But, in addition to these, e.g. in order to see a colour, a third element is needed—light. Light comes from the sun; although the sun does not see, it is a precondition for seeing. We can also apply this reasoning to the process of realizing (knowing); our soul realizes the things when it has been directed to the Truth, i.e. when the Truth gives its light to the realizing process. This element which gives a soul aiming, at the Truth the ability to know can according to Plato be named as the *Form of Good*. It is also the cause of the knowledge and the Truth because it can be reached by intelligence. This concept of the Good lies outside our consciousness. Plato's Good (to Agathon) involves both knowing and existing, but at the same time it is more than they are.[10]

In the following we make some comments which may clarify Plato's arguments. We must remember the teleological nature of the Grecian philosophy and thinking. This means that all existing things, both the actions and intentions of human beings and the life of animals and plants, are directed towards a certain purpose, *telos*. Thus, a man's will is always and of necessity directed towards the Form of Good. This ultimate purpose has been thought to be aiming at happiness, because the Greeks thought that happiness was the natural and principal good for a man. This puts forth the teleological *eudaimonism* prevailing the Grecian ethics. To aim at happiness is an in-built element in the Grecian model of human action.

According to Karl Popper,[11] an English social philosopher, Plato's doctrine of Forms has several functions in Plato's philosophy. First, it has a methodological task. It makes it possible to get pure scientific information about the Forms which can then be applied to in the world of altering and varying things. This is important because we cannot directly get real knowledge, *episteme*, from that changing world, but only opinions and beliefs, *doxa*. So, this lays the basis for the founding of political science. Second, it gives us the keys to form a theory of change, a theory of birth and death, and a way to understand our history better than before. Third, it gives a possibility to some kind of social technology. It gives a chance to develop resistance mechanisms against societal change by offering the ideal of the best state. We must remember that from Plato's point of view change represented a negative process in a societal sphere.

Plato's ethics involve strongly his ontological and epistemological stance. The thoughts presented above confirm to us that the ethics of Plato has a character of *ascetic transcendental eudaimonism*. In other words, to love the eternal Forms guarantees the soul the possibility to be with the Forms eternally, and this means that life is a means of reaching the purpose of the Good in the realm of the dead. While believing that the Forms are moral by their nature, Plato at the same time accepts the concept of *universal moral*. This concept has an existence which is independent of people's opinions. Another matter important in Plato's ethics is the doctrine of the immortal soul. It seems to me that he believed that body and soul are separable elements and soul will continue its life after the body's death.[12]

Like many other Greeks, also Plato conceives that *autarkia*, self-suffi-ciency, and the completeness of soul are the criteria for happiness. But he shows in his dialogues that neither of them alone is enough. Reason is necessary, but life also demands pleasure, *hedone*. Still there is a hierarchy of pleasures. The pleasure reached by knowing and realizing the Form of beauty is one of the highest pleasures.

Next, I will consider in detail some dialogues on the themes of management of leadership in Plato's thinking.

The Gorgias—a Critique on Rhetoric and an Early Attempt to Consider the "Management of Meaning"

The Gorgias is a dialogue in which Plato treats the main ethical problems of philosophy, e.g. the justification of manipulative action, i.e. the true na-ture of *rhetoric*. The Gorgias falls in three sections: in each of them Socrates has a different interlocutor, and each section establishes certain positions once and for all before passing on. The function of the first part is to dispose of the claims of rhetoric being a doctrine in which virtue is taught, and also to make a distinction between the two senses of *persua-sion*. Gorgias, a rhetor, is the upholder of the view that rhetoric, as an art of persuasion, is the means of attaining a man's supreme good. The supreme good is freedom and by freedom is meant the freedom to have one's own way in everything.

Gorgias himself does not seem to have claimed that he was a teacher of virtue: he taught the skills of rhetoric, developing in his students the abil-ity to persuade and convince the audience, and encouraging them to ac-quire the capability to respond to the audience's questions with confi-dence and self-possession.[13] The rhetor, the sophist, and the tyrant emerge in the Gorgias as the three icons of an antiphilosopher.

Socrates questions whether an orator needs the knowledge of right and wrong any more than he needs the knowledge of engineering. Gorgias is not entirely consistent at this point; he appears to argue that an orator on occasion needs to be a just man, but is vague about how he can become one. He presents rhetoric as such as a morally neutral technique which can be used for either the right or the wrong purposes: to put the blame on a teacher of rhetoric for its misuse by his pupils would be as silly as to accuse a teacher of boxing for the ways in which his pupils may use their craft afterwards.

The idea that the techniques of persuasion are morally neutral is a re-current one in the human society. But if the idea is to hold true that such techniques are neutral, it is also necessary to stick to it that it is morally irrelevant whether a man comes to a given belief by reasoning or in some irrational way.

The real sphere of rhetoric is the just and the unjust, the noble and the shameful, the good and the bad; its aim is not just to make an audience convinced, but to instruct them about matters where the question is about right and wrong; or about the policy which will prove beneficial. The orator will be ignorant of these subjects, for, as in Gorgias' case, it is partly because of his profession that he is capable of being more convincing in any sphere, even without any knowledge, than a man with the knowledge. Existing orators, then, are concerned only with appearances, not with reality; they deal with what appears to be good to their audience, because it is for the moment attractive and pleasant, not with what really is good. The teaching of rhetoric leads by an easy road to vice. If so, it is the very reverse of what education should be.[14]

To conclude, we can state that Plato reveals in this dialogue his conviction of the persuading nature of rhetoric as an antithesis of the real truth-seeking philosophy. A rhetoric action directed at manipulative goals is doomed. It is not real true-loving but only a *techne*, a means, to become more famous and wealthy.

The Republic; the Ideal State and the Ruling of It Versus Reality—Leadership as an Educational Catalyst in an Ideal State

What is the main issue in the dialogue of the Republic? There are several issues which Plato wants to consider. In this paper it is not possible to handle all his topics but some choices have to be made. Perhaps the most important issues from my point of view are the following:

- What the term "justice" really means
- The nature of leadership in an ideal state

The Republic opens with a request for a definition of "justice". After a long discussion Plato comes to the conclusion that it is not a matter of justice for the stronger to abuse his power over the weaker. Plato implements the Republic as a dialogue on the nature of justice: the ideal state is presented as social embodiment of justice. The division of functions in the State is the principle which indicates the nature of justice. A just social order is one where order and harmony are maintained by each class of citizens carrying out the tasks for which they are suited and not interfering with the work of others.[15] In this context I do not, however, consider it relevant to handle this matter more deeply. According to Popper,[16] behind the sociological points presented by Plato, there is the view that a state must be stable and in equilibrium. As long as these terms are put into practice, the power and the unity of the ruling class are guaranteed. To educate this class must be the first and foremost task of the leader of the State.

Next, we examine *more closely the tasks of the leader in an ideal state*. At least two tasks can be assumed to rest with the leader. The first of them is to control the implementation of education, and the second to control the propagation of thoughts. The function of the controllers in the State is considered important and therefore the controllers must be philosophers. The Popperian view is that Plato must have had political ambitions to think in that way. The main objective should be to raise the power of the Guardians as much as possible and in that way make it possible to get more and more Defenders in the State. But excellent military facilities are not enough to execute persistent power in the State. To lay basis for stable power in a state calls for supernatural or transcendental abilities from a leader, and mystical skills must be developed, to be used by the leader when ruling the state. Plato's leaders are not like human beings, they belong to the world of gods. In this way the *philosopher-king* can be seen to be descending from the ancient priest-kings of the earliest tribes. So, Platonic education may have a political basis. It leaves its mark on leaders, and on the other hand, sets up a borderline between the rulers and the ruled subjects. By this means Platonic wisdom gives mystical skills to leaders; they resemble ancient magicians.

And further, it is not allowed to give schooling to all citizens, but only to two upper classes, to the Rulers and the Defenders. Plato wants to train Defenders like dogs: a good dog is tender to his master and fierce to strangers, and in the same way the fury of the Defenders must be focused in the right way. The Defenders are citizens with the potential to grow and develop in the social hierarchy. Some of them can rise in the hierarchy and achieve as philosophers in ruling positions. But education is not enough because people are weak creatures tempted by many passions. What is needed is an ascetic way of life defined by the ruler-philosophers.

Also children ought to be educated to become proper citizens of the State.[17] The children of the Guardian class follow a curriculum with three elements, *mousike, gymnastike, and mathematics*. The successful development of a child's character depends on the balance maintained amongst these three sectors of education elements.

Homer, a Greek poet, has taught that the gods are a badly behaving bunch of creatures, but Plato wants to oppose this. He states that the gods are totally good and unchanging by their nature and to be obeyed. They are the *symbols of law*. Therefore, *stories* are an important means of education. In Plato's days, the Athenian children are brought up on an abundant diet of myths and legends, consisting especially of the stories embedded in the poems of Homer and Hesiod. The educational system proposed for the Guardians involves that virtually all the tales created by Homer and Hesiod are rejected: lies about the gods are unsuitable as educational material. Plato insists that stories about the gods and heroes must be truthful; a god is perfect, immutable, utterly truthful. The stories of divine immorality, of the gods who are shape-changing deceivers, thieves, liars, and adulterers have no place in education. In thus arguing, Plato is following the footsteps of Xenophanes and Heraclitus, both of whom were harshly critical of the foolish stories told about the gods. The interpreters of the myths had attempted to meet such criticism by producing elaborate allegorical interpretations of the myths which gave them an acceptable meaning. Plato refuses to accept that the existence of such interpretations would justify the use of the myths and legends he condemns. A story itself has the power to influence a child apart from the interpretations given to it. The stories used in the education of children must have an appropriate moral content. However, what is important, Plato states that telling lies is allowed to the Rulers for the sake of the State's best. Therefore, Rulers can serve a bunch of lies like a doctor doses a medicine for the sick. The benefit of the State comes first. Lying is not allowed to an individual citizen, only to the Rulers.[18]

Philosopher-King—Leadership as the Duty of a Philosopher

Plato is sure that there exists one and only one model of the ideal state. The most evident reason for the uselessness of the existing states is the lack of competent leaders. Those men who know what is best for the State and also have the strength to act according to that knowledge are philosophers. So, the philosophers have to be Rulers, philosopher-kings. Plato defines a philosopher by setting out an account of knowledge and belief and then contrasting the philosopher who has knowledge with the non-philosophical man who at his best has only a true belief or opinion.

Plato is at the core disappointed in the existing states because their leaders do not have any knowledge about the ultimate purposes of the state, neither do they have moral strength to act according to common good. Their objects are merely in individual gains and losses, and in their will to rule. A good leader is beneficial to his subjects in the same way as a good doctor to his patients. People cause only harm to themselves if they are so stupid that they do not want to be ruled by a philosopher-king.[19]

One of the most important tasks on the leader's agenda is to take care of the education of the different classes. The means used in the ruling of a state can be rude and, from our perspective, also quite questionable. Plato accepts the method, which I shall call *"management by lying"*. He states: "The Rulers of the State, if anybody, must be able to tell lies, if necessary, betraying both enemies and their own citizens. But no one else should do this".

The ideal state, according to Plato, shall have four main virtues. They are (1) prudence (2) courage (3) temperance and (4) justice. Prudence can be understood as the highest and best ability to give advice concerning the issues of governing the State as one unity. It is not a technical ability of or skill, but a virtue of ultimate purpose. This kind of knowledge is conserving. It helps to retain the stability in the State, and the Rulers with this knowledge are the most competent. Prudence is a gift typical of very rare people—philosophers, it is the understanding of the ultimate nature of the Forms. As Plato notices, the State can avoid disaster by choosing philosophers as rulers. This can happen by two means: either existing rulers become philosophers or philosophers become rulers. And rulers must be true philosophers who want to search out the ultimate truth instead of being egoists and motivated only by the gaining of power.

But it is very difficult to connect prudence and political power for two reasons. First, although a true philosopher would be available, people are blind and not ready to use their talents. Plato knows that politicians win their power by mutual fights and by courting the voters' favour. Therefore, an ideal leader needs an ideal public with the ability to choose the right leader. Second, connecting prudence and power is difficult because only a few people are true philosophers, and the most just pretend to be that. A true philosopher wants to rise into the spheres of esoteric meditation and is forced to accept rulership against his will.

It becomes apparent from the Republic that Plato's political idea was that the State should be governed by philosophers who would know with certainty the moral principles which should be the basis of the social order. Unfortunately, the one serious opportunity Plato had to make a ruler a philosopher failed utterly. The ideal remained, and Plato's Academia continued to disseminate the sort of education a philosopher-ruler would need, but Plato came to the point where he had to accept that the philosopher-ruler might prove to be an unattainable ideal.[20]

Statesman—Governing as a Special Skill

In his later dialogue, the Statesman, Plato does not any more consider ideas according to which the ideal state has to be organized. Instead, he believes that ruling is a special skill like the art of sailing or art of carrying on one's trade. Plato's method to analyze things in the Statesman represents a definitive technique. It is based on the dialectical process of out-separating. In the Statesman the Eleatic stranger uses this technique to demonstrate that the art of governing is indeed a form of knowledge. A Ruler who possesses that knowledge will be able to decide political questions with wisdom and understanding. In the absence of such a ruler, the State should be governed by law.[21]

As we can see above, Plato makes a distinction between the rule by someone who possesses the "art of ruling" and the rule by law. The rule by law can only be the second best: laws are necessarily imperfect, because they always use the same description, even if the circumstances are different. On the other hand, laws have positive value: they are largely based on experience, and have the right kinds of advocates for them, such as general descriptions. Provided, then, that they are based on the prevailing law, the existing forms of institution will offer some kind of framework for living in the absence of the true statesman. While Plato evidently considers it possible that true statesmen will turn up, he now asks whether it is likely that they will. In the Republic he was preoccupied with urging the need for a philosophical rule; in the Statesman, he views that ideal from the perspective of the conditions of ordinary life, and recognizes just how difficult it will be to achieve that philosophical rule.[22]

The Statesman offers a solution to the problem of the origin of the world. It contains a lengthy mythical account of the divine government of the world. The cyclical motion of the heavens is due to God's periodic action, infusing new vitality into the cycles. The myth's emphasis on the world's need for God's vitalizing influence is significant: the world is more than a mere matter.[23]

Best of all will be the rule of an expert individual, the true king, who is able to govern on the basis of knowledge of eternal verities as well as of practical skill, though it is the latter on which great stress is laid in this context. But men with prerequisite intellect, and moral qualities do not accede to the rulership naturally in the way the queen bee does in a hive. Therefore, men have to come together and draw up codes of law, pursuing the traces of the most rightful constitution; and as a result are the inferior types of rule. They are all difficult to live under, but they can be put in order of preference.[24]

To conclude, one can say that in the Statesman Plato wants to emphasize the Ruler's personal abilities to take good care of the State. He can have an inherent talent for this, but he can also learn the skill to rule by his own personal vision, notwithstanding the rules and laws binding the common citizen. A True Leader must have this charismatic trait, and also be able to apply it in practice, on his own agenda.

The Laws—Laws as a Paradigmatic Basis for Ruling a State

In his old age Plato remained intellectually active. His later dialogues show a mind still flexible and fertile. No doubt his contacts with the younger thinkers at the Academia helped him to retain his own intellectual vitality. The later dialogues may lack the sparkling humour and the vivid manner of expression which make the earlier dialogues so read-able, but they present new ideas, new forms of argument, and new tech-niques of dialectical reasoning; they address new questions, and ap-proach familiar questions in new ways. The *Laws* is Plato's last work. It is a substantial work, as large as the Republic. It suffers from faults in style and certain dryness: it is the work of an old man determined to write down and publish the ideas he believes to be important. Plato is racing with the calendar as he writes the Laws, the style is of little concern to him. And the things he has to say are new.[25]

The Laws is a work which also reminds us that Plato has an impartial interest in political philosophy. The Laws' concern is the nature of a soci-ety in which virtue is universally inculcated. In the first parts of this very comprehensive work the emphasis is upon the nature of the inculcation; in the later parts, there are discussions on practical proposals for legisla-tion to be enacted in the imaginary about-to-be-founded Cretan city of Magnesia. As with the society of the Republic, there is to be a hierarchical order of the rulers and the ruled in the city. As with the society of the Re-public, true virtue is only possible for those who belong to the clearly confined class of rulers. But in the Republic the whole emphasis lies upon the education of the rulers. In the Laws, nothing like this can be found. In the Republic the education of the rulers is put forth as further-going and more exact than that of the mass of the citizens, whereas in the Laws the positive development of desirable habits and traits takes the place of re-strictions. The citizens are encouraged to live in accordance with virtue, and both education and laws are to nurture them in this way of life. But when they live in this way, it is because they have been conditioned and habituated to such a way of life, and not because they would understand the point of it.[26] That understanding is still the privilege of the rulers. This opinion emerges most clearly in the discussion about the gods.

In the Laws the existence of the Divine has become the cornerstone of morals and politics. "The greatest question . . . is whether we do or do not think rightly about the gods and so live well". The Divine is important in the Laws because it is identified with the law: to be obedient before the law is to be obedient before the gods. The Divine also seems to represent the general primacy of spirit over matter, soul over body. Ordinary people are induced to believe in the gods, because it is important that all men who at-tend to human affairs and who are not subject to human weakness in that respect should believe in the gods. But the rulers are to be men who have toiled their way to acquire the complete confidence in the existence of the gods by intellectual effort. What others regard as a result of conditioning and tradition they have grasped by using rational proof. Plato's determina-tion to uphold paternalistic and totalitarian politics is clearly independent of any particular version of the theory of the Forms.

The Laws, like the Republic, pays a great deal of attention to education. Education is regarded as the cornerstone of the State—that is, education in virtue which is in essence understood in terms of educating our desires. Full virtue, no doubt, would still include wisdom, but the basic requirement is that we should desire the right things. Once again, it is asserted that virtuous life is the happiest; it is the best and most pleasant for us: if it were not, the task of persuading people to choose it would be difficult.[27]

The conclusion may be drawn that the Laws puts forth such a concept of leadership that stresses the meaning of laws and common rules in addition to the leader's personal power. He must obey and act according to the laws made by some common government organ. This practice will prevent the abuse of the leader's personal power.

Implications for Modern Leadership-Thinking

We can find several areas in Plato's discourse which come close to modern leadership debate. These issues are, for example:

- debates on charisma in leadership
- symbols and leadership; leadership as heroical action
- debate on the nature of managerial work, and especially, the possibility to be a statesman-leader in business, expressed by the words of Richard Norman[28]
- justice in managerial work: in many managerial routines is it possible to be a just leader of the organization?
- in the field of organizational theory: organizational equilibrium versus conflict
- the management of meaning
- truth-manipulating and totalitarian aspects of leadership

Of course, several other issues can be identified, but in my opinion those mentioned above are the most important topics. Next I will take some of them under closer scrutiny.

Discussion on Statesmen Leadership

In his book *Creative Leadership* (orig. publ. 1975), Richard Norman puts forth the concept of statesman leadership. He states that the function of a *statesman leader* (STL) is to balance the totality formed by several business branches. The main task of the STL is to take care that the political system of many businesses is functioning well. To handle and relax tensions existing between the various parts of an organization is one of the main tasks of the STL. But, contrary to Plato, Norman sees those tensions as creative and fruitful tools for making a better organization. The STL must be a person who is able to restrain these tensions, but he must also create new tensions in order to renew the organization.

Discussion on Charisma

Charisma, in terms used by Max Weber, means literally "the gift of grace". It is used by Weber to characterize self-appointed leaders followed by people who are in distress and who need to follow the leader because they believe him to be extraordinarily qualified. The charismatic leaders' actions are enthusiastic, and in such extraordinary enthusiasm, class and status barriers sometimes give way to fraternization and exuberant community sentiments. For this reason, charismatic heroes and prophets are viewed as truly revolutionary forces in history.[29] Weber emphasizes that the charismatic leader is self-ordained and self-styled. The background for this self-styling is the charismatic leader's "mission". This causes that his action is his destiny. The role of a follower is to acknowledge this destiny, and the authority of genuine charisma is derived from the duty of the followers to recognize the leader.[30] The very nature of charismatic authority is unstable; this is because the source of charisma is continuously "moving on". It will never be stable and unchanging.

Charismatic leadership usually arises in times of crisis when the basic values, the institutions, and the legitimacy of the organization are brought into question. Genuine charisma is connected with something "new". And in extraordinary situations this "new" calls forth a charismatic authoritarian structure so that charisma, at least temporarily, leads to actions, movements, and events which are extraordinary, not routine, and outside the sphere of everyday life. The evocation of pure charisma and charismatic leadership always leads, at least temporarily, away from the world of everyday life; it rejects or transcends routine life. Just because pure charisma and charismatic leadership conflict with the existing, the self-evident, the established order, they work like a catalyst in an organization. But charisma is the specifically creative force in an organization only briefly before being unavoidably transformed or routinized into some more solid form.[31]

The legitimacy of charisma and charismatic leadership is sociologically and psychologically an attribute of the belief of the followers and not so much the quality of the leader. The leader is in this respect important because he can "charismatically" evoke this sense of belief and can thereby demand obedience. Weber thought that the unavoidable fate of charisma is routinization and institutionalization. Pure charisma is personal, direct, radical, extraordinary, and the authority of charisma is based on belief, after which the charismatic leadership as a movement is successful, then charisma becomes ordinary; charismatic leadership becomes routinized, depersonalized, and deradicalized. Therefore, the nature of belief may also be transformed. Considering the features of the Weberian pure charisma it seems that this type of authoritarian structure describes more a pre-modern (like ancient Grecian) society and form of organization. Especially pure charisma and charismatic leadership as an antieconomic force, characterized by great pathos; followers constituting genuine discipleship; and charismatic leadership pointing in a revolutionary and antiroutine way to something transcendent, hint rather to the premodern direction.[32]

Charisma is foreign to economic and efficiency-based considerations. Hence, in modern business organizations, a tight reign has to be kept on charisma. Too much counting on charisma, and the economic survival of the firm may be threatened. More appropriate to a muddled organization is the notion that charisma can move from one person to another who makes different decisions. Charisma can provide a vital driving force to decision making viewed through the eyes of e.g. the "garbage can" describing of organizational action. In it the participants are coming to the can and leaving it, carrying along their solution: an impulse to participants, the problems, and the solutions how to merge them together and make a choice that could be of use. But different solutions will bring different individuals together. When the relation between the goal and the means is unclear and there are uncertainties over the goals to be reached, inspirational decision-making seems to be the only way for decision-makers to cause action. Charisma would offer a solution to this problem but there is no reason why charisma should permanently reside in one and the same person.[33]

Plato's view of leadership, as a normative standpoint, was that a leader must be a man of power with a sincerely truth-seeking vision. This point of view comes close to the Weberian concept of charisma discussed above. Plato sees that a leader must have charisma, the gift of grace, to be successful in his actions. Without it a leader is not able to do his job, to be the head of an organization. And this charisma is something mystical which cannot be obtained by force or by training. It is of divine origin.

Discussion on the Management of Meaning

Discussion about management's "new" imperatives, like management by objectives, management by results etc., have been evolving. One of them is the discussion called the management of meaning. It has many roots, e.g. Bennis (1984) would suggest a view of strategic management as "the management of meaning." This concept is later elaborated, with more conceptual depth, by Smircich and Morgan (1982) and Smircich and Stubbart (1985).

In the background is the idea that organizations are socially constructed systems of shared meanings. So, the task of management, especially strategic management, is to create symbolic reality, and to facilitate action. Smircich and Stubbart refer to recent studies, where "the management of meaning" has been shown to be accomplished through values and their symbolic expressions, dramas and language. Broms and Gahmberg have found some examples of classical myths used in situational applications. Such are, for instance, the myth of rebirth, or the story of the Phoenix bird, in occasions of crisis and turn-around operations, or the myth of the Argonauts in biographies of famous leaders.[34]

The key challenge for a leader is to manage meaning in such a way that individuals orient themselves to the achievement of desirable end. In this endeavor the use of language, ritual, drama, stories, myths, and symbolic construction of all kinds play an important role. They constitute important tools for the management of meaning. Through words and images, symbolic actions, and gestures, leaders can structure attention and evoke patterns of meaning which give them considerable control over the situation being managed. Leadership rests as much in these symbolic modes of action as in those instrumental modes of management, direction, and control which define the substance of the leader's formal organizational role.[35]

So, it is said in the modern leadership studies that the task of strategic management is to rule the new and continuously changing situation by creating and using myths, symbols, metaphors etc. As we have seen previously, Plato sees the myths, metaphors and "stories" as inevitable forces in societal life. In the same way, he considers that it belongs to a leader's normative agenda to develop such means of symbolical leading.

The connections to the charisma-debate are also clear, if a leader wants to be charismatic, he must develop his skill of using symbols, metaphors etc. in his managerial work. So, the management of meaning discussion, and the charisma discussion are heavily interwoven.

Ethical Evaluation of the Truth-Manipulating and Totalitarian Aspects of Leadership

The problem with the stability in charismatic leadership has to be acknowledged. This question is also connected with the truth-manipulating and totalitarian aspects of leadership. As it has been said, the tendency of charisma to be routinized is an in-built feature of this phenomenon. Max Weber recognized that a certain degree of routinization is bound to occur almost as soon as the initial charisma of the leader is acknowledged by others and the next stage of charisma is developing.

This means that pure charisma is stable by its nature. It means that a leader who wants to possess charisma must resist this tendency towards routinization because it may lead to a totalitarian system or truth-manipulating operations.

To evaluate the totalitarian or truth-manipulating aspects of leadership is not an easy task. In this evaluation we must rest on some traditional ethical theories, like deontologism and utilitarianism. A utilitarian charismatic leader may argue that he uses truth-manipulating means if the outcome of these kinds of actions will achieve the maximum good to a maximum number of people. This logic involves several problems, e.g. how to determine the measure of "good" and define the number of people whose happiness has to be maximized. Deontological ethical theories like Kantianism offer a better solution for a charismatic leader to evaluate his behaviour in complex ethical decision-making situations. The duty to obey moral law or human rights obliges the leader not to misuse his charisma for "bad" practices. The leader's own conscience can also show the way to ethically good decisions and actions. Often charismatic leaders fail in this task. Like Hitler or Stalin, they use their power for inhuman deeds. However, some leaders, like Jesus or Gandhi, are good examples of ethically good leaders. They have the power but they use it for well-meaning purposes. Plato is a question mark in this respect. He is said to be the forefather of the totalitarian constitution (Popper). However, as it has been put forth in this paper, Plato is seen more as speaker on behalf of good leadership with truth-seeking visions.

Final Comments

An excursion has been made of Plato's world of ideas. This consideration consists of many different areas. We have seen that Plato has been one of the most influential organizational thinkers through the ages. A long time ago he has presented many themes which have been thought to be "modern," and during the 20th century his ideas have been further developed by the leadership theoreticians of our time. First, Plato has put forth the theory of an organization as a harmony-seeking entity, and in this way given a benchmark for modern organizational theoreticians stressing the unitary and well-balanced nature of modern complex organizations. Second, the concept of the management of meaning, or *leadership* as the management of meaning, has been evolved. Putting focus on the way the meaning is created, sustained and changed in organizational settings provides us with powerful means to understand the fundamental nature of leadership as a social process. This social process includes all those means by which management creates new meanings by rituals, symbolizing and "naming". As we have seen, all these elements are included in

Plato's leadership philosophy. Third, the debate on the attributes of a powerful leader is also in the focus of Plato's thinking. This notion leads us to the present debate on *charisma*, and to its role in today's management practices. A leader must possess charisma, the gift of grace, in order to be successful in his actions. Without it the leader is not able to do his job, to be the head of some complex organization. Max Weber, the forefather of the modern charisma debate, may agree with us: Plato is an ancient, but still fresh and actual developer of the leadership theory. And it is a theory that is always needed.

Notes

1. See Yukl, p. 2.
2. See Sayles, p. 29.
3. Op. cit. Yukl, p. 3.
4. Op. cit. Yukl, p. 3.
5. See Yukl, pp. 3–4.
6. Knuutila, p. 34.
7. See Kanerva, p. 18.
8. See Kanerva, p. 19.
9. See Asmus, p. 27.
10. See Asmus, p. 63.
11. Popper, p. 14.
12. See Tenkku, p. 58.
13. See Melling, pp. 46, 51.
14. See Rowe, p. 153.
15. E.g., see Melling, p. 84.
16. See Popper, p. 210.
17. See Melling, p. 86.
18. See Melling, p. 86, Kanerva, p. 23.
19. See Tenkku, p. 78.
20. See Melling, p. 158.
21. Melling, p. 158.
22. Rowe, p. 157.
23. See Melling, p. 151.
24. See Rowe, p. 138.
25. See Melling, p. 158.
26. See Hamlyn, p. 54.
27. See Rowe, p. 141.
28. See Norman, pp. 150.
29. See Gerth and Mills, p. 52 (op. cit. Pekonen).
30. See Pekonen, p. 13.
31. See Pekonen, p. 14.
32. See Pekonen, p. 15.
33. See Butler, p. 244.
34. See Gahmberg, p. 152.
35. See Smircich and Morgan.

References

Original Sources
(Edition used in Finnish):
Platon: Teokset I–VII (Plato: Works (I–VII). Keuruu. 1977–1989.
Gorgias
Pidot (Symposium)
Valtio (Republic)
Valtiomies (Statesman)
Lait (Laws)

Other Sources
Alvesson, M.: 1987, "The Culture Perspective on Organizations", *Scandinavian Management Journal* 5(2), 123–136.
Asmus, V.: 1977, *Platon* (Moskova).
Aspelin, G.: 1953, *Ajatuksen tiet. Porvoo* (The Ways of Ideas, only in Finnish).
Banner, D. and J. Blasingame: 1988, "Towards a Developmental Paradigm of Leadership", *Leadership and Organizational Development Journal* 9(4).
Bennis, W.: 1984, "The 4 Competencies of Leadership", *Training and Development Journal* (August), 15–19.
Butler, R.: 1991, *Designing Organizations* (New York).
Deal, T. and A. Kennedy: 1982, *Corporate Culture* (New York).
Fiedler, F. E.: 1964, "A Contingency Model of Leadership Effectiveness", in L. Berkowitz (ed.) *Advances in Experimental Social Psychology* (New York).
Finley, K.: 1986, *Politics in Ancient World* (London).
Gahmberg, J.: 1990, *Metaphor Management: On the Semiotics of Strategic Leadership*, Teoksessa Turner, B.: Organizational Symbolism (New York).
Gerth, H. and C.W. Mills (eds.): 1964, *From Max Weber: Essays in Sociology* (New York).
Hamlyn, D.W.: 1987, *The Penguin History of Western Philosophy* (London).
Hofstede, G.: 1980, *Culture's Consequences* (London).
Knuutila, S.: 1981, Aristoteles (Aristotle). Teoksessa Kanerva, J. (toim.): Politiikan teorian klassikoita. Juva. 1981 (The Classics of Political Theory, only in Finnish).
Lewin, K., R. Lippit and R.K. White: 1939, "Patterns of Aggressive Behaviour in Experimentally Created 'Social Climates'", *Journal of Social Psychology* 10, 271–279.
Likert, R.: 1967, *The Human Organizations* (New York).
Mac Intyre, A.: 1980, *A Short History of Ethics* (London).
Melling, D.: 1988, *Understanding Plato* (Oxford).
Norman, R.: 1983, *Luova Yritysjohto*. Keuruu (Creative Leadership, only in Finnish).
Pekonen, K.: 1986, "Charismatic Leadership and the Role of Image in Modern Politics", *Studia Politica Jyvaskylaensia*.
Popper, K.: 1972, *Open Society and Its Enemies* (London).
Rowe, C.: 1984, *Plato* (Sussex).
Sayles, L. R.: 1979, *What Effective Managers Really Do and How They Do It* (New York).

Schein, E.: 1985, *Organizational Culture and Leadership* (San Francisco).
Smircich, L. and G. Morgan: 1982, "Strategic Management in an Enacted World", *Academy of Management Review* 10(4).
Stogdill, R.: 1974, *Handbook of Leadership* (New York).
Tarkiainen, T.: 1959, *Demokratia—Antiikin Ateenan Kansanvalta* (Helsinki) (On the Democracy of the Ancient Athens, only in Finnish).
Tenkku, J.: 1983, *Vanhan-ha Keskiajan moraalifilosofian historia* (Porvoo) (The History of Moral Philosophy in Antique and Medieval Times, only in Finnish).
Yukl, G.: 1989, *Leadership in Organizations* (New Jersey).

14

Napoleon's Tragic March Home from Moscow

Lessons in Hubris

MARK J. KROLL

LESLIE A. TOOMBS

PETER WRIGHT

> *Napoleon, supreme egoist that he was, ignored the significance of the omens until he and his host were completely and irrevocably committed to an undertaking that was doomed. Never did the gods punish hubris more severely.*
> —*M. de Fezensac*, **The Russian Campaign, 1812**[1]

In June of 1812, Napoleon Bonaparte was ruler of the Empire of France, King of Italy, and master of the European continent. At the head of The Grand Army, numbering over 500,000 men, the largest force ever assembled at that point in history, he set out to conquer the one nation in Europe he had not yet subjugated—Imperial Russia. In December of the same year, less than 20,000 of those men would make it home alive, and as a practical matter, all that Emperor Napoleon had accomplished in his meteoric career would soon be lost. The tragedy of the Russian campaign, the loss of life, and the horrible suffering of those on the march back from Moscow have been a source of fascination for historians ever since. Explanations for the disaster include poor planning, unusually bad weather, insightful leadership on the opposing side, and plain bad luck. But, as indicated by our epigraph, almost all accounts of the campaign include a recognition of the role played by hubris.[2]

Hubris has been defined as exaggerated pride, self-confidence, or arrogance, frequently resulting in retribution.[3] Hubris may be blamed for the

Reprinted with permission, from *Academy of Management Executive* 14, 1 (February 2000), pp. 117–127. Copyright Academy of Management.

resounding failure of Napoleon's campaign because Napoleon possessed all its symptoms: unbounded confidence given his past successes and the accompanying narcissism, the adulation that fed that narcissism, and his callous indifference toward the rules that governed 19th Century geopolitics. As a result, Napoleon was able to convince himself that, despite all of the obvious obstacles, he could, through force of will, succeed in bringing Russia and especially Emperor Alexander I, the sole power on the Continent that refused to pay him homage, to their knees. His campaign was much less about the need to thwart the hostile intentions of a rival power, and more about the need to satisfy a hubris-infected personality with an arrogant confidence about what great feats could be accomplished.

One frequently cited explanation for hubris is that leaders often hunger for reassurance and applause from others. This hunger may first arise when a child's narcissistic displays are fondly received by parents.[4] As such leaders grow and become a part of groups or organizations, however, they may seek the same adulation from organization members in response to their displays of skill.

Those who excel in select skills may receive positive feedback from others as they produce beneficial results. Napoleon clearly excelled in the skills of warfare, as he planned and implemented winning campaigns. Before the Russian attack, Napoleon had amassed a record of 35 wins versus only 3 losses. The losses were either early in his career, and then forgotten, or were only very temporary setbacks from which he quickly recovered. Through these warfare experiences, he developed a distinctive approach to command, along with considerable confidence in that approach. By the time of the Russian Campaign, however, this confidence had turned into arrogance and a sense of invincibility. Worse, given his record, he appears to have believed that unique problems of a war with Russia were minor details that the force of will could surmount.

In the contemporary corporate arena, actions such as takeovers, corporate expansion programs, and blatant disregard of the rules of the game may reflect the presence of hubris. These actions sometimes suggest that the firm's management believes that the world, and the major forces in it, including financial markets, government regulators, and competitors, are wrong, and that they are right, and are not governed by the same forces. As with Napoleon's Grand Army, corporate hubris is often punished severely. We will take a look at three circumstances in which hubris may set businesses and their leaders down a perilous path—corporate acquisitions, unbridled growth for its own sake, and disregard for the rules. Parallels are drawn with Napoleon's circumstances.

Corporate Acquisitions

Well before the invasion of Russia, Napoleon's top lieutenants argued that the chances of failure, and the cost in lives and materiel were high. Napoleon rejected their warnings, pointing out that his plans called for a quick, decisive, and therefore low-cost campaign. He had conducted such campaigns before, and saw no difference this time.[5] Richard Roll has suggested that all too frequently takeover attempts result from an executive's belief that he or she can greatly improve the target firm's efficiency. The executive rejects feedback from others and, in particular, the wisdom of the financial markets,[6] even though it is generally recognized that the securities markets provide accurate feedback by doing a fairly effective job of valuing publicly traded firms.[7] The premiums executives sometimes pay over target firms' prevailing market prices often reflect a Napoleonic logic: "I will be able to overcome all the obstacles and make the acquired business far more successful than its incumbent management; I can turn a profit on the deal in spite of the high price I am paying."

However, compelling research evidence shows that corporate acquisitions driven by managerial hubris are often financially harmful for the shareholders of acquiring firms.[8] It also appears that as the level of managerial hubris rises, so does the likelihood that a firm will grossly overpay for an acquisition.[9] Compounding the problem of overpayment is the possibility that managerial hubris will undermine the process of integrating the acquired and acquiring firms. There is the very real threat that the acquiring firm's management, imbued with a sense of conquest, will treat the acquired firm's management and employees as conquered supplicants. This is especially likely if the acquiring firm is perceived as having a better track record than the acquired firm.[10] The inevitable results are a failure to achieve potential synergies and a loss of talent from the acquired firm. Both outcomes will exacerbate the initial overpayment problem.

An example of potential corporate hubris in an acquisition is the buyout of WordPerfect by Novell in March 1994. Novell's CEO, Raymond Noorda, offered $1.4 billion for WordPerfect, in what industry observers suggested was an attempt to build a software empire comparable to Microsoft's. Following the acquisition, Novell reportedly ran roughshod over WordPerfect's management and culture, leading to a hemorrhage of managerial and technical talent and a significant deterioration in the performance of WordPerfect. In early 1996, Novell was forced to sell WordPerfect for about $124 million, or less than 10 percent of what it paid for the firm in 1994.[11]

Unbridled Growth for Its Own Sake

Hubris can also manifest itself in a drive to dominate others and engage in empire building for its own sake. Napoleon's determination to invade Russia was driven not only by a desire to take over that country, but also by a burning ambition to dominate Czar Alexander. The Czar was the only European monarch Napoleon had not subjugated, and by doing so Napoleon would have become the sole master of Europe. The same need for domination and empire building may surface in the corporate world. It is generally recognized that individual executives infected with hubris have narcissistic requirements that demand they control fiefdoms of such large scale as to justify their own importance.[12] An executive infected with hubris will likely see growth as a means of building a bureaucracy of sufficient size to reflect his or her prominence. For instance, the rise and fall of the Saatchi & Saatchi advertising empire in the l990s reflected the ambition of a pair of brothers who no longer concerned themselves with building a profitable advertising business.[13] Instead, they aspired for dominance by building an advertising empire that was the very biggest, only to be forced out of the business they had built. Similarly, Barclay's Bank under CEO Sir John Quinton went on a quest to become Britain's largest bank in the early l990s. This attempt also failed and Sir John was forced to abdicate.[14]

Blatant Disregard of the Rules

Napoleon rose to power during the French Revolution, having been an officer in the army of the First Republic.[15] After establishing a winning record at the head of the Grand Army, he decided that he merited the title of first council or dictator, and later named himself emperor. These blatant power grabs were undertaken in spite of his earlier pledges of fidelity to the republic and its democratic ideals. He evidently concluded that obligations to the French people and living up to oaths were for others to fulfill.[16]

Managers afflicted with hubris can also create a climate in which they and the organizations they govern do not play by the same rules as everyone else.[17] For example, observers have remarked on the indifference of the managers of Archer Daniels Midland Company to the laws they broke and how the long-time CEO, Dwayne O. Andreas, allowed an anything-goes culture to develop.[18] Such hubris-prone personalities are likely to perceive themselves as having made great sacrifices and contributions that entitle them to special dispensation.[19]

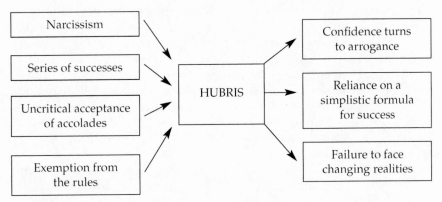

FIGURE 14.1   Sources and Implications of Hubris

Sources of Hubris

As illustrated in Figure 14.1, hubris has four sources: a personality prone to narcissism; a string of successes that feed the narcissism; blindly believing the accolades of others, particularly the media; and a history of getting away with breaking the rules. All these conditions can lead executives to believe that they are above the rules.[20]

Narcissism

Hubris derives from an overbearing sense of grandiosity, need for admiration, and self-absorption—in a word, narcissism. Narcissism is commonly found in many successful people, and it often compels them to seek leadership positions, with their accompanying power, status, and self-affirmation.[21] However, narcissism can drive executives to use their leadership roles to create a reality that further reinforces their narcissism.[22] Even very charismatic leaders may use their leadership talents to gain position and status in order to satisfy their narcissism at the expense of others.[23] In *War and Peace*, Tolstoy comments on Napoleon's narcissism: "He alone—with his ideal of glory and grandeur developed in Italy and Egypt, his insane self-adulation, could justify what had to be done."[24]

A number of business analysts have attributed Quaker Oats's disastrous acquisition of Snapple Beverages in part to the hubris of Quaker's management. Quaker's then CEO, William Smithburg, had made some very successful moves earlier in his tenure, often proving the pundits wrong. The company's Gatorade purchase won Smithburg praise in the business press. Observers believe he saw in Snapple an opportunity to surpass past triumphs and establish Quaker as a force to be reckoned with in the beverage industry. In spite of the consensus view of Wall Street analysts that Quaker was paying at least double what Snapple was worth, Quaker paid $1.7 billion for the firm. Even worse, perhaps owing to their extreme confidence in their ability to turn things around, Quaker's management went ahead with the purchase in spite of strong indications that Snapple was in the process of imploding. On the day the deal was announced, Quaker's stock dropped $7.38, or over 10 percent.[25]

It is possible that the need to create a reality that fits an executive's narcissistic vision, even though it materially departs from actual facts, may often lead to organizational underperformance. Narcissism may be reinforced by subordinates who, having little sense of control over the world around them, look to and idolize a leader they believe can deal with the helplessness they feel.[26] The leader's apparent confidence and pride fulfill the needs of followers for someone to bring order and stability to their lives.[27] They in turn feed the leader's narcissism, which transforms his or her self-confidence into arrogance.[28] Napoleon arrived on the French political stage in the midst of the confusion of post-revolutionary France. The population, exhausted by 10 years of violence and uncertainty, undoubtedly saw in Bonaparte the firm hand that could at last take the helm. Napoleon fed on that need. Having taken great pains to rid themselves of a royal monarchy in 1789, many French people embraced Napoleon as another type of monarch, consul for life, further contributing to his narcissism and hubris.

Series of Successes

Narcissism and hubris feed on further successes. As an executive accumulates a record of accomplishment, his or her susceptibility to hubris tends to grow.[29] Indeed, a consistent theme that runs through the various accounts of Napoleon's career is the inclination for his narcissism and hubris to grow with each successful campaign.[30] Following his successes in Italy, for instance, he remarked to one of his officers:

> They haven't seen anything yet, and the future holds successes for us far beyond what we have so far accomplished. Fortune is a woman, and the more she does for me, the more I will demand from her. In our day no one has conceived anything great; it is for me to give an example.[31]

In the context of contemporary business, the relationship between hubris and prior success and subsequent egoism makes particular sense when one recognizes that the executives of most organizations take disproportionate credit for high firm performance.[32] The valuable stock options and the lofty salaries American executives receive (mean executive total compensation in 1998 for the top 800 chief executives in the U.S. was $6.5 million) tend to reinforce the credit executives take for corporate performance.[33] Napoleon similarly took full credit for all the victories of the Grand Army. When Napoleon set off for Moscow at the head of an army of half a million soldiers, he had compiled an extraordinary win-loss record. In one 16-month period, beginning in November 1805, he had won the battles of Ulm, Austerlitz, Auerstadt, Eylau, and Freidland against the Austrians, Russians, and Prussians, making him the toast of Paris. This inclination on the part of most leaders to attribute successes primarily to their own actions[34] may be a natural one. Leaders may visualize how their own behavior brought about success and they may see a clear and linear connection between the two. If they had not initiated certain actions, accordingly, the desirable outcomes attained would probably not have occurred.

Uncritical Acceptance of Accolades

The third source of hubris is a natural outgrowth of the first—leaders come to believe the exaggerated accolades they receive from others. Praise from others, particularly the press, is likely to intensify hubris because it confirms and legitimizes an executive's narcissism and reinforces the executive's own feelings of grandiosity. As his or her fame spreads, especially in the media, the executive's hubris is in effect ratified.[35] Napoleon was widely heralded as a military genius of the first order. If he did not think of himself as the master of Europe early in his career, the newspapers of the day certainly helped him perpetuate this image. For instance, the *Journal de Paris* reported in 1807 that "He [Napoleon] was invincible, grateful to God, forceful, modest, clever, magnanimous . . . and he combined the qualities of all the great men of history."[36]

Contemporary leaders may become more susceptible to hubris as the press increasingly focuses on them. The press, however, may not present a balanced view of leaders.[37] An excellent example of someone who recognized the extremes in which the press can portray individuals is James Carville, a key strategist in President Clinton's 1992 campaign. Shortly after the 1992 election, Carville was heralded as a political strategy genius. He acknowledged the accolades, but also pointed out that he had managed failing campaigns, and had received a heavy dose of criticism in the press. He said he knew he was not as good as the press made him out to be following Clinton's election, just as he knew he was not as bad as the press had portrayed him in his defeats.[38]

Exemption from the Rules

Finally, those possessed by hubris tend to be part of a group that Freud referred to as "the exceptions" to the rules, people with a history of breaking the rules, inflicting sacrifice on others, and getting away with it.[39] Narcissistic personalities are predisposed to break the rules because they tend to possess a sense of independence from the norms that govern others. This sense of independence from norms not only may be accompanied by a willingness to exploit others, but also to lack of empathy for them.[40]

Napoleon's behavior dramatically illustrates these inclinations. He consistently broke all of the 18th century rules limiting the scope of destructiveness of warfare. He encouraged his troops to loot the countries through which they passed rather than rely on provisions from France. During the 1796 Italian campaign, he invaded the neutral Duchy of Parma in order to escape a trap laid by the Austrians. Having overrun the Duchy for convenience, he also took hostage the governor of the capital city of Piacenze to make it easier to loot the city.[41] Following the Russian campaign, with loss of life in the hundreds of thousands, he issued his famous 29th Bulletin, blaming the massive losses on the weather, but adding that "His Majesty's health has never been better."[42] On returning to Paris, Napoleon ordered lavish receptions and balls. An officer who attended one gala later commented: "I felt I was dancing on tombs."[43]

Breaking the rules has its counterpart in contemporary business. For instance, in August 1991, Salomon Brothers, a major bond trading house, admitted to a host of Treasury Department rule violations. These revelations caused the Treasury Department to suspend the firm's trading privileges and forced the resignation of the top three officers. From the accounts of both insiders and outsiders familiar with the firm, the violations were a direct result of what acting Salomon chairman Warren Buffett referred to as the firm's "macho and cavalier culture." Salomon's bond traders regularly flouted Treasury Department regulations designed specifically to rein in Salomon's excesses. Salomon's traders simply did not agree with the rules. This cultural deficiency appears to have been tolerated by Salomon's former CEO, John Gutfreund, who once told the *Economist* he was out for "the money, the power and the glory."[44]

Implications of Hubris

When senior managers succumb to hubris, they are likely to engage in behavior that reflects that hubris—confidence to the point of arrogance, relying on simplistic formulas for success, and failing to face changing realities.[45] All of these can be very costly to the firm in various ways.

Confidence Turns to Arrogance

Individuals possessed with hubris have an overbearing confidence in their abilities to make events conform to their will in spite of contrary external evidence. They believe that whatever external problems might arise will be easily and willfully overcome.[46] For example, Napoleon was advised by several of his senior officers that an attack on Russia was foolhardy. In fact, Napoleon's close friend and one-time ambassador to the Russian Court, General Armand Louis de Caulaincourt, recounted to Napoleon Czar Alexander's explanation of how Russia would defeat him:

> It will not be a one-day war. Your [Emperor] will be obliged to return to Paris to manage his affairs [after a long absence], and every advantage will be with the Russians. Then the winter, the cruel climate, and most important of all, my determination and avowed intention to prolong the struggle, and not, like so many monarchs, have the weakness to sign a peace treaty in my own capital. All these will take their toll.[47]

To this prophetic report, Napoleon responded with complete indifference, dismissing Czar Alexander's observations with the comment, "One good battle will knock the bottoms out of my friend Alexander's fine resolutions. He is fickle and feeble."[48]

This pattern of behavior is also evident in modern corporate takeovers. As mentioned earlier, the acquisition of Snapple by Quaker Oats appears to have been largely the result of management's assumption that it possessed unique talents that could breathe new life into Snapple. This high level of confidence appears to have been so strong that even a rapidly deteriorating situation at Snapple and an exorbitant price tag could not dissuade the Quaker Oats managers. The net result was Quaker's later having to divest Snapple and write off a $1.4 billion loss.[49]

Relying on a Simplistic Formula for Success

Another ramification of hubris is the tendency for leaders to develop what they perceive as their own unique and ingenious formulas for success. Such formulas, having served well in the past, are reapplied in many situations. In effect, leaders may reduce their strategy formulation and implementation to predictable action plans.[50] Napoleon's Russian campaign clearly reflected a reliance on what had worked well in the past, to the point that former innovations became standard operating procedure. This predictability served the Russians well, as General Michael Barclay de Tolly and Major General Prince Golenishchev-Kutuzov both consistently refused to play by Napoleon's established rules of warfare.

In an attempt to repeat past successes, Napoleon had sought to quickly engage the Russians early in the campaign in order to divide and destroy their army with overwhelming, decisive force. Quick and decisive engagements had worked well for Napoleon in Austria, Italy, and Prussia. Knowing this, both Russian commanders, and especially Kutuzov, baited the enemy with rear-guard attacks, followed by further retreats into Russia. These compelled Napoleon to follow the Russians, in the hope that perhaps at the next major city the sought-after engagement would occur. These pursuits progressively stretched his lines of supply and communication thinner.

Reliance on a simple formula has its counterpart in the world of business. A famous example is the strategy of General Motors in the 1970s. Company executives were committed to their big car, rear-wheel-drive formula for success despite the industry's changing around them. Well into the 1970s, and even after several oil shocks, GM's managers still clung to the belief that the land yacht products of the 1950s and 1960s would again prevail.[51] The commitment to this formula resulted in GM's market share dropping from 49 percent to 28 percent over two decades.[52]

Failure to Face Changing Realities

Another ramification of hubris is the tendency to create a simplified scanning process, selectively screening for external environmental cues that were previously relevant in implementing a time-tested formula for success. This screening process tends to exclude those environmental factors that have previously not been critical to implementing the formula for success. One of Napoleon's previous experiences had been that local populations often viewed him as a liberator. This reaction allowed him to provision his army and avoid attacks by partisans. Because Russia was a feudal society, he anticipated the same reaction from local peasants. Instead, he was subject to incessant attacks by roving bands of Cossack partisans.

Senior executives of General Motors similarly exercised an external scanning process so simple that they did not even consider it necessary to establish a consumer market research department until 1985.[53] In fact, GM's competitive analysis in the early 1970s consisted largely of assessing the threats that its own Pontiac and Buick divisions posed for each other. Rarely did the analysis scrutinize the threats posed by Ford and Chrysler, much less by the Japanese auto-makers.[54]

Given the obvious dangers hubris represents to a successful firm's future success, we will look at remedies both for the individual executive and the board of directors.

What Executives Can Do to Guard Against Hubris

A sincere self-examination of an executive's leadership behaviors may be the best place to start. Asking questions such as, "Am I willing to take the counsel of others when those ideas are counter to my own views of circumstances?" and "What do I need to do to improve my abilities to help the organization move forward?" will be helpful in this self-examination process.

Reflect on One's Own Performance

Managers sometimes exhibit the natural human tendency to attribute successes to their own actions, while blaming failures on external forces.[55] Those managers who have the capacity to recognize their own culpability in poor firm performance, however, tend to be more successful in the long-term.[56] Thus, to combat the tendency to blame externalities, managers need to confront their own failures. For instance, Daimler-Benz was an organization that by the 1980s had experienced enough success to infuse its managers with hubris. By the 1990s, according to industry observers, the firm had fallen victim to its managers' arrogance, as demonstrated by its deteriorating performance. Jurgen Schrempp had presided over the unbridled growth of Daimler's aerospace division before becoming the CEO. However, Schrempp was reflective enough to realize that the decline in Daimler-Benz's fortunes was due as much to internal problems as to the downturn in Europe's economy. Schrempp began reinventing Daimler-Benz, including taking such personally painful steps as owning up to his failure with the aerospace division and his allowing it to go into bankruptcy. The result was a 45-percent appreciation in Daimler's share price over a 12-month period.[57]

Listen to Naysayers

Executives exhibiting hubris tend to fall into the trap of listening only to people whose opinions are compatible with their own. Indeed, such executives tend to build teams with members whose conception of the desirable closely resembles their own. Such behavior tends to promote "groupthink" that normally leads to inferior alternatives and decision-making.[58] Alternatively, such managers may surround themselves with sycophants who echo what they believe the leader likes to hear, even if they inherently consider the leader's choices to be flawed. In 16th century Italy, Machiavelli observed: "Courts are always full of flatterers; men take such pleasure in their own concerns, and are so easily deceived, that this plague of flattery is hard to escape."[59]

To combat the limitations of groupthink and sycophants, senior executives need to make sure that their team is composed of members with diverse backgrounds as well as functional areas. Just as important, the members chosen must have the integrity and courage to argue for alternatives that may differ from those preferred by the senior executives. In fact, superior alternatives and strategizing are often the outcomes of groups whose members have dissimilar opinions and who are allowed to openly discuss their views without retribution.[60] Senior executives, however, must not only allow but also should encourage open discussions. Otherwise, even people of integrity and courage may be thwarted from fully contributing to discussions. Unfortunately, leaders often discourage open discourse. Napoleon's first wife, Josephine, for example, recorded in her memoirs: ". . . in his presence, no one had the right to hazard the slightest [contrary] observation."[61]

Appoint an Alter Ego

Senior executives may also benefit from an alter ego who can tell them when they are wrong.[62] This is especially important in organizations where personnel are inclined to nominally go along with the leader. The person who plays the role of alter ego should also serve as a mediator and a sounding board. Preferably, such a person should be non-threatening to the senior executive, having developed a relationship of mutual trust. This alter ego must be respected by the top leader and not criticized for expressing different opinions.

Not only Napoleon's confidant Caulaincourt, but most of his lieutenants, offered a host of reasons why Napoleon should not invade Russia. Napoleon invariably accused them of being timid, weak, and incapable of seeing what could be accomplished. However, following Napoleon's departure from Russia, Caulaincourt found him far more willing to listen to what he had to say about the Russian campaign. Caulaincourt was in fact amazed by how frankly he could talk to the Emperor compared with the period before the campaign. Unfortunately, this willingness to listen came only after an estimated 570,000 casualties.[63]

Model Behavior That Is in the Organization's Best Interest

Senior managers serve as role models for others employed by the company. Consequently, they should display behavior that contributes to firm performance. Herb Kelleher, CEO of Southwest Airlines, is a maverick who, by example, has created a culture in which employees can do things differently. In 1971, Southwest had three planes serving three

Texas cities. Today the company has over 240 aircraft serving 50 cities. This growth is largely the result of Kelleher's leadership style, which values creativity and efficiency. As Kelleher puts it: "We've always [encouraged that] work be done differently. You know, we don't assign seats. Used to be we only had about four people on the whole plane, so the idea of assigned seats just made people laugh. Now the reason is you can turn airplanes quicker at the gate. And if you can turn an airplane quicker, you can have it fly more routes each day. That generates more revenue, so you can offer lower fares."[64]

What Can Board Members Do to Control Hubris?

Monitor Executives for Signs of Hubris

We are hearing increasing calls for boards of directors, and especially outside board members, to take on a greater monitoring role in confronting the potential hubris of senior executives.[65] The departure of Ronald Allen as CEO of Delta Airlines resulted when outside board members took such action. Allen had led Delta through a series of acquisitions and painful cost-cutting programs that made him look decisive but were costly to employees and customers. Allen had plans to buy Continental Airlines and to continue cost cutting. However, the board became disheartened by declining employee morale, which was detracting from customer service. The board also saw a need for Delta to revert to its strategy of disciplined internal growth rather than acquisitions. Allen was replaced by Leo Mullin, who promised that customers and employees would not take a back seat to the company's stockholders.[66]

Promote a Heterogeneous Corporate Culture

Boards should ensure that views that run counter to conventional wisdom are tolerated or encouraged, and should promote the use of a more decentralized organizational structure.[67] Board members may also recommend that corporate codes of ethics and values be developed. Such codes should emphasize that firm decisions will promote the benefits of all stakeholders.

Develop a Strong Organizational Knowledge Base

As the world's economy continues to prove both turbulent and extremely competitive, the information needs of firms will continue to change rapidly. Prevailing systems have done well in gathering information within organizations.[68] But if internal reports are positive, managers may be prone to staying with simplistic formulas for success even if external conditions are changing, threatening the viability of the firm.

A Call to Action

In ancient Greece, hubris was considered a crime under Athenian law, and in Greek tragedy it was considered the greatest of sins, reflecting an arrogance growing out of a misplaced sense of one's own abilities rather than the generosity of the gods.[69] As we have seen, many historians have concluded that Napoleon fell victim to his own over-inflated sense of what he could accomplish, losing an army and an empire.

Financial and managerial markets also exact their own form of retribution for corporate hubris. People afflicted with corporate hubris often find it necessary to build an organization that reflects their narcissistic requirements through such conquests as acquisitions, even though acquisitions have not uniformly proven the path to quick riches for shareholders. The pursuit of narcissistic gratification can also inspire growth and investment decisions that may lead to a larger, but not necessarily more profitable, organization. Finally, hubris can lead to arrogance that justifies breaking rules.

Hubris tends to appear most frequently in people already prone to narcissism. A string of successes, some good press, and subordinates willing to feed that narcissism, can exacerbate hubris. As did Napoleon in a military context, corporate executives infected with hubris may come to believe they possess abilities and insights others do not have, and may trivialize the wisdom and contributions of others. Predictably, such executives come to believe that their formula for success is infallible and that additional information is largely irrelevant. The results of this process are especially unfortunate in competitive arenas such as war or commerce, as behavior becomes predictable and thus susceptible to attack in ways that are not part of the executive's model of reality. Tables 14.1 and 14.2 compare examples of the sources and implications of hubris.

The most practical way for an individual to combat hubris is to be introspective enough to realize one will never have all the answers and that the counsel of others is vital. One must also realize that success in an organizational context results from a complex interplay of the organization's various resources with the environment. While the leader may be a significant component in that success, it is dangerous to assume that the leader's role is the only factor. Executives should also work to insure that they have at least one confidant who is in a position to speak the truth.

The most practical way to combat hubris in an organizational setting is to ensure that top executives are monitored by a vigilant board with a reasonable number of outside directors. In addition, organizations should work to establish cultural norms that encourage the membership to disagree without being disagreeable. Organizations should also encourage the kind of continuous environmental surveillance necessary to avoid assuming that the future will conform to the predictable patterns that allowed for past glories.

Hubris does not affect every organization, but it is important to monitor for hubris because it can lead to devastating consequences. Boards must learn to distinguish between the confidence of an executive who, in the face of opposition, pursues an entrepreneurial vision, and the blind disregard of an executive suffering from hubris. Confidence and arrogance may be intertwined, as in the case of Napoleon, who was both a military genius and a slave to his own narcissism. However, the lesson of history is clear: All too often, successful leaders with many positive qualities become their own worst enemies by succumbing to their narcissistic inclinations and allowing hubris to cloud their vision. When an organization and its leader have achieved their ambitions, they must not allow hubris to erode their hard-earned accomplishments.

TABLE 14.1 Examples of the Sources of Hubris

Sources	Napoleon	Executives
Narcissism	Napoleon's need for position and self-aggrandization to satisfy his narcissism	Executives with hubris will seek out positions of power to satisfy their narcissism
Recent successes	Napoleon's hubris grew as his record of battlefield victories lengthened	A record of outstanding performance permits an executive to rationalize his or her hubris
Exaggerated accolades of others	Napoleon's hubris fed on the adulation showered on him by the French people and press	As executives receive praise from others and the media, their hubris is reinforced
Exemption from the rules	Napoleon regularly broke the rules that governed nineteenth-century Europe, and his hubris grew as he got away with more and more	A sense of entitlement accompanies hubris in executives as they break the rules and get away with it

TABLE 14.2   Examples of the Implications of Hubris

Implications	Napoleon	Executives
Confidence turns to arrogance	When Napoleon's officers pointed out the perils of the Russian campaign, he called them timid and weak	Executives with hubris appear to undertake mergers that are over-priced out of a sense that they know better than others what is best
Relying on a simplistic formula	Napoleon assumed the quick, hard-hitting attacks that had worked before would subdue Russia	Once executives believe they alone know the formula for success, they repeatedly trot out the same strategy regardless of circumstances
Unwillingness to see the obvious	Napoleon systematically refused to recognize the differences between the Russian campaign and earlier campaigns	Once absorbed with hubris and convinced of infallibility, executives may become blind to signals of environmental change

Notes

1. De Fezensac, M., translated by Lee Kennett, 1970, *The Russian campaign, 1812* (Athens, GA: The University of Georgia Press), viii.

2. Our discussion of the 1812 Russian campaign, and the geopolitical situation at the time of the campaign, is based on numerous sources. To avoid the bias of any single historian or account of the events, we have avoided taking any positions that are not reflected in at least two of the works listed below: Aldington, R., 1943, *The Duke: Being an account of the life and achievements of Arthur Wellesley, First Duke of Wellington* (New York: Viking); Aubry, O., 1938, *Napoleon: Soldier and emperor* (New York: Lippincott); Ballard, C. R., 1971, *Napoleon, an outline* (New York Books for Libraries); Burnett, C., 1978, *Bonaparte* (New York: Hill and Wang); Carr, A., 1941, *Napoleon speaks* (New York: Viking); Cate, C., 1985, *The war of the two emperors* (New York: Random House); Duffy, C., 1973, *Borodino and the War of 1812* (New York: Charles Scribner's Sons); De Fezensac, op. cit.; Fournier, A., 1913, *Napoleon 1* (New York: Henry Holt); Nicolson, N., 1985, *Napoleon 1812* (New York: Harper & Row); Tarle, E., 1942, *Napoleon's invasion of Russia 1812* (New York: Oxford University Press); Tolstoy, L. N., translated by Louise & Aylmer Maude, 1970, *War and Peace* (London: Oxford University Press).

3. Hayward, M.L.A. & Hambrick, D. C., 1997, Explaining the premiums paid for large acquisitions: Evidence of CEO hubris, *Administrative Science Quarterly* 42:103–127; Kets de Vries, M.F.R., 1990, The organizational fool: Balancing a

leader's hubris, *Human Relations* 43:751–770; Wilson, A., The Classics Pages, at http://www.globalnet.co.uk-loxias.

4. Kohut, H., 1978, Creativeness: charisma, group psychology, in P. Omstein (ed.), *The search for the self,* volume 2 (New York: International Universities Press).

5. Cate, op. cit., 9–11.

6. Roll, R., 1986, The hubris hypothesis of corporate takeovers, *Journal of Business* 59:197–216.

7. Fischer, D. E. & Jordan, R. J., 1995, Security analysis and portfolio management (Upper Saddle River, NJ: Prentice-Hall), sixth edition, 556.

8. Berkovitch, E. & Narayanan, M. P., 1993, Motives for takeovers: An empirical investigation, *Journal of Financial and Quantitative Analysis* 28:347–362; Bradley, M., Desai, A., & Kim, E. H., 1988, Synergistic gains from corporate acquisitions and their division between the stockholders of target and acquiring firms, *Journal of Financial Economics* 21:3–40; Jarrell, G. A. & Paulsen, A. B., 1989, The returns to acquiring firms in tender offers: Evidence from three decades, *Financial Management* (Autumn):12–19; Limmack, R. J., 1993, Bidder companies and defended bids: A test of Roll's hubris hypothesis, *Managerial Finance* 19:25–36.

9. Hayward, M. L. & Hambrick, D. C., op. cit., 103–127; Hitt, M., Harrison, J., Ireland, R. D., & Best, L., 1998, Attributes of successful and unsuccessful acquisitions of U.S. firms, *British Journal of Management* 9:91–114.

10. Hambrick, D. C. & Cannella, A. A. Jr., 1993, Relative standing: A framework for understanding departures of acquired executives, *Academy of Management Journal* 36:733–762.

11. *Business Week,* 1994, How sweet a deal for Novell? April 4, 38; *Wall Street Journal,* 1996, Software firm fights to remake business after ill-fated merger, January 12, AI, A8.

12. Kets de Vries, M.F.R. & Miller, D., 1985, Narcissism and leadership: An object relations perspective, *Human Relations* 38:583–601.

13. Goldman, K., 1997, *Conflicting accounts: The creation and crash of the Saatchi & Saatchi advertising empire* (New York: Simon and Schuster); *Forbes,* 1997, Hubris redeemed, January 13, 42–44.

14. *Economist,* 1992, The shake-up in the Barclay's boardroom, April 25, 83–84.

15. Barnett, op. cit., 36–53.

16. Lefebvre, G., 1969, *Napoleon 1799–1807* (New York: Routledge and Kegan Paul), 141.

17. Kets de Vries, M.F.R., 1991, Whatever happened to the philosopher-king? The leader's addiction to power, *Journal of Management Studies* 28:339–351.

18. *Business Week,* 1996, Archer Daniel's cleanup: Don't stop now, January 29, 37.

19. Frances, A. (Task Force Chair), 1994, *Diagnostic and statistical manual of mental disorders,* fourth edition (Washington, D.C.: American Psychiatric Association), 658–661; Miller, A., 1981, *Prisoners of childhood* (New York: Basic Books), 33–34.

20. The four sources of hubris we identify are derived from several works (which are listed below). As Hayward and Hambrick observe, there is no definitive set of factors that must always be present in significant amounts in order to engender hubris. However, there are clearly common threads that run through much of the hubris-related literature. We have distilled from that literature the

four sources we have discussed. It would of course be unrealistic to assume that hubris can exist only in an intense presence of all four of the sources we discuss. However, it seems reasonable to conclude that greater degrees of the four sources of hubris will lead to elevated levels of hubris. Also see: Brockner, J., 1988, *Self-esteem at work: Research, theory and practice* (Lexington, MA: Lexington Books); Hayward & Hambrick, op. cit., 103–127; Kets de Vries, The organizational fool, op. cit., 751–770; Kets de Vries & Miller, op. cit., 583–601; Salancik, G. R. & Meindl, J. R., 1984, Corporate attributions as strategic illusions of management control, *Administrative Science Quarterly* 29:238–254.

21. Kets de Vries, The organizational fool, op. cit., 764; Frances, op. cit., 658–661.

22. Sankowsky, D., 1995, The charismatic leader as narcissist: Understanding the abuse of power, *Organizational Dynamics* (Spring):57–71.

23. O'Connor, J., Mumford, M. D., Clifton, T. C., & Gessner, T. L., 1995, Charismatic leaders and destructiveness: An historiometric study, *Leadership Quarterly* 6:529–555.

24. Tolstoy, op. cit., 427.

25. *Business Week,* 1996, Crunch time at Quaker Oats, September 23, 71; *Business Week,* 1996, Putting the snap back in Snapple, July 22, 40; *Advertising* Age, 1995, Snapple is now up to Smithburg, October 30, 8; *Wall Street Journal,* 1994, Quaker Oats to buy Snapple for $1.7 billion, November 3, A3; Forbes, 1996, He who laughs last, January 1, 42–43; *Beverage World,* 1997, Snapped up, April 15, 92; *Fortune,* European ed., 1997, Quaker acts—At last, May 26, 30.

26. Kets de Vries, The organizational fool, op. cit., 765.

27. Kets de Vries & Miller, op. cit., 583–601.

28. Ibid., 589.

29. Brockner, op. cit.

30. Barnett, op. cit., 45.

31. De Raguse, D., 1857, *Memoires I* (Paris), 297.

32. Meindl, J. R. & Ehrlich, S. B., 1987, The romance of leadership and the evaluation of organizational performance, *Academy of Management Journal* 30:91–109. Also see: Staw, B. M., McKechnie, P., & Puffer, S. M., 1983, The justification of organizational performance, *Administrative Science Quarterly* 28:582–600; Bettman, J. R. & Weitz, B. A., 1983, Attributes in the board room: Causal reasoning in corporate annual reports, *Administrative Science Quarterly* 28:165–183.

33. *Forbes,* 1999, The scorecard, May 17, 216–286.

34. Clapham, S. E. & Schwenk, C. R., 1991, Self-serving attributions, managerial cognition, and company performance, *Strategic Management Journal* 12:219–229.

35. Chen, C. C. & Meindl, J. R., 1991, The construction of leadership images in the popular press: The case of Donald Burr and People Express, *Administrative Science Quarterly* 36:521–551; Hayward & Hambrick, op. cit., 109; Meindl, J. R., Ehrlich, S. B. & Dukerich, J. M., 1985, The romance of leadership. *Administrative Science Quarterly* 30:78–102.

36. Holtma, R., 1969, *Napoleonic propaganda* (New York: Greenwood Press), 33.

37. Chen & Meindl, op. cit., 521–551; Meindl, Ehrlich, & Dukerich, op. cit., 78–102.

38. James Carville, speech given before the student body and faculty of Louisiana State University, broadcast by CSPAN, November 1992.

39. Freud, S., 1957, Some character-types met with in psychoanalytic work, in J. Starchey (ed.), *The Standard Edition of the Complete Psychological Works of Sigmund Freud,* volume 14 (London: Hogarth Press and Institute of Psychoanalysis).

40. Kets de Vries, Philosopher-king, op. cit., 342.

41. Barnett, op. cit., 45.

42. Ibid., 182.

43. Nicolson, op. cit., 180.

44. *Economist,* 1991, Salomon brothers: Life after Gutfreund, August 24, 67–68; *Institutional Investor,* 1991, Who should run Salomon Brothers? September, 11–14.

45. While the three behaviors we discuss here are not the only ones manifested by a hubris-infected executive, for the sake of brevity we address these three as they likely have the greatest strategic consequences for the firm. Another behavior not discussed that may manifest itself in someone imbued with hubris is abuse of authority that leads to the alienation and departure of valued employees. A charismatic leader who is also consumed with hubris may use his or her talents to achieve a position of leadership and trust, only to betray that trust when it becomes expedient to do so in order to satisfy his or her personal needs. Throughout his career, Napoleon betrayed those to whom he had made commitments when it became expedient to do so, including his first wife Empress Josephine. Please see: Sankowsky, op. cit., 57–71.

46. Kets de Vries & Miller, op. cit.; Kets de Vries, The organizational fool, op. cit.

47. Nicholson, op. cit., 17.

48. Ibid., 18.

49. *Beverage World,* op. cit., 92.

50. Miller, D., 1993, The architecture of simplicity, *Academy of Management Review* 18:116–138.

51. Keller, M., 1989, *Rude awakening* (New York: Harper Pernnial).

52. *Business Week,* 1998, Slip slidin' away at General Motors, March 23, 38.

53. Keller, op. cit., 21.

54. Ibid., 51.

55. Clapham & Schwenk, op. cit., 227.

56. Ibid., 227.

57. *Forbes,* 1996, A tough deadline, April 22, 165–174; *Forbes,* 1997, Mercedes-Benz's bold niche strategy, September 8, 68–76; *Economist,* 1996, Neutron Jurgen? March 16, 72; Schrempp, J. E., 1997, Thriving on global economic changes, address delivered to the Economic Club of Detroit, Detroit, Michigan, January 6; *Fortune,* 1997, Neutron Jurgen ignites a revolution at Daimler-Benz, November 10, 144–152; *Business Week,* 1997, The bulldozer at Daimler-Benz, February 10, 52.

58. Filley, A. C., House, R. J., & Kerr, S., 1976, *Managerial process and organizational behavior* (Glenview, IL: Scott Foresman & Co.), 57–62; Janis, I. L., 1972, *Victims of groupthink* (Boston: Houghton Mifflin), 13–15.

59. Kets de Vries, The organizational fool, op. cit., 757.

60. Filley et al., op. cit., 353; Janis. op. cit.

61. Le Normand, M. A., 1895, The historical and secret memoirs of the *Empress Josephine* (London), 229.

62. Kets de Vries, The organizational fool, op. cit., 757.

63. Nicolson, op. cit., 162. The attentive reader may wonder at the 570,000 casualty figure, given that Napoleon entered Russia with an army of 500,000 and about 20,000 recrossed the Neiman River and escaped alive. However, several supplemental regiments of reinforcements joined the army at various points during the retreat, thus increasing the absolute number of men involved in the campaign. In addition to the 570,000 official casualties, there were many thousands of noncombatant casualties. Many of the officers brought with them wives, children, and personal servants who were not officially part of the army, but suffered the same fates as their husbands, fathers, and masters. In addition, early 19th Century armies were often accompanied by merchants who sold various items to the troops along the way, as well as by women camp followers, many of whom fared poorly, ibid., 172.

64. Kelleher, Herb, http://www.iflyswa.com/herb/herbie.html.

65. It is worth noting some scholars have argued that subordinate insiders will check the behavior of the CEO as they are natural competitors for control of the firm and their fortunes are tied to the firm's. For these reasons, they will act to cause the replacement of the CEO by influencing outside board members when the CEO's behavior is truly harmful to the firm. See Fama, E. F., 1980, Agency problems and the theory of the firm, *Journal of Political Economy,* 88, 288–307.

66. *Business Week,* 1997, Bailing out of Delta, May 26, 62; *Wall Street Journal,* 1997, Delta Air's Allen to quit three top posts, May 13.

67. As organizations become more decentralized and move toward the use of self-directed work teams, decision making occurs at lower levels in the organization. This is especially true in organizations where empowerment exists. In such organizations, hubris at the corporate level may be less of an issue in that control of decision making is reduced.

68. Drucker, P. F., Dyson, E., Handy, C., Saffo, P., & Senge, P. M., 1997, Looking ahead: Implications of the present, *Harvard Business Review* (September–October):22.

69. Wilson, op. cit.

15

The Greatest Man Churchill and Truman Ever Met

ALBERT R. HUNT

In a time when anniversaries from the monumental to the mundane are celebrated, today marks one of the more important, if little noticed, in modern American history: It was 55 years ago that George Catlett Marshall became Army chief of staff.

For the next dozen years General Marshall, as chief of staff, secretary of state and secretary of defense, left a legacy rivaled by few public servants in this century: He built and shaped the military machine that won World War II; launched the economic plan that put postwar Europe back on its feet, and reinforced the supremacy of civilian control when he recommended the firing of General Douglas MacArthur. Dwight Eisenhower, Winston Churchill, Harry Truman and countless others considered him the greatest man they'd ever met.

It's unclear whether this man of such vision and integrity would have been able to adapt to the exigencies of contemporary politics and statecraft. But Forrest Pogue's magnificent four-volume biography of General Marshall should be required reading for today's practitioners.

When George Marshall took over as chief of staff on Sept. 1, 1939, there were two stark realities: Hitler's powerful army had overrun Poland that day and was on the verge of dominating the continent of Europe to an extent not seen since Napoleon; and the U.S. Army numbered fewer than 200,000 soldiers, ranking behind 16 other nations. In less than five years General Marshall built an army of 8.3 million, the most powerful fighting machine the world had ever seen.

As secretary of state and later as secretary of defense, General Marshall was President Truman's right hand; no one played a larger role in constructing the policy that contained the menace of communism. The author of the Marshall Plan was the first military man to win the Nobel Peace Prize in peacetime.

The issues were so awesome, and General Marshall's involvement so central, that he made major mistakes. He didn't adequately anticipate a Japanese attack on Pearl Harbor in 1941; arguably, along with General Eisenhower and others, he underestimated Soviet intentions in 1945; and he was on the wrong side of the debate over recognizing Israel in 1948. But as big as these miscalculations are, they are dwarfed by his contributions.

The Marshall vision and sense of duty never were deterred by the prevailing political winds. It's easy to forget what a herculean task he performed in building the Army, overcoming initial public resistance. In 1938 a majority of the House voted for a constitutional amendment to require a national referendum before the U.S. could go to war. In 1941, less than four months before Pearl Harbor, the extension of the draft passed by one vote; without General Marshall's enormous influence on Capitol Hill it would have failed decisively.

The aftermath of World War II ushered in another new world order; despite the Soviet threat there was a strong tendency to look inward. But General Marshall and President Truman not only proposed the multibillion-dollar rescue of Europe but persuaded a Republican Congress to approve it.

General Marshall, an unusually secure man, spotted bright subordinates and then delegated huge responsibilities. In the Army, General Eisenhower, Omar Bradley, Matthew Ridgway and George Patton all were Marshall men. The Army chief of staff had no use for yes men. At the end of his first week, General Bradley once recalled, he summoned his top aides and expressed strong disappointment: "You haven't disagreed with a single thing I have done all week."

He was a military leader with a special sensitivity. When some expressed surprise that an Army general won the Nobel Peace Prize, he noted in his acceptance speech that "the cost of war is constantly spread before me, written neatly in many ledgers whose columns are gravestones. I am greatly moved to find some means or method of avoiding another calamity of war." Working with industrialists and Congress he made sure that his army was the best supplied and best cared for in the world.

This son of the Virginia Military Institute lacked the charisma of MacArthur or even Eisenhower, but he possessed a powerful presence that commanded trust and respect. Churchill, notoriously condescending to military commanders, quickly realized that George Marshall was different. Although he eschewed conventional politics he was a superb politician. During the war he was at the epicenter of an extraordinary collection of powerful personalities and egos—Churchill and Roosevelt, the Machiavellian commanders in chief with their own notions of military strategy, and in his own Army, MacArthur and Patton. Yet the single domineering military figure was George C. Marshall.

He loathed self-promotion. An oft-quoted Marshall dictum is that there's no end to what can be accomplished if you credit others; it's not clear whether he actually said it, but he certainly practiced it.

The most remarkable example of his character was when the time came to choose the supreme Allied commander for the invasion of Europe; most everyone, from Churchill to the entire American military establishment, thought General Marshall the perfect choice. Yet when President Roosevelt pressed him for a recommendation, General Marshall, with a devout belief in civilian control, refused to lift a hand on his own behalf, insisting the president must be free to make the choice. FDR said he would sleep better with General Marshall in Washington; General Eisenhower thus led what became the Normandy invasion. General Marshall never expressed any regret and reveled in his subordinate's success.

Yet as Forrest Pogue says, George Marshall was humble only "if you use the term correctly. He was quite aware of his ability to run the Army and the war better than anyone else." And he was secure enough not to react when he was viciously attacked by Joe McCarthy and the Republican right in the early 1950s.

Would General Marshall succeed as easily today? Mr. Pogue suspects not, worried that he would despise television's penchant for the instantaneous passions of the moment, the ever-reliance on polls, and the constant negative drumbeat about public service.

Whether it's politicians or generals or athletes, there is an irresistible temptation to suggest we don't make them like we used to. In that vein, it's good to remember that in 1888 Lord Bryce wrote his famous essay about American politics entitled "Why Great Men Are Not Elected President." Americans, over the next 60 years, then proceeded to elect Teddy Roosevelt, Woodrow Wilson, Franklin Roosevelt and Harry Truman.

Perhaps there's a George Marshall on the horizon. Let's hope so.

16

The Antileadership Vaccine

JOHN W. GARDNER

It is generally believed that we need enlightened and responsible leaders—at every level and in every phase of our national life. Everyone says so. But the nature of leadership in our society is very imperfectly understood, and many of the public statements about it are utter nonsense.

This is unfortunate because there are serious issues of leadership facing this society, and we had better understand them.

The Dispersion of Power

The most fundamental thing to be said about leadership in the United States is also the most obvious. We have gone as far as any known society in creating a leadership system that is not based on caste or class, nor even on wealth. There is not yet equal access to leadership (witness the remaining barriers facing women and Negroes), but we have come a long, long way from the family- or class-based leadership group. Even with its present defects, ours is a relatively open system.

The next important thing to be said is that leadership is dispersed among a great many groups in our society. The President, of course, has a unique, and uniquely important, leadership role, but beneath him, fragmentation is the rule. This idea is directly at odds with the notion that the society is run by a coherent power group—the Power Elite, as C. Wright Mills called it, or the Establishment, as later writers have named it. It is hard not to believe that such a group exists. Foreigners find it particularly difficult to believe in the reality of the fluid, scattered, shifting leadership that is visible to the naked eye. The real leadership, they imagine, must be behind the scenes. But at a national level this simply isn't so.

The Antileadership Vaccine," by John W. Gardner, president's essay, reprinted from the 1965 Carnegie Corporation of New York Annual Report.

In many local communities and even in some states there is a coherent power group, sometimes behind the scenes, sometimes out in the open. In communities where such an "establishment," that is, a coherent ruling group, exists, the leading citizen can be thought of as having power in a generalized sense: he can bring about a change in zoning ordinances, influence the location of a new factory, and determine whether the local museum will buy contemporary paintings. But in the dispersed and fragmented power system that prevails in the nation as a whole one cannot say "So-and-so is powerful," without further elaboration. Those who know how our system works always want to know, "Powerful in what way? Powerful to accomplish what?" We have leaders in business and leaders in government, military leaders and educational leaders, leaders in labor and in agriculture, leaders in science, in the world of art, and in many other special fields. As a rule, leaders in any one of these fields do not recognize the authority of leaders from a neighboring field. Often they don't even know one another, nor do they particularly want to. Mutual suspicion is just about as common as mutual respect—and a lot more common than mutual cooperation in manipulating society's levers.

Most of the significant issues in our society are settled by a balancing of forces. A lot of people and groups are involved and the most powerful do not always win. Sometimes a coalition of the less powerful wins. Sometimes an individual of very limited power gets himself into the position of casting the deciding ballot.

Not only are there apt to be many groups involved in any critical issue, but their relative strength varies with each issue that comes up. A group that is powerful today may not be powerful next year. A group that can cast a decisive vote on question A may not even be listened to when question B comes up.

The Nature of Leadership

People who have never exercised power have all kinds of curious ideas about it. The popular notion of top leadership is a fantasy of capricious power: the top man presses a button and something remarkable happens; he gives an order as the whim strikes him, and it is obeyed.

Actually, the capricious use of power is relatively rare except in some large dictatorships and some small family firms. Most leaders are hedged around by constraints—tradition, constitutional limitations, the realities of the external situation, rights and privileges of followers, the requirements of teamwork, and most of all the inexorable demands of large-scale organization, which does not operate on capriciousness. In short, most power is wielded circumspectly.

There are many different ways of leading, many kinds of leaders. Consider, for example, the marked contrasts between the politician and the intellectual leader, the large-scale manager and the spiritual leader. One sees solemn descriptions of the qualities needed for leadership without any reference at all to the fact that the necessary attributes depend on the kind of leadership under discussion. Even in a single field there may be different kinds of leadership with different required attributes. Think of the difference between the military hero and the military manager.

If social action is to occur, certain functions must be performed. The problems facing the group or organization must be clarified, and ideas necessary to their solution formulated. Objectives must be defined. There must be widespread awareness of those objectives, and the will to achieve them. Often those on whom action depends must develop new attitudes and habits. Social machinery must be set in motion. The consequences of social effort must be evaluated and criticized, and new goals set.

A particular leader may contribute at only one point to this process. He may be gifted in analysis of the problem, but limited in his capacity to communicate. He may be superb in communicating, but incapable of managing. He may, in short, be an outstanding leader without being good at every aspect of leadership.

If anything significant is to be accomplished, leaders must understand the social institutions and processes through which action is carried out. And in a society as complex as ours, that is no mean achievement. A leader, whether corporation president, university dean, or labor official, knows his organization, understands what makes it move, comprehends its limitations. Every social system or institution has a logic and dynamic of its own that cannot be ignored.

We have all seen men with lots of bright ideas but no patience with the machinery by which ideas are translated into action. As a rule, the machinery defeats them. It is a pity, because the professional and academic man can play a useful role in practical affairs. But too often he is a dilettante. He dips in here or there; he gives bits of advice on a dozen fronts; he never gets his hands dirty working with one piece of the social machinery until he knows it well. He will not take the time to understand the social institutions and processes by which change is accomplished.

Although our decentralized system of leadership has served us well, we must not be so complacent as to imagine that it has no weaknesses, that it faces no new challenges, or that we have nothing to learn. There are grave questions to be answered concerning the leadership of our society. Are we living up to standards of leadership that we have achieved in our own past? Do the conditions of modern life introduce new complications into the task of leadership? Are we failing to prepare leaders for tomorrow?

Here are some of our salient difficulties.

Failure to Cope with the Big Questions

Nothing should be allowed to impair the effectiveness and independence of our specialized leadership groups. But such fragmented leadership does create certain problems. One of them is that it isn't anybody's business to think about the big questions that cut across specialties—the largest questions facing our society. Where are we headed? Where do we want to head? What are the major trends determining our future? Should we do anything about them? Our fragmented leadership fails to deal effectively with these transcendent questions.

Very few of our most prominent people take a really large view of the leadership assignment. Most of them are simply tending the machinery of that part of society to which they belong. The machinery may be a great corporation or a great government agency or a great law practice or a great university. These people may tend it very well indeed, but they are not pursuing a vision of what the total society needs. They have not developed a strategy as to how it can be achieved, and they are not moving to accomplish it.

One does not blame them, of course. They do not see themselves as leaders of the society at large, and they have plenty to do handling their own specialized role.

Yet it is doubtful that we can any longer afford such widespread inattention to the largest questions facing us. We achieved greatness in an era when changes came more slowly than now. The problems facing the society took shape at a stately pace. We could afford to be slow in recognizing them, slow in coping with them. Today, problems of enormous import hit us swiftly. Great social changes emerge with frightening speed. We can no longer afford to respond in a leisurely fashion.

Our inability to cope with the largest questions tends to weaken the private sector. Any question that cannot be dealt with by one of the special leadership groups—that is, any question that cuts across special fields—tends to end up being dealt with by government. Most Americans value the role played by nongovernmental leadership in this country and would wish it to continue. In my judgment it will not continue under the present conditions.

The cure is not to work against the fragmentation of leadership, which is a vital element in our pluralism, but to create better channels of communication among significant leadership groups, especially in connection with the great issues that transcend any particular group.

Failure of Confidence

Another of the maladies of leadership today is a failure of confidence. Anyone who accomplishes anything of significance has more confidence than the facts would justify. It is something that outstanding executives have in common with gifted military commanders, brilliant political leaders, and great artists. It is true of societies as well as of individuals. Every great civilization has been characterized by confidence in itself.

Lacking such confidence, too many leaders add ingenious new twists to the modern art which I call "How to reach a decision without really deciding." They require that the question be put through a series of clearances within the organization and let the clearance process settle it. Or take a public opinion poll and let the poll settle it. Or devise elaborate statistical systems, cost-accounting systems, information-processing systems, hoping that out of them will come unassailable support for one course of action rather than another.

This is not to say that leadership cannot profit enormously from good information. If the modern leader doesn't know the facts he is in grave trouble, but rarely do the facts provide unqualified guidance. After the facts are in, the leader must in some measure emulate the little girl who told the teacher she was going to draw a picture of God. The teacher said, "But, Mary, no one knows what God looks like"; and Mary said, "They will when I get through."

The confidence required of leaders poses a delicate problem for a free society. We don't want to be led by Men of Destiny who think they know all the answers. Neither do we wish to be led by Nervous Nellies. It is a matter of balance. We are no longer in much danger, in this society, from Men of Destiny. But we are in danger of falling under the leadership of men who lack the confidence to lead. And we are in danger of destroying the effectiveness of those who have a natural gift for leadership.

Of all our deficiencies with respect to leadership, one of the gravest is that we are not doing what we should to encourage potential leaders. In the late eighteenth century we produced out of a small population a truly extraordinary group of leaders—Washington, Adams, Jefferson, Franklin, Madison, Monroe, and others. Why is it so difficult today, out of a vastly greater population, to produce men of that caliber? It is a question that most reflective people ask themselves sooner or later. There is no reason to doubt that the human material is still there, but there is excellent reason to believe that we are failing to develop it—or that we are diverting it into nonleadership activities.

The Antileadership Vaccine

Indeed, it is my belief that we are immunizing a high proportion of our most gifted young people against any tendencies to leadership. It will be worth our time to examine how the antileadership vaccine is administered.

The process is initiated by the society itself. The conditions of life in a modern, complex society are not conducive to the emergence of leaders.

The young person today is acutely aware of the fact that he is an anonymous member of a mass society, an individual lost among millions of others. The processes by which leadership is exercised are not visible to him, and he is bound to believe that they are exceedingly intricate. Very little in his experience encourages him to think that he might some day exercise a role of leadership.

This unfocused discouragement is of little consequence compared with the expert dissuasion the young person will encounter if he is sufficiently bright to attend a college or university. In those institutions today, the best students are carefully schooled to avoid leadership responsibilities.

Most of our intellectually gifted young people go from college directly into graduate school or into one of the older and more prestigious professional schools. There they are introduced to—or, more correctly, powerfully indoctrinated in—a set of attitudes appropriate to scholars, scientists, and professional men. This is all to the good. The students learn to identify themselves strongly with their calling and its ideals. They acquire a conception of what a good scholar, scientist, or professional man is like.

As things stand now, however, that conception leaves little room for leadership in the normal sense; the only kind of leadership encouraged is that which follows from the performing of purely professional tasks in a superior manner. Entry into what most of us would regard as the leadership roles in the society at large is discouraged.

In the early stages of a career, there is a good reason for this: becoming a first-class scholar, scientist, or professional requires single-minded dedication. Unfortunately, by the time the individual is sufficiently far along in his career to afford a broadening of interests, he often finds himself irrevocably set in a narrow mold.

The antileadership vaccine has other more subtle and powerful ingredients. The image of the corporation president, politician, or college president that is current among most intellectuals and professionals today has some decidedly unattractive features. It is said that such men compromise their convictions almost daily, if not hourly. It is said that they have tasted the corrupting experience of power. They must be status seekers, the argument goes, or they would not be where they are.

Needless to say, the student picks up such attitudes. It is not that professors propound these views and students learn them. Rather, they are in the air and students absorb them. The resulting unfavorable image contrasts dramatically with the image these young people are given of the professional who is almost by definition dedicated to his field, pure in his motives, and unencumbered by worldly ambition.

My own extensive acquaintance with scholars and professionals on the one hand and administrators and managers on the other does not confirm this contrast in character. In my experience, each category has its share of opportunists. Nevertheless, the negative attitudes persist.

As a result the academic world appears to be approaching a point at which everyone will want to educate the technical expert who advises the leader, or the intellectual who stands off and criticizes the leader, but no one will want to educate the leader himself.

Are Leaders Necessary?

For a good many academic and other professional people, negative attitudes toward leadership go deeper than skepticism concerning the leader's integrity. Many have real doubts, not always explicitly formulated, about the necessity for leadership.

The doubts are of two kinds. First, many scientific and professional people are accustomed to the kinds of problems that can be solved by expert technical advice or action. It is easy for them to imagine that any social enterprise could be managed in the same way. They envisage a world that does not need leaders, only experts. The notion is based, of course, upon a false conception of the leader's function. The supplying of technically correct solutions is the least of his responsibilities.

There is another kind of question that some academic or professional people raise concerning leadership: Is the very notion of leadership somehow at odds with the ideals of a free society? Is it a throwback to earlier notions of social organization?

These are not foolish questions. We have in fact outgrown or rejected several varieties of leadership that have loomed large in the history of mankind. We do not want autocratic leaders who treat us like inferior beings. We do not want leaders, no matter how wise or kind, who treat us like children.

But at the same time that we were rejecting those forms of leadership we were evolving forms more suitable to our values. As a result our best leaders today are not out of place in a free society—on the contrary, they strengthen our free society.

We can have the kinds of leaders we want, but we cannot choose to do without them. It is in the nature of social organization that we must have them at all levels of our national life, in and out of government—in business, labor, politics, education, science, the arts, and every other field. Since we must have them, it helps considerably if they are gifted in the performance of their appointed task. The sad truth is that a great many of our organizations are badly managed or badly led. And because of that, people within those organizations are frustrated when they need not be frustrated. They are not helped when they could be helped. They are not given the opportunities to fulfill themselves that are clearly possible.

In the minds of some, leadership is associated with goals that are dis-
tasteful—power, profit, efficiency, and the like. But leadership, properly
conceived, also serves the individual human goals that our society values
so highly, and we shall not achieve those goals without it.

Leaders worthy of the name, whether they are university presidents or
senators, corporation executives or newspaper editors, school superintendents or governors, contribute to the continuing definition and articulation of the most cherished values of our society. They offer, in short,
moral leadership. So much of our energy has been devoted to tending the
machinery of our complex society that we have neglected this element in
leadership. I am using the word "moral" to refer to the shared values that
must undergird any functioning society. The thing that makes a number
of individuals a society rather than a population or a crowd is the presence of shared attitudes, habits and values, a shared conception of the enterprise of which they are all a part, shared views of why it is worthwhile
for the enterprise to continue and to flourish. Leaders can help in bringing that about. In fact, it is required that they do so. When leaders lose
their credibility or their moral authority, then the society begins to disintegrate.

Leaders have a significant role in creating the state of mind that is the
society. They can serve as symbols of the moral unity of the society. They
can express the values that hold the society together. Most important,
they can conceive and articulate goals that lift people out of their petty
preoccupations, carry them above the conflicts that tear a society apart,
and unite them in the pursuit of objectives worthy of their best efforts.

PART FOUR

DILEMMAS AND PARADOXES

The study of leadership is laced with paradox. Individuals who possess all of the important characteristics and qualities of effective leaders don't necessarily succeed, and if they do, their efforts often result in great harm or tragedy to others. Moreover, leaders and followers often find themselves using unethical means to achieve worthy ends, and vice versa. An individual who is a successful leader in one situation or context may fail in another situation, even though he or she employs the same capacity, skill, or style, whereas other individuals (although not very many) are able to successfully lead in a variety of very different situations. This brings up the question of whether leaders are born or made. Although there is general agreement that leadership can be learned, it is certainly true that some find it much easier than others to learn the qualities of successful leadership. The paradoxes of leadership are many, real, and intense, making the study of the subject all the more relevant.

The varieties of ideas, approaches, and conclusions that have emerged from the study of leadership have not provided a consensus. Earlier, we found this discouraging. We now conclude that the dilemmas and paradoxes are strengths in better understanding leadership. The reality is that there are many languages, interpretations, and value sets associated with leadership.

Leaders must make choices. That they can do so in partnership with their followers is strength. Yet the reality is that the leader is ultimately responsible for and credited with the outcomes associated with the decision. If the choices were easy, there would be significantly fewer treatises on leadership. That many choices are difficult leads us to examine some of the contemporary dilemmas and paradoxes faced by our leaders.

A dilemma is defined as a choice between equally balanced alternatives or a predicament that seemingly defies a satisfactory solution. A common business dilemma relates to decisions about price competition.

The reality today is that consumers expect the highest quality at the lowest price. The Internet provides savvy consumers with almost complete information about alternative products and services. While producers may choose to differentiate on the basis of features or service, the reality is that many products and services are defined by the consumer in rather simple terms. Thus, armed with information from a variety of producers, the expected level of high quality allows consumers to choose the alternative with the lowest price. Business leaders are constantly faced with reducing the costs of production so that for the level of desired quality and differentiation, the price offered will be as low as possible. This leads to intricate supply chain structures and minimizing the non-value-added costs of administration and support.

With the above in mind, a shift in the economy or in the demand for a product can pose a challenge to the leader. Suddenly, the company is no longer competitive and the choices are to shift production to a low-cost labor force in another country or lose the market to foreign competitors. In both instances, the impact will be a reduction in employment, meaning that people will lose jobs, communities will lose the taxes and philanthropic support, and the influence of the business in the region will be reduced. This is a classic "lose-lose" scenario being played out globally in our highly competitive economic environment.

In the public sector, the most common dilemma is the desire for lower taxes with increasing expectations for services. All too often, we externalize our wants and needs as citizens, looking to government for better education, higher levels of public safety, a cleaner environment, better infrastructures, and more responsiveness in our elected officials. All of these require funding, but few candidates for office are willing to propose that we must pay. Thus, we hear pledges to reduce taxes, which endears to voters those candidates who will place the least financial burden on the electorate. Once elected, government leaders are faced with the reality that citizen expectations cannot be easily met.

Because of economics, similar scenarios are created in our not-for-profit organizations that provide arts and entertainment, social services, and spiritual support. There is increasing pressure to apply "cost-benefit" analysis in all organizational sectors—a cry to run organizations "like a business." The result has been an overemphasis on the business leadership model.

How the leader makes those choices is critical. The leadership dilemma is one of increasing the value of the business for owners and identifying ways in which employees can continue to have productive jobs in the future. Communicating the choices to employees can either be confrontational or lead to innovation and change in the company. Transformational leaders will address dilemmas with confidence and optimism, engaging followers to help identify other alternatives that will be in the best interests of the organization and, ultimately, themselves.

Other contemporary dilemmas deal with issues like investing in equipment friendly to the environment that may increase the cost of a product, demonstrating diversity by promoting minority candidates ahead of others, purchasing services rather than doing them in-house, and awarding dividends to owners and employees rather than reinvesting in capital development of the firm. And there are other such dilemmas, large and small. These are what many leaders describe as the "tough choices." Dilemmas become less traumatic when the followers are included in the ultimate choices.

Yet Robert Greenleaf's servant leadership remains an attractive construct. Many people believe that current trends should be reversed to focus on ideological outcomes to assess leadership effectiveness, not resource allocation. Perhaps the dominant dilemma is one of attempting to separate the economics from the other choices a leader must make.

A paradox is a statement that seems contradictory or unbelievable but that may well be true. Because of the diversity of leadership perspectives, there appear to be continuing paradoxes associated with the concept. We see situations where reason appears not to prevail. We accept assumptions about leadership that are not based upon fact or reality.

One example is that women and men are different as leaders because of gender. A great deal of discussion surrounds attempts to define the ways in which these differences are represented in style and even substance. Supporting evidence for the assertion is not compelling, yet the dialogue continues.

Another example is that "leaders are born, not made." This is often used as a reason for the failures in leadership training. Our response has been to link training with management effectiveness and concentrate on development as the path to effective leadership. The proclivity for leadership is a choice one makes, but as noted earlier, we believe that most people have the capacity to lead, if they are committed to do so.

In a sense, many of the paradoxes are artificial as we attempt easy answers to the questions about effective leadership. Our intent is to expose you to some of the contemporary paradoxes so that you can differentiate between what appears to be the case and the reality of leadership.

Leadership Perspectives

In each edition of this book, we turn to Warren Bennis for discourse on contemporary issues. He takes a radical position in "The End of Leadership: Exemplary Leadership Is Impossible Without Full Inclusion, Initiatives, and Cooperation of Followers" (Chapter 17). The paradox presented is that exemplary leadership and organizational change are not possible without a partnership with followers. The author describes the preeminence of top-down leadership, which is maladaptive, leading ultimately to failure. His notion of the end of leadership is truly a redirection, translated as a partnership between leaders and followers. Bennis suggests four themes. First, the leader must understand and embrace the power of appreciation in developing the followers. Second, the leader must continue reminding the people in the organization of what is important. Third, the leader must generate and sustain trust throughout the organization. Fourth, the leader and followers must emerge as intimate allies. Thus, Bennis sees great groups and organizations make great leaders.

"Do We Really Want More Leaders in Business?" (Chapter 18) is the dilemma posed by Andrea Giampetro-Meyer, Timothy Brown, S.J., M. Neil Browne, and Nancy Kubasek. The authors use a focus on ethics to compare differences between transformational, transactional, and servant leadership in organizations. They also examine leadership styles in terms of popularity in organizations without passing judgment. In a search for theories that allow reason to play more than a minimal role in ethical decision-making, they explore the best fit with the firm's desire to achieve efficiency in the short run. Their notion of the dilemma is a consideration of the short-run profit expectation relative to the costs associated with ensuring more ethical corporate cultures. This is easier to think about from afar than being on the firing line with analysts and owners in an uncertain economic environment.

Harriet Rubin presents a paradox of women business leaders and begins with the untested common assumptions in "We Won't See Great Leaders Until We See Great Women Leaders" (Chapter 19). She notes that women start a company on the average of one every sixty seconds but few such companies seem to grow large. The enemy is fear and the action is to embrace self-confidence and move forward. Essentially, Rubin suggests that the same issues confronting men in creating great companies are the challenges that women face. The reflection that in the new economy, everyone was born yesterday provides the opportunity and incentive to challenge the paradox in contemporary leadership.

In Chapter 20, we explore "Narcissistic Leaders: The Incredible Pros, the Inevitable Cons" with Michael Maccoby. The dilemma is that narcissists are good for companies that need people with vision and courage but are bad for companies when their narcissistic leaders refuse to listen to the advice of those around them when challenged with problems that can lead to trouble. Effective leaders all have some degree of ego, but the narcissistic leader must be cautious. The author suggests that the narcissistic leader must find a trusted sidekick to bring rationality to the leader's visions. In addition, the narcissistic leader has a wonderful opportunity to get people in the organization to identify with the lofty goals and to incorporate the goals into the fabric of the organization. We need narcissistic leaders to create visions for today's organizations, but they need to understand and accept their limits.

Finally, in "Level 5 Leadership: The Triumph of Humility and Fierce Resolve" (Chapter 21), Jim Collins reports on the results of research that explain what catapults a company from merely good to truly great. He has found that most powerfully transformative executives possess a paradoxical mixture of personal humility and professional will. They are timid and ferocious, shy and fearless. They are rare—and unstoppable. Does this chapter contradict the preceding one?

17

The End of Leadership

*Exemplary Leadership Is Impossible Without
Full Inclusion, Initiatives, and
Cooperation of Followers*

WARREN BENNIS

I've never fully approved of formal debates. The very premise of a debate, where issues are egregiously over-simplified, can't help but lose the subtly-nuanced distinctions we academics relish and thrive on. So when I was asked not long ago to participate in this kind of foolishness, I was naturally resistant to participate. Especially when the "resolution before the house" was phrased as follows: "All successful organizational change must originate at the top." To make matters worse, the organizers of the debate insisted that I take the opposite position of the "resolution of the house," casting me "against type," so to speak. I would have felt far more comfortable being on the side of strong leadership, a position more compatible with most of my recent writing. I did agree, however, despite my strong reservations primarily because the organizers were colleagues and I wanted an expense paid trip to the East Coast. In accepting, I was reminded of an old *NEW YORKER* cartoon showing Charles Dickens in his publisher's office, being told rather sternly by his editor: "Well, Mr. Dickens, it's either the best of times OR the worst of times. It can't be both."

What I discovered was that getting impaled on the horns of a false dichotomy was rather more fun than I anticipated. More importantly in preparing for the debate, I arrived at an unexpected conclusion, close to an epiphanic event. I came to the unmistakable realization that TOP-

Reprinted with permission, from *Organizational Dynamics* 28, 1 (Summer 1999), pp. 71–80.

down leadership was not only wrong, unrealistic and maladaptive but also, given the report of history, dangerous. And given certain changes taking place in the organizational landscape, this obsolete form of leadership will erode competitive advantage and destroy the aspirations of any organization that aims to be in the phone book beyond the year 2002.

I think it is now possible to talk about the end of leadership without the risk of hyperbole. Some of this change is organic and inevitable. But much of it is the legacy of our times ignited by that dynamic duo: globalization and relentlessly disruptive technology.

The Encompassing Tendency

The idea of traditional TOPdown leadership is based on the myth of the triumphant individual. It is a myth deeply ingrained in the American psyche and unfortunately fostered and celebrated in the daily press, business magazines, and much of academic and popular writing. My own work, at times, has also suffered from this deification of the icons of American business: the Welches, the Barneviks, the Gateses—fill in your own hero. Whether it is midnight rider Paul Revere or basketball's Michael Jordan or, more recently, Mark McGwire, we are a nation enamored of heroes—rugged self-starters who meet challenges and overcome adversity. Our contemporary views of leadership are entwined with our notions of heroism, so much so that the distinction between "leader" and "hero" (or "celebrity," for that matter) often becomes blurred.

In our society leadership is too often seen as an inherently individual phenomenon. It's Oprah and Michael (Jordan or Eisner) and Bill (Clinton or Gates) and Larry and Hillary and Monica. We are all victims or witnesses to what Leo Braudy calls the "frenzy of renown," the "peoplification" of society. Think of it: Can you imagine a best-selling magazine as popular as *PEOPLE* called *SYSTEM*?

And yet we do understand the significance of systems. After all, it is systems that encourage collaboration and systems which makes change not only effective but possible. A shrinking world in which technological and political complexity increase at an accelerating rate offers fewer and fewer arenas in which individual action, TOPdown leadership, suffices. And here is the troubling disconnect. Despite the rhetoric of collaboration, we continue to live in a "by-line" culture where recognition and status are conferred on individuals, *not teams of people* who make change possible.

But even as the lone hero continues to gallop through our imaginations, shattering obstacles with silver bullets, leaping tall buildings in a single bound, we know that that's a falsely lulling fantasy and that is not the way real change, enduring change, takes place. We know there is an alternative reality.

What's surprising is that this should surprise us. In a society as complex and technologically sophisticated as ours, the most urgent projects require the coordinated contributions of many talented people working together. Whether the task is building a global business or discovering the mysteries of the human brain, it doesn't happen at the top; TOPdown leadership can't hope to accomplish it, however gifted the person at the TOP is. There are simply too many problems to be identified and solved, too many connections to be made. So we cling to the myth of the Lone Ranger that great things are accomplished by a larger-than-life individual shouting commands, giving direction, inspiring the troops, sounding the tocsin, decreeing the compelling vision, leading the way and changing paradigms with brio and shimmer.

This *encompassing tendency* is dysfunctional in today's world of blurring, spastic, hyper-turbulent change, and will get us into unspeakable troubles unless we understand that the search engine, the main stemwinder for effective change, is the workforce and its creative alliance with top leadership.

A personal case in point. My colleague David Heenan and I wrote a book about the role of Number Twos in organizations, how they work and don't work. We thought it an original idea, one that was significant and astonishingly neglected in the literature. We entitled the book *Second Banana* and had chapters on some of the most·famous and successful partnerships between Ones and Twos in corporate life; for example, the fabled relationship between Warren Buffett and his Number Two, Charles Munger, known for containing Buffett's enthusiasm about investments and referred to by Buffett as the "Abominable No Man." And there was a chapter called "Banana Splits," on infamously unsuccessful partnerships such as the widely publicized split between Michael Eisner and Michael Ovitz. All twelve of the publishers who reviewed the book declined. One put it rather nicely. He said, "Warren, no one in America wants to be Number Two." He also quoted Leonard Bernstein who once proclaimed that "The hardest instrument to play in a symphony orchestra is second fiddle."

So David and I changed the title to *Co-Leaders* and added a subtitle, *The Power of Great Partnerships*. With that new title and a shift in emphasis away from being Number Two, it was published this year by John Wiley.

I give this example not to plug the book but to illustrate the power of this encompassing tendency of the Great Man which dominates our thinking and perverts our understanding of organizational life and how leading change really works.

The Argument

I will present my argument in an unorthodox way by drawing on sources a little out of the ordinary for management scholars: examples and analogies from poetry, history and theater, as well as the more traditional sources of experimental studies and business anecdotes. I'll start with an excerpt from a poem by Bertholt Brecht, the Marxist playwright.

Questions from a Worker

Who built the town of Thebes of Seven Gates?
The names of kings are written in the books.
Was it the kings who dragged the slab of rock?
And Babylon, so many times destroyed,
Who built her up again so many times?
Young Alexander conquered India.
All by himself?
Caesar beat the Gauls.
Not even a cook to help him with his meals?
Philip of Spain wept aloud when his Armada
Went down. Did no one else weep? Frederick the Great won the
   Seven Years War.
Who Else was the winner?
On every page a triumph.
Who baked the victory cake?
In every decade a great man. Who picked up the check?
So many reports.
So many questions.

"In every decade a great man." That encompassing tendency again. And it shows up throughout history. In Plutarch's great biography of Cato the Elder, he wrote: "Rome showed itself to be truly great, and hence worthy of great leaders." What we tend to forget is that greatness lies within nations and organizations themselves as much, if not more, than their leaders. Could Gandhi achieve his greatness without staying close to the people representing their greatness of spirit? So many questions . . . Now for a contemporary business example. I wrote an article in which I quoted one of my favorite management philosophers, The Great One, Wayne Gretzky, saying: " It's not where the puck is, it's where the puck will be." Soon after I received a rather sour letter from the Chairman and CEO of one of our largest FORTUNE 100 companies who wrote:

I was particularly interested in what you characterize as the Gretzky factor. I think I know where the puck is going to be—the problem is, we've got thousands and thousands of folk who don't want the puck to go there, would rather that it wasn't going there, and in the event that it is going there, aren't going to let us position ourselves to meet it until after we've skated past. *In plain English, we've got a bunch of people who want the world to be the way it used to be—and are very disinclined to accept any alternative forecast of the future.* (Emphasis mine.)

Now what's interesting about this "leader" is that (a) he was regarded as one of the most innovative and creative CEOs in his industrial sector and (b) his unquestionable "genius" was totally useless because he lacked a critical mass of willing followers. And he had no followers because he was unable to generate and sustain a minimum degree of trust with his workforce, widely known to be resistant to and—no exaggeration—*dyspeptic* with his pre-Copernican ego and macho style.

If there is one generalization we make about leadership and change, it is this: No change can occur without willing and committed followers.

Let us turn now to social movements and how they are led and mobilized. Mahatma Gandhi's singular American apostle was Dr. Martin Luther King, Jr. who was introduced to his teachings as a graduate student in Boston University's Divinity School in the early 1950's. I had gone to college with Coretta Scott and got acquainted with her future husband while she attended the New England Conservatory of Music and I was in graduate school at M.I.T. Recently, upon reading John Lewis's book, *Walking with the Wind*, I recalled how back then, light years ago, Coretta seemed the charismatic one and Martin shy and bashful. Lewis, one of King's acolytes in the Civil Rights Movement of the '60s, now a Congressman from Atlanta and one of the most respected African-American leaders, tells us in his book how much of the movement was a team effort, a "band of brothers and sisters," and how Dr. King "often joined demonstrations late or ducked out early." (I should add that Lewis was and is a devoted admirer of King.) Gary Wills writes that "he tried to lift others up and found himself lifted up in the process. *He literally talked himself into useful kinds of trouble.* King's oratory urged others on to heroic tasks and where they went he had to follow. Reluctant to go to jail, he was shamed into going—after so many young people responded to his speeches and found themselves in danger." (Emphasis mine.)

Don't be misled here. I'm not just reiterating one of those well-worn bromides about leadership; you know, where leaders carefully watch where their followers are going and then follow them. I'm saying something quite different. I'm saying that exemplary leadership and organizational change are impossible without the full inclusion, initiatives and co-operation of followers.

I mentioned earlier on that TOPdown leadership tendency is also *maladaptive* and I think it's time to return to that now. It's become something of a cliché to discuss the extraordinary complexity and ambiguity and uncertainties of our current business environment. As one of my CEO friends put it, "If you're not confused, you don't know what's going on." At the risk of oversimplifying his important work on leadership, Ron Heifetz asserts that with relatively simple, "technical problems," leadership is relatively "easy"; i.e. TOPdown leadership can solve them. But with "adaptive" problems, complex and messy problems, like dealing with a seriously ill cancer patient or cleaning up an ecological hazard, many stakeholders must be involved and mobilized. The truth is that adaptive problems require complex and diverse alliances. Decrees, orders, etc., *do not work*.

An elegant experiment dreamed up by one of the most imaginative, and least acknowledged social psychologists of his day, Alex Bavelas, dramatizes, if not proves, this point. Imagine a simple, wooden circular dining room table, about 10 feet in diameter with plywood partitions walling off the five participants from visible sight of each other. The table is constructed so that subjects can communicate only by passing messages written on 3 X 5 cards through narrow slots in the partitions. The cards are all color coded so that you can count how many messages were sent to whom and by whom. Also, the table was constructed so that different organizational forms can be simulated. For example, you can create a rough example of a typical bureaucratic, command-and-control organization by restricting the flow of messages to only one central person. We used three kinds of organizational models, the Wheel, which more or less resembles the typical organizational pyramid, the Chain, a slight modification of the Wheel and the Circle where everyone could communicate to the two participants adjacent to them. Not quite a completely connected network, but one of equality (see Figure 17.1).

The problem to be solved was relatively simple. Each subject was given a pillbox which contained six different colored marbles. They were what we used to called "purees," pure white, pure blue, pure green, red, etc., and easily identifiable. For each experimental trial, there was only one color that each subject had in common. On one trial, for example, it was the red, on another it was the green, and so on, randomly varied. There were 15 trials. As soon as the subject thought he had the correct color, he would drop the marble down a rubber tube in the table so that the experimenter could not only measure the accuracy for the group but also how long it took for all five subjects to deposit the marble. Our predictions were not surprising and they were confirmed. The Wheel, the

Wheel   Chain   Circle

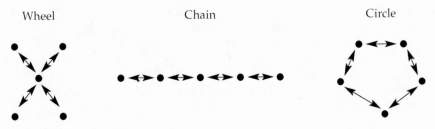

FIGURE 17.1   Organizational Networks

form most like the TOPdown leadership model was the most accurate and the most efficient; they were very, very quick. We did notice that in our post-experiment questionnaire, the central person reported having the highest morale and was wildly enthusiastic about his role while the other group members were, to be polite, pissed.

Expectable and not particularly exciting results. So we decided to change the task to a more "adaptive" problem and substituted for the primary colors, the so-called "purees," ambiguously colored marbles: cat's eyes, ginger ale-ish, bluish-green or greenish blue, all sorts of dappled colored marbles . . . Again, our predictions were confirmed. Now, under ambiguous and changing conditions, the Circle was the most efficient and accurate and all members claimed relatively high morale. On only one occasion, and we repeated this particular experiment about 50 times, did the Wheel perform better. In this one case, the central person was an exceptionally gifted artist and writer. She was also taking a minor in art history. Genius happens. Once in a blue moon.

The connection between that antediluvian experiment and the messy, changing business environment barely needs stating. But it dramatically illustrates my point that none of us is as smart as all of us, that the TOPdown model, in the present business context, is dysfunctional, maladaptive and, as I'll get to now, dangerous.

The dangers of TOPdown leadership, vivid examples of colossal folly and disaster, are so numerous that one doesn't know where to begin. Stalin's communal farms? Niemeyer's Brasilia? Hitler's Holocaust? Chainsaw Al's Follies? Napoleon's Russian campaign? LBJ's VietNam? Mao's Cultural Revolution? Maggie Thatcher's poll tax? Perhaps the best source to turn to in this respect is Barbara Tuchman's *March of Folly*, an ignored treasure for students of organizational behavior.

She argues that folly occurs when a governmental leader pursues policies contrary to the self-interest of the nation. But to be real Folly, the policy must have been perceived as counter-productive *in its own time*, not merely by hindsight. Secondly, there are always feasible alternative means that were available. She takes her notion of folly and refracts it through the prism of four major epochal events: the Trojan Horse escorted through the gates of Troy, led innocently (and stupidly) by Priam's own warriors (who had heard from Cassandra, among others, that it was probably a Greek ploy); the Renaissance Popes and how their actions brought about the Protestant Reformation; George III and the loss of the "colonies"; and LBJ and the VietNam War. Tuchman writes:

> Wooden-headedness, the source of self-deception, is a factor that plays a remarkable role in individuals. It consists in assessing a situation in terms of preconceived fixed notions while ignoring or rejecting any contrary signs. It is acting according to wish while not allowing oneself to be deflected by the facts. It is epitomized in a historian's statement about Philip II of Spain, the surpassing wooden-head of all sovereigns. "No experience of the failure of the policy could shake his belief in its essential excellence."

The New Leadership

So where does all of this lead us in terms of the current organizational context? What should be clear by now is that post-bureaucratic organization requires a new kind of alliance between leaders and the led. Today's organizations are evolving into federations, networks, clusters, cross-functional teams, temporary systems, ad hoc task forces, lattices, modules, matrices—almost anything but pyramids with their obsolete TOP-down leadership. The new leader will encourage healthy dissent and values those followers courageous enough to say no. It will go to the leader who exults in cultural differences and knows that diversity is the best hope for long-term survival and success. The title of this article was deliberately provocative but, I hope, not too misleading. It's not quite the *end* of leadership, actually, but it clearly points the way to a new, far more subtle and indirect form of influence for leaders to be effective. The new reality is that intellectual capital, brain power, know-how, human imagination has supplanted capital as the critical success factor and leaders will have to learn an entirely new set of skills that are not understood, not taught in our business schools, and, for all of those reasons, rarely practiced. I am going to suggest that there are four competencies that will determine the success of New Leadership.

1. *The New Leader understands and practices the Power of Appreciation. They are connoisseurs of talent, more curators than creators.*   We all pay lip service to acknowledgment and appreciation. To generalize just a tad, most organizations are woefully neglectful of bestowing either. And it is one of the

most powerful motivators, especially for knowledge workers. To take only one example out of numberless cases, many years ago, I sent my first book to the Dean and, in turn, received a perfunctory, dictated note saying that he would take the book on his next plane trip and read it then. That was it. That was the last word I ever heard from him about something I had spent over three years working on. Not very motivating or energizing, to say the least.

What I'm also getting at is that the leader is rarely the best or the brightest in the new organizations. The New Leader has a smell for talent and an imaginative rolodex, is unafraid of hiring people better than he is, and is often more a curator than a creator. In my book, *Organizing Genius*, I looked at the leadership of Great Groups and in most cases, the leader was rarely the cleverest or the sharpest. Peter Schneider, president of Disney's colossally successful Feature Animation studio, leads a group of 1,200 animators. He can't draw to save his life. Bob Taylor, former head of the Palo Alto Research Center, where the first commercial PC was invented, wasn't a computer scientist. J. Robert Oppenheimer, head of the befabled Manhattan Project which produced the first nuclear device, while a brilliant physicist, never matched the accomplishments of the future Nobel Laureates working for him at Los Alamos. It goes on and on. Perhaps a story about two of Britain's most famous 19th Century Prime Ministers illustrates this point. It was said about William Ewart Gladstone that when you had dinner with Mr. Gladstone, you felt that he was the world's most brilliant and provocative, the most intelligent and wittiest conversationalist you have ever met. But when you were dining with Mr. Disraeli, you felt that *you* were the world's most brilliant and provocative, the most . . .

Max DePree put it best when he said that good leaders "abandon their ego to the talents of others."

2. The New Leader keeps reminding people of what's important.   Organizations drift into entropy and the bureaucratization of imagination when they forget what's important. Simple to say, but that one sentence is one of the few pieces of advice I suggest to leaders: Remind your people of what's important. Even in my profession of teaching I will occasionally hear a colleague say, usually in half-jest, that the university would be a great place to work if only there weren't students around. What else is there but helping students to become successful at life. What can be more ennobling?

A powerful enough vision can transform what would otherwise be routine and drudgery into collectively focused energy—even sacrifice. Witness again the Manhattan Project. The scientists there were willing to put their careers on hold and to undertake what was, in essence, a massive engineering feat because they believed the free world depended on their doing so. Reminiscing about Los Alamos, Richard Feynman, the irreverent and future Nobel Laureate, told a story that illustrates how reminding people of "what's important" can give meaning and value to work. The U.S. Army had recruited talented engineers from all over the United States for special duty on the project. They were assigned to work on the primitive computers of the period (1943–'45), doing energy calculations and other tedious jobs. But the Army, obsessed with security, refused to tell them anything specific about the project. They didn't know that they were building a weapon that could end the war or even what their calculations meant. They were simply expected to do the work, which they did slowly and not very well. Feynman, who supervised the technicians, prevailed on his superiors to tell the recruits what they were doing and why. Permission was granted to lift the veil of secrecy, and Oppenheimer gave them a special lecture on the nature of the project and their own contribution.

"*Complete* transformation," Feynman recalled. "*They* began to invent ways of doing it better. They improved the scheme. They worked at night. They didn't need supervising in the night, they didn't need anything. They understood everything; they invented several of the programs we used." Ever the scientist, Feynman calculated that the work was done "nearly ten times as fast" after it had meaning.

Meaning. Charles Handy has it right in his book *The Hungry Spirit.* We are all hungry spirits craving purpose and meaning at work, to contribute something beyond ourselves and leaders can never forget to stop reminding people of what's important.

3. The New Leader generates and sustains trust. We're all aware that the terms of the new social contract of work have changed. No one can depend on life-long loyalty or commitment to any organization. Since 1985, 25% of the American workforce has been laid off at least once. That's about a half-million on average each year. In 1998, when the unemployment rate was the lowest in 30 years, roughly 110,000 workers were down-sized. At a time when the new social contract makes the times between organizations and their knowledge workers tenuous, trust becomes the emotional glue that can bond people to an organization. Trust is a small word with powerful connotations and is a hugely complex factor. The ingredients are a combination of competence, constancy, caring, fairness, candor and authenticity. Most of all the latter. And that is achieved by the New Leaders when they can balance successfully the tripod of forces working on and in most of us: ambition, competence and integrity. Authenticity, as Groucho joked, cannot be faked. To be redundant, it's real. The current cliché is "walk your talk." But it's far more than that. The best and perhaps the only way I know of to illustrate (as opposed to define) authenticity is to quote from Robert Bolt's Preface to his play, A Man for All Seasons:

> At any rate, Thomas More, as I wrote about him, became for me a man with an adamantine sense of his own self. He knew where he began and left off, what area of himself he could yield to the encroachments of his enemies, and what to the encroachments of those he loved. It was a substantial area in both cases, for he had a proper sense of fear and was a busy lover. Since he was a clever man and a great lawyer, he was able to retire from those areas in wonderfully good order, but at length he was asked to retreat from that final area where he located his self. And there this supple, humorous, unassuming and sophisticated person set like metal, was overtaken by an absolutely primitive rigor, and could no more be budged than a cliff.

4. The New Leader and the led are intimate allies.   Earlier I referred to how Dr. King's followers shamed him into going to jail because so many young people responded to his speeches and found themselves in danger. They were the unsung heroes. People you've never heard of: James Bevel, Diane Nash, Otis Moss and many others. All heroes. John Lewis tells us in his book how much of the Civil Rights Movement was a heroic team effort, referring to Henry V "band of brothers."

It's not too much of a stretch to consider Jakob Schindler, the protagonist of an epochal story immortalized in the film *Schindler's List*. The power of Spielberg's film is the transformation of Schindler from a sleazy, down-at-the-heels small-time con-man who moves to Poland in order to harness cheap Jewish labor to make munitions which he can then sell to the Germans at low cost. His transformation is the singular compelling narrative of the film. And it comes about over a period of time where Schindler interacts with his Jewish workers, most of all the accountant, Levin, but also frequent and achingly painful moments where he confronts the evil of the war, of the holocaust, of the suffering, of the injustice. In the penultimate scene, when the war is over and the Nazis have evacuated the factory, but before the American troops arrive, the prisoners give him a ring, made for him, from the precious metals used by the workers. As he tries to put the ring on, he begins crying, "Why, why are you doing this? With this metal, we could have saved three, maybe four, maybe five more Jews." And he drives off in tears.

I find it hard to be objective about a scene that tears at my soul, but I want to argue that though this was a unique, singular event, it portrays what New Leadership is all about: that great leaders are made by great groups and by organizations that create the social architecture of respect and dignity. And, through some kind of weird alchemy, some ineffable symbiosis, great leadership brings that about. Without each other, the leader and the led are culturally impoverished. Only a poet could sum up the majesty of this alchemy:

> *We are all angels with only one wing.*
> *We can only fly while embracing each other.*

These New Leaders will not have the loudest voice, but the most attentive ear. Instead of pyramids, these post-bureaucratic organizations will be structures built of energy and ideas, led by people who find their joy in the task at hand, while embracing each other—and not worrying about leaving monuments behind.

Selected Bibliography

There are several books I referred to in the article that would more likely be found on the book shelf of a history or English professor than a management scholar or practitioner but two of them, *Frenzy of Renown* by Leo Braudy, (Oxford, 1986) and Barbara Tuchman's *March of Folly* (Alfred Knopf, 1984), deserve to be. They are just terrific books on leadership. Braudy's is the first and only history of celebrity and is brilliantly written as might be expected but often found lacking in academic treatises. I've said enough about Tuchman in the text, I use it in my undergraduate leadership class and it's very useful. What historian Tuchman refers to as folly or woodenheadedness, we might refer to as cognitive dissonance. John Lewis's book, *Walking with the Wind* (Simon & Schuster, 1998) is a splendid personal memoir of the civil rights movement, written by one of the most important African-American leaders. In Jim O'Toole's *Leading Change* Jossey-Bass, 1995), the frontispiece of that book which I reproduced here underlines, with great wit and clarity, the basic premise of this important work; i.e., leaders better learn how to enroll willing followers. It could have also been written by a humanities professor, which he basically is, except with brio and a deep philosophical lens, he has written one of the most provocative and important books on leadership. Ronald Heifetz's book, *Leadership Without Easy Answers* (Belknap, 1994), more than lives up to its name and is not an easy read as the title suggests. But it is deep and complex and goes way beyond the domain of Corporate America, though he doesn't exclude that, into areas of community leadership, doctor/patient relationships among others. Gary Wills's book *Certain Trumpets* (Simon & Schuster, 1994) is already a classic. It has a lot in common with Howard Gardner's *Leading Minds* (Basic Books, 1995) which I should have referenced as well. Wills goes at leadership as a political scientist cum historian would, while Gardner is a cognitive psychologist. They both rely on fascinating narratives, but their choices of leaders, at the margins anyway, give away their world view, their range, and their informed biases. So while Wills chooses to focus on Cesare Borgia or King David, Gardner will take up Robert Maynard Hutchins or Jean Monet. At the same time, they often choose the same icon, like Martha Graham, Gandhi, Eleanor Roosevelt and Pope John XXIII. Two recent books I co-authored, one with Patricia Biederman, *Organizing Genius* (Perseus, 1997) and one with David Heenan, *Co-Leaders* (Wiley, 1999) provided some of the conceptual background for this article but try to put the spotlight not so much on leadership but on Great Groups and Partnerships.

I'll end this bibliographic narrative with Bertholt Brecht, who always liked to have the last word anyway. He disliked collaboration or partnership and was not capable of either, except for his wicked and bittersweet lyrics to Kurt Weill's *Threepenny Opera*. The poem I used came from Georg Tabori's book, *The World of Brecht* (Samuel French, 1964.)

18

Do We Really Want More Leaders in Business?

ANDREA GIAMPETRO-MEYER
TIMOTHY BROWN, S.J.
M. NEIL BROWNE
NANCY KUBASEK

A recent issue of *Fortune* proclaimed that "everyone thinks business needs better leadership" (1995). Many people both within and outside business are calling for more or better leadership to serve as an antidote to a broad array of businesses problems. The hope is that by turning mangers into leaders, leadership will transform problems into opportunities. Unfortunately, those who write in favor of better leadership are often unclear about what they want "better" leaders to do, and how they want "better" leaders to treat people. The ambiguity of leadership allows many of us to be in favor of it, without raising serious questions about whether it is possible to turn most managers into leaders. Even if such a development were possible, it is unclear whether this change will promote improved decision-making in organizations, at least from an ethical perspective. This article suggests that the potential for leadership to promote ethically sound corporate cultures depends on the kind of leadership one advocates or appreciates, as well as the measures a company or individual managers take to correct some harsh consequences of commonly practiced forms of leadership.

Three Kinds of Leadership

JoAnne Ciulla, a professor in the leadership and ethics program at the Jepson School of the University of Richmond, recently published a com-

Reprinted with permission, from *Journal of Business Ethics* 17 (1998), pp. 1727–1736. Copyright 1998 by Kluwer Academic Publishers.

prehensive review of leadership research (1995). In that review, Ciulla stimulates interest in dissecting the idea of leadership. She points out that most researchers do not disagree about what leadership is. Ciulla explains that most definitions focus on "some kind of process, act, or influence that in some way gets people to do something." She suggests that instead of considering the question "What is leadership?" we should be asking "What is good leadership?" When we consider what constitutes good leadership, Ciulla urges us to consider both ethics and competence. She points out that people long for highly ethical leaders (Ciulla, 1995).

In her article, Ciulla presents a brief discussion of three kinds of leadership: *transformational*, *transactional*, and *servant* leadership. *Transformational or charismatic leaders* inspire their followers to pursue the leader's clear vision for the company (Steers and Black, 1994, p. 420). Transformational leaders demonstrate self-confidence, the ability to articulate a vision, a willingness to pursue the vision even if they must assume high personal risks, and an ability to promote change (Steers and Black, 1994). *Transformational leaders* look at leadership as a social exchange process among leaders and followers (Steers and Black, 1994). An effective transactional leader is one who makes it clear that those who give something to the organization get something in return. The transactional leader says to her followers, "I will look out for your interests if you look out for mine (and the company's)" (Steers and Black, 1994). *Servant leaders* make serving employees, customers and the community their number one priority (Spears, 1995, p. 3). A servant leader asks whether those the leader serves grow as persons. The servant leader asks, "Do those I serve become wiser, healthier, freer, more autonomous, more likely themselves to become servants?" (Spears, 1995).

This article makes a few basic observations about these three kinds of leadership. These observations focus on differences about how each definition of leadership outlines what the leader is supposed to achieve, and how the leader treats people in the organization while striving to achieve the organization's goals. We also consider which leadership styles are likely to be most popular in organizations that strive to maximize short-run profits. The article presents these three kinds of leadership as dichotomous theories, and suggests some problems with these leadership styles. While we present transformational, transactional and servant leadership as three separate theories, it is possible to look a leader and see someone who is both charismatic or transformational, and looks at the leader/follower relationship as a transaction. We also present problems associated with leadership as dichotomous problems. For example, we raise the problem of conformity under the topic of transactional leadership, but it is possible that transformational leaders can also be associated with problems related to conformity. We present concepts as dichotomous to enhance clarity. We are making an attempt to move the debate about leadership in a more productive direction. Our point is to show that the idea of leadership demands deeper consideration.

We start with transformational leadership because this is the leadership style most people envision when they say they want more or better leaders. Then, we consider transactional leadership as the primary alternative to transformational leadership. Finally, we consider servant leadership because it holds special promise as a way to improve organizations from an ethical perspective. We are not touting or degrading any of these theories. We will, however, point out which theories allow reason to play more than a minimal role in the ethical decision-making, as well as those that are most consistent with a firm's desire to achieve efficiency in the short run.

Transformational Leadership: Absolutist Behavior and the Problem of Narcissism

Do we want more leaders who can make their vision a reality by inspiring their followers to work toward the leader's vision? Our answer is, it *depends*. Our primary point in this section is that transformational or charismatic leaders tend to inspire followers more when they demonstrate absolutist behavior. Inspirational leaders are *certain* a particular action is right or wrong from an ethical perspective. They rarely admit that the moral issues individuals and business face are often "tangled webs of frequently subtle, ill-defined problems" (Shaw and Barry, 1995). We also point out that transformational leaders are probably more likely than others to demonstrate problems created by narcissism. Finally, we will explain how the transformational leader's behavior is often rewarded by financial markets (Korten, 1996).

A good example of a transformational leader is Lee Iacocca. Iacocca turned the Chrysler Corporation around, manufactured and marketed the popular Ford Mustang, and restored the Statue of Liberty. At one point, he was a potential candidate for the presidency of the United States. Iacocca demonstrates many characteristics of a transformational or charismatic leader. He shows self-confidence and an ability to articulate a vision; he can promote change. David Pincus, in his book about leadership and the importance of strong communication skills, describes Iacocca as a corporate top dog with a "powerful, engaging personal style" who articulated a vision and made that vision a reality (1994). Iacocca could speak in a way that inspired many people to rally to help him achieve his important goals.

Can we count on transformational leaders like Lee Iacocca to promote good organizational decision-making from an ethical perspective? This question is difficult to answer. From an ethical perspective, strength in decision-making comes from reflection, as well as the ability to recognize the ambiguity of ethical dilemmas. Strong decision-making also shows respect for analytical decision-making based upon principles rooted in moral philosophy. A serious limitation to the transformational leader's ability to promote improved ethical decision-making is that followers tend to be more inspired by assertions expressed with certainty rather than uncertainty. It is more powerful for leaders to say "I'm sure I'm right" than to say "this situation is confusing and difficult to resolve." Unfortunately, a leader who sees situations as tangled webs can look limp rather than wise to followers.

It would be all right for the leader to demonstrate self-confidence about an ethical decision if this decision came about after the leader and followers went through an analytical, reflective reasoning process. Often, leaders and followers make decisions much more simply. A good example is Iacocca's decision to manufacture and market the Ford Pinto. In this situation, Lee Iacocca demonstrated a clear vision, and his leaders followed his inspiring vision. This vision was to manufacture and market a car that weighed no more than 2000 pounds and cost no more than 2000 dollars. In their rush to achieve the $2000/2000 pound goal, Lee Iacocca's followers designed and manufactured a car they knew would lead to many burn deaths. The company's notorious cost-benefit analysis allowed Iacocca's followers to conclude they should not correct the Pinto's design because it was cheaper to pay for burn injuries and deaths than to change the car's design (Strobel, 1980). Ford's decision to manufacture and market the Pinto occurred after the company determined (perhaps incorrectly) how it could maximize its short-run profits, not after it engaged in analytical decision-making based upon principles rooted in moral philosophy. The Pinto case shows that it is not clear that transformational leaders engage in behavior that moves organizations toward becoming more morally courageous, democratic or reasonable.

Transformational or charismatic leaders also present the problem of narcissism, which sometimes encourages the leader to inspire her followers to pursue questionable goals. Some provocative work on the behavior of leaders has been conducted by Manfred Ket de Vries, an economist and psychoanalyst who has considered the dark side of leadership (1993). What makes his work compelling is that he sees and explains how traits we typically associate with leaders (especially transformational leaders) can drive organizations toward a wide range of outcomes, some of which are disastrous. The trait Ket de Vries considers that deserves the most attention is narcissism. In Ket de Vries' most recent book, he states that most leaders are narcissistic. He explains that the consequences of this trait are complex. He writes that "[n]arcissism is a strange thing, a double-edged sword. Having either too much or too little of it can throw a person off balance" (1995). Narcissism drives leaders to achieve, which obviously helps organizations thrive. Narcissism is especially helpful when combined with positive leadership traits such as competence, vision, humor, and determination (1993). However, narcissistic leaders are not always constructive. Sometimes, leaders use their power toward ends that show a lack of empathy. Some leaders develop what Ket de Vries calls a "grandiose sense of self-importance." This grandiosity sometimes leads to disastrous consequences in the end.

Lee Iacocca is a good example of a transformational leader who used his talents toward both constructive and destructive ends. With the Pinto decision, we see the dark side of leadership. The self-confidence that allows leaders like Lee Iacocca to change the world also blinds them to the real, human consequences of their decisions. In his best-selling autobiography, Iacocca reflects briefly about the Pinto decision. His reflection omits a discussion about how his leadership allowed the company to make the decision to manufacture and market the car, or about how his employees were willing to follow his direction no matter the consequences (Iacocca, 1984). In a recent interview in *Fortune*, he reflects on his life in the auto industry. Iacocca reminds us he is a "bottom line guy." He says that in his life he got some notoriety, and made some money in the car business. Iacocca says, "I made some mistakes, but it averaged out pretty good. Now that chapter has closed, and I don't think much about cars anymore" (Taylor, 1996). His lack of empathy for the families who suffered as a consequence of his leadership demonstrates the narcissistic side of his personality.

Under what circumstances do we want more transformational leaders? Generally, we do not need transformational leaders who view the world in absolute terms, or whose narcissism promotes questionable behavior, if our goal is to improve corporate cultures from an ethical perspective. One important way transformational leaders *could* promote improved ethical decision-making is if the leader recognizes and models for followers a comparative, pragmatic approach to ethics. If the transformational leader demonstrates an acceptance of policies or thought processes that encourage empathy in decision-making, we might want more transformational leaders. One strategy is that managers can engage in what Christopher Stone calls "responsible reflection" (1982). Responsible reflection is important because it fills the need of the corporation to act as if it has a conscience. Responsible reflection requires managers to not only obey laws, but also to engage in a cognitive process that allows them to engage in intellectual, analytical reasoning. When faced with a decision within the organization, the manager who engages in responsible reflection does not act on impulse, takes full measure of his or her accountability, considers the needs and interests of others, and acts with a sense of duty (Stone, 1982). Some transformational leaders do appear to engage in responsible reflection.

More recently, this idea of responsible reflection has taken the form of value-based ethics training. Some transformational or charismatic leaders advocate ethics programs that take a comparative, pragmatic approach to ethics. Robert D. Haas, Chairman of the Board and Chief Executive Officer of Levi Strauss & Co., is a proponent of value-based organizational approaches to ethics. Haas says that "high ethical standards can be maintained only if they are modeled by management and woven into the fabric of the company" (Mitchell, 1994). He challenges managers to "do the right thing" by adhering to an approach to ethics based upon six ethical principles: Honesty, promise-keeping, fairness, respect for others, compassion, and integrity. Haas' approach recognizes the complexity of ethical decision-making in organizations. The company addresses ethical issues by identifying which ethical principles are relevant in a specific situation. Then, the company considers the needs and interests of not only those the company has a clear financial interest in pleasing (shareholders, employees, business partners), but also those affected by their decisions (customers, members of local communities, and public interest groups) (Mitchell, 1994). This approach to ethics allows the company to trust the judgment of their workers, and shows appreciation for the competing interests of various groups the company's decisions affect. Values-based ethical decision-making is an example of responsible reflection and is consistent with improved corporate cultures from an ethical perspective.

Not everyone benefits from cultures that implement policies that encourage responsible reflection to counteract the harsh consequences of transformational leadership. It is not clear financial markets reward responsible reflection. David Korten, author of *When Corporations Rule the World*, explains that financial markets reward CEOs of companies that "abandon accountability to all stakeholders but one: the global financial market" (1996). These CEOs are "hellbent on maximizing short-run financial returns to shareholders." As long as corporate managers are "captives of the system," their individual willingness to pursue responsible reflection is undermined by a capitalistic system that rewards something else. Do we want more transformational leaders? Employees and communities might be better off with more transformational leaders if these leaders are not too narcissistic, engage in responsible reflection, and resist the temptation to engage in absolutist behavior. Shareholders are probably better off with transformational leaders who inspire their followers in a certain, absolute style. Although leading the corporate charge toward the bottom line financial position of the company is not consistent with an improved ethical climate, it is crucial to most companies to maximize short-run financial returns to shareholders.

Transactional Leaders: Relativistic Behavior and the Problem of Conformity

Do we want more leaders who look at their relationship with followers as a social exchange process based upon self-interest? Our answer is, *it depends*. Our primary point in this section is that transactional leaders tend to follow what we call craft ethics. Craft ethics is a form of ethical relativism by which the moral agent discovers what his craft mandates in particular situations and follows that mandate. This form of relativism omits reflection about what the agent personally believes would be moral; instead, there is a looking outward for what those in the craft say is right and wrong. This craft ethic is followed on the job, even when its principles directly conflict with those the moral agent abides by outside the firm. This form of ethics often inspires ethically questionable behavior from both leaders and followers. We also explain the problem of conformity, which makes it more likely that individuals in organizations will follow craft ethics. Finally, we explain that transactional leaders, like transformational leaders, can provide an important outcome: they can help firms maximize short-term financial returns to shareholders. For that reason, some people want "better" leaders to develop the skills that will make them strong transactional leaders.

A good example of a transactional leader is Daniel E. Gill, chairman and chief executive of Bausch and Lomb. In fall of 1995, *Business Week* reported on questionable practices at Bausch and Lomb. Specifically, the article described how Gill pressured executives to maintain double digit sales and earnings growth, which stimulated unethical behavior throughout the organization. Driven to "make the numbers," in large part by a compensation system relying heavily on attaining these goals, corporate managers did what was expedient, even when such behaviors were unlawful or unethical, including giving customers extraordinarily long payment terms, knowingly feeding grey markets, threatening to cut off distributors if they didn't take huge quantities of unwanted goods, and shipping goods before they were ordered and reporting these shipments as sales (Maremont, 1995). Gill created a culture that was "tenacious, demanding—and very numbers-oriented" (Maremont, 1995). The behavior of these Bausch and Lomb managers is consistent with earlier research arguing that a company's reward structure can "influence the ethical/unethical behavior of its members through specific rewards and punishment" (Trevino, 1990). Gill's behavior suggests he believed the leader/follower relationship is based upon the notion that "I will look out for your interests in you look out for mine and the company's" (Steers and Black, 1994).

Astra U.S.A., Inc.'s President and Chief Executive Officer, Lars Bildman, is another example of a transactional leader. In May of 1996, *Business Week* reported on the corporate culture at Astra. This article described a company led by a man who is a "very disciplined, goal-oriented guy" (Maremont, 1996). His drive led the company to a position of financial strength in the pharmaceutical industry. He was a powerful leader who inspired fear and action from followers by establishing a controlling, domineering atmosphere at Astra. The company's culture generated much financial success, but also allowed an environment that perpetuated a sexually hostile environment toward women. Both male and female employees accepted the company's norms, which included widespread sexual harassment by Bildman and several senior managers. Employees condoned the sexual harassment because Bildman and other managers made it clear it was in their best interests to conform. Those who failed to conform left the company; some filed lawsuits.

Can we count on transactional leaders like Gill and Bildman to promote good organizational decision-making from an ethical perspective? Both Astra U.S.A. and Bausch & Lomb established corporate cultures that were relativistic. The kind of corporate relativism accepted by employees at both organizations is not uncommon in firms today, and is encouraged by transactional leadership styles. It is a relativism whereby what is right and wrong is determined by what those at the upper reaches of the corporate hierarchy say is right or wrong. And in most corporations, it could be summed up by the phrase, "whatever it takes to get the job done." As an ethical moral agent, the manager's over-riding responsibility is to interpret and follow the corporate culture.

Probably the most important work on the topic of ethics in bureaucratic organizations was done by Robert Jackall in the late 1980's. His work shows how transactional leadership leads to questionable corporate decision-making. Jackall went into a number of organizations to study the ways through which the organizational bureaucracy shaped managers' moral consciousness, and the occupational ethics of these managers (Jackall, 1988). What he found could be summed up as "What is right in the corporation is what the guy above you wants from you" (Jackall, 1988, p. 6). In this kind of culture, it is crucial to be a team player. When Jackall describes what it takes to survive in the corporate culture, his description sounds almost exactly like the definition of transactional leadership. To survive, Jackall explains that the manager must identify what his superior wants, and then do whatever is necessary to attain the superior's objectives as expediently as possible. The problem with this kind of decision-making is that when followers are faced with a moral dilemma, they attempt to strip the dilemma of anything like the commitments that define the reflective moral self and ask instead what outcome would be most congruent with the objectives of one's institution (Jackall, 1988, p. 124). By transforming personal decisions into team decisions, and thus keeping managers from feeling individually responsible for the consequences of their decisions, the firm further turns moral questions into questions of what is in the best interests of the firm. Thus, the good corporate manager identifies the goals of his CEO and does whatever is necessary to meet those goals. One may thus undertake actions that one would consider wrong, even immoral, outside the firm, but these actions are acceptable within the firm because what is moral is what one's boss desires. Transactional leadership encourages this behavior. Both Bildman and Gill created corporate cultures that inspired managers to follow craft ethics. The managers at Bausch & Lomb wanted to make their numbers no matter what or how, while managers at Astra U.S.A. wanted to get ahead even if it meant they were the perpetrators or victims of sexual harassment.

Jackall's work demonstrated that managers tend to refrain from making their own judgments in situations in which the leader is clear and certain about the "right" or "wrong" course of action. His observations are not surprising to those who have studied problems created by conformity. Many studies have documented the strength of individuals' propensity to comply with authority figures (Milgram, 1974). Strong transactional leaders would expect their workers to comply with their wishes. It would be in the follower's best interests to do so. Sometimes, conformity is good for an organization, and society. Most organizations count on conformity to get their employees to help the company achieve its mission. However, sometimes conformity presents significant problems. Occasionally, followers lack the conviction to refrain from following the authority figure's command, even when they know they are hurting others (Milgram, 1974). Even when no one's life is at stake, conformity presents serious problems. Studies of organizational dynamics show that employees in the corporate world are reluctant to speak up when they see something happening in the organization that troubles them. Most people are not willing to bring bad news to the attention of powerful people in their organizations (Jackall, 1988). The idea of conformity helps us understand why most managers are willing to comply with craft ethics. Most managers are willing to act upon the belief that "what is right in the corporation is what the guy above you wants from you" (Jackall, 1988). This would be especially true when "the guy above you" is a strong transactional leader who expects self-interest to guide corporate behavior. Managers at both Astra and Bausch & Lomb demonstrated incredible conformity to powerful leaders who appealed to the employees' and company's self-interests.

Under what circumstances do we want more transactional leadership? Definitions of transactional leaders are not all the same. Some writers who describe transactional leaders add a discussion of certain values to the description. Ciulla, for instance, explains that transactional leaders are interested in values that are consistent with improving the "means of an act" (Ciulla, 1995). She explains that transactional leadership rests on values such as responsibility, fairness, honesty, and promise-keeping. Her explanation is more positive. She explains that transactional leadership is a "form of leadership [that] helps leaders and followers reach their own goals by supplying lower level wants and needs so that they can move up to higher needs."

If transactional leaders make the values of responsibility, fairness, honesty, and promise-keeping an important part of their analysis, perhaps we do want more transactional leaders. If these values are foremost in the leader's mind, their behavior might be consistent with the behavior Robert Haas of Levi Strauss envisions. In fact, it is possible we could describe Haas as a transactional leader whose beliefs are value-based. However, we must be cautious. It is likely that many of the managers and leaders Jackall described in his book believe in all those values—responsibility, fairness, honesty and promise-keeping. Within the context of corporate cultures it is difficult to act on the basis of these values. Self-interest discourages managers from following these values.

Transactional leadership styles do, however, benefit shareholders, even if the transactional leader does not embrace values-based ethical decision-making. Shareholders in both Astra and Bausch & Lomb benefited from the behavior their corporate leaders inspired. In the short run, both corporations enjoyed tremendous financial success. Bausch & Lomb's focus on the bottom line and quarterly results made the company a financial success. Under Gill's leadership, Bausch & Lomb's sales and earnings tripled within a decade (Maremont, 1995). Bildman similarly led Astra to a strong financial position. If organizations strive to maximize short-run profit positions, transactional leaders have much to offer.

Servant Leadership: Reflective Behavior and the Problem of Efficiency

Do we want more leaders who lead because they want to serve others? (Greenleaf, 1977). Our answer is, it depends. Our primary point in this section is that the idea of servant leadership holds the most promise for ethically improved corporate cultures because it is the form of leadership most likely to promote reflective behavior. We also explain the limited usefulness of servant leadership in business. We explain why scholars must be cautious about thinking servant leadership is THE solution to the problem of how to harness the best in corporations. Although servant leadership is consistent with improved corporate cultures, it is not consistent with short-run profit maximization. If global competitiveness requires short-run effi-ciency, servant leaders will hinder corporate financial success.

When people write about servant leadership, they do not tell stories about corporate top dogs who achieved great things. They usually do not start with a story about any businessperson. Instead, they tell the story from Herman Hesse's *Journey to the East* (Spears, 1995). Robert Greenleaf originally used this story to demonstrate what servant leadership means. In Hesse's story, a servant, Leo, carries bags and does chores for a group on a spiritual journey to the East. He solidifies the group through songs and just by his presence. At one point, Leo disappears. The group loses its way. As Hesse's story progresses, the book's main character, HH, dis-covers that Leo was actually the leader. This story shows Greenleaf's main point, that *leaders serve followers.*

Servant leadership is not rooted in a quest for power, fame, or any self-centered goal. It is something a person discovers, not a leadership style one leader can teach another. A servant leader is a genius; the servant leader is truly human. He or she listens well and feels the human condi-tion. Servant leaders are concerned with the least privileged in society and strive to help others grow as persons. Servant leaders want to help those they serve become "healthier, wiser, freer, more autonomous, and more likely themselves to become leaders" (Greenleaf, 1977). Servant leaders show awareness of how the decisions they inspire affect others.

Although books about leadership give examples from the business world of servant leadership in action, the stories are not of famous people like Lee Iacocca (Spears, 1995). Instead, the stories focus on unknown managers who treat others well on a daily basis. Servant leaders are most likely to be managers who do not strive to be leaders. Instead, those the leader serves discover that a particular person is leading them by serving.

Can we count on servant leaders like Leo (in the form of a corporate manager) to promote good organizational decision-making from an ethi-cal perspective? Compared to transformational and transactional leader-ship, servant leadership is most consistent with the idea of responsible reflection. Note, for instance, how Max DePree, author of *Leadership Jazz*, describes leadership. He says "[a]bove all else, leadership is a position of servanthood. Leadership is a forfeiture of rights." He lists twelve traits of successful leadership. These characteristics are the keys to becoming a successful leader: Integrity, vulnerability, discernment, awareness of the human spirit, courage in relationships, sense of humor, intellectual en-ergy and curiosity, respect for the future, regard for the present, under-standing of the past, predictability, breadth, comfort with ambiguity, presence" (Spears, 1995, p. 111). Certainly, leaders who demonstrate these characteristics are likely to engage in responsible reflection. Re-sponsible reflection leads organizations toward goals that show respect for many stakeholders, including employees, consumers and members of the community.

Under what circumstances do we want more servant leaders? Initially, servant leadership is exciting to those who are discouraged by the behavior of leaders like Bildman, Gill, and Iacocca. It is hard to imagine who would be discouraged by leaders who promise behavior based upon ideas like integrity, empathy and awareness. One stakeholder in particular would be hurt by better leadership in the form of the servant leader. Shareholders would be impatient with the servant leader; the leader who is not aggressive, cannot or will not articulate a vision, and does not strive to maximize short-run profits. Servant leadership clashes with the idea of efficiency.

Perhaps servant leadership is more promising to nonprofit organizations or organizations that are such market leaders they can afford to engage in responsible reflection even if they give up some measure of short-run profits. For instance, Johnson & Johnson can afford to have servant leaders. Even if some of their corporate managers consider needs other than short-run efficiency, the corporate bottom line will not suffer significantly. Additionally, it is possible for individual managers within large, competitive companies to admire servant leaders and strive to demonstrate the traits of servant leaders even if their organizations are unlikely to reward this kind of leadership. The servant leader is most likely to be able to remain true to his or her individual beliefs, no matter what their corporation's norms. The servant leader is least likely to end up believing that "much of the actual work of management is senseless" (Jackall, 1988). If the servant leader can help those they serve become healthier, wiser, freer, more autonomous, and more likely themselves to become leaders, the servant leader will have achieved significant success in his or her working life, no matter what their contribution to the corporation's bottom line.

Conclusion

Ciulla urged scholars who are interested in leadership ethics to ask questions like, "What sort of person should lead?" and "What are the moral responsibilities of leadership?" In this article, we started at a basic level. We are not as sure as Ciulla that ethics is at the heart of leadership, at least not as leadership is currently practiced in most corporations. Thus, we asked whether we really want more leaders in business. Years ago Christopher Stone explained that the best hope for ethical transformation of business lies in the hands of management (1982). Today, we count on managers to play a strong role in challenging the leader. We want them to serve as a balance to the leader's power. We also hope managers will strive to find ways to remain true to their own beliefs in the context of organizations that want them to follow the leader blindly. From a societal perspective, we must ask how many corporate top dogs we really want. We must consider how much short-run profit we're willing to give up in exchange for more ethical corporate cultures. Only then can we engage in a meaningful dialogue about what kind of leaders we might really want in business.

References

Callahan, E.S. and R. Dworkin: 1994, "Why Blow the Whistle to the Media," and "Why: Organizational Characteristics of Media Whistleblowers," *American Business Law Journal*, 32, 151–179.

Ciulla, J.: 1995, "Leadership Ethics: Mapping the Territory," *Business Ethics Quarterly* 5, 5–28.

Greenleaf, R.: 1977, *Servant Leadership* (Paulist Press, New York).

Haas, R.: "Ethics—A Global Business Challenge," *Vital Speeches of the Day* LX, 506–509.

Iacocca, L.: 1984, *Iacocca: An Autobiography* (Bantam Books, New York).

Jackall, R.: 1988, *Moral Mazes: The World of Corporate Managers* (Oxford University Press, New York).

Ket de Vries, M.: 1989, *Prisoners of Leadership* (Wiley, New York).

Ket de Vries, M.: 1993, *Leaders, Fools, and Imposters* (Jossey-Bass Inc., San Francisco, California).

Ket de Vries, M.: 1995, "Leaders Who Go off the Deep End: Narcissism and Hubris," in Ket de Vries (ed.), *Life and Death in the Executive Fast Lane* (Jossey-Bass Inc., San Francisco, California).

Korten, D.: 1996 (May–June), "Let's Get Real About Business Responsibility," *Business Ethics* 61.

Maremont, M.: 1995 (Oct. 23), "Blind Ambition: How the Pursuit of Results Got Out of Hand at Bausch & Lomb," *Business Week*, 78–92.

Maremont, M.: 1996 (May 13), "Abuse of Power: The Astonishing Tale of Sexual Harassment at Astra U.S.A.," *Business Week*, 86–98.

Milgram, S.: 1974, *Obedience to Authority: Experimental View* (Harper & Row, New York).

Mitchell, R.: 1994 (Aug. 1), "Managing by Values: Is Levi Strauss' Approach Visionary—Or Flaky?" *Business Week*, 46–52.

Pincus, D.: 1994, *Top Dog* (McGraw-Hill, New York).

Shaw, W. and V. Barry: 1995, *Moral Issues in Business* (Wadsworth Publishing Company, Belmont, CA).

Spears, L. (ed.): 1995, *Reflections on Leadership: How Robert K. Greenleaf's Theory of Servant-Leadership Influenced Today's Top Management Thinkers* (John Wiley & Sons, Inc., New York).

Steers, R. and J.S. Black: 1994, *Organizational Behavior* (HarperCollins College Publishers, New York), p. 420.

Stone, C.: 1975. *Where the Law Ends: The Social Control of Corporate Behavior* (Waveland Press, Prospect Heights, Illinois).

Stone, C.: 1982, "Corporate Accountability in Law and Morals," in O. Williams and J. Houck (eds.), *The Judeo-Christian Vision and the Modern Corporation* (University of Notre Dame Press, Notre Dame, Indiana).

Stratford, S.: 1995 (Nov. 27), "How Tomorrow's Best Leaders Are Learning Their Stuff," *Fortune*, 90–102.

Strobel, L.P.: 1980, *Reckless Homicide? Ford's Pinto Trial* (And Books, South Bend, Indiana).

Taylor, A. III: 1996 (June 24), "How I Flunked Retirement," *Fortune*, 50–61.

Trevino, L. and K. Nelson: 1990, *Managing Business Ethics: Straight Talk About How to Do It Right* (John Wiley & Sons, Inc., New York).

19

We Won't See Great Leaders Until We See Great Women Leaders

HARRIET RUBIN

Women are canaries in the coal mine of power. They fall over dead whenever work gets stifling. They groove wherever new models of business behavior are emerging: consensual management, flextime, the belief that work should have meaning. Women are early adopters of technology: They enthusiastically took to the skies right after Kitty Hawk, and they brought appliances into the home and typewriters into the office. If you want to know what's new in the world of business, look to women.

For that reason, we won't see great leaders until we see great women leaders. As role models, men are going flat, and men themselves are beginning to realize that. Carly Fiorina's name was added to the list of candidates for Hewlett-Packard's presidency by Lew Platt, the company's then CEO and president. Platt added Fiorina to the list during a painful winter: His wife was dying, and he was beginning to see just how strong a force she had been in holding their family together. So he hatched the notion that a woman would be a stronger leader than he had been.

As president and CEO of Hewlett-Packard, Fiorina has a tremendous opportunity ahead of her—one that she'll grasp neither by caring strictly about reputation nor by focusing on the creation of her personal brand. To realize the call of leadership, she must heed the call of legend. Legend is the missing ingredient in leadership—although you often see it in women. All attention today goes to the Brand Called You. The action and the meaning of legend are unknown.

Reprinted with permission, from *Fast Company Magazine*, January–February 2000, pp. 248–252. All rights reserved.

How is a legend different from a brand? An alternative spelling of "legend" is g-u-t-s. A legend is someone who not only attains the heights but also does something to expand the envelope. Legends are people who act so daringly that they become bigger than life. In legend, there is an element of the inexplicable, the irrational.

Why is a legend a good thing? Because beyond all of the honing of reputations and the building of brands, what ultimately matters is stretching the container of leadership. Do the unusual, the unexpected, and you give yourself a wider platform on which to operate: Others expect you to be comfortable with risk, and they trust you with risk. Just as important, you give others permission to think outside the box. Legend involves a leadership feedback loop that people don't like to talk about, because it's trouble.

As women reach higher into the leadership stratosphere, they are doing all of the right things—but none of the "wrong" ones. Doing the wrong things means committing rough, difficult actions. You see this kind of behavior in bad-boy leaders. Larry Ellison does something wild, and his legend grows. Stories about Steve Jobs's bad-boy reputation are rife. Even today, Jobs dresses in his signature black; it's a sign that he's still the pirate, the outlaw, the misfit. Read about the greatest founders of all—the founding fathers of this country—and you'll see that using the action language of legend is not a bad thing. George Washington and Benjamin Franklin consistently used that language: They did the outrageous; they put themselves in danger. Franklin used to chase storms to learn more about them; Washington once had several horses shot out from under him—and survived.

Look at the great female leadership legends: Benazir Bhutto, Margaret Thatcher, Golda Meir. It doesn't matter if you disagree with their politics, or deplore their triumphs or their losses. What matters is that they walked on the wild side. They burned, baby; they burned. They were bad girls. They weren't afraid to risk their reputation, and they didn't give a whit about brand. Start to build your legend, and you stop worrying about criticism. You begin to do something that fits into no known category. You give yourself latitude. You start to play on a bigger playing field. And then you begin to think that you can triumph. You begin to experience the kind of leadership that turns people at the top into heroes.

As part of my ongoing education in how leadership works, I recently had a choice: I could go uptown to hear a handful of *Fortune*'s "50 Most Powerful Women in American Business" give the same old speech about the opportunities for women at the top. Or I could go downtown to a little theater accurately named the Flea, where a women's circus called "Volcano Love" was holding court.

I went downtown. I wasn't the only one to make that choice. Also in the audience at "Volcano Love" were Sigourney Weaver and Madonna.

Excluded from the gathering of *Fortune*'s "most powerful women," these actresses have portrayed some of the most powerful characters in modern legend: Weaver starred as Dian Fossey in *Gorillas in the Mist*; she also played the heroine in the *Alien* movies. And Madonna, of course, has not only played Evita; she also plays the living legend known as Madonna.

Dian Fossey expanded the container of what women are. For Fossey, everything was difficult. She was afraid of heights, afraid even to walk downstairs in her native San Francisco. Yet she took herself to the jungles of Rwanda, where she bounded down ravines so that she could study mountain gorillas in the wild. There are stories of how she would light bonfires to keep the poachers away. They stayed away not because they were scared of the flames but because, when they saw her feed the fire with dollar bills, they thought that she must be crazy and dangerous.

The decision to go downtown was a no-brainer. "Volcano Love" makes it clear what the uptown girls are missing. The women in that show are doing what heroes do: challenging the rational. "Volcano Love" is the creation of Sarah East Johnson, a fire-eater, juggler, stilt dancer, and trapeze artist who founded the New York City–based dance company Lava. "I want to expand the models of what women can be, to see what all the possibilities are," she says. Johnson named her company after the fiery heat of Earth's inner forces, thereby celebrating the Earth's struggle to rearrange its known categories. The disruptive force of a volcano also had its appeal. "What gets in your way can take you to someplace new," says Johnson.

Johnson has a role model that I'm sure wasn't mentioned uptown: "There is so much to learn from things that are beautiful and powerful. I drove across the country several years ago. And when I reached the Rocky Mountains, I felt that I wanted to *be* a Rocky Mountain. There are very few things in the world that you see and say, "That's what I want to be—particularly if you're a woman. How many role models are there that are really inspiring?"

What's interesting here is that Johnson doesn't just want to get to the top. She wants to be a powerhouse. The *Fortune* women say again and again in their magazine interviews that it wasn't very hard to get to the top. Maybe that's because the game that they're playing is way too easy. Maybe that's why, when you look at a comparable list of the most powerful male CEOs in America, you get builders, shapers, dazzlers: Jeff Bezos, Bill Gates, Jay Walker. Not people who get along by going along. Not people who get swept up in the current and pulled along by it, as the *Fortune* "most powerful women in business" have done.

Why isn't there a woman leader to rival Steve Jobs or Bill Gates? Forget the old argument that women haven't invested generations in business. Neither have the new male rich. In the new economy, everybody was born yesterday.

The most "powerful" women are good girls writ large and rational. And so their influence is small.

Why aren't women going out and building the kinds of businesses that build society? After all, women start twice as many businesses as men do. Every 60 seconds in the United States, a woman starts a company. But such companies don't grow very large. Why is it that most businesses that are started by women, or run by women, never reach the stage of becoming big-time players? Why do they never achieve the status of legend?

Legends reach into the realm of the heroic—testing themselves, daring to look ridiculous. (You think fighting a green monster is elegant?) Heroes, according to the mythologist Joseph Campbell, test themselves, put themselves into unfamiliar territory, risk their identity, and come back from an ordeal or adventure with a gift for the community. Heroes go on a personal journey that makes them whole. Having a special skill or talent isn't enough. The risk, the challenge—that's what makes a hero's abilities increase.

As I sat in the audience at "Volcano Love," I imagined the uptown scene. I thought about the uptown girls engaging in what they do best: genteel talk between morning fruit and afternoon salad.

The downtowners were willing not just to talk but also to do—to face the enemy. But the enemy isn't men. Nor is it the intransigent corporation. The enemy is fear. Watching those women soar changed my metabolism, as if I'd just eaten a peach and sugar were flooding my brain. Their display of fearlessness makes you move. You enter their world to a blast of Johnny Cash: It burns, burns, burns a ring of fire. The Lava women have learned to move past their fear.

"Fear is something that comes up all the time in this particular kind of work," says Sarah Johnson.

> Sometimes, that fear is about how much something is going to hurt: "I can't stay in this handstand for another minute," or "I can't do one more handstand." And sometimes it's a fear of a specific act, such as jumping backward through a hoop. You're afraid that you're going to fall on your head and that it's going to hurt. But you tell yourself that you can do it, and then you have to do it—even though you're afraid.

The rest of us talk about the glass ceiling. Lava women fly right up to it and make it look like a cloud that might disappear if you blew on it. The rest of us groan about jumping through hoops. Lava women plunge through hoops—backward and in high heels. Lava women put themselves at risk. They face embarrassment at every moment. They are riveting to watch because you worry about them; you expect a spill. The *For-*

tune women keep reassuring the rest of us through interviews how easy their rise was. Would Steve Case ever say that it wasn't difficult to get to the top?

Okay, the downtown girls are not changing the world. But they do offer a lesson in what's missing, not only from the world of women's leadership but also from the world of leadership in general. Look at the latest dotcom startups: puny businesses, thin ideas, no risks. Something big is called for—something irrational.

Time for a little volcano in the world of leadership. Says Johnson: "A volcano destroys everything around it—but it brings new earth to the surface, and it has the ability to create an island. At the same time, it can destroy every house and plant and tree."

20

Narcissistic Leaders

The Incredible Pros, the Inevitable Cons

MICHAEL MACCOBY

Many leaders dominating business today have what psychoanalysts call a narcissistic personality. That's good news for companies that need passion and daring to break new ground. But even productive narcissists can be dangerous for organizations. Here is some advice on avoiding the dangers.

There's something new and daring about the CEOs who are transforming today's industries. Just compare them with the executives who ran large companies in the 1950s through the 1980s. Those executives shunned the press and had their comments carefully crafted by corporate PR departments. But today's CEOs—superstars such as Bill Gates, Andy Grove, Steve Jobs, Jeff Bezos, and Jack Welch—hire their own publicists, write books, grant spontaneous interviews, and actively promote their personal philosophies. Their faces adorn the covers of magazines like *Business Week, Time,* and the *Economist.* What's more, the world's business personalities are increasingly seen as the makers and shapers of our public and personal agendas. They advise schools on what kids should learn and lawmakers on how to invest the public's money. We look to them for thoughts on everything from the future of e-commerce to hot places to vacation.

There are many reasons today's business leaders have higher profiles than ever before. One is that business plays a much bigger role in our lives than it used to, and its leaders are more often in the limelight. Another is that the business world is experiencing enormous changes that

Reprinted with permission, from the *Harvard Business Review* (January–February 2000). Copyright 2000 by the Harvard Business School Publishing Company.

call for visionary and charismatic leadership. But my 25 years of consulting both as a psychoanalyst in private practice and as an adviser to top managers suggest a third reason—namely, a pronounced change in the personality of the strategic leaders at the top. As an anthropologist, I try to understand people in the context in which they operate, and as a psychoanalyst, I tend to see them through a distinctly Freudian lens. Given what I know, I believe that the larger-than-life leaders we are seeing today closely resemble the personality type that Sigmund Freud dubbed narcissistic. "People of this type impress others as being 'personalities,'" he wrote, describing one of the psychological types that clearly fall within the range of normality. "They are especially suited to act as a support for others, to take on the role of leaders, and to give a fresh stimulus to cultural development or damage the established state of affairs."

Throughout history, narcissists have always emerged to inspire people and to shape the future. When military, religious, and political arenas dominated society, it was figures such as Napoleon Bonaparte, Mahatma Gandhi, and Franklin Delano Roosevelt who determined the social agenda. But from time to time, when business became the engine of social change, it, too, generated its share of narcissistic leaders. That was true at the beginning of this century, when men like Andrew Carnegie, John D. Rockefeller, Thomas Edison, and Henry Ford exploited new technologies and restructured American industry. And I think it is true again today.

But Freud recognized that there is a dark side to narcissism. Narcissists, he pointed out, are emotionally isolated and highly distrustful. Perceived threats can trigger rage. Achievements can feed feelings of grandiosity. That's why Freud thought narcissists were the hardest personality types to analyze. Consider how an executive at Oracle describes his narcissistic CEO Larry Ellison: "The difference between God and Larry is that God does not believe he is Larry." That observation is amusing, but it is also troubling. Not surprisingly, most people think of narcissists in a primarily negative way. After all, Freud named the type after the mythical figure Narcissus, who died because of his pathological preoccupation with himself.

Yet narcissism can be extraordinarily useful—even necessary. Freud shifted his views about narcissism over time and recognized that we are all somewhat narcissistic. More recently, psychoanalyst Heinz Kohut built on Freud's theories and developed methods of treating narcissists. Of course, only professional clinicians are trained to tell if narcissism is normal or pathological. In this article, I discuss the differences between productive and unproductive narcissism but do not explore the extreme pathology of borderline conditions and psychosis.

Leaders such as Jack Welch and George Soros are examples of productive narcissists. They are gifted and creative strategists who see the big picture and find meaning in the risky challenge of changing the world and leaving behind a legacy. Indeed, one reason we look to productive narcissists in times of great transition is that they have the audacity to push through the massive transformations that society periodically undertakes. Productive narcissists are not only risk takers willing to get the job done but also charmers who can convert the masses with their rhetoric. The danger is that narcissism can turn unproductive when, lacking self-knowledge and restraining anchors, narcissists become unrealistic dreamers. They nurture grand schemes and harbor the illusion that only circumstances or enemies block their success. This tendency toward grandiosity and distrust is the Achilles' heel of narcissists. Because of it, even brilliant narcissists can come under suspicion for self-involvement, unpredictability, and—in extreme cases—paranoia.

It's easy to see why narcissistic leadership doesn't always mean successful leadership. Consider the case of Volvo's Pehr Gyllenhammar. He had a dream that appealed to a broad international audience—a plan to revolutionize the industrial work place by replacing the dehumanizing assembly line caricatured in Charlie Chaplin's *Modern Times*. His wildly popular vision called for team-based craftsmanship. Model factories were built and publicized to international acclaim. But his success in pushing through these dramatic changes also sowed the seeds for his downfall. Gyllenhammar started to feel that he could ignore the concerns of his operational managers. He pursued chancy and expensive business deals, which he publicized on television and in the press. On one level, you can ascribe Gyllenhammar's falling out of touch with his workforce simply to faulty strategy. But it is also possible to attribute it to his narcissistic personality. His overestimation of himself led him to believe that others would want him to be the czar of a multinational enterprise. In turn, these fantasies led him to pursue a merger with Renault, which was tremendously unpopular with Swedish employees. Because Gyllenhammar was deaf to complaints about Renault, Swedish managers were forced to take their case public. In the end, shareholders aggressively rejected Gyllenhammar's plan, leaving him with no option but to resign.

Given the large number of narcissists at the helm of corporations today, the challenge facing organizations is to ensure that such leaders do not self-destruct or lead the company to disaster. That can take some doing because it is very hard for narcissists to work through their issues—and virtually impossible for them to do it alone. Narcissists need colleagues and even therapists if they hope to break free from their limitations. But because of their extreme independence and self-protectiveness, it is very difficult to get near them. Kohut maintained that a therapist would have to demonstrate an extraordinarily profound empathic understanding and sympathy for the narcissist's feelings in order to gain his trust. On top of that, narcissists must recognize that they can benefit from such help. For their part, employees must learn how to recognize—and work around—narcissistic bosses. To help them in this endeavor, let's first take a closer look at Freud's theory of personality types.

Three Main Personality Types

While Freud recognized that there are an almost infinite variety of personalities, he identified three main types: erotic, obsessive, and narcissistic. Most of us have elements of all three. We are all, for example, somewhat narcissistic. If that were not so, we would not be able to survive or assert our needs. The point is, one of the dynamic tendencies usually dominates the others, making each of us react differently to success and failure.

Freud's definitions of personality types differed over time. When talking about the erotic personality type, however, Freud generally did not mean a sexual personality but rather one for whom loving and above all being loved is most important. This type of individual is dependent on those people they fear will stop loving them. Many erotica are teachers, nurses, and social workers. At their most productive, they are developers of the young as well as enablers and helpers at work. As managers, they are caring and supportive, but they avoid conflict and make people dependent on them. They are, according to Freud, outer-directed people.

Obsessives, in contrast, are inner-directed. They are self-reliant and conscientious. They create and maintain order and make the most effective operational managers. They look constantly for ways to help people listen better, resolve conflict, and find win-win opportunities. They buy self-improvement books such as Stephen Covey's *The 7 Habits of Highly Effective People*. Obsessives are also ruled by a strict conscience—they like to focus on continuous improvement at work because it fits in with their sense of moral improvement. As entrepreneurs, obsessives start businesses that express their values, but they lack the vision, daring, and charisma it takes to turn a good idea into a great one. The best obsessives set high standards and communicate very effectively. They make sure that instructions are followed and costs are kept within budget. The most productive are great mentors and team players. The unproductive and the uncooperative become narrow experts and rule-bound bureaucrats.

Narcissists, the third type, are independent and not easily impressed. They are innovators, driven in business to gain power and glory. Productive narcissists are experts in their industries, but they go beyond it. They also pose the critical questions. They want to learn everything about everything that affects the company and its products. Unlike erotica, they want to be admired, not loved. And unlike obsessives, they are not troubled by a punishing superego, so they are able to aggressively pursue

---

EXHIBIT 20.1 *Fromm's Fourth Personality Type*

Not long after Freud described his three personality types in 1931, psycho-analyst Erich Fromm proposed a fourth personality type, which has become particularly prevalent in today's service economy. Fromm called this type the "marketing personality," and it is exemplified by the lead character in Woody Allen's movie *Zelig*, a man so governed by his need to be valued that he becomes exactly like the people he happens to be around.

Marketing personalities are more detached than erotics and so are less likely to cement close ties. They are also less driven by conscience than ob-sessives. Instead, they are motivated by a radar-like anxiety that permeates everything they do. Because they are so eager to please and to alleviate this anxiety, marketing personalities excel at selling themselves to others.

Unproductive marketing types lack direction and the ability to commit themselves to people or projects. But when productive, marketing types are good at facilitating teams and keeping the focus on adding value as defined by customers and colleagues. Like obsessives, marketing personalities are avid consumers of self-help books. Like narcissists, they are not wedded to the past. But marketing types generally make poor leaders in times of crisis. They lack the daring needed and are too responsive to current, rather than future, customer demands.

---

their goals. Of all the personality types, narcissists run the greatest risk of isolating themselves at the moment of success. And because of their inde-pendence and aggressiveness, they are constantly looking out for ene-mies, sometimes degenerating into paranoia when they are under ex-treme stress. (For more on personality types, see Exhibit 20.1.)

Strengths of the Narcissistic Leader

When it comes to leadership, personality type can be instructive. Erotic personalities generally make poor managers—they need too much ap-proval. Obsessives make better leaders—they are your operational man-agers: critical and cautious. But it is narcissists who come closest to our collective image of great leaders. There are two reasons for this: they have compelling, even gripping, visions for companies, and they have an ability to attract followers.

Great Vision

I once asked a group of managers to define a leader. "A person with vi-sion" was a typical response. Productive narcissists understand the vision thing particularly well, because they are by nature people who see the big picture. They are not analyzers who can break up big questions into manageable problems; they aren't number crunchers either (these are usually the obsessives). Nor do they try to extrapolate to understand the future—they attempt to create it. To paraphrase George Bernard Shaw, some people see things as they are and ask why; narcissists see things that never were and ask why not.

Consider the difference between Bob Allen, a productive obsessive, and Mike Armstrong, a productive narcissist. In 1997, Allen tried to expand AT&T to reestablish the end-to-end service of the Bell System by reselling local service from the regional Bell operating companies (RBOCs). Although this was a worthwhile endeavor for shareholders and customers, it was hardly earth shattering. By contrast, through a strategy of combining voice, telecommunications, and Internet access by high-speed broad-band telecommunication over cable, Mike Armstrong has "created a new space with his name on it," as one of his colleagues puts it. Armstrong is betting that his costly strategy will beat out the RBOCs' less expensive solution of digital subscriber lines over copper wire. This example illustrates the different approaches of obsessives and narcissists. The risk Armstrong took is one that few obsessives would feel comfortable taking. His vision is galvanizing AT&T. Who but a narcissistic leader could achieve such a thing? As Napoleon—a classic narcissist—once remarked, "Revolutions are ideal times for soldiers with a lot of wit—and the courage to act."

As in the days of the French Revolution, the world is now changing in astounding ways; narcissists have opportunities they would never have in ordinary times. In short, today's narcissistic leaders have the chance to change the very rules of the game. Consider Robert B. Shapiro, CEO of Monsanto. Shapiro described his vision of genetically modifying crops as "the single most successful introduction of technology in the history of agriculture, including the plow" (*New York Times*, August 5, 1999). This is certainly a huge claim—there are still many questions about the safety and public acceptance of genetically engineered fruits and vegetables. But industries like agriculture are desperate for radical change. If Shapiro's gamble is successful, the industry will be transformed in the image of Monsanto. That's why he can get away with painting a picture of Monsanto as a highly profitable "life sciences" company—despite the fact that Monsanto's stock has fallen 12% from 1998 to the end of the third quarter of 1999. (During the same period, the S&P was up 41%.) Unlike Armstrong and Shapiro, it was enough for Bob Allen to win against his competitors in a game measured primarily by the stock market. But narcissistic leaders are after something more. They want—and need—to leave behind a legacy.

Scores of Followers

Narcissists have vision—but that's not enough. People in mental hospitals also have visions. The simplest definition of a leader is someone whom other people follow. Indeed, narcissists are especially gifted in attracting followers, and more often than not, they do so through language. Narcissists believe that words can move mountains and that inspiring speeches can change people. Narcissistic leaders are often skillful orators, and this is one of the talents that makes them so charismatic. Indeed, anyone who has seen narcissists perform can attest to their personal magnetism and their ability to stir enthusiasm among audiences.

Yet this charismatic gift is more of a two-way affair than most people think. Although it is not always obvious, narcissistic leaders are quite dependent on their followers—they need affirmation, and preferably adulation. Think of Winston Churchill's wartime broadcasts or J.F.K.'s "Ask not what your country can do for you" inaugural address. The adulation that follows from such speeches bolsters the self-confidence and conviction of the speakers. But if no one responds, the narcissist usually becomes insecure, overly shrill, and insistent—just as Ross Perot did.

Even when people respond positively to a narcissist, there are dangers. That's because charisma is a double-edged sword—it fosters both closeness and isolation. As he becomes increasingly self-assured, the narcissist becomes more spontaneous. He feels free of constraints. Ideas flow. He thinks he's invincible. This energy and confidence further inspire his followers. But the very adulation that the narcissist demands can have a corrosive effect. As he expands, he listens even less to words of caution and advice. After all, he has been right before, when others had their doubts. Rather than try to persuade those who disagree with him, he feels justified in ignoring them—creating further isolation. The result is sometimes flagrant risk taking that can lead to catastrophe. In the political realm, there is no clearer example of this than Bill Clinton.

Weaknesses of the Narcissistic Leader

Despite the warm feelings their charisma can evoke, narcissists are typically not comfortable with their own emotions. They listen only for the kind of information they seek. They don't learn easily from others. They don't like to teach but prefer to indoctrinate and make speeches. They dominate meetings with subordinates. The result for the organization is greater internal competitiveness at a time when everyone is already under as much pressure as they can possibly stand. Perhaps the main problem is that the narcissist's faults tend to become even more pronounced as he becomes more successful.

Sensitive to Criticism

Because they are extraordinarily sensitive, narcissistic leaders shun emotions as a whole. Indeed, perhaps one of the greatest paradoxes in this age of teamwork and partnering is that the best corporate leader in the contemporary world is the type of person who is emotionally isolated. Narcissistic leaders typically keep others at arm's length. They can put up a wall of defense as thick as the Pentagon. And given their difficulty with knowing or acknowledging their own feelings, they are uncomfortable with other people expressing theirs—especially their negative feelings.

Indeed, even productive narcissists are extremely sensitive to criticism or slights, which feel to them like knives threatening their self-image and their confidence in their visions. Narcissists are almost unimaginably thin-skinned. Like the fairy-tale princess who slept on many mattresses and yet knew she was sleeping on a pea, narcissists—even powerful CEOs—bruise easily. This is one explanation why narcissistic leaders do not want to know what people think of them unless it is causing them a real problem. They cannot tolerate dissent. In fact, they can be extremely abrasive with employees who doubt them or with subordinates who are tough enough to fight back. Steve Jobs, for example, publicly humiliates subordinates. Thus, although narcissistic leaders often say that they want teamwork, what that means in practice is that they want a group of yes-men. As the more independent-minded players leave or are pushed out, succession becomes a particular problem.

Poor Listeners

One serious consequence of this oversensitivity to criticism is that narcissistic leaders often do not listen when they feel threatened or attacked. Consider the response of one narcissistic CEO I had worked with for three years who asked me to interview his immediate team and report back to him on what they were thinking. He invited me to his summer home to discuss what I had found. "So what do they think of me?" he asked with seeming nonchalance. "They think you are very creative and courageous," I told him, "but they also feel that you don't listen." "Excuse me, what did you say?" he shot back at once, pretending not to hear. His response was humorous, but it was also tragic. In a very real way, this CEO could not hear my criticism because it was too painful to tolerate. Some narcissists are so defensive that they go so far as to make a virtue of the fact that they don't listen. As another CEO bluntly put it, "I didn't get here by listening to people!" Indeed, on one occasion when this CEO proposed a daring strategy, none of his subordinates believed it would work. His subsequent success strengthened his conviction that he had nothing to learn about strategy from his lieutenants. But success is no excuse for narcissistic leaders not to listen.

Lack of Empathy

Best-selling business writers today have taken up the slogan of "emotional competencies"—the belief that successful leadership requires a strongly developed sense of empathy. But although they crave empathy from others, productive narcissists are not noted for being particularly empathetic themselves. Indeed, lack of empathy is a characteristic shortcoming of some of the most charismatic and successful narcissists, including Bill Gates and Andy Grove. Of course, leaders do need to communicate persuasively. But a lack of empathy did not prevent some of history's greatest narcissistic leaders from knowing how to communicate—and inspire. Neither Churchill, de Gaulle, Stalin, nor Mao Tse-tung were empathetic. And yet they inspired people because of their passion and their conviction at a time when people longed for certainty. In fact, in times of radical change, lack of empathy can actually be a strength. A narcissist finds it easier than other personality types to buy and sell companies, to close and move facilities, and to lay off employees—decisions that inevitably make many people angry and sad. But narcissistic leaders typically have few regrets. As one CEO says, "If I listened to my employees' needs and demands, they would eat me alive."

Given this lack of empathy, it's hardly surprising that narcissistic leaders don't score particularly well on evaluations of their interpersonal style. What's more, neither 360-degree evaluations of their management style nor workshops in listening will make them more empathic. Narcissists don't want to change—and as long as they are successful, they don't think they have to. They may see the need for operational managers to get touchy-feely training, but that's not for them.

There is a kind of emotional intelligence associated with narcissists, but it's more street smarts than empathy. Narcissistic leaders are acutely aware of whether or not people are with them wholeheartedly. They know whom they can use. They can be brutally exploitative. That's why, even though narcissists undoubtedly have "star quality," they are often unlikable. They easily stir up people against them, and it is only in tumultuous times, when their gifts are desperately needed, that people are willing to tolerate narcissists as leaders.

Distaste for Mentoring

Lack of empathy and extreme independence make it difficult for narcissists to mentor and be mentored. Generally speaking, narcissistic leaders set very little store by mentoring. They seldom mentor others, and when they do they typically want their protégés to be pale reflections of themselves. Even those narcissists like Jack Welch who are held up as strong mentors are usually more interested in instructing than in coaching.

Narcissists certainly don't credit mentoring or educational programs for their own development as leaders. A few narcissistic leaders such as Bill Gates may find a friend or consultant—for instance, Warren Buffett, a superproductive obsessive—whom they can trust to be their guide and confidant. But most narcissists prefer "mentors" they can control. A 32-year-old marketing vice president, a narcissist with CEO potential, told me that she had rejected her boss as a mentor. As she put it, "First of all, I want to keep the relationship at a distance. I don't want to be influenced by emotions. Second, there are things I don't want him to know. I'd rather hire an outside consultant to be my coach." Although narcissistic leaders appear to be at ease with others, they find intimacy—which is a prerequisite for mentoring—to be difficult. Younger narcissists will establish peer relations with authority rather than seek a parentlike mentoring relationship. They want results and are willing to take chances arguing with authority.

An Intense Desire to Compete

Narcissistic leaders are relentless and ruthless in their pursuit of victory. Games are not games but tests of their survival skills. Of course, all successful managers want to win, but narcissists are not restrained by conscience. Organizations led by narcissists are generally characterized by intense internal competition. Their passion to win is marked by both the promise of glory and the primitive danger of extinction. It is a potent brew that energizes companies, creating a sense of urgency, but it can also be dangerous. These leaders see everything as a threat. As Andy Grove puts it, brilliantly articulating the narcissist's fear, distrust, and aggression, "Only the paranoid survive." The concern, of course, is that the narcissist finds enemies that aren't there—even among his colleagues.

Avoiding the Traps

There is very little business literature that tells narcissistic leaders how to avoid the pitfalls. There are two reasons for this. First, relatively few narcissistic leaders are interested in looking inward. And second, psychoanalysts don't usually get close enough to them, especially in the workplace, to write about them. (The noted psychoanalyst Harry Levinson is an exception.) As a result, advice on leadership focuses on obsessives, which explains why so much of it is about creating teamwork and being more receptive to subordinates. But as we've already seen, this literature is of little interest to narcissists, nor is it likely to help subordinates un-

---

EXHIBIT 20.2   *The Rise and Fall of a Narcissist*

The story of Jan Carlzon, the former CEO of the Scandinavian airline SAS, is an almost textbook example of how a narcissist's weakness can cut short a brilliant career. In the 1980s, Carlzon's vision of SAS as the businessperson's airline was widely acclaimed in the business press; management guru Tom Peters described him as a model leader. In 1989, when I first met Carlzon and his management team, he compared the ideal organization to the Brazilian soccer team—in principle, there would be no fixed roles, only innovative plays. I asked the members of the management team if they agreed with this vision of an empowered front line. One vice president, a former pilot, answered 'no.' "I still believe that the best organization is the military," he said. I then asked Carlzon for his reaction to that remark. "Well," he replied, "that may be true, if your goal is to shoot your customers."

That rejoinder was both witty and dismissive; clearly, Carlzon was not engaging in a serious dialogue with his subordinates. Nor was he listening to other advisers. Carlzon ignored the issue of high costs, even when many observers pointed out that SAS could not compete without improving productivity. He threw money at expensive acquisitions of hotels and made an unnecessary investment in Continental Airlines just months before it declared bankruptcy.

Carlzon's story perfectly corroborates the often-recorded tendency of narcissists to become overly expansive—and hence isolated—at the very pinnacle of their success. Seduced by the flattery he received in the international press, Carlzon's self-image became so enormously inflated that his feet left the ground. And given his vulnerability to grandiosity, he was propelled by a need to expand his organization rather than develop it. In due course, as Carlzon led the company deeper and deeper into losses, he was fired. Now he is a venture capitalist helping budding companies. And SAS has lost its glitter.

---

derstand their narcissistic leaders. The absence of managerial literature on narcissistic leaders doesn't mean that it is impossible to devise strategies for dealing with narcissism. In the course of a long career counseling CEOs, I have identified three basic ways in which productive narcissists can avoid the traps of their own personality.

Find a Trusted Sidekick

Many narcissists can develop a close relationship with one person, a sidekick who acts as an anchor, keeping the narcissistic partner grounded. However, given that narcissistic leaders trust only their own insights and view of reality, the sidekick has to understand the narcissistic leader and what he is trying to achieve. The narcissist must feel that this person, or in some cases persons, is practically an extension of himself. The sidekick must also be sensitive enough to manage the relationship. Don Quixote is a classic example of a narcissist who was out of touch with reality but who was constantly saved from disaster by his squire Sancho Panza. Not surprisingly, many narcissistic leaders rely heavily on their spouses, the people they are closest to. But dependence on spouses can be risky, because they may further isolate the narcissistic leader from his company by supporting his grandiosity and feeding his paranoia. I once knew a CEO in this kind of relationship with his spouse. He took to accusing loyal subordinates of plotting against him just because they ventured a few criticisms of his ideas.

It is much better for a narcissistic leader to choose a colleague as his sidekick. Good sidekicks are able to point out the operational requirements of the narcissistic leader's vision and keep him rooted in reality. The best sidekicks are usually productive obsessives. Gyllenhammar, for instance, was most effective at Volvo when he had an obsessive COO, Hakan Frisinger, to focus on improving quality and cost, as well as an obsessive HR director, Berth Jonsson, to implement his vision. Similarly, Bill Gates can think about the future from the stratosphere because Steve Ballmer, a tough obsessive president, keeps the show on the road. At Oracle, CEO Larry Ellison can afford to miss key meetings and spend time on his boat contemplating a future without PCs because he has a productive obsessive COO in Ray Lane to run the company for him. But the job of sidekick entails more than just executing the leader's ideas. The sidekick also has to get his leader to accept new ideas. To do this, he must be able to show the leader how the new ideas fit with his views and serve his interests. (For more on dealing with narcissistic bosses, see Exhibit 20.3, "Working for a Narcissist.")

Indoctrinate the Organization

The narcissistic CEO wants all his subordinates to think the way he does about the business. Productive narcissists—people who often have a dash of the obsessive personality—are good at converting people to their point of view. One of the most successful at this is GE's Jack Welch. Welch uses toughness to build a corporate culture and to implement a daring business strategy, including the buying and selling of scores of companies. Unlike other narcissistic leaders such as Gates, Grove, and Ellison, who have transformed industries with new products, Welch was able to transform his industry by focusing on execution and pushing companies to the limits of quality and efficiency, bumping up revenues and wringing out costs. In order to do so, Welch hammers out a huge corporate culture in his own image—a culture that provides impressive rewards for senior managers and shareholders.

EXHIBIT 20.3   *Working for a Narcissist*

Dealing with a nacissistic boss isn't easy. You have to be prepared to look for another job if your boss becomes too narcissistic to let you disagree with him. But remember that the company is typically betting on his vision of the future—not yours. Here are a few tips on how to survive in the short term:

- Always empathize with your boss's feelings, but don't expect any empathy back. Look elsewhere for your own self-esteem. Understand that behind his display of infallibility, there hides a deep vulnerability. Praise his achievements and reinforce his best impulses, but don't be shamelessly sycophantic. An intelligent narcissist can see through flatterers and prefers independent people who truly appreciate him. Show that you will protect his image, inside and outside the company. But be careful if he asks for an honest evaluation. What he wants is information that will help him solve a problem about his image. He will resent any honesty that threatens his inflated self-image and will likely retaliate.

- Give your boss ideas, but always let him take the credit for them. Find out what he thinks before presenting your views. If you believe he is wrong, show how a different approach would be in his best interest. Take his paranoid views seriously, don't brush them aside— they often reveal sharp intuitions. Disagree only when you can demonstrate how he will benefit from a different point of view.

- Hone your time-management skills. Narcissistic leaders often give subordinates many more orders than they can possibly execute. Ignore the requests he makes that don't make sense. Forget about them. He will. But be careful; carve out free time for yourself only when you know there's a lull in the boss's schedule. Narcissistic leaders feel free to call you at any hour of the day or night. Make yourself available, or be prepared to get out.

Welch's approach to culture building is widely misunderstood. Many observers, notably Noel Tichy in *The Leadership Engine*, argue that Welch forms his company's leadership culture through teaching. But Welch's "teaching" involves a personal ideology that he indoctrinates into GE managers through speeches, memos, and confrontations. Rather than create a dialogue, Welch makes pronouncements (either be the number one or two company in your market or get out), and he institutes programs (such as Six Sigma quality) that become the GE party line. Welch's strategy has been extremely effective. GE managers must either internalize his vision, or they must leave. Clearly, this is incentive learning with a vengeance. I would even go so far as to call Welch's teaching brain-washing. But Welch does have the rare insight and know-how to achieve what all narcissistic business leaders are trying to do—namely, get the organization to identify with them, to think the way they do, and to become the living embodiment of their companies.

Get into Analysis

Narcissists are often more interested in controlling others than in knowing and disciplining themselves. That's why, with very few exceptions, even productive narcissists do not want to explore their personalities with the help of insight therapies such as psychoanalysis. Yet since Heinz Kohut, there has been a radical shift in psychoanalytic thinking about what can be done to help narcissists work through their rage, alienation, and grandiosity. Indeed, if they can be persuaded to undergo therapy, narcissistic leaders can use tools such as psychoanalysis to overcome vital character flaws.

Consider the case of one exceptional narcissistic CEO who asked me to help him understand why he so often lost his temper with subordinates. He lived far from my home city, and so the therapy was sporadic and very unorthodox. Yet he kept a journal of his dreams, which we interpreted together either by phone or when we met. Our analysis uncovered painful feelings of being unappreciated that went back to his inability to impress a cold father. He came to realize that he demanded an unreasonable amount of praise and that when he felt unappreciated by his subordinates, he became furious. Once he understood that, he was able to recognize his narcissism and even laugh about it. In the middle of our work, he even announced to his top team that I was psychoanalyzing him and asked them what they thought of that. After a pregnant pause, one executive vice president piped up, "Whatever you're doing, you should keep doing it, because you don't get so angry anymore." Instead of being trapped by narcissistic rage, this CEO was learning how to express his concerns constructively.

Leaders who can work on themselves in that way tend to be the most productive narcissists. In addition to being self-reflective, they are also likely to be open, likable, and good-humored. Productive narcissists have perspective; they are able to detach themselves and laugh at their irrational needs. Although serious about achieving their goals, they are also playful. As leaders, they are aware of being performers. A sense of humor helps them maintain enough perspective and humility to keep on learning.

The Best and Worst of Times

As I have pointed out, narcissists thrive in chaotic times. In more tranquil times and places, however, even the most brilliant narcissist will seem out of place. In his short story *The Curfew Tolls*, Stephen Vincent Benet speculates on what would have happened to Napoleon if he had been born some 30 years earlier. Retired in prerevolutionary France, Napoleon is depicted as a lonely artillery major boasting to a vacationing British general about how he could have beaten the English in India. The point, of course, is that a visionary born in the wrong time can seem like a pompous buffoon.

Historically, narcissists in large corporations have been confined to sales positions, where they use their persuasiveness and imagination to best effect. In settled times, the problematic side of the narcissistic personality usually conspires to keep narcissists in their place, and they can typically rise to top management positions only by starting their own companies or by leaving to lead upstarts. Consider Joe Nacchio, formerly in charge of both the business and consumer divisions of AT&T. Nacchio was a super-salesman and a popular leader in the mid-1990s. But his desire to create a new network for business customers was thwarted by colleagues who found him abrasive, self-promoting, and ruthlessly ambitious.

Two years ago, Nacchio left AT&T to become CEO of Qwest, a company that is creating a long-distance fiber-optic cable network. Nacchio had the credibility—and charisma—to sell Qwest's initial public offering to financial markets and gain a high valuation. Within a short space of time, he turned Qwest into an attractive target for the RBOCs, which were looking to move into long-distance telephony and Internet services. Such a sale would have given Qwest's owners a handsome profit on their investment. But Nacchio wanted more. He wanted to expand—to compete with AT&T—and for that he needed local service. Rather than sell Qwest, he chose to make a bid himself for local telephone operator U.S. West, using Qwest's highly valued stock to finance the deal. The market voted on this display of expansiveness with its feet—Qwest's stock price fell 40% between last June, when he made the deal, and the end of the third quarter of 1999. (The S&P index dropped 5.7% during the same period.)

Like other narcissists, Nacchio likes risk—and sometimes ignores the costs. But with the dramatic discontinuities going on in the world today, more and more large corporations are getting into bed with narcissists. They are finding that there is no substitute for narcissistic leaders in an age of innovation. Companies need leaders who do not try to anticipate the future so much as create it. But narcissistic leaders—even the most productive of them—can self-destruct and lead their organizations terribly astray. For companies whose narcissistic leaders recognize their limitations, these will be the best of times. For other companies, these could turn out to be the worst.

21

Level 5 Leadership

The Triumph of Humility and Fierce Resolve

JIM COLLINS

In 1971, a seemingly ordinary man named Darwin E. Smith was named chief executive of Kimberly-Clark, a stodgy old paper company whose stock had fallen 36% behind the general market during the previous 20 years. Smith, the company's mild-mannered in-house lawyer, wasn't so sure the board had made the right choice—a feeling that was reinforced when a Kimberly-Clark director pulled him aside and reminded him that he lacked some of the qualifications for the position. But CEO he was, and CEO he remained for 20 years.

What a 20 years it was. In that period, Smith created a stunning transformation at Kimberly-Clark, turning it into the leading consumer paper products company in the world. Under his stewardship, the company beat its rivals Scott Paper and Procter & Gamble. And in doing so, Kimberly-Clark generated cumulative stock returns that were 4.1 times greater than those of the general market, outperforming venerable companies such as Hewlett-Packard, 3M, Coca-Cola, and General Electric.

Smith's turnaround of Kimberly-Clark is one the best examples in the twentieth century of a leader taking a company from merely good to truly great. And yet few people—even ardent students of business history—have heard of Darwin Smith. He probably would have liked it that way. Smith is a classic example of a *Level 5 leader*—an individual who blends extreme personal humility with intense professional will. According to our five-year research study, executives who possess this paradoxical combination of traits are catalysts for the statistically rare event of transforming a good company into a great one.

"Level 5" refers to the highest level in a hierarchy of executive capabilities that we identified during our research. Leaders at the other four levels in the hierarchy can produce high degrees of success but not enough to elevate companies from mediocrity to sustained excellence. (For more details about this concept, see Exhibit 21.1.) And while Level 5 leadership is not the only requirement for transforming a good company into a great one—other factors include getting the right people on the bus (and the wrong people off the bus) and creating a culture of discipline—our research shows it to be essential. Good-to-great transformations don't happen without Level 5 leaders at the helm. They just don't.

Not What You Would Expect

Our discovery of Level 5 leadership is counterintuitive. Indeed, it is countercultural. People generally assume that transforming companies from good to great requires larger-than-life leaders—big personalities like Iacocca, Dunlap, Welch, and Gault, who make headlines and become celebrities.

Compared with those CEOs, Darwin Smith seems to have come from Mars. Shy, unpretentious, even awkward, Smith shunned attention. When a journalist asked him to describe his management style, Smith just stared back at the scribe from the other side of his thick black-rimmed glasses. He was dressed unfashionably, like a farm boy wearing his first J.C. Penney suit. Finally, after a long and uncomfortable silence, he said, "Eccentric." Needless to say, the *Wall Street Journal* did not publish a splashy feature on Darwin Smith.

But if you were to consider Smith soft or meek, you would be terribly mistaken. His lack of pretense was coupled with a fierce, even stoic, resolve toward life. Smith grew up on an Indiana farm and put himself through night school at Indiana University by working the day shift at International Harvester. One day, he lost a finger on the job. The story goes that he went to class that evening and returned to work the very next day. Eventually, this poor but determined Indiana farm boy earned admission to Harvard Law School.

He showed the same iron will when he was at the helm of Kimberly-Clark. Indeed, two months after Smith became CEO, doctors diagnosed him with nose and throat cancer and told him he had less than a year to live. He duly informed the board of his illness but said he had no plans to die anytime soon. Smith held to his demanding work schedule while commuting weekly from Wisconsin to Houston for radiation therapy. He lived 25 more years, 20 of them as CEO.

EXHIBIT 21.1   *The Level 5 Hierarchy*

The Level 5 leader sits on top of a hierarchy of capabilities and is, according to our research, a necessary requirement for transforming an organization from good to great. But what lies beneath? Four other layers, each one appropriate in its own right but none with the power of Level 5. Individuals do not need to proceed sequentially through each level of the hierarchy to reach the top, but to be a full-fledged Level 5 requires the capabilities of all the lower levels, plus the special characteristics of Level 5

LEVEL 5   Level 5 Executive
Builds enduring greatness through a paradoxical combination of personal humility plus professional will

LEVEL 4   Effective Leader
Catalyzes commitment to and vigorous pursuit of a clear and compelling vision; stimulates the group to high performance standards

LEVEL 3   Competent Manager
Organizes people and resources toward the effective and efficient pursuit of predetermined objectives

LEVEL 2   Contributing Team Member
Contributes to the achievement of group objectives; works effectively with others in a group setting

LEVEL 1   Highly Capable Individual
Makes productive contributions through talent, knowledge, skills, and good work habits

Smith's ferocious resolve was crucial to the rebuilding of Kimberly-Clark, especially when he made the most dramatic decision in the company's history: sell the mills.

To explain: shortly after he took over, Smith and his team had concluded that the company's traditional core business—coated paper—was doomed to mediocrity. Its economics were bad and the competition weak. But, they reasoned, if Kimberly-Clark was thrust into the fire of the *consumer* paper products business, better economics and world-class competition like Procter & Gamble would force it to achieve greatness or perish.

And so, like the general who burned the boats upon landing on enemy soil, leaving his troops to succeed or die, Smith announced that Kimberly-Clark would sell its mills—even the namesake mill in Kimberly, Wisconsin. All proceeds would be thrown into the consumer business, with investments in brands like Huggies diapers and Kleenex tissues. The business media called the move stupid, and Wall Street analysts downgraded the stock. But Smith never wavered. Twenty-five years later, Kimberly-Clark owned Scott Paper and beat Procter & Gamble in six of eight product categories. In retirement, Smith reflected on his exceptional performance, saying simply, "I never stopped trying to become qualified for the job."

Not What We Expected Either

We'll look in depth at Level 5 leadership, but first let's set an important context for our findings: we were not looking for Level 5 or anything like it. Our original question was can a good company become a great one, and, if so, how? In fact, I gave the research teams explicit instructions to downplay the role of top executives in their analyses of this question so we wouldn't slip into the simplistic "credit the leader" or "blame the leader" thinking that is so common today.

But Level 5 found us. Over the course of the study, research teams kept saying, "We can't ignore the top executives even if we want to. There is something consistently unusual about them." I would push back, arguing, "The comparison companies also had leaders. So what's different here?" Back and forth the debate raged. Finally, as should always be the case, the data won. The executives at companies that went from good to great and sustained that performance for 15 years or more were all cut from the same cloth—one remarkably different from that which produced executives at the comparison companies in our study. It didn't matter whether the company was in crisis or steady state, consumer or industrial, offering services or products. It didn't matter when the transition took place or how big the company was in crisis or steady state, consumer or industrial, offering services or products. It didn't matter when the transition took place or how big the company—the successful organizations all had a Level 5 leader at the time of transition.

Furthermore, the absence of Level 5 leadership showed up consistently across the comparison companies. The point: Level 5 is an empirical finding, not an ideological one. And that's important to note, given how much the Level 5 finding contradicts not only conventional wisdom but much of management theory to date. (For more about our findings on good-to-great transformations, see Exhibit 21.2.)

Humility + Will = Level 5

Level 5 leaders are a study in duality: modest and willful, shy and fearless. To grasp this concept, consider Abraham Lincoln, who never let his ego get in the way of his ambition to create an enduring great nation. Author Henry Adams called him "a quiet, peaceful, shy figure." But those who thought Lincoln's understated manner signaled weakness in the man found themselves terribly mistaken—to the scale of 250,000 Confederate and 360,000 Union lives, including Lincoln's own.

EXHIBIT 21.1   *Not by Level 5 Alone*

Level 5 leadership is an essential factor for taking a company from good to great, but it's not the only one. Our research uncovered multiple factors that deliver companies to greatness. And it is the combined package—Level 5 plus these other drivers—that takes companies beyond unremarkable. There is a symbolic relationship between Level 5 and the rest of our findings: Level 5 enables implementation of the other findings, and practicing the other findings may help you get to Level 5. We've already talked about who Level 5 leaders are; the rest of our findings describe what they do. Here is a brief look at some of the other key findings.

First, Who: We expected that good-to-great leaders would start with the vision and strategy. Instead, they attended to people first, strategy second. They got the right people on the bus, moved the wrong people off, ushered the right people to the the the right seats—and then they figured out where to drive it.

Stockdale Paradox: This finding is named after Admiral James Stockdale, winner of the Medal of Honor, who survived seven years in a Vietcong POW camp by hanging on to two contradictory beliefs: his life couldn't be worse at the moment, and his life would someday be better than ever. Like Stockdale, people at the good-to-great companies in our research confronted the most brutal facts of their current reality—yet simultaneously maintained absolute faith that they would prevail in the end. And they held both disciplines—faith and facts—at the same time, all the time.

Buildup-Breakthrough Flywheel: Good-to-great transformations do not happen overnight or in one big leap. Rather, the process resembles relentlessly pushing a giant, heavy flywheel in one direction. At first, pushing it gets the flywheel to turn once. With consistent effort, it goes two turns, then five, then ten, building increasing momentum until—bang!—the wheel hits the breakthrough point, and the momentum really kicks in. Our comparison companies never sustained the kind of breakthrough momentum that the good-to-great companies did; instead, they lurched back and forth with radical change programs, reactionary moves, and restructurings.

The Hedgehog Concept: In a famous essay, philosopher and scholar Isaiah Berlin described two approaches to thought and life using a simple parable: The fox knows a little about many things, but the hedgehog knows only one big thing very well. The fox is complex, the hedgehog simple. And the hedgehog wins. Our research shows that breakthroughs require a simple hedgehog-like understanding of three intersecting circles: what a company can be the best in the world at, how its economics works best, and what best ignites the passions of its people. Breakthroughs happen when you get the hedgehog concept and become systematic and consistent with it, eliminating virtually anything that does not fit in the three circles.

Technology Accelerators: The good-to-great companies had a paradoxical relationship with technology. On the one hand, they assiduously avoided

(Continues)

jumping on new technology bandwagons. On the other, they were pioneers in the application of carefully selected technologies, making bold, farsighted investments in those that directly linked to their hedgehog concept. Like turbochargers, these technology accelerators create an explosion in flywheel momentum.

A Culture of Discipline: When you look across the good-to-great transformation, they consistently display three forms of discipline: disciplined people, disciplined thought, and disciplined action. When you have disciplined people, you don't need hierarchy. When you have disciplined thought, you don't need bureaucracy. When you have disciplined action, you don't need excessive controls. When you combine a culture of discipline with an ethic of entrepreneurship, you get the magical alchemy of great performance.

It might be a stretch to compare the 11 Level 5 CEOs in our research to Lincoln, but they did display the same kind of duality. Take Colman M. Mockler, CEO of Gillette from 1975 to 1991. Mockler, who faced down three takeover attempts, was a reserved, gracious man with a gentle, almost patrician manner. Despite epic battles with raiders—he took on Ronald Perelman twice and the former Coniston Partners once—he never lost his shy, courteous style. At the height of the crisis, he maintained a calm business-as-usual demeanor, dispensing first with ongoing business before turning to the takeover.

And yet, those who mistook Mockler's outward modesty as a sign of inner weakness were beaten in the end. In one proxy battle, Mockler and other senior executives called thousands of investors, one by one, to win their votes. Mockler simply would not give in. He chose to fight for the future greatness of Gillette even though he could have pocketed millions by flipping his stock.

Consider the consequences had Mockler capitulated. If a share-flipper had accepted the full 44% price premium offered by Perelman and then invested those shares in the general market for ten years, he still would have come out 64% behind a shareholder who stayed with Mockler and Gillette. If Mockler had given up the fight, it's likely that none of us would be shaving with Sensor, Lady Sensor, or the Mach III—and hundreds of millions of people would have a more painful battle with daily stubble.

Sadly, Mockler never had the chance to enjoy the full fruits of his efforts. In January 1991, Gillette received an advance copy of *Forbes*. The cover featured an artist's rendition of the publicity-shy Mockler standing on a mountaintop, holding a giant razor above his head in a triumphant pose. Walking back to his office, just minutes after seeing this public acknowledgment of his 16 years of struggle, Mockler crumpled to the floor and died from a massive heart attack.

Even if Mockler had known he would die in office, he could not have changed his approach. His placid persona hid an inner intensity, a dedication to making anything he touched the best—not just because of what he would get but because he couldn't imagine doing it any other way. Mockler could not give up the company to those who would destroy it, any more than Lincoln would risk losing the chance to build an enduring great nation.

A Compelling Modesty

The Mockler story illustrates the modesty typical of Level 5 leaders. (For a summary of Level 5 traits, see Exhibit 21.3.) Indeed, throughout our interviews with such executives, we were struck by the way they talked about themselves—or rather, didn't talk about themselves. They'd go on and on about the company and the contributions of other executives, but they would instinctively deflect discussion about their own role. When pressed talk about themselves, they'd say things like, "I hope I'm not sounding like a big shot," or "I don't think I can take much credit for what happened. We were blessed with marvelous people." One Level 5 leader even asserted, "There are lot of people in this company who could do my job better than I do."

By contrast, consider the courtship of personal celebrity by the comparison CEOs. Scott Paper, the comparison company to Kimberly-Clark, hired Al Dunlap as CEO—a man who would tell anyone who would listen (and many who would have preferred not to) about his accomplishments. After 29 months atop Scott Paper, Dunlap said in *Business Week*: "The Scott story will go down in the annals of American business history as one of the most successful, quickest turnarounds ever. It makes other turnarounds pale by comparison." He personally accrued $100 million for 603 days of work at Scott Paper—about $165,000 per day largely by slashing the workforce, halving the R&D budget, and putting the company on growth steroids in preparation for sale. After selling off the company and pocketing his quick millions, Dunlap wrote an autobiography in which he boastfully dubbed himself "Rambo in pinstripes." It's hard to imagine Darwin Smith thinking, "Hey, that Rambo character reminds me of me," let alone stating it publicly.

Granted, the Scott Paper story is one of the more dramatic in our study, but it's not an isolated case. In more than two-thirds of the comparison companies, we noted the presence of a gargantuan ego that contributed to the demise or continued mediocrity of the company. We found this pattern particularly strong in the unsustained comparison companies— the companies that would show a shift in performance under a talented yet egocentric Level 4 leader, only to decline in later years.

EXHIBIT 21.3   *The Yin and Yang of Level 5*

Personal Humility	**Professional Will**
Demonstrates a compelling modesty, shunning public adulation; never boastful	Creates superb results, a clear catalyst in the transition from good to great
Acts with quiet, calm determination; relies principally on inspired standards, not inspiring charisma, to motivate	Demonstrates an unwavering resolve to do whatever must be done to produce the best long-term results, no matter how difficult
Channels ambition into the company, not the self, sets up successors for even more greatness in the next generation	Sets the standard of building an enduring great company; will settle for nothing less
Looks in the mirror, not out the window, to apportion responsibility for poor results, never blaming other people, external factors, or bad luck	Looks out the window, not in the mirror, to apportion credit for the success of the company—to other people, external factors, and good luck

---

Lee Iacocca, for example, saved Chrysler from the brink of catastrophe, performing one of the most celebrated (and deservedly so) turnarounds in U.S. business history. The automaker's stock rose 2.9 times higher than the general market about halfway through his tenure. But then Iacocca diverted his attention to transforming himself. He appeared regularly on talk shows like the *Today Show* and *Larry King Live*, starred in more than 80 commercials, entertained the idea of running for president of the United States, and promoted his autobiography, which sold seven million copies worldwide. Iacocca's personal stock soared, but Chrysler's stock fell 31% below the market in the second half of his tenure.

And once Iacocca had accumulated all the fame and perks, he found it difficult to leave center stage. He postponed his retirement so many times that Chrysler's insiders began to joke that Iacocca stood for "I Am Chairman of Chrysler Corporation Always." When he finally retired, he demanded that the board continue to provide a private jet and stock options. Later, he joined forces with noted takeover artist Kirk Kerkorian to launch a hostile bid for Chrysler. (It failed.) Iacocca did make one final brilliant decision: he picked a modest yet determined—perhaps even a Level 5—as his successor. Bob Eaton rescued Chrysler from its second near-death crisis in a decade and set the foundation for a more enduring corporate transition.

An Unwavering Resolve

Besides extreme humility, Level 5 leaders also display tremendous professional will. When George Cain became CEO of Abbott Laboratories, it was drowsy family-controlled business, sitting at the bottom quartile of the pharmaceutical industry, living off its cash cow, erythromycin. Cain was a typical Level 5 leader in his lack of pretense; he didn't have the kind of inspiring personality that would galvanize the company. But he had something much more powerful: inspired standards. He could not stand mediocrity in any form and was utterly intolerant of anyone who would accept the idea that good is good enough. For the next 14 years, he relentlessly imposed his will for greatness on Abbott Labs.

Among Cain's first tasks was to destroy one of the root causes of Abbott's middling performance: nepotism. By systematically rebuilding both the board and the executive team with the best people he could find, Cain made his statement. Family ties no longer mattered. If you couldn't become the best executive in the industry, within your span of responsibility, you would lose your paycheck.

Such near-ruthless rebuilding might be expected from an outsider brought in to turn the company around, but Cain was an 18-year insider—and a part of the family, the son of a previous president. Holiday gatherings were probably tense for a few years in the Cain clan—"Sorry I had to fire you. Want another slice of turkey?"—but in the end, family members were pleased with the performance of their stock. Cain had set in motion a profitable growth machine. From its transition in 1974 to 2000, Abbott created shareholder returns that beat the market 4.5:1, outperforming industry superstars Merck and Pfizer by a factor of two.

Another good example of iron-willed Level 5 leadership comes from Charles R. "Cork" Walgreen III, who transformed dowdy Walgreens into a company that outperformed the stock market 16:1 from its transition in 1975 to 2000. After years of dialogue and debate within his executive team about what to do with Walgreens' food-service operations, this CEO sensed the team had finally reached a watershed: the company's brightest future lay in convenient drugstores, not in food service. Dan Jorndt, who succeeded Walgreen in 1988, describes what happened next:

> Cork said at one of our planning committee meetings, "Okay, now I am going to draw the line in the sand. We are going to be out of the restaurant business completely in five years." At the time we had more than 500 restaurants. You could have heard a pin drop. He said, "I want to let everybody know the clock is ticking." Six months later we were at our next planning committee meeting and someone mentioned just in passing that we had only five years to be out of the restaurant business. Cork was not a real vo-

ciferous fellow. He sort of tapped on the table and said, "Listen, you now have four and a half years. I said you had five years six months ago. Now you've got four and a half years." Well, that next day things really clicked into gear for winding down our restaurant business. Cork never wavered. He never doubted. He never second-guessed.

Like Darwin Smith selling the mills at Kimberly-Clark, Cork Walgreen required stoic resolve to make his decisions. Food service was not the largest part of the business, although it did add substantial profits to the bottom line. The real problem was more emotional than financial. Walgreens had, after all, invented the malted milk shake, and food service had been a long-standing family tradition dating back to Cork's grandfather. Not only that, some food-service outlets were even named after the CEO—for example, a restaurant chain named Corky's. But no matter, if Walgreen had to fly in the face of family tradition in order to refocus on the one arena in which Walgreens could be the best in the world—convenient drugstores—and terminate everything else that would not produce great results, then Cork would do it. Quietly, doggedly, simply.

One final, yet compelling, note on our findings about Level 5: because Level 5 leaders have ambition not for themselves but for their companies, they routinely select superb successors. Level 5 leaders want to see their companies become even more successful in the next generation, comfortable with the idea that most people won't even know that the roots of that success trace back to them. As one Level 5 CEO said, "I want to look from my porch, see the company as one of the great companies in the world someday, and be able to say, 'I used to work there.'" By contrast, Level 4 leaders often fail to set up the company for enduring success—after all, what better testament to your own personal greatness than that the place falls apart after you leave?

In more than three-quarters of the comparison companies, we found executives who set up their successors for failure, chose weak successors, or both. Consider the case of Rubbermaid, which grew from obscurity to become one of *Fortune*'s most admired companies—and then, just as quickly, disintegrated into such sorry shape that it had to be acquired by Newell.

The architect of this remarkable story was a charismatic and brilliant leader named Stanley C. Gault, whose name became synonymous in the late 1980s with the company's success. Across the 312 articles collected by our research team about Rubbermaid, Gault comes through as a hard-driving, egocentric executive. In one article, he responds to the accusation of being a tyrant with the statement, "Yes, but I'm a sincere tyrant." In another, drawn directly from his own comments on leading change, the "I" appears 44 times, while the word "we" appears 16 times. Of course, Gault had every reason to be proud of his executive success: Rubbermaid generated 40 consecutive quarters of earnings growth under his leadership—an impressive performance, to be sure, and one that deserves respect.

But Gault did not leave behind a company that would be great without him. His chosen successor lasted a year on the job and the next in line faced a management team so shallow that he had to temporarily shoulder four jobs while scrambling to identify a new number-two executive. Gault's successors struggled not only with a management void but also with strategic voids that would eventually bring the company to its knees.

Of course, you might say—as one *Fortune* article did—that the fact that Rubbermaid fell apart after Gault left proves his greatness as a leader. Gault was a tremendous Level 4 leader, perhaps one of the best in the last 50 years. But he was not at Level 5, and that is one crucial reason why Rubbermaid went from good to great for a brief, shining moment and then just as quickly went from great to irrelevant.

The Window and the Mirror

As part of our research, we interviewed Alan L. Wurtzel, the Level 5 leader responsible for turning Circuit City from a ramshackle company on the edge of bankruptcy into one of America's most successful electronics retailers. In the 15 years after its transition date in 1982, Circuit City outperformed the market 18.5:1.

We asked Wurtzel to list the top five factors in his company's transformation, ranked by importance. His number one factor? Luck. "We were in a great industry, with the wind at our backs." But wait a minute, we retorted, Silo—your comparison company—was in the same industry, with the same wind, and bigger sails. The conversation went back and forth, with Wurtzel refusing to take much credit for the transition, preferring to attribute it largely to just being in the right place at the right time. Later, when we asked him to discuss the factors that would sustain a good-to-great transformation, he said, "The first thing that comes to mind is luck. I was lucky to find the right successor."

Luck. What an odd factor to talk about. Yet the Level 5 leaders we identified invoked it frequently. We asked an executive at steel company Nucor why it had such a remarkable track record of making good decisions. His response? "I guess we were just lucky." Joseph F. Cullman III, the Level 5 CEO of Philip Morris, flat out refused to take credit for this company's success, citing his good fortune to have great colleagues, successors, and predecessors. Even the book he wrote about his career—which he penned at the urging of his colleagues and which he never intended to distribute widely outside the company—had the unusual title *I'm a Lucky Guy*.

At first, we were puzzled by the Level 5 leaders' emphasis on good luck. After all, there is no evidence that the companies that had progressed from good to great were blessed with more good luck (or more bad luck, for that matter) than the comparison companies. But then we began to notice an interesting pattern in the executives at the comparison companies: they often blamed their situations on bad luck, bemoaning the difficulties of the environment they faced.

Compare Bethlehem Steel and Nucor, for example. Both steel companies operated with products that are hard to differentiate, and both faced a competitive challenge from cheap imported steel. Both companies paid significantly higher wages than most of their foreign competitors. And yet executives at the two companies held completely different views of the same environment.

Bethlehem Steel's CEO summed up the company's problems in 1983 by blaming the imports: "Our first, second, and third problems are imports." Meanwhile, Ken Iverson and his crew at Nucor say the imports as a blessing: "Aren't we lucky; steel is heavy, and they have to ship it all the way across the ocean, giving us a huge advantage." Indeed, Iverson saw the first, second, and third problems facing the U.S. steel industry not in imports, telling a gathering of stunned steel executives in 1977 that the real problems facing the industry lay in the fact that management had failed to keep pace with technology.

The emphasis on luck turns out to be part of a broader pattern that we came to call *the window and the mirror*. Level 5 leaders, inherently humble, look out the window to apportion credit—even undue credit—to factors outside themselves. If they can't find a specific person or event to give credit to, they credit good luck. At the same time, they look in the mirror to assign responsibility, never citing bad luck or external factors when things go poorly. Conversely, the comparison executives frequently looked out the window for factors to blame but preened in the mirror to credit themselves when things went well.

The funny thing about the window-and-mirror concept is that it does not reflect reality. According to our research, the Level 5 leaders were responsible for their companies' transformations. But they would never admit that. We can't climb inside their heads and assess whether they deeply believed what they saw in the window and the mirror. But it doesn't really matter, because they acted as if they believed it, and they acted with such consistency that it produced exceptional results.

Born or Bred?

Not long ago, I shared the Level 5 Finding with a gathering of senior executives. A woman who had recently become chief executive of her company raised her hand. "I believe what you've told us about Level 5 leadership," she said, "but I'm disturbed because I know I'm not there yet, and maybe I never will be. Part of the reason I got this job is because of my strong ego. Are you telling me that I can't make my company great if I'm not Level 5?"

"Let me return to the data," I responded. "Of 1,435 companies that appeared on the Fortune 500 since 1965, only 11 made it into our study. In those 11, all of them had Level 5 leaders in key positions, including the CEO role, at the pivotal time of transition. Now, to reiterate, we're not saying that Level 5 is the only element required for the move from good to great, but it appears to be essential."

She sat there, quiet for a moment, and you could guess what many people in the room were thinking. Finally, she raised her hand again, "Can you learn to become Level 5?" I still do not know the answer to that question. Our research, frankly, did not delve into how Level 5 leaders come to be, nor did we attempt to explain or codify the nature of their emotional lives. We speculated on the unique psychology of Level 5 leaders. Were they "guilty" of displacement—shifting their own raw ambition onto something other than themselves? Were they sublimating their egos for dark and complex reasons rooted in childhood trauma? Who knows? And perhaps more important, do the psychological roots of Level 5 leadership matter any more than do the roots of charisma or intelligence? The question remains: Can Level 5 be developed?

My preliminary hypothesis is that there are two categories of people: those who don't have the Level 5 seed within them and those who do. The first category consists of people who could never in a million years bring themselves to subjugate their own needs to the greater ambition of something larger and more lasting than themselves. For those people, work will always be first and foremost about what they get—the fame, fortune, power adulation, and so on. Work will never be about what they build, create, and contribute. The great irony is that the animus and personal ambition that often drives people to become a Level 4 leader stands at odds with the humility required to rise to Level 5.

When you combine that irony with the fact that boards of directors frequently operate under the false belief that a larger-than-life, egocentric leader is required to make a company great, you can quickly see why Level 5 leaders rarely appear at the top of our institutions. We keep putting people in positions of power who lack the seed to become a Level 5 leader, and that is one major reason why there are so few companies that make a sustained and verifiable shift from good to great.

The second category consists of people who could evolve to Level 5; the capability resides within them, perhaps buried or ignored or simply nascent. Under the right circumstances—with self-reflection, a mentor, loving parents, a significant life experience, or other factors—the seed can begin to develop. Some of the Level 5 leaders in our study had significant life experiences that might have sparked development of the seed. Darwin Smith fully blossomed as a Level 5 after his near-death experience with cancer. Joe Cullman was profoundly affected by his World War II experiences, particularly the last-minute change of orders that took him off a doomed ship on which he surely would have died; he considered the next 60-odd years a great gift. A strong religious belief or conversion might also nurture the seed. Colman Mockler, for example, converted to evangelical Christianity while getting his MBA at Harvard, and later, according to the book *Cutting Edge*, he became a prime mover in a group of Boston business executives that met frequently over breakfast to discuss the carryover of religious values to corporate life.

We would love to be able to give you a list of steps for getting to Level 5—other than contracting cancer, going through a religious conversion, or getting different parents—but we have no solid research data that would support a credible list. Our research exposed Level 5 as a key component inside the black box of what it takes to shift a company from good to great. Yet inside that black box is another—the inner development of a person to Level 5 leadership. We could speculate on what that inner box might hold, but it would mostly be just that, speculation.

In short, Level 5 is a very satisfying idea, a truthful idea, a powerful idea, and, to make the move from good to great, very likely an essential idea. But to provide "ten steps to Level 5 leadership" would trivialize the concept.

My best advice, based on the research, is to practice the other good-to-great disciplines that we discovered. Since we found a tight symbiotic relationship between each of the other findings and Level 5, we suspect that conscientiously trying to lead using the other disciplines can help you move in the right direction. There is no guarantee that doing so will turn executives into full-fledged Level 5 leaders, but it gives them a tangible place to begin, especially if they have the seed within.

We cannot say for sure what percentage of people have the seed within, nor how many of those can nurture it enough to become Level 5. Even those of us on the research team who identified Level 5 do not know whether we will succeed in evolving to its heights. And yet all of us who worked on the finding have been inspired by the idea of trying to move toward Level 5. Darwin Smith, Colman Mockler, Alan Wurtzel, and all the other Level 5 leaders we learned about have become role models for us. Whether or not we make it to Level 5, it is worth trying. For like all basic truths about what is best in human beings, when we catch a glimpse of that truth, we know that our own lives and all that we touch will be the better for making the effort to get there.

About the Editors and Contributors

Editors

William E. Rosenbach is Evans Professor of Eisenhower Leadership Studies and professor of management at Gettysburg College. Formerly professor and head of the Department of Behavioral Sciences and Leadership at the U.S. Air Force Academy, he is the author or coauthor of numerous articles and books on leadership topics. He is especially interested in the elements of effective followership and is an active consultant to private and public organizations in North America, Europe, and Australia on executive leadership development.

Robert L. Taylor is professor of management and dean, College of Business and Public Administration at the University of Louisville. Formerly professor and head of the Department of Management at the U.S. Air Force Academy and the Carol N. Jacobs Professor of Business and the University of Wisconsin–Stevens Point, he has been a student of leadership for nearly thirty years. Most recently, Dr. Taylor served as board chair of AACSB: The International Association for Management Education. His interests have resulted in undergraduate and graduate seminars, presentations, and consultancies, with a primary focus on the elements of effective leadership.

Contributors

Warren Bennis is university professor and distinguished professor of business administration at the University of Southern California and the founding chairman of USC's Leadership Institute. He has written eighteen books, including: *On Becoming a Leader* (which was translated into nineteen languages), *Why Leaders Can't Lead*, and *The Unreality Industry*, co-authored with Ian Mitroff. Bennis was successor to Douglas McGregor as chairman of the organization studies department at MIT. He also taught at Harvard and Boston Universities. Later, he was provost and executive vice president of the State University of New York–Buffalo and president of the University of Cincinnati. He has published over 900 articles, and two of his books have earned the coveted McKinsey Award for the Best Book on Management. He has served in an advisory capacity to the past four U.S. presidents and served as consultant for many corporations and agencies and for the United Nations. Awarded eleven honorary degrees, Bennis has also received numerous awards, including the Distinguished Service Award of the American Board of Professional Psychologists and the Perry L. Rohrer Consulting Practice Award of the American Psychological Association.

Robert Birnbaum is a professor at Columbia University and has held that position since 1989. His fundamental scholarly interest is in studying colleges and universities as institutions, and as social and interpretive systems. Dr. Birnbaum has published eight books, including: *Making Sense of Administrative Leadership: The "L" Word in Higher Education,* ASHE/ERIC Higher Education Report (Washington, D.C.: Association for the Study of Higher Education, 1989), with E. Bensimon and A. Neumann; *Faculty in Governance: The Role of Senates and Joint Committees in Academic Decision Making. New Directions for Higher Education,* No. 75 (San Francisco: Jossey-Bass, 1991) (editor); and *How Academic Leadership Works: Understanding Success and Failure in the College Presidency* (San Francisco: Jossey-Bass, 1992).

Michael Brown is a doctoral candidate studying management and organizational behavior at the Smeal College of Business Administration, Pennsylvania State University. His primary research interests focus on the ethical dimensions of leadership and e-business leadership, with a particular focus at the executive level. His ongoing research explores some of the antecedents and consequences of ethical leadership to develop a theoretical model of ethical leadership at the executive level.

Rev. Timothy Brown, S.J., came to Loyola College in Maryland in 1987 to teach courses in the Law and Social Responsibility Department of the Sellinger School of Business and Management. Currently, Father Brown serves as special assistant to the president, associate professor of law and codirector of the college's Center for Values and Service. He has coauthored numerous articles for a variety of publications. Among his fields of research are business ethics, child labor, and public-policy interests in smoking and gambling. Ordained in 1986, Brown received his Master of Divinity from Weston School of Theology in Cambridge, Massachusetts, that same year. Four years earlier, he earned his Juris Doctor from George Mason University School of Law in Arlington, Virginia. Father Brown, who also has an M.A. in philosophy from New York's Fordham University, received his B.S. in foreign service from Georgetown University in 1974.

M. Neil Browne joined the Bowling Green State University faculty in 1968. He received his J.D. from the University of Toledo in 1981, his Ph.D. at the University of Texas in 1969, and his B.A. from the University of Houston in 1965. His major areas of academic interest are methodology, history of economic thought, and labor economics. Neil Browne has won several prestigious awards in recent years, which include: the National Endowment for the Humanities Distinguished Scholar, University of Hartford, for 1994–1995 and CASE Ohio Professor of the Year in 1989.

Jim Collins operates a management research laboratory in Boulder, Colorado. He is coauthor, with Jerry I. Porras, of *Built to Last: Successful Habits of Visionary Companies* (Harper Business, 1994). His new book *Good to Great* will be published by Harper Business in 2001.

Richard A. Couto holds the George Matthews and Virginia Brinkley Modlin Chair in Leadership Studies at the University of Richmond. He has a B.A. in history from Marist College, an M.A. in political science from Boston College, and a

Ph.D. in political science from the University of Kentucky. His published work has addressed the labor movement, the NAACP, health care and the homeless, women and poverty, welfare reform, and race relations. His book *Ain't Gonna Let Nobody Turn Me Around: The Pursuit of Racial Justice in the Rural South* (1991) was named an Outstanding Book by the Gustavus Myers Center for the Study of Human Rights.

Robert M. Fulmer is a respected scholar of leadership. A distinguished visiting professor at the Graziadio School of Business at Pepperdine University, he was previously the W. Brooks George Professor of Management at the College of William and Mary and a visiting scholar at the Center for Organizational Learning at MIT. He also taught at Columbia University's Graduate Business School and served as director of executive education at Emory University. Beyond academia, he was director of corporate management development for Allied Signal, Inc., and president of two management consulting firms specializing in human resource issues. The coauthor of *Leadership by Design* and four editions of *The New Management*, Dr. Fulmer has designed and delivered leadership initiatives in twenty-two countries. Dr. Fulmer received his MBA from the University of Florida and his Ph.D. from UCLA. He lives in Santa Barbara, California.

John W. Gardner served six presidents of the United States in various leadership capacities. He was secretary of health, education, and welfare, founding chairman of Common Cause, cofounder of Independent Sector, and president of the Carnegie Corporation and the Carnegie Foundation for the Advancement of Teaching. The author of *On Leadership*, he served as Miriam and Peter Haas Centennial Professor at Stanford Business School.

Andrea Giampetro-Meyer is associate professor of law in the Department of Strategic and Organizational Studies in the Sellinger School of Business and Management at Loyola College. Her teaching career at Loyola began in 1986 after she graduated from the Marshall-Wythe School of Law at the College of William and Mary. Professor Giampetro's undergraduate degree is in business administration (concentration in economics). She graduated from Bowling Green State University in Ohio in 1983. She has published several scholarly articles that focus on her areas of research, which include legal responses to gender discrimination in employment, corporate social responsibility, and pedagogy. In August 1999, the Academy of Legal Studies in Business named her the recipient of the Holmes-Cardozo award for excellence in legal scholarship. She won this award for her article entitled "Recognizing and Remedying Individual and Institutional Gender-Based Wage Discrimination in Sport," which analyzes and evaluates legal claims brought by women who coach at the college level.

Daniel Goleman consults internationally and lectures frequently to business audiences and professional groups and on college campuses. He is founder of Emotional Intelligence Services, an affiliate of the Hay Group in Boston. A psychologist who for many years reported on the brain and behavioral sciences for the *New York Times*, Dr. Goleman was previously a visiting faculty member at Harvard. Dr. Goleman has received many journalistic awards for his writing, including two nominations for the Pulitzer Prize for his articles in the *Times* and a Career Achievement Award for Journalism from the American Psychological Association. In recognition of his efforts to communicate the behavioral sciences to the public, he was elected a Fellow of the American Association for the Advancement of Science. Dr. Goleman attended Amherst College, where he was an Alfred P. Sloan Scholar and graduated magna cum laude. His graduate education was at Harvard, where he was a Ford Fellow, and he received his M.A. and Ph.D. in clinical psychology and personality development.

David P. Hamilton, a reporter in the San Francisco bureau of the *Wall Street Journal*, covers the semiconductor industry, Internet computing, and the technological and economic evolution of the Internet. He joined the *Journal* as a reporter in the Tokyo bureau in November 1992, and moved to San Francisco in January 1999. Mr. Hamilton began his journalism career in 1989 as a reporter-researcher for the *New Republic Magazine* in Washington, D.C. From 1990 to 1992, he was a staff reporter for *Science Magazine*, also in Washington. He received both a bachelor's degree and a master's degree in electrical engineering from the Massachusetts Institute of Technology.

Laura Pincus Hartman, J.D., is the associate director of DePaul University's Institute for Business and Professional Ethics, held the Wicklander Chair in Professional Ethics and is an Associate Professor of Legal Studies and Ethics at DePaul's Kellstadt Graduate School of Business. Hartman has done extensive research on the ethics of the employment relationship, employee rights, and employer responsibilities and has published the first business-school textbook in the field, *Employment Law for Business*, as well as other textbooks. She has also published articles in, among other journals, *Hofstra Law Review, Columbia Business Law Journal, Harvard Journal of Law and Technology, American Business Law Journal, Labor Law Journal, Journal of Individual Employment Rights*, and *Journal of Legal Studies Education*.

Albert R. Hunt is executive editor for the Washington, D.C., bureau of the *Wall Street Journal* and *Dow Jones*. He joined the *Journal* in 1965 as a reporter in New York City. He transferred to the Boston bureau in 1967 and to Washington in 1969. From 1972 to 1983, Hunt covered Congress and national politics, becoming Washington bureau chief in 1983. He was named executive Washington editor in 1993. Hunt writes a weekly editorial column and has been a panelist on the Public Broadcasting Service program *Washington Week in Review* and NBC's *Meet the Press*. He has also been a political analyst on the *CBS Morning News* and a member of CNN's *The Capital Gang* since its inception in 1988.

Mark J. Kroll is professor of management and the George W. and Robert S. Pirtle Distinguished Professor in Free Enterprise at the University of Texas at Tyler. He received his D.B.A. in management from Mississippi State University. His current research interests are business policy and strategy, agency problems, and corporate acquisitions.

Nancy Kubasek joined the Bowling Green State University faculty in 1982. She received her J.D. from the University of Toledo College of Law in 1981, and her B.A. from Bowling Green State University in 1978. Her major areas of academic interest are environmental law and women's legal issues. Professor Kubasek is currently vice president of the Tri-State Regional Academy of Legal Studies in Business. She was a cofounder in 1995 of the Environment and Business Section of the Academy of Legal Studies in Business and currently serves as the organization's co-chair and editor of its newsletter.

Polly LaBarre is senior editor of *Fast Company* magazine. She has edited the magazine's "Report from the Future" section—which focuses on the new culture of success and the future of working, competing, and living. Before joining FC, Polly was New York bureau editor of *Industry Week*, a biweekly management magazine. There she was book review editor and covered a broad arena of management theory. She also coproduced IW's interactive service and a series of executive conferences. In a previous life, Polly, twenty-seven, did time in New York's book publishing scene as an assistant literary scout for foreign book publishers and Steven Spielberg's production house, Amblin, with Maria Campbell Associates. She graduated summa cum laude from Yale University with a BA in Literature.

Michael Maccoby, author of *The Gamesman* and *The Leader*, is a consultant on issues of leadership, strategy, and organization to business, government, and unions. He is president of The Maccoby Group in Washington, D.C., where he lives.

Thane S. Pittman is professor of psychology and former chair of the Department of Psychology at Gettysburg College.

Earl H. Potter III is dean of the College of Business at Eastern Michigan University and former director of organizational development at Cornell University. He has a doctorate in organizational psychology from the University of Washington and over twenty-five years of experience in research and consulting on issues of leadership, team effectiveness, and organizational change. As a leader, he has headed polar diving explorations, sailed a square-rigged ship with a crew of 200 as executive officer, and chaired countless faculty meetings.

Harriet Rubin, Working Diva's director, is a writer, consultant, and lecturer on leadership issues. She is author of the international bestseller *The Princessa: Machiavelli for Women* (Dell, 1998) and *Soloing: Realizing Your Life's Ambition* (HarperCollins, November 1999). She is a contributing editor and columnist for *Fast Company* magazine. Her articles have been published in the *New York Times*, the *Wall Street Journal, Inc.* magazine, and other publications. She has appeared on *The Today Show, Politically Incorrect*, and National Public Radio's *Marketplace*. She has lectured on leadership throughout the United States, Europe, Africa, and South America. In 1989, she founded Currency/Doubleday, which became the leading publisher of business books. Rubin is currently finishing a book on the roots of power and freedom, to be published by HarperCollins in 2001.

Marshall Sashkin is professor of human resource development of the Graduate School of Education and Human Development at the George Washington University.

Peter Senge is director of the Center for Organizational Learning at MIT's Sloan School of Management. He is a founding partner of a consulting and training firm—Innovation Associates—and is associated with the Learning Circle, an organization founded to develop a worldwide community of learning organization practitioners.

T. Takala is associate professor of organizations and management in the School of Business and Economics, University of Iyvdskyia, Finland. His main research interests are themes on ethical business, managerial ethics, leadership thinking, and social responsibility issues. He is publishing the scientific ethics journal, *Elec-*

tronic Journal of Business and Organizational Ethics, as editor-in-chief. He has published articles in numerous journals, including *Scandinavian Journal of Management, Journal of Business Ethics, European Journal of Marketing, Electronic Journal of Business* and *Organizational Ethics, Journal of Finnish Business Studies,* and *Journal of Finnish Administrative Studies.*

Neal Thornberry is associate professor of management at Babson College.

Leslie A. Toombs is associate professor of management at the University of Texas at Tyler. Her primary teaching fields are strategic management, business research, organizational behavior, and quality management. She received her Doctor of Business Administration from Louisiana Tech University. Dr. Toombs has written many articles on quality and strategic management topics, which have appeared in publications such as the *Strategic Management Journal* and *Academy of Management Executive.* In addition, she has served as a consultant to business organizations in the areas of strategic management and quality management.

Linda Klebe Trevino is professor of organizational behavior and chair of the Department of Management and Organization at Penn State University. She holds a Ph.D. in management from Texas A&M University. Her research and writing on the management of ethical conduct in organizations is widely published and well known internationally. She coauthored a textbook with Katherine Neson of William M. Mercer Consulting, entitled *Managing Business Ethics: Straight Talk About How to Do It Right.* The second edition was published in 1999. She has presented her research findings to business groups, including the Conference Board, the Conference Board of Canada, and the Ethics Officers Association.

Matthew Valle is assistant professor of management at Wichita State University. He received his Ph.D. in business administration from the Florida State University in 1995. His research interests include organizational politics and politics perceptions, leadership in the public sector, and product and process improvement initiatives.

Peter Wright is professor of management and holds the University of Memphis Endowed Chair in Free Enterprise Management. He received his undergraduate degree from Ohio State University and his Ph.D. degree from Louisiana State University. His research focuses on agency theory and the valuation of firm strategies.